The Goddess and the Bull

PRAISE FOR *THE GODDESS AND THE BULL* FROM ALL QUARTERS

From the profession . . .

"Michael Balter takes us on a fascinating journey through the excavations at one of the world's great archaeological sites. He provides an engrossing chronicle of one of the world's earliest farming villages and of the personalities and thought of the archaeologists engaged in the research—the human side of archaeology." —*Brian Fagan, University of California, Santa Barbara*

"A superb biography of a super archaeological site!" —*Bruce Trigger, McGill University, Montreal*

"If you're interested in when people first began to settle down in villages and towns, and you can read only one book, this is the one to choose. If you're interested in how archaeologists reconstruct the social organization, economy and religion of prehistoric communities and why they often disagree, this again is the book you want. And if you think learning interesting stuff often means plowing through a lot of dull prose and technical detail, you'll be pleased to find that this is a book you'll have a hard time putting down." —*Richard Klein, Stanford University*

From librarians . . .

"A canny narrative history of a wondrous archaeological site, full of personality and personalities, and ripe with thoughtful conjectures." —*Kirkus Reviews*

From the press . . .

"(Balter) has produced a compelling read, one that achieves the double act of educating and entertaining." —*Science Magazine*

"What else makes this book a cut above the normal look-what-we-dug-up text is its digressions. Balter spins off to the politics of getting a site to dig, goddess worship, just what makes scholars tick. He tells the story of real archaeologists doing real work." —*Providence Journal*

"All in all, this book is an exciting read. Balter knows his stuff and anyone interested in the origins of civilization and the ultimate foundations of the modern world we live in will enjoy and learn from it. Besides that, there is basically an undergraduate education in archaeological theory included." —*Political Affairs*

"This is a book for anyone interested in the history of the Middle East or in archeology, of course, but will appeal as well to those who love to read about the history of science. It should win awards." —*Books in Canada*

"He leaves no controversy or good yarn untouched. This all makes for a readable book that is as much an academics' soap-opera as it is a factual account." —*Current Archaeology*

THE GODDESS AND THE BULL

Çatalhöyük: An Archaeological Journey to the Dawn of Civilization

MICHAEL BALTER

Illustrations by John-Gordon Swogger

WALNUT CREEK, CALIFORNIA

LEFT COAST PRESS, INC.
1630 North Main Street, #400
Walnut Creek, CA 94596
http://www.LCoastPress.com

ISBN 1-59874-069-5 paperback

Original hardcover edition of this book was published by Free Press, New York.

Library of Congress Cataloging-in-Publication Data:
The goddess and the bull / Michael Balter
p. cm.
Added t.p. title: Çatalhöyük : An Archaeological Journey to the Dawn of Civilization
Includes bibliographical references (p.) and index
1.Çatalhöyük Mound (Turkey) 2. Turkey—Antiquities. 3. Excavations (Archaeology)—Turkey.
I.Title: Çatalhöyük : An Archaeological Journey to the Dawn of Civilization
II. Title
GN776.32.T9B35 2005
939.2—dc22
2004057413

Printed in the United States of America

The paper used in this publication meets the minimum requirements of American National Standard for Information Sciences—Permanence of Paper for Printed Library Materials, ANSI/NISO Z39.48–1992.

06 07 08 09 10 5 4 3 2 1

Cover illustrations: Bulgarian archaeologist Tatiana Stefanova examining a bull figurine. Female "goddess" figurine uncovered in 2004 at the site. Illustrations courtesy of the Çatalhöyük Research Project.

For Catherine and Emma

and

in memory of Rick Harmon

Contents

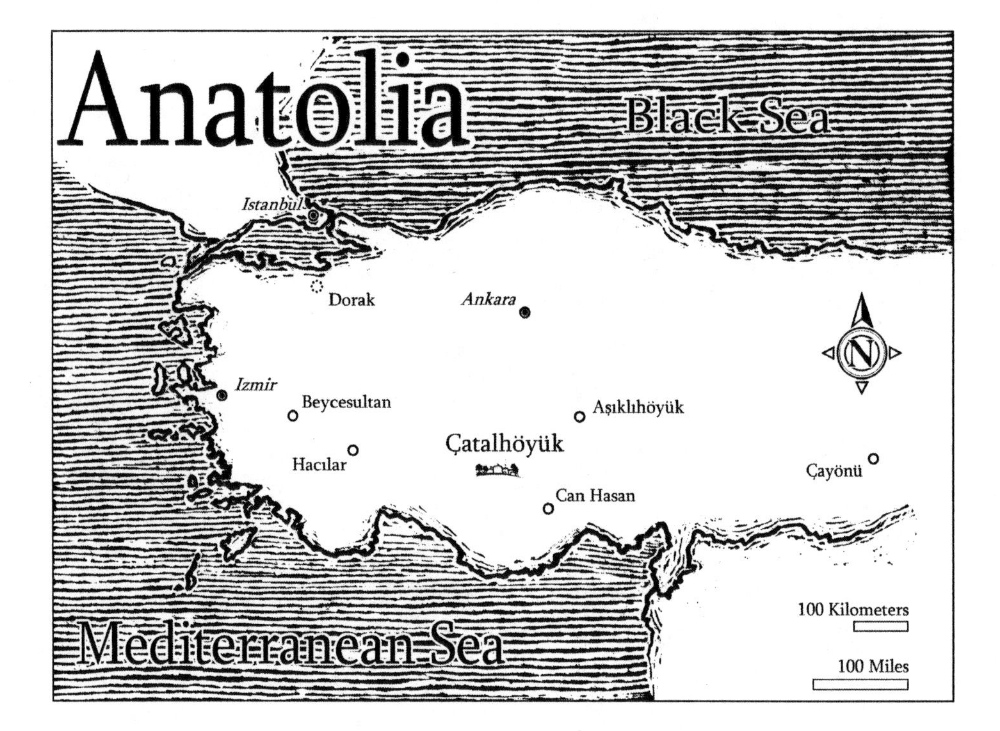
Anatolia
Black Sea
Istanbul
Dorak
Ankara
Izmir
Beycesultan
Aşıklıhöyük
Çatalhöyük
Hacılar
Çayönü
Can Hasan
N
100 Kilometers
100 Miles
Mediterranean Sea

Preface to the Paperback Edition

FOR ANY AUTHOR, the publication of a paperback edition of his or her book is a major event, equivalent to a rebirth and a renewal. I certainly feel that way about the paperback you are holding in your hands. Since its original publication in January 2005 by Free Press, *The Goddess and the Bull* has received a very positive reception from archaeologists, anthropologists, and the general public, despite occasional quibbles over certain points (about which more in a moment). Even in hardback, the book has already been adopted as a required text in a number of university courses in prehistory and archaeological theory. And I have received many kind e-mail messages from amateur archaeology buffs around the world telling me how much they learned from the book and how much they enjoyed it. With the paperback, the story of 9,500-year-old Çatalhöyük in Turkey—the largest early farming community ever discovered, and a site key to understanding the origins of civilization—should find many new readers, in the archaeological community and far beyond.

When the book was first published, I had only a few clear ideas about who its readers might be. Çatalhöyük, the prototypical Neolithic (New Stone Age) village, is certainly well known to archaeologists and prehistorians, and is discussed in nearly all textbooks covering early civilizations. And since its spectacular wall murals and sculptures of bulls, vultures, and "goddesses" represent the earliest known art created on human-made surfaces, the site often pops up in the first chapter of art history books, just after the section on Paleolithic (Old Stone Age) cave art. Another Çatalhöyük constituency is the feminist spirituality movement, particularly that segment which practices worship of a Mother Goddess; indeed, claims by the original excavator of Çatalhöyük, James Mellaart, that such a deity was worshipped there—and even that it was the home of a matriarchal society where women dominated—have made the site the equivalent of Mecca for the Mother Goddess movement.

I have been surprised, however, to find out how many people unassociated with any of these natural audiences for the book have not only heard of Çatalhöyük but actually developed a "thing"—in some cases, almost an obsession—about the place. That certainly happened to me, as I describe in the book's original Introduction. In my case, I was attracted not only by the site's fascinating archaeology but also by the fascinating people digging there. For others, the amazing preservation of Çatalhöyük's mudbrick houses, art, and artifacts makes the site a unique window into a time when humans were first settling down into organized communities and giving up the nomadic, hunting-and-gathering way of life. And the works of art, which motivated Mellaart and now the current dig director, Ian Hodder, to devote their careers to digging there, provide tantalizing glimpses into the minds of our prehistoric ancestors. Moreover, archaeologists digging at Çatalhöyük come literally face to face with these ancestors every season. Thus the book begins and ends with the discovery of human skulls buried under the floors of the houses and treated with special care, a rare and haunting evocation of the ties and emotions that once bound the settlement's inhabitants together into a thriving community.

David Bowie, who was kind enough to provide a comment for the back cover of this edition, suggests that burying the dead under the floors is a good way to remember where you put them. I think that there is a grain of truth to this amusing remark. The latest round of radiocarbon dating at Çatalhöyük shows that its inhabitants stayed rooted to this spot for about 1,200 years, roughly equal to fifty generations. In those first days of farming and settled life, prehistoric humans needed to anchor themselves symbolically to their land and to create the traditions and continuity necessary to hold their communities together. Although humans began to bury their dead during the Paleolithic period, only in the Neolithic did they literally live right on top of their ancestors—a highly effective way to foster the kind of remembering that Bowie hints at.

The excavations at Çatalhöyük were still under way when I finished this book, and Ian Hodder has indicated that they will continue until at least the year 2018. A number of readers have told me that they found the book's ending frustrating and somewhat arbitrary, implying that I should have waited a little longer before I wrote this story. Indeed, although there are seldom final answers in archaeology, I share their frustration. Just days after I finished writing the Epilogue—which covers most of the 2004 excavation season—and sent it directly from Çatalhöyük by e-mail to the book's editor in New York, yet more discoveries were made. The plastered skull I describe in the last paragraphs upon further digging turned out to be cradled in the arms of another skeleton. Yet again, Çatalhöyük had shown that archaeologists really can dig up evidence of emotional links between specific humans in the past.

And the 2005 season saw more dramatic finds, some of which may "bear" on the question of whether a Mother Goddess was actually worshipped at Çatalhöyük. One such discovery was a beautiful clay "stamp seal," an artifact commonly found in Near Eastern digs and which was probably used to stamp designs on clothing or other items to show ownership. This particular seal depicts an animal, quite likely a bear, with its front and hind legs raised upwards. Mellaart found a number of similar motifs in the form of sculptures on house walls—which usually had their heads and feet cut off—and interpreted them as goddesses. But the heads and feet of the stamp seal remain, leading Hodder to conclude that Mellaart's supposed goddess sculptures also depicted animals and not deities. Nevertheless, figurines clearly depicting females continue to be found, as evidenced by a bizarre discovery the same season: the front of one figurine resembled a typical Mother Goddess–style statuette, with full breasts on which the female's arms rest and a swollen belly possibly indicating pregnancy; but the back of the object seemed to represent the bones of a skeleton, with ribs and vertebrae clearly etched in a macabre fashion. Hodder is still thinking about how to interpret this figurine, with its suggestive juxtaposition of life and death.

Also in 2005, the Hodder team found, inside one mudbrick house, its first full "bucranium," the plastered skull of a bull. Next to the bucranium was a separate installation of bull horns embedded in a plastered bench. I don't want to give away the ending to Chapter 16, but the animal bone team's conclusions about whether the cattle at Çatalhöyük were wild or tame may shed light on the symbolic meaning of this dramatic find.

The female figurine mentioned above, by the way, was found by a new team from Istanbul University's prehistory department that began working at Çatalhöyük in 2005. In the view of many outside archaeologists, this is a long-overdue development: although many Turkish archaeology students have worked at the site over the years, this marks the first time that a Turkish-led team has dug at this largely Anglo-American excavation. The Istanbul team is led by Mihriban Özbaşaran, who makes a brief appearance in Chapter 9, when Hodder's team visits two Neolithic digs in Cappadocia that Özbaşaran co-led. Özbaşaran and her colleagues are looking at the earliest levels of occupation at Çatalhöyük. Meanwhile, a second Turkish group, from Selcuk University, is just now beginning to excavate Hellenistic, Roman, and Byzantine occupation just to the east of the Neolithic mound.

Future seasons will no doubt produce even more spectacular finds, and I can only hope that this book will stimulate readers to follow the dig's progress on its newly redesigned Web site (www.catalhoyuk.com).

I mentioned earlier that this book, like any other, has not been above criticism. For example, some, although certainly not all, Mother Goddess believers have attacked *The Goddess and the Bull* for denigrating their religion. As I point out in some detail, Ian Hodder and most archaeologists now working at Çatalhöyük are very skeptical about earlier claims that a Mother Goddess was worshipped at the site and that the settlement was organized along matriarchal lines—claims first advanced by Mellaart and later taken up by the late Marija Gimbutas. One such reviewer called the book "a gigantic cheap shot" and suggested that I would not have dared to treat Christianity with such disrespect. But most Goddess worshippers have been much kinder in their reviews, acknowledging the importance of understanding the current team's interpretations of this important site whether or not they agree with them. Most important, these more reasonable adherents recognize that the issue of whether or not a Mother Goddess was worshipped at Çatalhöyük is above all an archaeological question that must be addressed with archaeological evidence; this is an entirely different question from whether or not such a deity as a Mother Goddess actually exists, which is a matter of religion and faith.

• • •

THIS BOOK BEGAN as an assignment for *Science*, for which I have worked for the past fifteen years. I am grateful to the journal's editors for allowing me to continue to cover the discoveries at Çatalhöyük, which keeps my reporting on the site up-to-date. I also want to thank my editor at Free Press, Elizabeth Stein, for her friendship and support both during and after the writing of this book. And I am particularly pleased that Mitch Allen, publisher of Left Coast Press Inc., has agreed to take on the paperback edition of *The Goddess and the Bull.* Mitch and I began talking about this project shortly after he attended a panel at Cody's Bookstore in Berkeley in spring 2005, which included myself, Ian Hodder, and Ruth Tringham, the leader of the Berkeley contingent at Çatalhöyük. His enthusiasm for the book, and faith in its future, are much appreciated.

Michael Balter
Paris, France
January 2006

Introduction

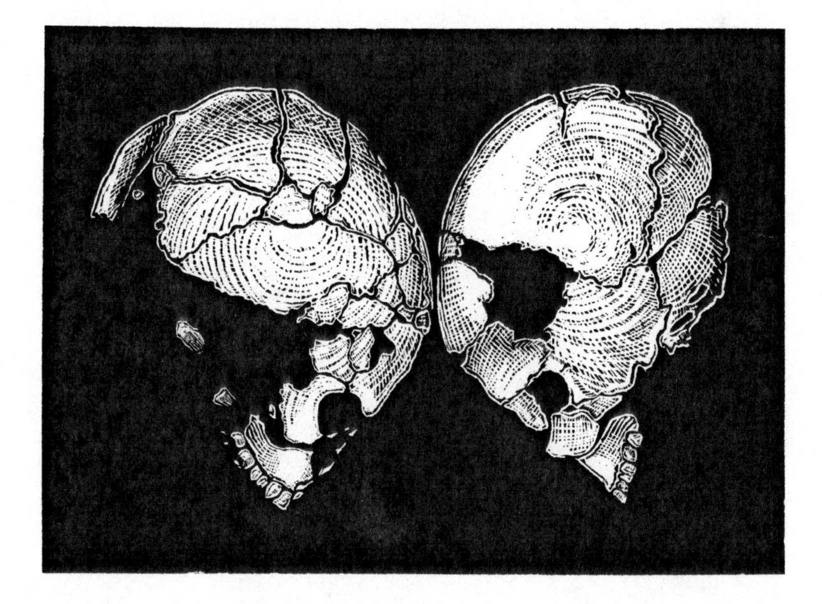

The archaeologist is digging up, not *things*, but *people*.

—MORTIMER WHEELER, *Archaeology from the Earth*

ONE HOT DAY in August 1999, archaeologists excavating at Çatalhöyük (pronounced "Chah-tahl-hew-yook"), a 9,500-year-old prehistoric village in south central Turkey, found two detached human skulls lying on the floor of what had once been a mud-brick house. The skulls had taken on a faint reddish color from the dense soil that had kept them hidden down through the ages. They were slightly crushed but still remarkably intact. The physical anthropologists working at Çatalhöyük took a close look at the skulls and concluded that one was that of a boy perhaps twelve years old, while the other was that of a young woman in her twenties. The skulls were lying together face to face, their foreheads lightly touching. With just a little imagination, one could picture a moment of tenderness between a mother and child or a brother and sister. Indeed, the anthropologists found that both crania shared an unusual pattern of bone sutures, a hint that they may well have been related.

When I visited the Çatalhöyük excavations about a week later, the team was still buzzing about the "finds." This is the dispassionate term archaeologists often use to refer to even the most exciting discoveries. Everyone was aware that this kind of find was rare. How often, after all, does an archaeologist dig up tangible evidence of an emotional tie between two specific human beings who lived so long ago? Almost never. One scientific specialist on the team suggested to me privately that the skulls could have rolled together by chance and just happened to touch foreheads. When I tried this explanation out on some of the excavators, they just laughed. The supervisor of that particular prehistoric house, they pointed out, was Mirjana Stevanovic, an archaeologist at the University of California at Berkeley with nearly thirty years of digging experience. Mirjana herself did not really want to speculate about the skulls, but she had no doubts about what she had found. "All I know," she told me, "is that they were put that way deliberately."

I made my first trip to Çatalhöyük in 1998, as a reporter for the American journal *Science*, to write an article called "The Mystery of Communities." We were tackling the question of why, around 10,000 years ago, human beings began giving up their former hunting and gathering existence, invented agriculture, and crammed themselves into close-knit villages made of stone or mud brick. Archaeologists often refer to this crucial step in human development—which took place first in the ancient Near East, then independently in several other parts of the world—as the "Neolithic Revolution." The phrase was coined by the Australian prehistorian V. Gordon Childe in the early part of the twentieth century, although the term *Neolithic* (meaning "New Stone Age") was first used by the British antiquarian Sir John Lubbock in his 1865 book *Prehistoric Times*, one of the first works to bring archaeology to the general public. Lubbock distinguished the Neolithic period from what he called the Paleolithic, or "Old Stone Age," which preceded it.

Today archaeologists usually date the beginning of the Paleolithic to about 2.5 million years ago, when humans first began using stone tools. This date also roughly corresponds to the first appearance of the genus

Homo in the fossil record. Just why our ancestors did not get around to inventing agriculture any earlier is one of the big questions archaeologists specializing in the Neolithic period, including the archaeologists working at Çatalhöyük, are trying to answer. After all, 10,000 years is not much more than a statistical blip in our long evolutionary history. The question can also be put another way: why did humans bother to invent agriculture and settle down in such close quarters, instead of continuing to romp across the landscape, hunting and gathering?

The Neolithic Revolution was a crucial turning point in human cultural and technological development. For better or worse, the first roots of civilization were planted along with the first crops of wheat and barley, and the mightiest of today's skyscrapers can trace its heritage to the Neolithic architects who built the first houses from stone, mud, and timber. Nearly everything that came afterwards, such as art and architecture, organized religion, writing, cities, social inequality, warfare, population explosions, global warming, traffic jams, mobile phones, the Internet—in short, all the blessings and curses of modern civilization—can be traced to that seminal moment in human prehistory when people decided that they wanted to live together in communities.

Biologist Jared Diamond, in his Pulitzer Prize–winning book *Guns, Germs, and Steel,* has even argued that today's division of the world into haves and have-nots can be traced back to the Neolithic Revolution. Those living in the right place at the right time—such as in the Near East, where the wild ancestors of wheat, barley, sheep, goats, and cattle made their home, or in Europe, where the agricultural revolution later spread like wildfire—reaped the major benefits of these momentous changes, as did their descendants, while those whom the revolution passed by, including the peoples of Africa, are still suffering the consequences today, in terms of poverty and lagging technological development. While not everyone agrees with Diamond's thesis, there is little argument that the Neolithic period marked a point of departure for the entire human race.

Çatalhöyük is one of the largest and most populated Neolithic settlements ever unearthed. This enormous village on Turkey's Konya Plain, discovered in 1958 by the flamboyant British archaeologist James Mellaart, was home to as many as 8,000 people at the height of its thousand-year lifetime. Mellaart dug here for four seasons during the early 1960s before Turkish authorities ejected him from the country under somewhat murky circumstances. Mellaart's findings, which included remarkably well preserved mud-brick houses and spectacular artworks depicting leopards, vultures, bulls, and what he interpreted as "Mother Goddesses," made the site internationally famous. Today Çatalhöyük merits a mention in many textbooks of archaeology and histories of architecture as the prototypical Neolithic village.

The current excavations are directed by Ian Hodder, who spent much of his career at Cambridge University and is now based at Stanford University in California. In the early 1980s Hodder launched a controversial rebellion against traditional approaches to archaeology, which culminated in his reopening of Çatalhöyük in 1993. An international team, made up of more than one hundred archaeologists and other experts, has flocked to join him. It includes archaeologists, physical anthropologists, cultural anthropologists, paleoenvironmentalists, climatologists, botanists, architects, geologists, geophysicists, chemists, computer experts, and even a psychoanalyst. This collective expertise probably represents the greatest concentration of scientific firepower ever focused on an archaeological dig. The team wants to know what brought thousands of people together on the Konya Plain, how they went about their daily lives, what they ate, why they buried their dead under the floors of their houses, what they believed, and what they were trying to express through the dramatic paintings and sculptures that adorned the walls of their homes.

In 1999, the year after my first visit, I returned to Çatalhöyük. Ian Hodder spotted me walking across the gravel courtyard of the "dig house" and came over to greet me. "Is this a business trip or a social call?" he asked with a smile. That was a good question: why had I come? *Science*'s news editor had expressed little enthusiasm for a follow-up article so soon after "The Mystery of Communities." No doubt I had been drawn back in part by Çatalhöyük's near-mythical celebrity and the fascination of witnessing one of the world's most important digs. Yet there was something else. The team of archaeologists at Çatalhöyük was one of the most interesting and diverse collections of individuals I had ever encountered. They were working at a site that dated from the dawn of civilization, probing some of the most fundamental questions about human existence. In the process they had formed their own community, with its own unique blend of friendships, rivalries, traditions, and rituals.

Science did end up publishing my article about the 1999 season, and several others since. And the day after Ian posed his perceptive question about why I had come, I decided to write this book. I have now been back to the site every season since that first visit. The team members have become used to my poking around and asking them personal questions about their childhoods and why they became archaeologists in the first place. One day, while consulting the dig's Web site (www.catalhoyuk.com), I was surprised to see that without my knowledge I had been designated as the excavation's official "biographer." At first I was a little concerned. I even thought about asking them to take my name off. Wouldn't being a member of the team jeopardize my reputation as an objective journalist? Indeed, I had often secretly wondered whether I kept going back to Çatalhöyük so that I could write this book, or whether I wrote this book so that I could keep going back to Çatalhöyük. But in the end, it really doesn't matter; either way, the story comes out the same.

That story begins on a cold day in 1958, when the history of archaeology, and of our understanding of our own origins, was changed forever.

1 / "It's Neolithic!"

LATE IN THE AFTERNOON of November 10, 1958, a green Land Rover lurched down a narrow dirt road in south central Turkey, about thirty miles southeast of the city of Konya. Three British archaeologists were packed inside. A frigid wind gusted from the south, blowing swirls of cold dust over the surrounding wheatfields. The Land Rover pulled up to the edge of a massive hill that stood out prominently from the flat plain. The archaeologists already suspected that this was no ordinary hill. The crunch of the tires went silent, and the three men climbed out to have a closer look.

The leader of the group was James Mellaart, thirty-three years old, pudgy, round-faced, his eyes darting to and fro excitedly behind dark-rimmed glasses. Mellaart lit a cigarette and stared out at the mound. The motor of a tractor droned in the distance. A flock of gray-throated great bustards circled overhead, their large wings swishing in the air. At

Mellaart's side, buttoning his coat against the cold, stood David French. Mellaart and French were visiting scholars at the British Institute of Archaeology at Ankara, the BIAA. Both men specialized in the prehistory of Anatolia, the vast plateau that makes up most of modern Turkey. (Prehistory is, in short, everything that had happened to humanity before the invention of writing some 5,000 years ago, during the Near Eastern Bronze Age.)

The third archaeologist was Alan Hall, a student at the University of Edinburgh in Scotland. Hall was studying the Classical period in Anatolia, from about the eighth century B.C. to the fourth century A.D., when Greek and Roman cultures spread from Europe into Asia. Mellaart had never learned how to drive, and Hall, whose Land Rover it was, had been kind enough to lend it for the mission. For more than a week the threesome had crisscrossed the Konya Plain, looking for signs of early human settlements. In theory this archaeological survey was meant to record any and all signs of ancient occupation, from all epochs, with an eye to possible future excavations. But Mellaart had come to Turkey with a mission: he was out to prove that Anatolia had played a pivotal role in prehistory. He had little interest in anything later than the Bronze Age. Despite the considerable remains of Classical civilization he and his colleagues came upon, Mellaart would dismiss even the most interesting of these ruins as "F.R.M.," short for "filthy Roman muck."

French shared Mellaart's passion for ancient Anatolia. Earlier that same year, he had dug with Mellaart at Hacilar, a 7,500-year-old village in western Turkey. Those excavations were already pushing back the earliest evidence for civilization in the region by several thousand years. Turkey was still relatively untouched by archaeological trowels. The unexplored horizons of its austere landscape beckoned to young archaeologists like French and Mellaart eager to make important discoveries and names for themselves. Yet as late as 1958, Anatolia was a passion in which few other archaeologists partook. Most experts believed that the Anatolian plateau was little more than a backwater during prehistoric times. The real action, they were convinced, had been farther east, at Neolithic sites like Jericho in Palestine and Jarmo in Iraq. There, some of the earliest known farming villages, 10,000 years old and more, had been unearthed in the early 1950s.

That dismissive attitude, however, had left a dilemma. Archaeologists were confident that the earliest farming settlements had sprouted in the Near East. A few thousand years later, Neolithic villages began cropping up in Greece, then the rest of Europe. It was logical to assume that farming had spread overland, from Asia to Europe, by the most direct route: via Anatolia. But there was little evidence to support this idea. Anatolia, the supposed land bridge for the westward spread of farming and settled life, had nothing to show for itself. As late as 1956, Mellaart's boss, Seton Lloyd—the BIAA's director in Ankara and a veteran of three decades of archaeological campaigns in the Near East—had written that "the greater part of modern Turkey, and especially the region more correctly described as Anatolia, shows no sign whatever of habitation during the Neolithic period." Some experts proposed instead that farmers had traveled from Asia to Greece by sea. This notion grew in popularity after excavations on Cyprus during the 1930s and 1940s revealed a sophisticated Neolithic community on that Mediterranean island, which later radiocarbon dating showed to be nearly 8,000 years old.

As Mellaart fidgeted and French shivered, they could hardly dare to believe that they were about to prove the experts wrong. Nor did they imagine that they would do far more than simply score points in what, to nonexperts, might have seemed like a fairly esoteric debate. In just a few years, discoveries at the impressive mound they now stood before would make headlines around the world, electrify the archaeological community, and revolutionize our picture of Neolithic technology, art, culture, and religion. And they would make Mellaart's reputation as one of the most brilliant, as well as most controversial, figures in archaeological history.

At the moment, however, all that lay in the future. During the previous week or so, the three archaeologists had already accomplished enough to make their meandering journey worthwhile. Their survey had charted more than a dozen new settlements dated to the Chalcolithic, or Copper Age, the epoch sandwiched between the earlier Neolithic and the later Bronze Age. Most archaeologists were willing to accept that Anatolia had been occupied during the Chalcolithic. Yet before Mellaart had begun trekking the plateau some years before, few of these sites had been recorded. Not that they were so difficult to find. To the great convenience of archaeologists searching for ancient villages, early Near Eastern settlers had two enduring habits. First, they often constructed their houses in mud brick, a building material with a lifetime of less than one hundred years. Second, when they rebuilt their homes, they usually did so on the same spot, using the ruins of the earlier structures as new foundations. Over hundreds of years, as these successive building levels lifted the villages higher and higher above the surrounding landscape, they eventually formed considerable mounds—or, in archaeological parlance, *tells*, after the Arabic word for "tall."

Long before Mellaart began working in Turkey, archaeologists had been mapping mounds across the Near East. One pioneer was the British archaeologist Max Mallowan. Accompanied by his wife, mystery writer Agatha Christie, Mallowan recorded hundreds of tells in Iraq during the 1930s while working for the British School of Archaeology in Baghdad. Seton Lloyd, who later took over this project, expanded the list to more than 5,000 mounds by the time he left Iraq for Turkey in 1948. But while Near Eastern mounds are relatively easy to find, some of them are layered with so many thousands of years of occupation that earlier levels tend to be compressed and distorted by later ones. As a result, archaeologists trying to understand their stratigraphy—that is, which occupation level belongs to which time period—often face a daunting challenge. A good example was Jericho, a complex site tackled by the British archaeologists John Garstang in the 1930s and Kathleen Kenyon in the 1950s. Garstang and Kenyon had to make sense of more than 10,000 years of archaeological deposits, which were first laid down when Jericho was a seasonal camp for hunter-gatherers and then continued to build up during the Neolithic period, the Bronze Age, and the Iron Age.

The tell that now loomed before Mellaart and his colleagues looked equally daunting. The oval-shaped mound was huge, a third of a mile long and some sixty feet high at its highest point. It was blanketed with wild grass and ruin weed, a bushy plant often found growing on Near Eastern tells. French and Hall trudged up the hill to have a look at the top, while Mellaart stayed below. As he prowled around the perimeter, eyes glued to the ground, Mellaart began spotting shards of a burnished, chocolate-brown pottery. He also spied hundreds of small pieces of glassy black volcanic obsidian, some fashioned into blades shaped like long prisms. Mellaart's heart began to race. He knew this pottery. He knew this obsidian. During the late 1930s, after Garstang had finished his work at Jericho, the pioneering archaeologist went on to excavate a large Neolithic settlement near the Turkish city of Mersin, on the Mediterranean coast. Mellaart had long thought that Garstang's discoveries should have opened archaeologists' eyes to the importance of Anatolia. But Mersin was so close to northern Syria that the experts didn't associate it with Anatolia at all. They preferred to lump it in with better-known Neolithic cultures in Syria and Mesopotamia.

The pottery and obsidian under Mellaart's feet were nearly identical to the Neolithic artifacts that Garstang had found at Mersin. The shards were practically oozing out of the mound. But what was at the top? At Mersin, Garstang's Neolithic village had been overbuilt with Chalcolithic, Bronze Age, Hittite, Greek, Byzantine, and finally Arab settlements. Mellaart looked up to see French and Hall racing down the tell towards him. "It's Neolithic! It's Neolithic at the top!" they shrieked. Mellaart shouted back, hardly believing his ears, "It's bloody Neolithic at the bottom!"

On this bitterly cold November day, Mellaart, French, and Hall had proved once and for all that Anatolia had been occupied during the Neolithic period. But they had done much more. They had discovered the biggest and best-preserved prehistoric settlement found to date. It sheltered a thousand years of pure Neolithic occupation, from bottom to top, with nothing—certainly no filthy Roman muck—to disturb its delicate mud-brick stratigraphy.

THAT EVENING the three checked into a hotel in the nearby town of Çumra, where they toasted their discovery long into the night with glasses of raki, the potent, aniseed-flavored Turkish liqueur. The next morning they returned briefly to collect samples of pottery and obsidian, and, as Mellaart later said, "to make sure it was still there." Mellaart's maps told him that this hill was called Çatal Hüyük, which meant "mound at the forked road" in Turkish. (Many years later Turkish authorities modernized the spelling to the present-day *Çatalhöyük.*) Local villagers confirmed that he had the right mound.

In Mellaart's later report on the discovery, published in *Anatolian Studies*, the BIAA's journal, his excitement had not abated. After briefly mentioning the fourteen new Chalcolithic sites the survey had found, Mellaart wrote, "Even more important is the discovery of one huge *Neolithic town-site*...this mound is nearly three times the size of Jericho...were excavations undertaken here, some extremely important conclusions might be reached about the earliest settlement on the Anatolian plateau." As the senior member of the survey team, Mellaart, according to archaeological tradition, had first dibs on the right to excavate the site. Certainly no one would question whether he was the right man for the job.

TO HIS FRIENDS, he has always been Jimmy. His enemies call him Jimmy too. Both friend and foe agree that Mellaart was an archaeological genius, with an unequaled nose for sniffing out ancient settlements. If the legend was born on the Anatolian plateau, the man himself came into the world in London, on November 14, 1925. According to Mellaart's account of his family's history, his father's ancestors were Highland Scots who eventually settled in Holland. Mellaart's father was a Dutch national who had emigrated to England shortly before Mellaart was born; his mother came from Northern Ireland. His father was an art expert who had studied with the Dutch Rembrandt scholar Abraham Bredius, who is perhaps best known for being taken in by the notorious Vermeer forgery *Supper at Emmaus*.

Mellaart spent his early childhood in a fine house in the West London borough of Chelsea, surrounded by art and talk of art. His father made a good living advising connoisseurs on their purchases, especially of Old Master drawings. But when Mellaart was seven years old, everything changed. The 1929 Wall Street crash, and the worldwide depression that followed, had dried up the art market. By 1932 his father gave up and moved the family, which now also included Mellaart's younger sister, to Amsterdam. Soon after, his mother died. Mellaart was never told how or why. His father refused to talk about it. But his mother's death marked him indelibly, especially after his father remarried.

Mellaart's father moved the family several times, from Amsterdam to Rotterdam to The Hague, where the boy started high school. Then, in May 1940, the Germans invaded and occupied the Netherlands. When Hitler began building his Atlantic Wall right through the coastal suburb where they lived, Mellaart's father picked the family up again and settled in an eighteenth-century castle near Maastricht. But right after Mellaart took his final exams at the local high school, he received a letter from German authorities ordering him to report to the Maastricht railroad station. He was to be sent to Germany to join the Nazis' slave labor force. Instead he went underground. Mellaart's father had many friends in Dutch museums; one of them found a job for him at the National Museum of Antiquities in Leiden, where he was put to work mending broken pottery and making plaster casts of archaeological finds.

In high school Mellaart had developed a keen interest in ancient Egypt. In Leiden he was befriended by a professor of Egyptology at Leiden University, Adriaan de Buck, who was best known for his extensive translations of texts found on ancient Egyptian coffins. Since the Nazis had closed the university, the elderly de Buck had no one to teach. He encouraged Mellaart to study Egyptian languages. Each week the young man would come around for tea and tutoring sessions. But Mellaart, surrounded by the fabulous riches in the museum, had already decided he wanted to be an archaeologist rather than a linguist. In those days the best places in Europe to study archaeology were London and Oxford.

In 1947 Mellaart landed a place in the undergraduate archaeology program at University College London. He continued to pursue his fascination with ancient Egypt and, in particular, with the origins of the so-called Sea Peoples, raiders and plunderers who plagued the eastern Mediterranean beginning around the thirteenth century B.C. They made a number of attempts to conquer Egypt, an ambition that was ultimately defeated by Pharoah Ramses III around 1170 B.C. The Sea Peoples were more successful in the Levant, the region along the eastern Mediterranean coast. One group of Sea Peoples, the Philistines, became the biblical enemies of the Israelites. Just where the Sea Peoples came from is still a matter of debate. Much of their pottery, which has been unearthed at sites they apparently destroyed—the pottery lies in stratigraphic layers just above the destroyed settlements—is similar to that made by the Mycenaeans from Bronze Age Greece.

Some archaeologists have put the finger farther west, on the Sardinians, Sicilians, or the Etruscans. Mellaart, while a student in London, became an enthusiast of yet another minority viewpoint: the Sea Peoples who harassed Egypt and the Levant, he decided, must have come from the north—that is, from Anatolia. Before long, the pursuit of this iconoclastic hypothesis would take Mellaart to Turkey. But first he had to learn to dig.

AT THE TIME MELLAART was coming of age as an archaeologist, in the late 1940s and early 1950s, British field archaeology had long been dominated by two giants: Kathleen Kenyon and her mentor, Mortimer Wheeler. In North America the so-called Wheeler-Kenyon school of excavation had its parallels in what is more simply called the Stratigraphic Revolution, exemplified by Alfred Kidder's meticulous work on the Pueblo cultures of the American Southwest. This generation of archaeologists had borrowed the concept of stratigraphy, meaning "stratification," from geologists who used the term to describe the strata that made up the earth's crust. Just as volcanoes, rivers, and lakes had deposited successive layers of rocks and sediments on the earth's surface, so did successive waves of ancient peoples leave behind the stratified deposits of their civilizations. The archaeologist's job, Wheeler and his like-minded colleagues insisted, was to carefully record the position of each find—whether it be a pottery shard, a grinding stone, or a human burial—so that it could be correctly assigned to the culture that had produced it.

Today it may seem obvious that the most recent occupation layers at an archaeological site will usually be found at the top and the oldest at the bottom, but a full appreciation of this basic premise was slow in coming. For one thing, it meant treating the biblical account of creation, which put the age of humankind at no more than 6,000 years, with considerable skepticism. It was also necessary to acknowledge that our own species is the fruit of millions of years of biological and cultural evolution. Before the middle of the nineteenth century, when scholars finally began to accept these once-radical notions, it was difficult for archaeology to take off as a scientific discipline in its own right. An early and notable exception was the work of Thomas Jefferson, whom Wheeler himself credited with conducting "the first scientific excavation in the history of archaeology"—a carefully recorded 1784 trench through a burial mound on Jefferson's property in Virginia. Unfortunately, as Wheeler lamented, Jefferson was too far ahead of his time: "This seed of a new scientific skill fell upon infertile soil."

Two major events finally gave archaeology the lift it needed. One was the publication in 1859 of Charles Darwin's *On the Origin of Species*, which put the theory of evolution on a firm scientific basis. The other, also in 1859, was the visit of a delegation of eminent British scientists to France's Somme River. Since 1837 amateur archaeologist Jacques Boucher de Crèvecoeur de Perthes had been claiming to have found human-made stone axes buried in the river's banks, in intimate association with the bones of extinct animals. Until the British confirmed his conclusions, Boucher de Perthes, the director of a local customs house, was hard put to convince anyone that the Ice Age humans who made the tools had lived long before the great flood described in the Bible.

Many more years would pass before archaeologists would adopt the rigorous scientific methods Wheeler and others had begun advocating by the 1920s. "There is no right way of digging, but there are many wrong ways," Wheeler, ever the scold, declared. He was particularly disdainful about the celebrated excavations at Troy and Mycenae carried out in the 1870s by the German banker and adventurer Heinrich Schliemann—the Indiana Jones of his day—which had done so much to stoke the public's appetite for the romance of archaeology. "We may be grateful to Schliemann" for uncovering these fabulous sites, Wheeler wrote, "because he showed us what a splendid book had in fact been buried there; but he tore it to pieces in snatching it from the earth, and it took us upwards of three-quarters of a century to stick it more or less together again and to read it aright." A more worthy hero, Wheeler believed, was General Augustus Lane-Fox Pitt-Rivers, who brought military discipline and precision to his excavations in southern England in the 1880s and 1890s.

Wheeler, a former military man himself, would conduct a number of archaeological campaigns across England and India during his long career. The young Kathleen Kenyon—daughter of the biblical scholar Frederick Kenyon, a leading advocate of the literal truth of the Bible—caught up with Wheeler in 1930 at Verulamium, near Saint Albans in Hertfordshire. Verulamium is still heralded as one of the best excavations of a Roman British town. Wheeler put his twenty-four-year-old protégée in charge of excavating a Roman theater. By the end of the decade Kenyon had become his leading disciple.

When James Mellaart caught up with Kenyon in 1948, she was making a name for herself at Sutton Walls, an Iron Age hill fort in southwest England. Mellaart spent three Easter vacations digging with Kenyon at Sutton Walls, learning how to decipher stratigraphic layers by the differences in the color and texture of their soils, a technique Wheeler and Kenyon had championed. He also learned how to excavate human burials. A battle had apparently taken place at or near the hill fort, as evidenced by a large grave filled with the skeletons of men and boys who had met a violent death.

Kenyon told Mellaart that she was planning to dig at Jericho beginning in 1952 and invited him to join her when the time came. But Mellaart was graduating from University College London in June 1951. He needed something to do in the meantime. In that case, Kenyon said, the new British Institute of Archaeology at Ankara was offering scholarships to young archaeologists. It would give him some experience in the Near East. Why not apply?

BY THE LATE 1940S, the sun was beginning to set on the British Empire. But archaeologically speaking, the end of World War II sparked a resurgence of foreign research in the Near East, as the British, Americans, French, and even Germans rushed back in to grab the best sites. The British, with schools and institutes of archaeology in Baghdad, Jerusalem, Cairo, Amman, Athens, and Rome, among other spots, were well positioned to get their fair share, but they had no institutional presence in Turkey. In 1946 Garstang—who had been forced to suspend his dig at Mersin during the war—returned for a final season. While there, he hatched a plan to found a new institute. The French and German archaeological institutes were based in romantic Istanbul; Garstang insisted that the British should set up shop in Ankara, the capital. Turkish authorities quickly gave their blessing to the project. In January 1948 the BIAA was officially inaugurated. Garstang asked Seton Lloyd, who had worked with him at Mersin in the late 1930s, to serve as the BIAA's director. Lloyd, having spent most of the war in Baghdad and Jerusalem, was happy to have a change of scene.

Mellaart's application to the BIAA for a two-year scholarship, submitted in February 1951, was nothing if not ambitious. In his search for the origins of the Sea Peoples, he proposed to "explore those areas from Mersin to the Aegean"—that is, almost the entire Mediterranean coast of Turkey—"for sites of ancient habitation." Mellaart also suggested, although he conceded that "there may not be enough time," a similar investigation of Turkey's western seaboard. Just how realistic the BIAA considered these plans is not recorded, but in May his application was accepted. He was awarded the grand sum of £150 to last the entire two years. A few months later he was on his way to Turkey.

From the moment Mellaart set foot within its borders, Turkey's archaeological landscape was transformed. His first sweeping surveys across the southern part of the country, in 1951 and 1952, put some four hundred new pre-Classical sites on the map, where before there had been mostly blank spaces. Since Mellaart didn't drive—and even if he had, there was no vehicle available—he crossed most of this territory on foot, occasionally using trains and buses to get him to the next study region. He collected thousands of pottery shards. Most of the sites were tells dating from the Copper Age (beginning around 5500 B.C.) or later, although even then he thought that some of the pottery might date from the Neolithic, some 2,000 years earlier. Mellaart would later say that one day in 1952, while surveying in the Konya region, he had spotted the imposing mound of Çatalhöyük six miles in the distance. But a lingering bout of dysentery, and the heavy bags of potshards slung over his shoulder, made him postpone the visit for another time.

In 1952 and 1953, on breaks from his Anatolian surveys, Mellaart served as one of Kenyon's many field supervisors at Jericho. The first season, he discovered a Bronze Age tomb and excavated it with the help of a crew of Palestinian workmen. Mellaart's confidence in himself, which was already considerable, only grew. The following year, when Kenyon thought she might have reached bedrock in one part of the tell, Mellaart was convinced that there might still be archaeological remains farther down. "Go ahead, Jimmy, you always know best," Mellaart recalled Kenyon saying. Another five meters of digging revealed three stone walls, one on top of the other. Behind those walls, after Mellaart had left, Kenyon later found the remains of a massive stone tower some thirty feet in diameter—one of the most amazing feats of Neolithic architecture ever discovered.

Meanwhile, back in Turkey, Mellaart's energy and enthusiasm were a godsend for BIAA director Seton Lloyd, who was trying to put his new institute on the map. His young protégé was finding ancient sites faster than anyone could excavate them. During his 1952 survey, a local history teacher had led Mellaart to the mound of Beycesultan, on the upper stretches of the Meander River in western Turkey, where Lloyd and Mellaart would later excavate a spectacular Bronze Age palace dated to about 1800 B.C. In 1956 another local teacher from a village near the southwest city of Burdur showed Mellaart a mound littered with shards of brilliantly painted pottery. This was Copper Age Hacilar, site of the first excavation Mellaart would direct by himself, from 1957 to 1960. During the last season at Hacilar—the year before he began digging at Çatalhöyük—the excavations would also lay bare an earlier Neolithic village that dated from around the time Çatalhöyük was abandoned.

As Mellaart's digs took him ever deeper into the past—Bronze Age Beycesultan, Copper Age Hacilar, and soon to come, Neolithic Çatalhöyük—his star at the BIAA rose higher and higher. His findings were appearing in nearly every issue of *Anatolian Studies.* Mellaart was fast becoming a major figure in Near Eastern archaeology. In 1958 the institute's governing council appointed Mellaart as assistant director to Seton Lloyd. His discovery of Çatalhöyük that same year mooted Lloyd's declaration, just two years earlier, that Anatolia had not been occupied during the Neolithic. Lloyd seemed happy to be proved wrong: "J. Mellaart's West Anatolian survey made nonsense of all these theories," he wrote later.

Everyone soon forgot that Mellaart had originally come to Turkey to search for traces of the Sea Peoples. Mellaart never did find any evidence for these mysterious invaders, although he still counts himself among a minority of archaeologists who think that Anatolia is a good bet for their origins. But perhaps more important, he found a partner to accompany him on the ups, and then the downs, of his archaeological career. Her name was Arlette.

• • •

ARLETTE CENANI came from an upper-class Istanbul family. Her stepfather, Kadri Cenani, was descended from a long line of Ottoman Empire viziers and diplomats. In 1939, when Arlette was fifteen years old, the family moved to a sprawling *yali*, as a waterside wooden house is called in Turkish. Arlette's *yali* was on the Asian side of the Bosphorus, not far from Istanbul. There her mother kept three grand pianos and entertained such celebrated visitors as Agatha Christie and Somerset Maugham. Archaeology had long been a family passion. Kadri's great-grandfather had been the Ottoman governor of Syria. His collection of Syrian artifacts was later housed in Istanbul's Museum of the Ancient Orient. In the early 1950s Arlette began sitting in on the German archaeologist Kurt Bittel's classes at Istanbul University. Bittel was an expert on the Hittites, who had ruled Anatolia for some eight hundred years beginning about 2000 B.C. He was also the former director of the German Archaeological Institute in Istanbul, one of the BIAA's rival institutions.

In late 1952 Arlette was digging with Bittel at Fikirtepe, near Istanbul, one of the first excavations in Turkey to show evidence of Chalcolithic settlement. One day Bittel brought over an earnest young man who was visiting the dig for a week. It was James Mellaart. Bittel asked Arlette, who spoke English fluently, to take Mellaart in hand. Arlette, for whom all archaeologists were dashing figures, was happy to oblige. Mellaart, for his part, took a quick look at the handsome young woman who stood before him—at her long, straight nose and serious brown eyes—and made no objection either. Before long the two were down on their hands and knees digging together. They soon uncovered a rare find: a beautiful, completely intact, red burnished pot. Mellaart thought it might be Neolithic, but Bittel dismissed the suggestion with a wave of his hand.

In April 1954 James and Arlette were married at the *yali*, with the entire Cenani family in attendance. The following year their son Alan was born in Istanbul. From that time on, Arlette would accompany Mellaart on all his digs, as translator, photographer, and housekeeper. She also served as secretary in the BIAA's Ankara headquarters for several years.

The couple spent the summers in Ankara or in the field. The rest of the year they lived in the *yali*, where Mellaart set up a study in a room overlooking the Bosphorus. Turkey was now his home.

Many years later, after radiocarbon dating had become a well-established technique, archaeologists concluded that the earliest stratigraphic levels at Fikirtepe were indeed Neolithic. Mellaart had been right about that pot. You can see it today in Istanbul's Archaeological Museum.

2 / A Prehistoric Art Gallery

From the moment James Mellaart discovered Çatalhöyük in November 1958, he began hatching plans to excavate the mound. But first he had to complete his dig at Hacilar. For James and Arlette, Hacilar was a team effort. While Mellaart supervised the excavations, Arlette handled the housekeeping and accounting, and took the photographs of her husband's stunning finds. David French catalogued the abundant pottery: beautiful cream-colored dishes, bowls, and jugs decorated with brilliant red stripes, still rated as some of the most spectacular ceramics from the Near East. Most of the hard work, however, was performed by a team of several dozen Turkish workmen Mellaart and Seton Lloyd had trained at Beycesultan. These local men had honed their skills on Beycesultan's huge Bronze Age palace, a sprawling complex of chambers covering more than an acre. They knew when to keep digging—to "move earth," as archaeologists say—and when to put down their shovels and call Mellaart over to look at what they had found. At Hacilar the crew quickly became expert at negotiating the intricacies of fragile mud-brick architecture.

During the last few days of the final season at Hacilar, in 1960, Mellaart and his crew found nearly twenty intact female figurines on the plastered floors of some of the mud-brick houses. Some of these statuettes, which ranged from about three to five inches tall, were made of baked clay; others were still unbaked, as if they were waiting to be put in the oven. They depicted tall, voluptuous women, some standing and some sitting, some with their hands at their sides and others holding their heavy, pendulous breasts. The figurines sparked a media sensation when Mellaart published Arlette's photographs of them in *Anatolian Studies* early the next year. "Mellaart has discovered the remains of a culture so sophisticated as to shatter all previous notions about Late Neolithic man," declared *Time* magazine, which also published one of Arlette's photos of a sitting figurine. The British press was equally ebullient: the "statuettes of the 'Mother Goddess,'" the *Daily Telegraph* reported, "are the first of their sort in the history of art."

Suddenly Mellaart was a media star. He cranked up the media hype even more when he published a three-page color spread on the figurines in the *Illustrated London News*, a popular magazine that often reported on archaeological finds. And he spelled out his views on their religious and artistic significance in his *Anatolian Studies* report. The statues, he wrote, most likely represented "the Anatolian 'Fertility Goddess,' the prototype of Hepat, Kupapa, Cybele, and the Magna Mater": that is, the Hacilar figurines presaged a long line of later goddesses worshipped across Asia and Europe. As for the ancestral origins of these sacred images, Mellaart continued, "it can only be hoped that the continuation of excavations of still older sites will reveal the earlier stages, if not the beginning, of this truly remarkable art." Even as he wrote these words, he knew exactly where to look.

ON MAY 17, 1961, Mellaart arrived at Çatalhöyük. He was armed with an excavation permit from the Turkish antiquities department and a $2,400 grant from the Wenner-Gren Foundation for Anthropological Research in New York, plus a number of other donations toward the dig's expenses. Arlette was there, camera at the ready, as was their son, Alan, now nearly six years old. The crew also included an American expert in stone tools, an architect from London to draw the plans of the buildings, an artist to sketch the finds, an archaeology student from Istanbul University, and thirty-five workmen from Beycesultan. Arlette had arranged housing for all of them in school buildings at Küçükköy, a village just up the dirt road from the mound.

David French, however, was absent. French, with Mellaart's encouragement, had decided to launch his own excavations at Can Hasan, a small mound about thirty-five miles southeast of Çatalhöyük that Mellaart had first seen during a survey in 1954. French and Mellaart, along with Alan Hall, had visited the site again during their 1958 survey.

Mellaart decided to break Çatalhöyük's ground in the southwest section of the tell, where in 1958 he had seen traces of burnt mud-brick walls exposed by the erosion of the southern wind. Under his attentive direction, the Turkish workmen began digging into the *fill*—a complex combination of plaster, mud-brick, ash, and rubbish—with which the Neolithic settlers had packed their abandoned houses. Before long they were exposing the surfaces of the walls, which were covered with multiple layers of cream-colored plaster. On the second day of the dig, a swatch of plaster on the wall of one building fell off, revealing what at first seemed like a blotch of thick red paint on the plaster layer underneath. Mellaart stared at the blotch, waiting for his eyes to focus. Suddenly a red stag with bristling antlers was leaping out at him from the wall.

With the entire crew crowded around, Mellaart used a small knife to carefully pare away the plaster. After several hours the scene, spread across more than four feet of plaster surface, was laid bare. Five or six red men, some dressed in animal skins, appeared to be chasing a herd of seven red deer. The men brandished bows and arrows. One of them was holding what appeared to be a lasso. The deer were fleeing toward the right-hand side of the picture. Some had their heads turned sharply backward toward the hunters, as if in terror. One stag, already fallen to its knees, was flanked by two men who seemed about to kill it.

Mellaart gazed at the tableau in amazement. None of the Neolithic digs over the previous decades had uncovered wall paintings, even if other forms of art—especially figurines—were already well known from

Jericho and other sites. At that time the earliest known wall murals in the Near East were from Teleilat Ghassul, a Chalcolithic site in Palestine several thousand years younger than Çatalhöyük. But wall painting was rare even during the Chalcolithic. Archaeologists had long been puzzled by the wide time gap between the last of the magnificent Upper Paleolithic paintings at caves like Lascaux in France and Altamira in Spain—estimated at 13,000 to 15,000 years old—and the much later resurgence of pictorial art exemplified by the vivid palace frescoes of Late Bronze Age Greece and Crete, beginning about 1600 B.C. Whether this discontinuity was due to poor archaeological preservation of prehistoric paintings that once did exist, or whether Neolithic and Chalcolithic peoples preferred to express themselves in other ways, was not clear. Now the gap seemed to be filled. At the very least, Mellaart had found the earliest known paintings on human-made surfaces.

Over the four seasons that he dug at Çatalhöyük, Mellaart found dozens of wall paintings, as well as painted plaster wall sculptures, depicting hunting scenes, giant bulls, leopards, vultures, female breasts, and "goddesses." One painting, he thought, seemed to represent a "town plan" of the Neolithic village, with an erupting volcano looming overhead. Mellaart became obsessed with the search for more and more of these works of art. While some experts on prehistoric art have cautioned against reading too much into these images, suggesting that ancient peoples might have engaged in "art for art's sake," most archaeologists have assumed that they are symbolic expressions of the psyche of ancient peoples. Çatalhöyük's plethora of artworks seemed to provide an unprecedented opportunity to get into the minds of Neolithic settlers.

Such an understanding would complement what archaeologists had already discovered about early farmers. During the previous decade, two other key digs had thrown open new windows onto the Neolithic way of life. At Jericho, the earliest known permanent settlement, Kathleen Kenyon had documented the transition between hunter-gatherer and sedentary modes of human existence and laid bare important details of Neolithic architecture and burial practices. At Jarmo in Iraq, the American Robert Braidwood had found evidence for the earliest known domestication of wheat and barley, thus pinpointing the dawn of the agricultural revolution in the so-called Fertile Crescent of the Near East. Now, at Çatalhöyük, the canvas of Neolithic symbolic and religious life was being unveiled—if, that is, the meaning of the art could be deciphered.

Thrilling as the unexpected discovery of that first painting was for Mellaart and his team, it also presented a major emergency. For some 9,000 years, the pigments, the plaster, and the mud brick had been protected from the ravages of the Anatolian sun by a high level of moisture within the tell, thanks to the relatively high water table on the semiarid Konya Plain. As soon as the artworks were exposed to sunlight and the dry air, they began to dessicate and crack. Some of the brilliant red pigment began turning gray, and green fungus began spreading across the surface of some paintings. Mellaart was not sure what to do. Then he learned that Ernest Hawkins, an expert on fresco conservation with the Byzantine Institute of America, was working in Istanbul. Hawkins answered the call and arrived at Çatalhöyük a few days later. He immediately realized that the paintings could not be left in place if there was to be any hope of saving them. Hawkins' advice, based on his experience with Byzantine frescoes, was to coat their surfaces with the resin polyvinyl acetate. Once dry, the surfaces were covered with muslin or tissue, and then the paintings—or segments of them in the case of the larger works—were cut out of the wall, mud-brick backing and all.

A number of paintings were removed that way and placed onto wooden boards for the jarring, 150-mile Land Rover journey to the archaeological museum in Ankara. Conservators at the museum then laid the mud-brick backings onto wet plaster of paris, which, when dry, provided some additional stability. Miraculously, many of the paintings survived this treatment, and some were eventually put on display at the museum. But despite the great care taken by the Beycesultan men, who prepared the works for the journey, others did not survive. In at least one case, the plaster adhered to the covering cloth and fell away with it. Other paintings, particularly those that were already in poor condition, simply fell apart and could not be saved. Fortunately, thanks to the dig's artists and Arlette's camera, their images were captured on paper and film for the archaeological record.

AN ARCHAEOLOGIST can dig in only two directions: horizontally and vertically. Prior to the Stratigraphic Revolution, horizontal excavation—

that is, the laying bare of broad swaths of an ancient city, town, or settlement—was the general rule. Vertical excavation, in which the archaeologist peels away sequential stratigraphic layers to reveal their chronological sequence, was an antidote to the sometimes superficial horizontal approach. But Mortimer Wheeler, the British champion of stratigraphic excavation, argued that these two ways of attacking an archaeological site were complementary, even if the archaeologist—depending on what he or she was trying to find out—often had to give priority to one or the other. Vertical excavation alone, Wheeler commented with his customary metaphoric flourish, "is the railway timetable without a train" which "leaves us in the dark as to those very factors which fit a past culture or civilization into the story of human endeavor and so make its recovery worthwhile." Horizontal excavations alone, on the other hand, "were trains without a time-table. The trains sometimes ran vigorously enough, but we knew not when they were running or where they started, or their intermediate stopping-places, or their destination."

At Çatalhöyük, Mellaart managed to do both, and on an amazingly speedy schedule. During that first season, which lasted thirty-nine working days, the Beycesultan men railroaded through forty mud-brick buildings, a rate of one per day. Early each morning, to avoid the heat, Mellaart's crew climbed to the top of the mound with its picks and shovels. As the Anatolian sun rose higher in the sky, Mellaart paced up and down the mud-brick walls, supervising the work and smoking furiously. By the end of the dig in 1965, he had exposed nearly two hundred buildings, covering about an acre of the tell. Although this represented only about 3 percent of the thirty-two-acre mound, it was enough to provide an unprecedented picture of the layout of a Neolithic settlement. Çatalhöyük was so huge that Mellaart soon took to calling it a city, leapfrogging over the more modest designations of "village" or "town" used to classify other Neolithic sites. The notion that Çatalhöyük was a city received a major boost a few years later when Jane Jacobs, the respected Canadian expert on urban life, repeated the claim in her book *The Economy of Cities.*

Mellaart complemented his extensive horizontal exposure of Çatalhöyük with vertical plunges into the depths of the settlement. This necessarily meant destroying the houses as he went down. Since the

Neolithic villagers had built their houses one atop the other over a period of at least a thousand years, the only way to reveal the building underneath was to dismantle the one above. Working downward in selected parts of the mound, Mellaart eventually identified at least thirteen occupation levels, although he never reached virgin soil. Following the Wheeler-Kenyon guidelines, he numbered the layers with Roman numerals: the top, or most recent, level was designated 0, followed by I, II, III, and so forth, down to XII, the earliest level he reached, with a "deep sounding" during the last days of the 1963 season. One particularly well preserved layer identified during the first season, Level VI, apparently corresponded to the period of the settlement's maximum population. Mellaart also found considerable evidence that Level VI had been ravaged by a series of ferocious fires.

By the end of Mellaart's first excavation season, it had become clear that each house was built according to the same basic scheme. The walls were made of long, rectangular mud bricks fashioned from clay quarried from the alluvial soils of the surrounding landscape. The bricks were strengthened with added straw and sometimes small pieces of reed, and dried in the sun. They were then placed one atop the other, with a layer of thick black mortar—composed largely of ash and ground animal bones—sandwiched in between. The walls and floors were covered with coats of plaster. Some of the coats were quite thin, like whitewash, but other layers were much thicker and seemed to correspond to annual replasterings. By counting the number of these thicker coats, Mellaart was able to get an idea of the lifespan of a house. The average was about eighty years, although some houses in Level VII had as many as 120 plaster layers.

The Neolithic residents dismantled the roofs and knocked down much of the walls when rebuilding their houses, leaving little trace of the roofs and the upper halves of the buildings. But Mellaart surmised that the roofs were made of wood beams covered by bundles of reeds and mud and held up by timbers placed against the walls. This conclusion was supported by the wide scars these timbers had left in the wall plaster, as well as deep postholes in the floors where the beams had once stood. Mellaart's crew also found a great number of charcoal lumps on house floors and in the fill, the apparent remains of timbers that had been burned in accidental or deliberate fires.

The houses were arranged in a honeycomb pattern, with their outer walls jammed one against the other. Every so often a cluster of houses was interrupted by a large space that Mellaart called a "courtyard." This claustrophobic arrangement of the Neolithic neighborhood raised a question: how did the residents get in and out of their homes? While many houses had what appeared to be small storerooms demarcated by interior walls, and tight passageways that allowed the inhabitants to enter these cubicles, there were no exterior doorways. Nor did Mellaart find any evidence for streets or alleys in the part of the tell that he excavated. There seemed to be only one possible answer: the villagers had entered through holes in the roofs.

Indeed, the plaster on the south wall of nearly every house was scarred with a diagonal mark, which Mellaart concluded was the trace of a wooden ladder that had once rested there. At the bottom of these "ladder scars," with equal regularity, he found ovens or hearths set partly into the walls. The ovens, many of which were still remarkably well preserved, were made of large, dome-shaped shells of hardened clay or plaster. The hole in the roof apparently served not only as an entryway to let people in, but as a chimney to let the smoke from the fire out.

The south wall seemed to be devoted to public or domestic activities such as cooking and entry and exit. The layout of the rest of the house was apparently designed to provide more private spaces. In the standard arrangement, there was a series of raised platforms or benches built up from plaster: a small, square platform in the northeast corner, a longer platform against the east wall, and a narrow bench not far from the ladder. Often there would be a platform against the north wall as well, although this seemed to vary from house to house. Mellaart surmised that the platforms, which were probably covered with mats made of reeds or other material, were sat on during the daytime and slept on at night. If this assumption is correct, then the living were literally sleeping with the dead.

No sooner had the Beycesultan men begun breaking through the plaster platforms and floors of the first tier of houses than the bodies began turning up. Over the four seasons of Mellaart's dig, the team unearthed about 480 skeletons. Almost all of them were found beneath the platforms along the walls, although in Level VI, which corresponds to the most densely populated phase of the settlement, there were so many skeletons that some were buried in oval pits in the middle of the floor.

Mellaart calculated that the average number of burials in each building was about eight, but this varied greatly: one house had forty-two skeletons and a few had none at all. (This accounting is, however, incomplete, because the floors of many houses had not yet been excavated when the dig had to end.) Most of the bodies had been flexed tightly, knees to chest, and placed on their left sides with their heads facing the center of the room and their feet to the wall. But there were numerous exceptions to this general rule. Some skeletons were fully extended on their backs, and a few were even buried sitting up.

The apparent reverence with which the living regarded the dead had its limitations. In many cases the bones were quite jumbled up. This somewhat disorganized arrangement of the skeletons, along with evidence that the plaster platforms had been cut into repeatedly, made it clear that skeletons that had been buried earlier were sometimes pushed aside to make room for later burials. Mellaart also concluded that most of the interments were "secondary" rather than "primary" burials. In archaeological parlance, a primary burial is one in which a body is laid to rest shortly after death and then allowed to remain in more or less eternal repose without further disturbance. Secondary burial follows from the widespread tendency of ancient peoples—or people nowadays, for that matter—to mess about with the bones of their loved ones. In today's western world, for example, putting a body straight into a coffin and burying it in a cemetery would be an example of primary burial; having the remains cremated and keeping them in an urn on the living room mantel would count as secondary burial.

At Çatalhöyük a small number of skeletons were buried after their skulls had been removed, although the majority had kept their heads. Mellaart became convinced that the dead bodies were first put outdoors to decompose before their final burial. "Upon death the corpse of the deceased was probably removed to a mortuary outside the settlement where vultures cleaned the corpses down to the bones and dry ligaments," Mellaart wrote in his 1967 book about the excavations, *Çatal Hüyük: A Neolithic Town in Anatolia*. "Presumably the dead were exposed on platforms, accessible to the birds and insects, but not to dogs or other scavengers which carry off bones." The idea that vultures might be lending a helping beak to the mortuary ritual was suggested by wall paintings depicting these carrion-eating birds swooping down on headless people. Another painting, found in a Level VI building, showed what Mellaart thought was a gabled "charnel house" filled with numerous stylized skulls. But some other members of Mellaart's team questioned whether the bodies were really allowed to decompose to such a great extent before being buried. If not, the vulture paintings might have greater symbolic than literal significance.

Mellaart also concluded, based on preliminary determinations of the sexes of the skeletons later carried out by physical anthropologists, that there were important differences in the way men and women had been buried. The adult male skeletons seemed concentrated under the small, northeast platforms of the houses, while females were usually found under the longer platform along the east wall. And while none of the burials was particularly rich in so-called grave goods—that is, objects buried together with the deceased—there were clues that men and women might have played different gender roles even in those ancient days. Thus males were often found with weapons such as stone mace heads or flint daggers with bone handles, as well as bone belt hooks and the occasional bead and pendant; females were adorned with jewelry such as necklaces made from beads and shells, or copper and bone finger rings. One astonishing item, however, was found only in female burials: shiny mirrors made from large lumps of black obsidian, a glassy rock formed when molten lava cools. The obsidian had been ground into the shape of a hemisphere and the flat side finely and skillfully polished until it produced an optically accurate reflection.

Mellaart found at least eight obsidian mirrors during these excavations. Like so many other things unearthed at Çatalhöyük, the mirrors are the earliest known. But perhaps more important, they provide tantalizing hints about how aware prehistoric peoples might have been of themselves and the world around them. What did the people of Çatalhöyük see, or hope to see, in the reflected faces staring back at them? Mellaart would soon formulate some definite ideas about how these Neolithic settlers saw their place in the material and spiritual universes in which they lived. But first he wanted to assign Çatalhöyük to its proper place within the sweep of ancient Near Eastern civilizations. To do that, he needed to know how old the settlement really was.

• • •

WHEN MELLAART FIRST started working as an archaeologist in the early 1950s, dating a site was still largely a matter of guesswork, often based on sequences of pottery types and other highly inexact approaches. In a few cases, especially when archaeologists had access to written records, they could do better. For example, the many texts left behind by the ancient Egyptians have allowed scholars to accurately date each of their dynasties—New Kingdom, Middle Kingdom, Old Kingdom, and so on—going as far back as about 3000 B.C. Fortunately for Mellaart, however, the radiocarbon revolution in archaeology was just about to erupt.

The radiocarbon method was invented in the late 1940s by the American chemist Willard Libby, who won the 1960 Nobel Prize for his accomplishment. It was based on the discovery that a very small portion of carbon atoms are radioactive. These take a form known as carbon 14, as compared to the normal state of carbon, which is carbon 12. Over time, the carbon 14 atoms give off their radioactivity and "decay" to become normal nitrogen atoms, which are designated nitrogen 14. Carbon atoms, of course, are key constituents of most molecules necessary for life, including proteins and DNA. While animals and plants are alive, they maintain a small but steady intake of carbon 14, for example from the food that animals eat or the carbon dioxide that plants take in from the atmosphere. But once the organisms die, the radioactive stores in plant or animal tissues are no longer replenished. Those radioactive carbon atoms that remain continue to decay at a predictable and measurable rate, allowing dating experts to extrapolate backward and estimate how much time has passed since the organism's death.

Archaeologists began taking the potential of radiocarbon dating seriously when Libby and his coworkers published their analysis of a number of samples whose ages were already known, including acacia wood from the 2750 B.C. coffin of the Old Kingdom Egyptian pharaoh Zoser and a 2,900-year-old chunk of California redwood the longevity of which had been determined from counting its tree rings. Although there was room for improvement—and improvement there would be over the coming years—the new method proved to be fairly accurate even in those early days. Soon a number of radiocarbon dating laboratories sprang up, especially in the United States and France. Excavators from all over the world began flooding them with samples of organic materials such as charcoal, seeds, and bones.

A basic check of the technique was whether an occupation layer known to be older from its stratigraphic location gave an earlier radiocarbon date than one known to be later, and vice versa. Mellaart had given the method a try at Hacilar and found that the resulting dates passed this test of internal consistency very well. The lower stratigraphic levels at Hacilar came out at about 5600 B.C., middle layers at roughly 5400 B.C., and the higher levels at about 5200 B.C. Mellaart had assumed based on a comparison of its pottery and other artifacts that Çatalhöyük was somewhat older than Hacilar. The radiocarbon dates from Çatalhöyük proved that this assumption was correct. They also showed that this huge settlement could take its rightful place in the pantheon of Near Eastern Neolithic sites.

As the Beycesultan men dug ever deeper into Çatalhöyük, Mellaart collected samples for radiocarbon dating from each stratigraphic level. Some samples were chunks of charcoal from timbers that had held up the mud-brick buildings or from fires in the ovens. Others came from grain found in storage bins, ovens, or on the floors. One even came from a bit of human brain that had been miraculously preserved inside a skull. In all, twenty-seven samples were analyzed by technicians at radiocarbon laboratories at the University of Pennsylvania and at a French facility near Paris.

The earliest date obtained, for Level X, came out at 6385 B.C., with a statistical margin of error of about a hundred years older or younger. But since Mellaart never reached the very bottom of the settlement, he considered it likely that the site had been founded one or two hundred years earlier. The latest date, for Level II, came out at 5797 B.C., plus or minus seventy-nine years; Mellaart assumed that Levels 0 and I, which were on the mound's highly eroded surface and did not provide suitable samples for radiocarbon dating, represented an additional century of occupation. His conclusion, based on the best technology of the time: Çatalhöyük was founded around 8,500 years ago and was continuously inhabited for at least eight hundred years. This meant that the settlement, and Anatolia as a whole, could not be considered a Johnny-come-lately to the Neolithic Revolution. Although the Neolithic settlement at Jericho, the earliest known, was founded perhaps 2,000 years earlier, Çatalhöyük had thrived at the same time as Jarmo and many other Neolithic sites to the east of Anatolia.

While Çatalhöyük was not the earliest farming community, it was a major participant in the cultural and economic changes that had swept across the Near East. And its strategic location in Anatolia made it a bridgehead for the spread of the Neolithic way of life to Europe and beyond.

Mortimer Wheeler, in his introduction to Mellaart's 1967 book, *Çatal Hüyük: A Neolithic Town in Anatolia,* expressed the reverence with which archaeologists have long regarded Çatalhöyük: "After its primary precursor, the eighth-millennium walled oasis-town of Jericho in Jordan, it occupies a sort of midway position in the emergence of Civilized Man. As such, it may fairly be regarded as something more than just another archaeological excavation; it represents an outstanding human accomplishment in the upward grade of social development, and may be expected therefore to be of general interest even to a modern age which may have lost something of the easy Victorian certainty of Progress."

When Mellaart unearthed the voluptuous "goddess" figurines at Hacilar in 1960, the discovery quickly captured the imagination of the news media. He now wasted little time getting word out about his new discoveries at Çatalhöyük. A week before the first season ended, the *Daily Telegraph* ran an enthusiastic account headlined "Stone Age 'Painted Hall' Found in Turkey." Mellaart himself published the first comprehensive article on the 1961 findings in the American journal *Archaeology*, an eleven-page spread adorned with many of Arlette's color photographs. As he dug Çatalhöyük ever wider and deeper over the following years, the international media continued to report his progress. And once again, the *Illustrated London News* opened its lavish color pages to him. In February 1963 James and Arlette published a stunning two-part photo-essay on the dig's spectacular finds. The dramatic photographs depicted the latest wall paintings and also the plastered skulls of bulls—with menacing, protruding horns—that Mellaart and his team had found mounted on the walls of some of the mud-brick buildings.

All of this media exposure came at a propitious time for the young archaeologist. Despite the acclaim his discoveries had brought him, his future career in archaeology was not at all certain. Nowadays nearly every major university harbors either an archaeology department (especially in the United Kingdom) or a department of anthropology in which archaeologists form an important subgroup (as is the case more often in the United States). Nevertheless, university jobs in archaeology, as in most academic fields, are scarce. Most excavators today work as contract archaeologists on so-called rescue digs undertaken at construction sites where developers are usually obliged by law to pay the bill. Back in Mellaart's day, the job situation was even bleaker. By the time he began digging at Çatalhöyük, Mellaart had already applied for—and failed to land—a number of positions in England.

The excavations at Çatalhöyük also coincided with unsettling changes taking place at the British Institute of Archaeology at Ankara. For the previous decade the BIAA had supported Mellaart financially—although not always generously, in Mellaart's view. As the Çatalhöyük dig began in 1961, Seton Lloyd, who had been the institute's director since its founding in 1948, decided to step down and return to England. Lloyd took over Max Mallowan's professorship in western Asiatic archaeology at the prestigious Institute of Archaeology in London, which Mortimer Wheeler and Kathleen Kenyon had founded during the 1930s.

Lloyd's departure meant that Mellaart was losing his mentor and chief protector. While some members of the BIAA's London-based governing council had found Mellaart troublesome—for example, when he complained incessantly about bank transfers that went astray, or when he went around the council and publicly lobbied for the continuation of the Hacilar excavations—Lloyd tended to indulge his star protégé. After all, Mellaart had discovered and excavated Beycesultan, Hacilar, and now Çatalhöyük. He had done more than anyone else to put the BIAA on the map.

But now Lloyd was leaving Turkey. The council, which had twice extended Mellaart's tenure as the BIAA's assistant director, made it clear that his job would also end. Fortunately, Mellaart was able to negotiate a lectureship in prehistoric archaeology at the University of Istanbul, although this was not the kind of permanent position he was seeking. Lloyd's replacement, effective July 1961, was Michael Gough, an expert on the early Christian period in Turkey. Gough, a former major in the British Army, had been a student fellow at the BIAA just before Mellaart arrived but had left to take a position at the University of Edinburgh.

From the beginning, there was little love lost between Gough and Mellaart. Gough specialized in just the kind of "filthy Roman muck" that Mellaart abhorred. Mellaart felt that the new director had no real interest in the Neolithic period in Turkey. Gough, whose military background had given him a strong sense of decorum, quickly concluded that the unpredictable Mellaart was a source of trouble.

Over the next few years Mellaart continued to dig Çatalhöyük fiendishly, knowing that each season might be his last. As the Beycesultan men sent the dirt flying, the maze of mud-brick buildings stretched out ever wider before him, and the inventory of artworks and other artifacts piled up ever higher. From this archaeological raw material, Mellaart began constructing his imaginative vision of what life at Çatalhöyük might have been like.

3 / The Dorak Affair

JAMES MELLAART never had a big staff at Çatalhöyük. Except for the Beycesultan men, the team of archaeologists and other specialists seldom included more than about a dozen people. While Konya, the original home of the Whirling Dervishes, is on some tourist stops today, during the early 1960s the hinterlands of Turkey were considered fairly remote even by archaeologists. Nevertheless, a handful of intrepid souls did make their way to the dig. One of them was an archaeology student at the University of Birmingham named Ian Todd.

Todd, a tall young man who wore glasses and a beard, had written to Mellaart in 1961 asking if he could come work with him. Mellaart had never answered. Some months later Todd attended a lecture in London that Mellaart was giving about Hacilar. He went up to Mellaart afterward and reminded him about the letter. "I never answer letters like that," Mellaart said. Yet after a few minutes' conversation, he asked, "So when are you coming to Çatalhöyük?" Todd was floored but immediately agreed to come out for the 1962 season. "And be sure to shave off that beard before you get there," Mellaart said.

For the next three seasons Ian Todd served as Mellaart's assistant director at Çatalhöyük. Most of his time was spent on his knees in the mud-brick houses exposing the artworks. All day long, with the Anatolian sun burning overhead, he pared away the plaster walls with X-Acto knives and dental tools. It was not an easy task. The outer layer of plaster—that is, the last coat the Neolithic villagers laid down before abandoning their houses—was never painted. And yet this last layer was often almost an inch thick. The Turkish workmen would empty the houses of their fill and clean the tops of the mud-brick walls so that the upper edge of the plaster layers was exposed. If Todd was lucky, bits of red or black paint would give clues as to which layers had been painted. The idea was to press gently against the plaster so that it flaked off without damaging the painting underneath. Some of the smaller paintings could be cleaned in a day or two. But others—like one mural of a huge bull that covered an entire wall—took several weeks of painstaking work.

The process was so slow and tiring that nearly everyone on the team had to take a turn at it. During the 1963 season Todd got a lot of help from a young woman named Viola Pemberton-Pigott. Viola, the daughter of a British diplomat and a distant cousin of Seton Lloyd, had met the Mellaarts at a dinner party in London the previous year. Mellaart had gladly accepted her offer to come out and help. While Ian and Viola worked away at the artworks, Mellaart would pass by every so often to see what was developing. Sometimes the subject of a painting would not reveal itself until they were nearly done. A series of parallel black lines would suddenly coalesce as a vulture's wing; a patch of red would come into focus as an abstract geometric pattern. The plaster relief sculptures, mounted on the walls, were sometimes more obvious. A marvelous pair of spotted leopards, facing each other, adorned the wall of one building; when the building immediately below it was later excavated, a nearly identical pair popped up on the corresponding wall. Ian and Viola discovered that the leopards changed their spots. As they flaked away at the animals' flanks, it became clear that they had been painted and repainted a number of times. Each time the spots were of a different design.

Then there were the female breasts. At least, Mellaart thought that these rounded plaster wall sculptures, which occurred singly, in pairs, or in rows, were breasts. Many of them certainly had what looked like nipples in their centers. But within these clay hemispheres, danger lurked. Out of the nipples jutted the beaks of vultures or the lower jaws and tusks of wild boars, and the skulls of these animals were sometimes found hidden within the plaster. Other "breasts" harbored the skulls of foxes and weasels. Mellaart interpreted these sculptures as symbolizing the juxtaposition of life and death—mother's milk versus the carrion-eating vulture—and linked them to the Mother Goddess he now felt sure was worshipped at Çatalhöyük.

Mellaart also saw the Mother Goddess in wall reliefs of humanlike figures with outstretched arms and legs. This motif was repeated at least a dozen times in different buildings and stratigraphic levels. One of these figures seemed to have long tresses flowing out to one side, as if the wind were blowing through its hair. He was certain that these sculptures represented deities of some sort. Before abandoning their houses, the Neolithic settlers had made most of the figures "ritually harmless": that is, they had taken away their powers by obliterating their faces and sometimes their hands and feet as well. But what clinched the Mother Goddess theory for Mellaart was the discovery of dozens of female figurines during the four seasons of excavation. There were "goddesses" galore: goddesses sitting, standing, and squatting; goddesses giving birth; goddesses holding children in their arms; naked goddesses, goddesses wearing robes, goddesses wearing leopard skins; single goddesses, twin goddesses, and a goddess and a "god" locked in embrace.

The most spectacular of the statuettes, found in a grain bin, depicts a fat woman with pendulous breasts sitting on a throne, her hands on the heads of two leopards that stand on each side of her. Mellaart believed that she was captured in the process of giving birth, as evidenced by a round protrusion—the head of her child?—peeking out from between her legs. The original is displayed today in the archaeological museum in Ankara, and replicas are on sale in tourist shops across Turkey. For Mellaart there was no doubt what it represented: "A belief in a goddess of fertility and abundance is clearly demonstrated by the figurines," he wrote in one of his early reports in *Anatolian Studies*, adding that the Çatalhöyük figurines were the "ancestors of the remarkable series found in Late Neolithic Hacilar in 1960."

Moreover, Mellaart thought that his excavations had unearthed the goddess cult's special houses of worship. All of the mud-brick buildings had the same basic arrangement: ovens and ladders on the south wall, platforms and benches along the north and east walls, and so on. But roughly a third of the buildings seemed much richer in paintings and sculptures than others. In addition, many of the more elaborate buildings featured enormous bull heads, complete with giant horns, either mounted on the walls or on special pedestals or benches on the floors. In some cases real bull skulls were used; in others, the horn cores were embedded in stylized plaster sculptures of the massive heads. One alarming arrangement, found in a building in Level VI, consisted of a row of seven sharply pointed horn cores protruding menacingly from a long plaster bench.

Mellaart concluded that these special buildings were "shrines" devoted to the worship of the Mother Goddess and her son, a deity who sometimes took the form of a bull and who was both her child and her lover. Mellaart was inspired in this imaginative reconstruction of Neolithic religion by the parallels he saw with the later gods and goddesses of Crete, Greece, and Rome. This often bewildering array of deities included a number of mother-son pairings, some of which were incestuous. Among them were Demeter, goddess of agriculture, and her son Plutus, god of abundance; and Rhea, goddess of fruitfulness, whose son Zeus was the chief protector of gods and men. Closer to home, Mellaart saw a resemblance between the Çatalhöyük Mother Goddess and Agdistis, who was first worshipped in the land of Phrygia, in what is today west central Turkey. Agdistis, whom the Greeks called Cybele, was the Great Mother of the gods. She fell in love with her son Attis, a god of vegetation and fertility. But things did not end happily. Phrygian myth relates that Agdistis, upon learning that Attis was about to marry, suffered a fit of jealousy and struck her son with a spell of madness, whereupon the crazed Attis castrated himself under a pine tree.

To Mellaart the notion that Neolithic farmers would call upon gods and goddesses of agriculture and fertility to give them spiritual guidance and bless their harvests seemed obvious. Archaeologists working at other Near Eastern Neolithic sites both before and since Mellaart's day have often interpreted their own figurines in similar ways. Mellaart, however, put a particular Anatolian spin on Çatalhöyük's religious practices, a twist which would do much to draw attention to the site.

None of Çatalhöyük's figurines, relief sculptures, or wall murals, he noted, showed the sexual organs of the figures they represented. The absence of phalluses and vulvae was remarkable, Mellaart thought, because they were often portrayed in the art of Upper Paleolithic and Neolithic cultures outside Anatolia. In Mellaart's view, the meaning of this was simple: since "emphasis on sex in art is invariably connected with male impulse and desire," he concluded, the goddess cult at Çatalhöyük was led by women, not by men.

It took only one more logical leap for Mellaart to decide that Çatalhöyük, which he believed was the spiritual, cultural, and trade center of this region of ancient Anatolia, had been a matriarchical society. "As the only source of life," he wrote in his 1967 book, women "became associated with processes of agriculture, with the taming and nourishing of domesticated animals, with the ideas of increase, abundance, and fertility. Hence a religion which aimed at exactly that same conservation of life in all its forms, its propagation and the mysteries of its rites connected with life and death, birth and resurrection, [was] evidently part of her sphere rather than that of man."

Mellaart's contention that women were dominant at Çatalhöyük is probably the most controversial claim he ever made about the site. Because he was writing during the 1960s, when feminist movements around the world were just taking off, the notion was electrifying. In particular, it was seized upon by the Lithuanian-born archaeologist Marija Gimbutas, for whom the religious imagery at Çatalhöyük and other ancient sites across Asia and Europe was proof that today's male-dominated societies had superseded earlier communities where warfare was unknown and men and women lived in harmony. This nostalgia for a lost egalitarian paradise, where women were empowered rather than trodden underfoot, is central to the beliefs of today's goddess cults. Every year goddess worshippers from around the world make the pilgrimage to Çatalhöyük, the mother of all matriarchies.

IF, AS MELLAART BELIEVED, Çatalhöyük in its day was the spiritual and economic center of central Anatolia, what made it so? That this community was unequaled in size and population seems clear from Mellaart's archaeological surveys of the surrounding region. An estimated 5,000 to

8,000 people may have lived here, based on calculations from the number of burials under the mud-brick houses. No other Neolithic site in the area came close to it in size. To help him figure out the basis for the settlement's apparent prosperity, Mellaart put out the call to some of the world's leading specialists.

One of the first to show up was paleobotanist Hans Helbaek, an expert in fossil plant remains from the Danish National Museum in Copenhagen. Helbaek had earlier worked with Robert Braidwood at Jarmo, where he found the burnt remains of the earliest known domesticated wheat and barley. Helbaek was bowled over by the abundance of domesticated plants he found at Çatalhöyük. "The deposits of carbonized grains and seeds excavated at Çatal Hüyük are the largest and best preserved finds of their kind ever recovered from so early periods in the Old World," he enthused in his preliminary report in *Anatolian Studies.* Helbaek identified at least fifteen edible plant species, including large quantities of domesticated wheat, barley, and peas. Some of the grains were still in their storage bins. One grain bin, in a Level VI house, contained a gallon of carbonized plant remains. The inhabitants also gathered nuts—such as pistachios, almonds, and acorns—and hackberries. One pile of almonds was found in an oven, as if they had just been roasted.

If Çatalhöyük's fields were bountiful, so too, a leading expert concluded, were its animal herds. Mellaart asked the American archaeological zoologist Dexter Perkins Jr. to analyze the animal bones unearthed during the excavations to see which species were domesticated and which were wild. Perkins found the remains of sheep, goats, red deer, boar, ass, dogs, and cattle. When he compared the sizes and shapes of these bones to those found at other archaeological sites, he came to a startling conclusion: other than the dogs, only the cattle seemed to be domesticated. Moreover, the domestication process seemed to have taken place during the millennium-long occupation of the site. If correct, this fact would make Çatalhöyük, as Perkins later reported in the journal *Science,* the earliest known center of cattle domestication. Perkins's findings that cattle made up more than 90 percent of the population's meat diet also implied that these animals were central to Çatalhöyük's apparently booming economy, a development for which, he remarked, "there is no known parallel in the Near East."

Perkins' pronouncement was surprising, because many faunal experts had assumed that sheep and goats were domesticated before cattle throughout the Near East. If he was right, it would mean that the process of animal domestication followed a different course in Anatolia. Perkins speculated that this difference might have been due to a more plentiful supply of cattle on the Anatolian plains. Whatever the case, knowing the status of the cattle—tame or wild—is critical not only for understanding the basis of Çatalhöyük's economy but also for deciphering the symbolic meaning of the vivid bull imagery created by the community's artists.

Although Çatalhöyük was clearly a highly productive agricultural community, it did not live in splendid isolation. Neolithic villages apparently traded with each other. This trade may also have been a key to Çatalhöyük's wealth. Mellaart received a visit from British archaeologist Colin Renfrew, who together with other colleagues at Cambridge University was tracing the exchange of obsidian in the Near East. This black volcanic glass was evidently highly prized, especially because very sharp tools could be fashioned from it. Renfrew's group had found that obsidian from different volcanic sources differed in the amounts of trace elements found in the glass when it was analyzed using a technique known as spectrography. The relative amounts of barium and zirconium, in particular, were reliable indicators of where the obsidian had come from. Renfrew's research had identified two primary sources in the Near East: a pair of extinct volcanoes in central Anatolia and two other volcanoes near Lake Van in Turkey's far eastern corner.

Ian Todd drove Renfrew around the area in his Land Rover. As might be expected, the obsidian that Renfrew collected from the region around Çatalhöyük, as well as from the site itself, came from the central Anatolian sources. But so also did the obsidian unearthed at contemporaneous Neolithic sites much farther away in the Levant, including Jericho, Byblos in present-day Lebanon, and Khirokitia on Cyprus. On the other hand, the obsidian at Jarmo in Iraq, Ali Kosh in Iran, and other large Neolithic settlements farther east came from the Lake Van area. Renfrew concluded that settlements closer to the volanoes—like Çatalhöyük, where some 80 percent of the stone tools were made from obsidian—were getting their supplies directly from the source. Villages farther away, on the other hand, had a smaller proportion of obsidian tools and were more likely to have acquired them through trade. This evidence alone did not prove that Çatalhöyük was controlling the obsidian trade in the Levant, but as the largest community in Anatolia, it certainly could have had a large piece of the action.

By 1963, Mellaart's third excavation season at Çatalhöyük, these and other scientific studies were already providing important new information about life during the Neolithic. But there was so much left to do. Although he had exposed some thirteen occupation levels, Mellaart had yet to reach the very earliest phases of the community. He still knew little about its origins and why its first inhabitants had decided to settle here. Nor did he understand why, after nearly a millennium of apparent prosperity, this huge village had been abandoned. Had famine, overpopulation, or warfare put an end to it? Did the people resettle elsewhere? Just across a dry riverbed from the main mound, Mellaart had discovered a second, smaller tell that appeared to date from the early Chalcolithic period. Perhaps the people of Çatalhöyük had simply moved across the river. Excavations at this second mound might prove or refute this hypothesis. Mellaart figured he needed at least another ten years' work to solve Çatalhöyük's remaining mysteries.

He wouldn't get it. In early March 1964 Mellaart and Arlette were visiting the University of St Andrews on Scotland's windswept North Sea coast. The university faculty had invited Mellaart to give a lecture about his Çatalhöyük discoveries. The couple just about to sit down for dinner with their hosts when a letter for Mellaart, forwarded from London, was delivered to the table. It was from the Turkish Department of Antiquities in Ankara. Mellaart's permit application for the 1964 season had been refused, with no explanation. "We were devastated," Arlette later recalled. There was nothing to do but put on brave faces for their hosts and glumly eat their dinner.

Back in London, Mellaart went straight to the Turkish ambassador to the United Kingdom. The ambassador listened to his story and then asked, "Who is your enemy in Ankara? Find him and you will know the reason." Meanwhile, in Turkey, Arlette's father, Kadri Cenani, began making his own inquiries into the matter, questioning his many contacts in the government. But all he heard in answer to his questions was one word: Dorak.

In November 1959 Mellaart had published, in the *Illustrated London News*, details of a fabulous Bronze Age treasure supposedly found near the village of Dorak in northern Turkey. Ever since, Turkish authorities had been trying to locate the treasure, which Mellaart claimed that he had been shown by a mysterious young lady he had met on a train. It was never seen again, and the authorities assumed that it had been smuggled out of the country. While there was no evidence that Mellaart was involved in its disappearance, suspicions about his role had lingered over the years. It now appeared that those suspicions had caught up with him.

With nowhere to dig, Mellaart spent that year working on his final report on the Hacilar excavations. Ian Todd embarked on a survey of sites in central Anatolia, especially in the picturesque Cappadocia region. Acting on a tip from an archaeologist who had been searching for Hittite remains in the area, he discovered a large Neolithic mound near the Cappadocia town of Aksaray, about a hundred miles northeast of Çatalhöyük. On the surface of this tell, which was called Aşikli Höyük, Todd found enormous amounts of obsidian as well as other tools made from stone and bone. Judging by the style of these tools, Todd estimated that Aşikli had been abandoned shortly before Çatalhöyük was founded. Later radiocarbon dates would confirm this hypothesis. Had Çatalhöyük been settled by the descendants of Aşikli? As its discoverer, archaeological tradition said, Todd had priority to dig the new site.

Viola Pemberton-Pigott spent the summer of 1964 at the archaeological museum in Ankara, along with a young art conservator named Pamela Pratt—the future Mrs. David French. Viola and Pamela continued to apply coats of preservatives to shore up the paintings, trying to get them ready for eventual display at the museum. While there, Viola searched the storeroom for a small wooden box that she had uncovered during the 1963 season. At no other Near Eastern site had wooden implements managed to survive the ravages of time, but Çatalhöyük delivered up the fragments of a number of carved boxes and bowls. Viola had pumped the nearly intact box full of preservative, carefully wrapped it in cloth, and sent it off to the museum, hoping for the best. Now she carefully unwrapped her treasure. It had turned to dust.

• • •

THERE ARE TWO main theories about the Dorak treasure. The first is that it never existed and that Mellaart made it all up. A few experts have gone so far as to question the authenticity of the Dorak finds in print. The second theory holds that the treasure was real and that everything Mellaart said about it was true. This is what Seton Lloyd believed for most of his life, although he may have begun to harbor some doubts before his death in 1996. It was also the conclusion of a committee of inquiry convened in 1968 by the British Institute of Archaeology at Ankara and chaired by Kathleen Kenyon. The Kenyon committee accepted Mellaart's account. There is, however, a third possibility, which is suggested by some of Mellaart's friends. The Dorak treasure may have actually existed, in whole or in part, but Mellaart might have stretched the truth about where, when, and how it was found.

Indeed, Mellaart's own accounts varied in some details over time. According to his "official" version, reported in a letter to Turkish authorities more than two years after the supposed events, here is what happened: One day in the spring of 1958 he was traveling by train from Denizli, in southwestern Turkey, to the city of Izmir on the Aegean coast. He was making the trip to look at some ancient Greek artifacts in Izmir's archaeological museum. Mellaart fell into conversation with a young woman in his compartment, who later gave her name as Anna Papastrati. Anna spoke English well, with a trace of an American accent. The subject of archaeology soon came up. Anna told him that she had some "antiquities" that she would like to show him, on the condition that they remained secret. Mellaart was skeptical: "Usually when people wish to show you something, it is nearly always things like coins, Roman lamps or Byzantine bronzes which do not interest me as a prehistorian."

Nevertheless, he agreed to have a look. Upon their arrival in Izmir, Anna and Mellaart took the ferry to Anna's home in Karsiyaka, a suburb across the waters of the Gulf of Izmir. They were greeted by Anna's father, "an elegant but sick and plaintive old man." Suddenly Mellaart noticed that Anna was wearing what appeared to be a prehistoric bracelet, or at least a very good copy of one. "My hopes rose steadily," Mellaart wrote. They rose even higher when, after "a fairly late bottle of wine and a tête-à-tête meal," Anna brought out some gold earrings and the remains of a "Trojan" silver bracelet. Mellaart decided at once that the objects were genuine. Other artifacts followed, and Mellaart, with Anna's permission, began to draw them.

Mellaart ended up staying with Anna and her father for nearly a week, drawing and tracing the glittering hoard set before him: silver and gold bracelets, pitchers, swords and daggers; jewelry of amber, turquoise, and ivory; and a fabulous collection of female figurines made from bronze and silver and adorned with miniature silver and gold skirts, aprons, and necklaces. Anna showed Mellaart some notes and photographs that indicated that the collection had been unearthed some thirty-five years earlier, during the 1920s war between Turkey and Greece. The treasure supposedly came from four graves found near the village of Dorak on the southern shore of Lake Apolyont, in northern Turkey. But Anna would not say how her family had come to possess the objects. Nor did she allow Mellaart to call in a photographer to record them. Anna did, however, promise to mail him some photographs later on, as well as give him written permission to publish his drawings. Just before leaving, Mellaart noted the address of the house: 217 Kazim Dirik Street.

After returning to Ankara, Mellaart kept quiet for a few months, waiting to hear from Anna. Finally excitement got the better of him. He told Seton Lloyd what he had found. The discovery of such a fabulous hoard would get any archaeologist's juices flowing. But for Mellaart and Lloyd, the Dorak treasure had a much more fundamental significance. "Almost miraculously," as Lloyd later wrote, Mellaart had found something among the artifacts that allowed the treasure to be dated: a fragment of gold leaf, apparently from a wooden throne, bearing hieroglyphic symbols that referred to Sahure, the second king of the Fifth Dynasty of Egypt's Old Kingdom. That would put the Dorak finds at about 2300 B.C.—exactly contemporary with "Priam's treasure," the cache of gold ornaments that Heinrich Schliemann had found in the Second Settlement at Troy during the previous century. Had not Mellaart, after a visit to Troy with Seton in 1955, postulated in *Anatolian Studies* that the destruction of Troy II marked the end of a powerful Bronze Age kingdom that controlled the land and sea routes into northwestern Anatolia? The Dorak treasure, located more than a hundred miles east of Troy's site on the Aegean coast—and with an opulence that indicated it must have come from a royal tomb—represented stunning confirmation that just such a vast kingdom once did exist.

Lloyd was eager to see the Dorak finds published. But Anna had yet to send Mellaart the promised photographs, despite Mellaart's repeated letters to the address on Kazim Dirik Street. The photographs never did materialize. Finally, in October 1958, Anna responded. "Dear James," she wrote, "Here is the letter you want so much. As the owner, I authorise you to publish your drawings of the Dorak objects, which you drew in our house. You always were more interested in these old things than in me! Well, there it is. Good luck and goodbye." At the bottom Anna had typed "Love" and then signed her name.

On November 25, 1959, the *Illustrated London News* published Mellaart's four-page report on the discovery, complete with color illustrations by Lloyd's wife, Hydie, redrawn from Mellaart's sketches. The headline was sure to attract attention: "The Royal Treasure of Dorak—a first and exclusive report of a clandestine excavation which led to the most important discovery since the Royal tombs of Ur." The article certainly drew the attention of Turkey's Department of Antiquities, for which the revelation of such a rich and important cache seemed to come as a complete shock. Turkish authorities were already touchy about the illicit antiquities trade, which has robbed the nation of much of its ancient heritage. Museums and private collections around the world have long been stuffed with artifacts from the Greek, Roman, Byzantine, and other cultures that once flourished in Asia Minor. And it was not the first time that Mellaart's name had come up in this connection: as early as 1957, beautiful red-striped pots and jars, supposedly from Hacilar, had begun turning up at markets in Istanbul.

Mellaart claimed that he reported the Dorak finds to antiquities authorities soon after telling Seton Lloyd about them. But Kathleen Kenyon's committee of inquiry later faulted Mellaart on this point, concluding that he had not told the department until April 1959, and then only briefly, in the course of a much longer report about the survey of the Konya Plain and the discovery of Çatalhöyük. Moreover, early on, Mellaart made an error that would compromise his credibility. When he first told Lloyd about the treasure, he claimed that he had actually found it six years earlier—that is, in 1952 rather than 1958—but had been sworn to secrecy until recently. Mellaart later changed his story, explaining that he had originally lied because he was worried that Arlette, whom he married in 1954, would not be happy to learn that he had spent a week in the house of a pretty young woman. Lloyd apparently accepted this explanation.

The Turks, however, would not be satisfied until they had located Anna and the treasure. When the authorities went to Izmir to investigate, they could find neither. Kazim Dirik Street, they concluded, was in a commercial district of the city and had no private houses. Mellaart was in trouble. He quickly became suspect number one in what the authorities assumed was an attempt to smuggle the Dorak treasure out of the country. As the investigation dragged on, Mellaart stuck to his story. His situation was not helped any when, in March 1962, Sotheby's—the London auction house—listed two figurines and two pottery vessels from Hacilar in its catalogue.

Mellaart maintained that the traffic in Hacilar artifacts—some of which were genuine, while others were fakes—could be traced to local villagers who had pillaged the site both before and after his excavations. No one has ever tied Mellaart to this illicit trade. But for the Turkish press, it was just more grist for the mill. Two months after the auction, the leading Turkish newspaper *Milliyet* launched a three-part attack on Mellaart. The articles included quotes from Dorak villagers who claimed that a "fair-haired, fat, middle-aged foreigner" had been seen in the area in 1955 or 1956. Mellaart, who would have been somewhat pudgy but only thirty years old at that time, didn't fit the description very well. Yet *Milliyet*'s reporters also found a local youth who, when shown a photograph of Mellaart, supposedly identified him as the visitor.

A number of years later two investigative reporters with the London *Sunday Times*, Kenneth Pearson and Patricia Connor, traveled to Turkey to try to get to the bottom of the strange affair. Among other things, they solved, at least partly, the mystery of the house on Kazim Dirik Street. The pair discovered that there had once been two streets with that name in Izmir. The authorities had apparently gone to the one in Izmir's city center, rather than to the one in the suburb of Karsiyaka. Meanwhile, during the intervening years, the name of the street in Karsiyaka had been changed, as well as its numbering system. Pearson and Connor never did find Anna or her house. But their detailed two-part report, published in the *Sunday Times* in November 1966—as well as a book-length treatment that came out the following year, called *The Dorak Affair*—ultimately concluded that Mellaart was innocent of any wrongdoing. At worst, the reporters suggested, Mellaart had been the innocent victim of antiquities smugglers who had used Anna to lure him into authenticating the Dorak artifacts so they could later be sold at a high price.

This delayed exoneration came too late to salvage Mellaart's reputation in Turkey. But he did manage to dig at his beloved site one last time. When the excavations were suspended in 1964, the BIAA's new director, Michael Gough—as well as Seton Lloyd, who was now on the institute's governing council in London—began looking for a way to save the dig. The problem, they found, was not just the Dorak affair, but also a growing animosity against Mellaart from Turkish archaeologists who thought he was getting too much attention. "Quite apart from straightforward professional jealousy," Lloyd wrote to a fellow council member after a visit to Ankara, "they resent the personal character of the publicity which has attended all his archaeological successes." Lloyd also reported on a conversation he had in Ankara, during a visit to the city in the summer of 1964, with the director general of the Antiquities Department. The Turkish official had suggested that the excavations might be able to continue if, as Lloyd put it, they were directed by "someone capable of greater tact and discretion" than James Mellaart.

The department's attitude toward Mellaart did not change when, in early 1965, the case against him was dismissed on a technicality. The court looking into the Dorak affair ruled that under the terms of a general amnesty declared in 1960, Mellaart could not be prosecuted for any crimes he might have committed before that time. Turkish authorities, despite continuing press coverage of the Dorak scandal, were no more eager than the BIAA to see Çatalhöyük shut down. Lloyd and Gough came up with a solution that was acceptable to everyone, including Mellaart: they appointed Oliver Gurney, the editor of *Anatolian Studies*, as the formal director of the excavation. Gurney was the nephew of BIAA founder John Garstang and also an expert on the Hittites, the peoples who ruled much of Anatolia during the Middle and Late Bronze Age. He knew little about digging Neolithic remains. The antiquities authorities seemed to know full well that Mellaart would still be running the dig. They apparently hoped that this arrangement would avoid attracting any additional attention from the scandal-hungry Turkish press.

In July 1965, with Gurney nominally in charge and Ian Todd designated as Gurney's assistant director, Mellaart and Arlette returned to Çatalhöyük. The Beycesultan men, who by then were also working at David French's dig at Can Hasan, were there to do the heavy lifting. The site was in a bad state. Two winters had passed since the last excavations, and the rains had made a mess of the mud-brick buildings. Mellaart's 1963 deep sounding, with which he had tried to find the earliest levels of the settlement, was now a stagnant mosquito pool and had to be filled in. Nevertheless, that last two-month season was one of the most successful yet. Several dozen more buildings were exposed, along with some of the most spectacular artworks, including more leopard wall sculptures and the wall-length mural of a huge red bull being taunted by little red men. And by August Mellaart was making good progress on a new deep sounding. Then disaster struck once again.

Turkish antiquities regulations require that a full-time government representative be present on all archaeological digs that take place in the country. That year the department decided to post two such representatives at Çatalhöyük. One of them was a petite, serious young archaeologist named Nemika Altan, who had trained at Istanbul University. Altan took charge of listing every artifact found during the dig in an inventory. One day in early September, on a visit to Konya, she wandered into the shop of an antiques dealer. She saw on display two vases supposedly from Hacilar and three figurines—two human figures and a leopard or tiger—identified as coming from Çatalhöyük. "How did you obtain them?" Altan asked the dealer, pointing to the Çatalhöyük artifacts. He told her that he had bought them from the workers at the excavation.

Nemika Altan asked the dealer to come to Çatalhöyük and bring the figurines with him. When Mellaart and Ian Todd had a look at them, it was clear that the objects had come from the site. The dealer then pointed out four of the Beycesultan men who, he said, had sold him the artifacts. Protesting their innocence, the men immediately quit and persuaded the rest of the Beycesultan crew to leave with them. Ian Todd had the unpleasant job of transporting them by Land Rover into the nearby town of Çumra. With two weeks of excavation season left to go, Mellaart had to make do with a much smaller crew of six local men from two nearby villages. The deep sounding to the lowest levels of Çatalhöyük, which had been his primary objective, had to be abandoned for lack of manpower. On September 25, 1965, the season wrapped up. Nemika Altan had to report to her superiors in the Department of Antiquities everything that had happened. Another thirty years would pass before Mellaart set foot on Çatalhöyük's soil again.

THE ALLEGED LOOTING at Çatalhöyük could have been the last straw for the antiquities authorities. Their decision to allow Mellaart to participate in the dig, let alone actually run it, had not been popular among many Turkish archaeologists, and the national press had been critical of it as well. On the other hand, had Mellaart left things alone, he might eventually have been able to return to Çatalhöyük after the dust settled from this latest scandal. Looting at archaeological sites was not uncommon in Turkey or anywhere else in the world, and no one was accusing Mellaart of complicity in the stealing of artifacts from his own dig. Moreover, at least in his written correspondence with Michael Gough after the 1965 season, the Turkish director general of antiquities seemed much more concerned with the difficulties of conserving the many wall paintings than with the issue of thievery at Çatalhöyük. But leaving things alone was not Mellaart's style. As even his friends have noted, Mellaart was his own worst enemy. The proof, they say, was the "Toronto letter." If there was a last straw, this was it.

One of Mellaart's major financial backers at Çatalhöyük was the Royal Ontario Museum in Toronto, which had supported the dig for several years. The museum published a confidential newsletter, destined for its donors and other selected individuals. Mellaart was asked to provide an account of the 1965 season for the newsletter, which he apparently dashed off and sent along. He later insisted that he was expecting museum officials to edit the manuscript before publication. But they didn't. Mellaart's four-page report, in the February 1966 issue of the newsletter, began by explaining the circumstances under which his excavation permit had been refused in 1964: "A change of the Director General of Antiquities allowed certain xenophobic elements aided by the gutter press and the Cyprus crisis of 1964 to put strong pressure to bear on the Department and through envy and jealousy our application for a dig-permit for Çatal Hüyük was refused." During the 1965 season, he continued, "we had not less than five people to spy on us; two servants planted on us as agents provocateurs [and] a museum guard on the site with the manners of a Gestapo man."

Unfortunately, the select group of subscribers to the newsletter included a Turkish scholar at New York University, who made his displeasure about Mellaart's attacks on his countrymen known to the BIAA. It wasn't long before Mellaart's words were echoing in the Turkish press. Inspired by the Toronto letter—and later that year by the publication of Pearson and Connor's two-part series in the *Sunday Times*, despite its exoneration of Mellaart—*Milliyet* and several other Turkish newspapers began a renewed campaign of attacks on the archaeologist, digging up the Dorak affair and the Hacilar artifacts all over again. The press campaign went on for nearly two more years. Long before it was over, however, the BIAA council decided that enough was enough. The press campaign was endangering not only the future of Çatalhöyük but all British archaeological work in Turkey. At its meeting in London on October 28, 1966—during much of which Mellaart, who had been elected to the council in March of that year, was made to stand out in the hall—the council discussed in detail how Mellaart's indiscretions had damaged the institute. The governing body, which included Seton Lloyd, Kathleen Kenyon, and a number of other noted archaeologists, then voted unanimously to dissociate itself from the Toronto letter and to "discontinue the Institute's sponsorship of Mr. Mellaart's excavations in Turkey."

This was the final blow. Without the BIAA's support, Mellaart, who had made so many contributions to Anatolian archaeology, could no longer work in the country. Fortunately for his financial stability, the previous year he had been appointed as a lecturer at the Institute of Archaeology, a post he held until his retirement in 1991. Mellaart and Arlette moved to London, returning to Turkey only during holidays to spend time at Arlette's family *yali* on the Bosphorus. Over the following years, Mellaart made a number of attempts to get Çatalhöyük back, to no avail. Nor was he interested in starting all over again in another part of the Near East. Instead of digging Çatalhöyük, he had to be content with lecturing about it to a new generation of archaeologists.

Ian Todd, who had discovered Aşikli Höyük, never got to dig the site that was rightfully his; the scandal associated with Çatalhöyük had touched him as well. Instead a team of Turkish archaeologists eventually excavated Aşikli beginning in the 1980s, making important discoveries about the origins of the Neolithic in Anatolia. As a consolation, Todd did discover a small wall painting at a Neolithic site on Cyprus.

David French continued his work at Can Hasan. In 1969 he replaced Michael Gough as BIAA director, the beginning of a tenure in Ankara that lasted more than two decades. He spent much of that time trying to undo the damage that the Dorak affair had caused to British archaeology in Turkey. Pamela Pratt, who had met David during a visit to Can Hasan and later married him, spent the first few years after Çatalhöyük shut down making periodic visits to the Ankara museum in an attempt to keep the wall paintings from deteriorating. And Viola Pemberton-Pigott, whose career in conservation began at Çatalhöyük, went on to become chief painting conservator to Queen Elizabeth II of England. She finally retired from her studio in St. James's Palace in 2002.

One day in 1976, the Cenanis' waterside *yali* burned down to the ground. The Mellaarts were in London at the time. Arlette suspected that a servant had left a fire unattended. As she later wrote in an article about the house in the Turkish magazine *Cornucopia*, "A plume of smoke was seen rising from the roof, then a whirlwind of fire engulfed the *yali* and its contents—furniture, books, a Steinway grand piano, objets d'art, mementoes and family portraits. From my husband's point of view, the worst disaster was the loss of drawings, plans and photographs which were to be published in the reports of his excavations."

About the time that the *yali* burned down, James and Arlette Mellaart moved to a modest apartment in London's Finsbury Park district. Nearly thirty years later, they are still there. The living room walls are covered with Turkish carpets. The bookshelves lining Mellaart's dusty study are bulging with books about the archaeology of Turkey, Egypt, and other regions of the Near East. In one corner sits a large cardboard box stuffed with original drawings and tracings of Çatalhöyük's wall paintings. And stuffed into one drawer there is a cardboard box containing a typewritten manuscript, some 60,000 words long, describing the Dorak treasure. It is a monograph that the BIAA had once intended to publish but never did. Also in the box are original drawings, tracings, and rubbings of the Dorak artifacts. The text of the manuscript includes an analysis of the treasure's importance, followed by detailed descriptions of dozens of objects that Mellaart had supposedly seen at the home of Anna Papastrati.

If Mellaart invented the Dorak treasure out of whole cloth—if he painstakingly made up all of these details—why would he do it? By 1959, the year he published his account of the treasure in the *Illustrated London News,* Mellaart's discoveries of Beycesultan and Hacilar had launched his career as an archaeologist and made him Seton Lloyd's golden boy. He certainly did not need the glory. On the other hand, the Dorak discovery confirmed his prized theory that the Second Settlement at Troy was part of a much larger kingdom. Could he have gone to that much trouble just to prove a point? Of course, as some archaeologists have suggested, there is always the possibility that the treasure did exist, in whole or in part, but that Anna did not; according to this theory, Mellaart might have been shown the artifacts by a dealer or other individual whose identity he wanted to protect.

If the Dorak treasure did indeed exist, and if Mellaart, as he now claims, was just the fall guy in a plot by Anna Papastrati and her cohorts to put a greater value on the objects, then his losing Çatalhöyük could be seen as a great injustice. But if he made it all up, he was the less-than-innocent victim of his own folly. Either way, the real loser was humanity itself. During the three decades that passed before Ian Hodder was able to reopen and resanctify Çatalhöyük, humankind was deprived of a cornerstone of its heritage.

4 / Ian Hodder

"ÇATALHÖYÜK AND I, we bring each other into existence. It is in our joint interaction, each dependent on the other, that we take our separate forms." Ian Hodder wrote these words in a 1990 book about the Neolithic Revolution in Europe. It was published three years before he began digging at Çatalhöyük. Ian had already been thinking about Çatalhöyük for more than twenty years, ever since 1969, when he took James Mellaart's class in Near Eastern prehistory at the Institute of Archaeology in London. Ian sat toward the back of the institute's musty, airless ground-floor lecture hall. Mellaart walked down the aisle and stood behind the large oak desk at the front of the room. The lights went out and the slide projector began to hum. Speaking without notes, Mellaart paced back and forth, his excitement—and that of the entire class—growing steadily as the vivid images flashed on the large white screen behind him: bulls, vultures, goddesses, leopards, all discoveries he had made just a few years earlier. Like a time traveler, Ian was transported out of the dark hall and back into prehistory, when people lived in mud-brick houses and were first learning how to farm the land. Mellaart brought Çatalhöyük to life with his infectious enthusiasm and the sheer power of his imagination.

As he watched and listened, it never occurred to Ian that one day he might excavate Çatalhöyük himself, let alone give over his entire career to working there. Indeed, the road to Çatalhöyük would be long and winding.

IAN HODDER WAS BORN in Bristol, England, on November 23, 1948. He was the product of a postwar love affair between his father, a British soldier who had been seriously wounded in Italy and had spent time in a German prisoner of war camp, and his mother, who was from Glasgow. At the time of Ian's birth, his father—whose working-class parents were officers in the Salvation Army—had just begun his freshman year at Oxford University, thanks to a government program that allowed ex-servicemen to get a higher education. Ian's mother had gone to Bristol, where her Salvation Army in-laws were stationed, to have her baby. She then moved to Oxford to join her husband.

Ian's father, Bramwell William Hodder, took an Oxford degree in geography. When Ian was three years old, his father landed his first teaching job, at the University of Malaya in Singapore. For B. W. Hodder, as he called himself professionally, it was the beginning of a long and distinguished career as a tropical geographer. For Ian, young as he was, this Asian adventure provided the first inkling that there were other worlds besides that of provincial England. The noise and excitement of Singapore, the press of the crowds, the flash of lights and golden dragons on Chinese New Year, all fired the imagination of this precociously sensitive and impressionable boy. He was also dimly aware that Singapore, then living out its last days as a British colony, was itself divided into two worlds: that of the privileged foreign compound in which his family lived, with its swimming pools and formal dinner dress, and the mass of Singaporeans who surged through the busy streets.

When Ian was seven years old, the love affair between his parents came to an end. At the time, however, little was explained to Ian and his younger brother and sister. All he knew was that the family was engulfed in a swirl of hurt and confusion, and that his mother was moving back to Oxford and taking the children with her. He would later come to see the breakup as the event that most marked his life and shaped his personality. In his father's absence, Ian, the oldest child, had to take on more and more family responsibilities, as his mother struggled to support her brood with a series of low-paying jobs. For the first few years they moved often within the Oxford area, from one rented apartment or house to another. Ian felt lost and made few friends. Finally he found the stability he craved. When he was eleven years old, his mother rented a comfortable apartment in a gabled brick building on Bardwell Road, a quiet, sycamore-lined street in middle-class North Oxford. Ian won a scholarship that allowed him to attend Magdalen College School, an exclusive private school for boys that overlooks Oxford's idyllic Cherwell River.

Ian thrived at Magdalen. While the pain from his parents' separation had left him feeling shy and insecure behind the glasses he now wore, with his tall, slim frame he hovered over most of the other boys. And since he had been obliged to take a leading role in his family when still very young, Ian soon became a leader among his more privileged schoolmates, despite his reserved nature. Magdalen had an excellent academic reputation, but the school's real passions—and Ian's—were sports and music. Before long he became head of the rugby team, head of the boating team, head of the orchestra, and head of one of the school's four houses.

Meanwhile Ian's father had moved from Singapore to Nigeria, where he taught at the University of Ibadan, about a hundred miles north of Lagos, the country's chief port. Once or twice a year, during school holidays, Ian would journey to visit him. These trips were high adventures for the boy, who began making them when he was just ten years old. In London Ian—often accompanied by his younger brother and sister—would board a propeller-driven Super Constellation for the bumpy flight to Lagos. At that time B.W. Hodder was studying the rural markets of the Yoruba people, which are largely run and controlled by the tribe's women. Ian loved wandering from market to dusty market with his father, breathing in the pungent aromas of casaba melons, yams, and leather goods while listening to the chatter of the thousands of women dressed in multicolored sarongs.

At Magdalen the headmaster, who was a Classical scholar, encouraged Ian to focus his studies on the Classics, ancient Greek, and Latin, subjects in which he had a limited interest. He was, however, fascinated by philosophy and read a great deal on his own. He was particularly drawn to the writings of the British philosopher Alfred Jules Ayer, a proponent of logical positivism—a school of philosophy that holds that the only valid knowledge is that which can be scientifically verified. When Ian was fifteen years old, he learned that some archaeologists were excavating at a church just outside Oxford. Always in search of extracurricular activities, he volunteered to help out on weekends. The experience of engaging in an outdoor, physical activity that was also mentally stimulating immediately appealed to him. To Ian the past seemed like a puzzle. Excavation was a hands-on way to try to solve it. And he found the sociability and camaraderie of the archaeologists, the way they banded together into a group with a definite goal, much easier to cope with than the unsettling upper-crust competitiveness at Magdalen.

Ian began volunteering to work on digs during the summers, which is when most academics carry out their excavations. In the summer, when there are no classes to attend, the cheap student labor on which most university-run digs rely is plentifully available. One year he worked at Fishbourne in West Sussex, where the British archaeologist Barry Cunliffe was excavating the monumental 75 A.D. Roman palace of King Togidubnus. The palace had everything a budding young archaeologist could desire: mosaic floors, lavish baths, and painted wall plaster. Ian spent most of the time on his hands and knees in the villa's central courtyard, scraping the soil with a trowel to uncover the ancient flower beds of a Roman garden.

There were hundreds of digs Ian could volunteer for in England, but before long he decided to go farther afield. His trips to see his father in Africa had kindled a love for travel. And after all those years of helping his mother take care of the family, he was desperate to get away from Oxford for a while. Ian quickly learned that doing archaeology was a great way to see the world. While still a teenager, he traveled to Greece to work on an excavation run by Eric Higgs, the Cambridge University archaeologist. Higgs had founded an influential school within archaeology called paleoeconomy, which focused on the relationship between prehistoric peoples and their environments. Higgs maintained that archaeologists needed to look beyond the narrow perimeters of their sites and search the surrounding landscape for evidence of the resources that ancient communities had exploited. But he was also notorious for the grueling conditions at his excavations. He apparently believed that archaeologists had to be toughened up if they were to face the challenges of digging in the hot sun. The volunteers slept out in the open with no tents, shared cans of beans for dinner, and were required to raise their hands if they wanted to go to the toilet. Ian, unaware of Higgs' reputation, had signed up for two weeks; after the first week he left in disgust, joining the steady turnover of disillusioned students who learned early that archaeology is not always all fun and games.

Despite this negative experience, by the time Ian was seventeen years old, he had decided that archaeology was the life for him. But his ambivalence about the courses he was taking at Magdalen caught up with him when it came time to take his final exams: his grades were not good enough to get him into Oxford or Cambridge. At first Ian was bitterly disappointed. Then he had a lucky break. The Institute of Archaeology in London, which since its founding in 1937 by Mortimer Wheeler had provided only specialized training, decided to open its doors and offer an undergraduate degree in archaeology. In 1968, after taking a year off to bum around Europe and do more digging, Ian became one of the eighteen students admitted to the institute's first undergraduate class.

At the time Ian entered the institute, he knew little about archaeological theory. To him, archaeology meant digging, working with his hands. Interested as he was in philosophy, he nevertheless did not see himself as an intellectual. The archaeology books he had read in his spare time at Magdalen—Mortimer Wheeler's *Archaeology from the Earth* and Kathleen Kenyon's *Beginning in Archaeology*, among others—were mostly about stratigraphy and other methodological issues. But while a student at the institute, he soon got wind of the theoretical upheavals that were then rocking the field of archaeology to its foundations. There was a revolution brewing: it was called the New Archaeology. At that time in his life, revolution was just Ian's cup of tea.

• • •

EVER SINCE THE RISE of modern archaeology during the nineteenth century, the field has been in a perpetual identity crisis about its primary purpose. Archaeologists have never entirely agreed among themselves about what they are doing and why they are doing it. "What in fact is Archaeology? I do not myself really know," Mortimer Wheeler admitted in *Archaeology from the Earth.* To the general public, brought up on the swashbuckling of Indiana Jones and the glitter of King Tutankhamen's gold, archaeology must often seem to be about treasure hunting. Museums around the world are stuffed with the fabulous things that archaeologists have dug up: painted pottery, silver bracelets, polished jade axes, marble statues, sarcophagi stuffed with embalmed mummies. These objects are usually considered valuable collector's items. In the aftermath of the 2003 war in Iraq, the National Museum in Baghdad was looted by desperate people—and, apparently, professional thieves—looking for things to sell. Thousands of archaeological sites throughout Iraq were ripped apart in the search for objects. Yet few people would consider such acts of theft and vandalism to be the equivalent of archaeological excavation. Most archaeologists would agree with one of Wheeler's most eloquent statements: "The archaeologist is digging up, not *things,* but *people.*"

The study of people, or humankind, falls into the domains of both the natural sciences—such as biology, chemistry, and physics—and the social sciences, such as history, sociology, and economics. Archaeology's identity crisis has taken many forms over the years. One of the most persistent debates has been over whether it is, or should be, a natural or a social science—or, put more simply, whether archaeologists are primarily scientists or historians. Until the 1960s, despite the early emphasis on stratigraphy and rigorous methodology by pioneers like Mortimer Wheeler in the United Kingdom and Alfred Kidder in the United States, archaeology was most closely identified with history.

The written word is no doubt the primary raw material of history, whether it be the cuneiform inscriptions of ancient Mesopotamia, the hand-copied parchment scrolls of medieval Europe, or the church records of colonial Virginia. For archaeologists specializing in prehistory, however, the past speaks not in words but in artifacts. Beginning in the 1920s, prehistorians increasingly used artifacts to track what came to be called the "culture history" of the geographical regions they were interested in. They assumed that the objects they dug up directly reflected the culture of the peoples they were studying. Culture, in turn, was defined as a shared body of ideas, values, and beliefs. In his 1929 book, *The Danube in Prehistory*, V. Gordon Childe—the Australian archaeologist who coined the term *Neolithic Revolution*—clearly defined the basic assumptions of culture history: "We find certain types of remains—pots, implements, ornaments, burial rites, and house forms—constantly recurring together. Such a complex of associated traits we shall term a 'cultural group' or just a 'culture.' We assume that such a complex is the material expression of what today would be called a 'people.'"

The culture historians put a great deal of effort into classifying artifacts into types based on different pottery styles or variations in techniques of stone tool manufacture. They then used this typology to trace the movements of peoples and cultural ideas through time and space. In fact, before radiocarbon dating was invented, this method was the only way to guess the dates of archaeological sites. When cultural changes appeared in the archaeological record—either at one excavation site or across a geographical region—archaeologists assumed either that the prehistoric peoples had migrated and colonized other regions or that their ideas had spread and been adopted by other peoples. Indeed, the main purpose of the careful stratigraphic recording so strenuously advocated by Wheeler and like-minded archaeologists was to define the sequence of cultural changes. Alfred Kidder, a leader of the Stratigraphic Revolution in the United States, is perhaps best remembered for promoting the Pecos Classification, which organized the Native American Pueblo cultures of the American Southwest into stages that supposedly reflected increasing social and technological complexity over time. Likewise, so-called biblical archaeologists working in Palestine, including the American William F. Albright and the Israeli Yigael Yadin, traced the destinies of Israelites, Philistines, and Canaanites through their distinctive pottery and architecture.

James Mellaart, despite his embrace of radiocarbon dating, paleobotany, and other scientific methods, was firmly entrenched in the culture history school of archaeology. His primary aim, at Çatalhöyük and at Hacilar, was to prove that Anatolia had been center stage in the sweep of cultural and technological changes that accompanied the Neolithic

Revolution. Mellaart's impatience to establish Anatolia's cultural sequence was so great that he publicly chastised his old friend David French, who was excavating the Neolithic and Chalcolithic levels of nearby Can Hasan, for not doing enough to help fill in the cultural gaps between Can Hasan and Çatalhöyük. "Here then are the beginnings for a correlation between the two sites, which are not facilitated by the summary nature of my friend's preliminary reports," Mellaart wrote in the 1965 volume of *Anatolian Studies*.

French was also committed to establishing the Anatolian sequence, but he had other priorities as well. In contrast to the frenetic pace at which Mellaart moved earth at Çatalhöyük, French dug Can Hasan in a slow and meticulous fashion, determined to get as much information from this smaller and more modest mound as he could. "It is this kind of material, to some perhaps unspectacular, which is providing fundamental evidence on the problems of the environment," French countered in the same issue of *Anatolian Studies*.

Even as Mellaart dug Çatalhöyük in the early 1960s, the growing use of scientific methods was fanning the first sparks of a rebellion against the culture history school. David French and a number of other archaeologists had begun to explore new questions about the past. The work of Cambridge archaeologist Eric Higgs on ancient environments, and the American Robert Braidwood's attempts to trace the origins of agriculture at Jarmo in Iraq, relied heavily on scientific techniques. In the years before his death in 1957, V. Gordon Childe, the culture historian *par excellence*, became dissatisfied with merely categorizing chronologies and sequences and began to ask *why* cultural and economic changes had taken place—why, for example, the Neolithic Revolution had swept across the ancient Near East.

The rebellion, when it came, erupted almost simultaneously on both sides of the Atlantic Ocean. The New Archaeology—as it was called derisively by its critics and admiringly by its enthusiasts—was most closely associated with two charismatic but very different men: Lewis Binford in the United States and David Clarke in the United Kingdom. Binford was almost stereotypically American, tall and powerfully built, a child of 1930s depression-era Virginia who loved the outdoors. He filled university lecture halls with his deep, booming voice and sported a white, Hemingway-style beard. Clarke was nearly the exact opposite. He was a child of academia, educated at Cambridge University, short and rotund, with a characteristically bouncy walk. He wore tweed jackets and sported flowery, psychedelic ties.

It was Binford who fired the first shot across the bow of culture history. As a graduate student at the University of Michigan during the 1950s, he had his fill of typology and classification schemes—particularly the Midwestern Taxonomic Method, a rough equivalent of the Pecos Classification but applied to the central and eastern United States. In 1961 he began teaching at the University of Chicago. Sitting in his office late one night, and feeling frustrated that, as he later wrote, "archaeologists were all little Linnaean beings classifying things for the sake of classification," he put a sheet of paper in his typewriter and began furiously tapping the keys. By morning he had written a manifesto entitled "Archaeology as Anthropology," which was published in 1962 in the journal *American Antiquity*. Binford declared that archaeology should be not a servant of culture history but a proud branch of the field of anthropology: the science of humankind in all of its aspects. He argued that while archaeology had done an "admirable" job unearthing and describing past cultures, it had done essentially nothing to help explain why cultural change took place.

Moreover, Binford maintained, archaeologists had been working with an entirely erroneous concept of what culture was. It was not just a shared body of ideas, values, and beliefs that had somehow taken shape in human minds. Binford adopted the view of one of his heroes at the University of Michigan, the anthropologist Leslie White, that culture was the extrasomatic—literally, the "out of body"—means whereby human beings adapted to their environments. Just as early humans had won the physical struggle for survival by walking upright on two feet and evolving intricately dexterous hands, so too did our large brains invent culture as our way of mentally adapting to the challenges of life on earth. Archaeology's greatest sin, Binford and other New Archaeologists argued, was its lack of self-awareness about what it was doing, its failure to critically examine the unstated theories and assumptions that archaeologists carried into the field with them and that guided their interpretations of the archaeological record they dug up. "We cannot afford to keep our theoretical heads buried in the sand," Binford concluded in his 1962 paper.

David Clarke expressed similar concerns. In his most famous paper, "Archaeology: the loss of innocence," published in the March 1973 issue of the British journal *Antiquity*, Clarke contended that archaeologists cannot innocently pretend that they are simply gathering "facts" and have no need for theory: "Practical men who believe themselves to be quite exempt from any intellectual influences are, as Lord [John Maynard] Keynes pointed out, usually the unwitting slaves of some defunct theorist." Such a lack of methodological self-consciousness, Clarke insisted, made archaeology too reliant on unsubstantiated speculation and the pronouncements of authority figures, rather than on rigorous methods for deciphering what the artifacts were saying about the societies that produced them. "It is apparent that archaeologists need to know about knowing and the limits of what they can and cannot know from the data and to know this by critical appraisal, not simply by assertion," he wrote in his typical tongue-twisting style.

While Binford and Clarke were concerned with how archaeologists know what they know about the past, they both tended to sidestep the issue of whether archaeologists were scientists or historians—although they did so in somewhat different ways. Binford was most insistent that archaeologists should use a strictly scientific approach to analyze their data. In the early years of the New Archaeology, he was influenced by the logical positivist writings of the German-born philosopher Carl Gustav Hempel. Following Hempel, he argued that hypotheses about what had happened in the past must undergo rigorous testing to determine whether they could withstand scrutiny, just as new hypotheses in biology or physics had to be tested by laboratory experiments. Moreover, Binford ridiculed the notion, held by many culture historians, that artifacts directly reflected a society's shared ideas, and he dismissed attempts to get into the minds of ancient peoples as "paleo-psychology."

Clarke agreed with Binford about the importance of rigorous methodology; indeed, he was an early and enthusiastic advocate of the use of computers to analyze archaeological data. But while he shared Binford's basic critique of the limitations of the culture history school, he was much more interested than his American counterpart in culture in its own right, not just as an adaptation to the environment. And he was not quite so eager as Binford to cloak himself in a white laboratory coat. "Certainly, scientific aids no more make archaeology a 'science' than a wooden leg makes a man into a tree—isotope dating, chemical analysis, and proton magnetometers remain adjuncts," he cautioned in his 1968 book *Analytical Archaeology*. Nor did he go along with the idea that archaeology should be subsumed into anthropology. "Archaeology, is archaeology, is archaeology," he countered.

In 1968, the year that student protests against the Vietnam War reached their heights and workers and students built barricades in the streets of Paris, both Binford and Clarke published their first book-length expositions of the New Archaeology. The revolution against the culture historians had begun in earnest. On both sides of the Atlantic, the troops began to rally. Binford, first at the University of Chicago and then at the University of New Mexico, gathered together a group of like-minded graduate students. Meanwhile, at Cambridge University, Clarke was recruiting his own band of disciples, who would go forth and spread the word. One of them was Ian Hodder.

IAN DID NOT LEARN about the New Archaeology in his classes at the institute. The revolution had not yet come to London in 1968, his freshman year at the drab gray stone building on Gordon Square. James Mellaart and most of the other teaching staff were still steeped in the culture history school. A bronze bust of V. Gordon Childe met the students as they entered the institute's library. Ian would often pass Mortimer Wheeler—still flamboyant in his late seventies—as he strolled the halls wearing a large white carnation in his lapel. The library did, however, purchase the Binford and Clarke books when they came out, and toward the end of his three-year course Ian discovered them. He thought these new ideas were very exciting. He was particularly struck by Binford's enthusiasm for Hempel's logical positivism, which recalled his own fascination with the writings of British logical positivist Alfred Jules Ayer while still a student at Magdalen. But when he tried to discuss the books in class, he was amazed to learn that none of his lecturers had read them.

The students were required to write a thesis on an archaeological topic before they could graduate. Ian decided to tackle an ambitious project: an analysis of the spacing and distribution of towns and cities during the Roman occupation of Great Britain in the first centuries A.D.

Ian relied on an idealized model then popular among geographers, called Central Place Theory, which predicts that the distribution of urban centers will follow the pattern that is most economically advantageous for all of the centers concerned. While preparing the thesis, he got a lot of help from one of Britain's leading geographers—B. W. Hodder. In 1963 B. W. Hodder had landed a teaching position at the University of London, where he spent the rest of his career. He commuted to London from Cambridge. Ian began to see a lot of him. Ian's thesis was well received by the institute's faculty, and he graduated with first-class honors in 1971. That same year the prestigious British journal *Man* published a shorter version of the thesis, Ian's first academic paper. He sent a copy to David Clarke, who responded with two proposals: first, that it be published as a chapter in a new edited volume he was preparing, called *Models in Archaeology*, which included contributions by Lewis Binford and other leading lights of the New Archaeology; second, that Ian come to Cambridge to do his doctoral work. Ian was over the moon. At the tender age of twenty-three years, he was about to take his place among the revolutionary cadre.

During the three years that Ian spent at Cambridge working on his Ph.D., the New Archaeologists launched some of their biggest assaults against the culture history school. Binford challenged the work of French archaeologist François Bordes, who had spent years classifying the stone tools used by Neandertals and Cro-Magnons (modern humans) in southern France. Bordes argued, based on differences in the styles of the stone tools they used, that the Neandertals were divided into four ethnic or cultural groups. But Binford countered that the cultural "styles" these tools seemed to reflect could be more easily explained as representing different functions; that is, the tools were being used to do different jobs.

Another blow to the culture history approach was dealt by Colin Renfrew, the British archaeologist who had earlier analyzed the obsidian from James Mellaart's excavations at Çatalhöyük. Renfrew, who was David Clarke's chief rival for leadership of the New Archaeology movement in the United Kingdom, overturned the traditional view of how megalithic monuments—such as the huge stone pillars of Stonehenge in England or the long rows of standing stones at Carnac in Brittany—had come to dominate the landscape of prehistoric Western Europe.

Earlier archaeologists, most notably the British prehistorian Glyn Daniel, had concluded from stylistic similarities and differences among stone monuments that the earliest of them were constructed on Crete, Malta, and other sites in the Mediterranean. After that, the cultural idea of "megalithism" had supposedly diffused westward. But Daniel had drawn these conclusions before radiocarbon dating was available. Renfrew used the flurry of new, calibrated radiocarbon dates then coming out of megalithic sites to show that the earliest monuments in Western Europe—some of which were more than 6,000 years old—predated their Mediterranean counterparts by thousands of years. They were, Renfrew concluded, local inventions and not the passive result of cultural diffusion.

Ian's own contribution to the New Archaeology's arsenal of scientific methodology followed from his undergraduate thesis on the spatial distribution of towns and cities in Roman Britain. David Clarke had devoted a long chapter in *Analytical Archaeology* to the potential contribution that computers could make to archaeological analysis. Ian set about trying to fulfill some of that promise. For his doctoral work he developed a series of statistical methods that allowed archaeologists to rigorously compute the distribution of ancient sites within a geographical region, as well as compare the artifacts found within these sites. The culture historians, who had been mostly concerned with establishing chronologies and sequences, had often failed to take advantage of what could be learned by comparing the similarities and differences among towns and settlements that had existed more or less contemporaneously, and when they did do so, it was usually by eyeballing maps of dubious accuracy and completeness. Ian spent thousands of hours feeding thousands of punch cards into Cambridge University's mainframe computers, which obligingly spit out the data he used to compile charts and maps showing the detailed distribution of Roman coins, Roman pottery, and Bronze Age axes. A number of interesting and revealing patterns emerged from this work: for example, Ian was able to trace the adoption of one specific pottery style up and down a particular Roman road, a level of detail that archaeologists dream of but seldom achieve.

The thesis was well received. Ian had no trouble landing a position. In 1974 he was hired as a lecturer at the University of Leeds. Yet even as his career advanced on the strength of his doctoral work, he had a nagging feeling that something was wrong with the basic principles of the New Archaeology. As he tested various hypotheses about why a particular spatial distribution had come to be, he sometimes found that more than one hypothesis could lead to the exact same pattern—a phenomenon that scientists and philosophers often call "equifinality." If even the most objective scientific testing could not always distinguish between two or more possibilities, how could archaeologists be certain that their interpretations of the archaeological record were correct? For the moment he put these doubts out of his mind.

Then, in 1976, a tragic event occurred that would dramatically alter Ian's life as well as the future course of archaeology. David Clarke, convalescing at home after being hospitalized for an intestinal infection, suddenly developed a blood clot and died at age thirty-eight. Clarke was a much-loved figure at Cambridge, even by those who did not agree with all of his ideas. His early death shook up the archaeological community. Hundreds of colleagues and former graduate students crowded into Cambridge's Little St. Mary's Church for the memorial service.

Clarke's death had wide-ranging consequences, some of which would not be felt for many more years. However, there were two immediate repercussions. One was that Colin Renfrew, who was more closely allied with the New Archaeology's Binfordian tendency than with its more culture-oriented Clarkian version, became the movement's primary torchbearer in Great Britain. The other was that Cambridge University now needed someone to take over Clarke's teaching responsibilities. Many applied for the job; Ian Hodder was chosen.

WHEN IAN WAS STILL a graduate student at Cambridge in the early 1970s, he made a visit one day to his alma mater, the Institute of Archaeology in London. There he ran into Andrew Garrard, an old friend from his undergraduate days who was teaching at the institute. Garrard introduced Ian to a slim, attractive Frenchwoman named Françoise Hivernel, who was doing her Ph.D. on the stone tool technology of early humans in East Africa. Ian and Françoise starting seeing each other, fell in love, and in 1975 they were married. Françoise was spending part of each year excavating a Paleolithic (old Stone Age) site near Kenya's Lake Baringo, in a beautifully green, mountainous region of the country. Whenever he could, Ian would go to Kenya and help her dig. He had not forgotten his childhood experiences visiting his father in Nigeria, when he had first gotten an inkling of the amazing cultural diversity among human beings. As Ian worked away with his trowel in the excavation trench, every now and then he would gaze up at the colorfully dressed men and women passing by on their way to and from the local villages. There were three main tribes living in the Baringo area—the Tugen, the Njemps, and the Pokot—and all dressed differently. It struck Ian that they were actually wearing their cultures on their bodies.

Suddenly Ian had what seemed like a brilliant idea. If he brought his spatial analysis techniques to Kenya, perhaps he could crack the code of what these cultural differences meant. At that time, archaeologists were becoming increasingly excited by the promise of what was called "ethnoarchaeology," the study of present-day cultures as an aid to the interpretation of past societies. If archaeologists wanted to understand why prehistoric peoples buried their ancestors under the floors of their houses or why they decorated their pots in a certain way, they could try to dream up various explanations out of their own heads. A better approach might be to ask the Tikopia people of Polynesia why they bury their own dead under the floors, or to query the Navajos of the American Southwest about the distinctive stylistic flourishes on their pottery. The answers might not directly explain what prehistoric peoples had in mind, but they would at least present a range of possibilities and help generate plausible hypotheses.

Some early enthusiasts of this approach called it "living archaeology," although others were skeptical about how much it could really contribute. "I like to keep my archaeology dead," David Clarke once remarked to a leading ethnoarchaeologist. The enthusiasts included Lewis Binford, who in the late 1960s and early 1970s began his own ethnoarchaeological work among the Nunamiut peoples of Alaska. Binford had been grappling with the problems that cropped up during his attempts to test hypotheses about the past: archaeologists did not know enough about how the archaeological record had been created—that is, how pots, tools, and bones had come to be deposited where they were, and in the state that they were in—to be confident about the inferences they made about past human behaviors. In his studies of the Nunamiut, Binford focused on the way that they hunted and consumed the large caribou that roamed the Alaskan tundra—especially on where the bones ended up after the animals had been slaughtered and eaten. He used this new knowledge to interpret the patterns of bones and stone tools found at Paleolithic hunter-gatherer sites, for example in Africa. Binford was able to convince himself and many other archaeologists and anthropologists that early humans had probably not been such mighty hunters as previously believed; it was more likely that our ancestors were opportunistic scavengers who cleaned up after the hyenas and other wild animals that got to the carcasses first.

Ian, with some strategic help from the famous Kenyan anthropologist Richard Leakey, decided to launch his own ethnoarchaeology studies among the Baringo tribes. For several weeks each year, during vacations from teaching at the University of Leeds—and continuing after he moved to Cambridge in 1977—he would camp in the Tugen Hills near Lake Baringo with a small group of interpreters and graduate students. Each day they would divide up into smaller groups and spread out across the landscape. Ian and the students, armed with questionnaires, drawing pads, and cameras, would interview the bemused tribespeople, recording the clothes and beaded jewelry they wore, the styles of the leather flaps hanging from the ears of the women and the spears brandished by the men, the decorations on their pots, the weave of their baskets—anything and everything that could eventually be quantified and entered into a computer.

In carrying out this exhaustive work, Ian was guided by one of the key assumptions of the New Archaeology: that culture was the extrasomatic means whereby humans adapted to their environment. By then most archaeologists understood that the environment consisted not only of the physical landscape, the climate, and the flora and fauna, but also of other human beings with whom one could either compete or cooperate. Binford and other New Archaeologists postulated a fairly direct and predictable link between adaptive human behavior and the cultural styles it produced. Just as Binford had argued, in his debate with the French prehistorian François Bordes, that the Neandertals used different tools for different tasks, so did he and like-minded colleagues contend that different cultures reflected different adaptive strategies. In the 1960s and 1970s most prehistorians and ethnoarchaeologists believed that cultural similarities and differences among human groups reflected, to a great extent, the degree of contact and cooperation among them. The more interaction between two groups, the greater the cultural similarities would be, while competition would lead to greater cultural distinctions.

As Ian's data from Baringo piled up, he found that sometimes these predictions seemed to work and sometimes they didn't. For example, the women of the Tugen, Pokot, and Njemps tribes all wore different patterns of beaded decorations on their leather earflaps, which were inserted into large holes in their earlobes. Yet the men of the three tribes carried almost identical spears. To make matters worse, when a Tugen woman visited a Pokot village or compound, she would take her Tugen earflap off and replace it with a Pokot earflap, which she carried with her. Ian found similar inconsistent patterns in the pottery the tribespeople used and the utensils they made from calabash shells. He couldn't explain this inconsistency, but for the time being he set aside the data that didn't work and focused on the correlations that seemed to fit, publishing several papers on his Baringo work over the next few years.

In 1977, the year he took up his post at Cambridge, Ian went to Zambia to study the Lozi people, hoping that with a little more data he might be able to sort out the problems with his research. But in Zambia he found that things were even more confusing. Meanwhile, in Cambridge, where he had been hired to teach archaeological theory, Ian began to attract a group of bright graduate students. As one of the top two universities in the United Kingdom—the other is Oxford—Cambridge had its pick of the most brilliant doctoral candidates. Ian often found that he had as much to learn from them as they did from him. Some of his students—especially Henrietta Moore, who had done an undergraduate degree in both archaeology and anthropology at Durham University—introduced him to the latest thinking in cultural anthropology and the other social sciences. In seminars Ian and his students began reading the French anthropologist Claude Lévi-Strauss on the hidden structures in human minds and the French sociologist Pierre Bourdieu on the symbolic meaning of the Berber house of North Africa, as well as the anthropologists Mary Douglas and Victor Turner on symbolism and the meaning of rituals. They were reading social theorists that no sane archaeologist of the day, whether New Archaeologist or culture historian, would dream of touching. All of these thinkers agreed on one key concept: culture had to be taken seriously as a phenomenon in its own right.

For a long time, however, Ian made little connection between the intellectual questions posed by the reading he was doing and the down-to-earth problems he was having with his ethnoarchaeology research in Africa. Then, one day in the Nuba Hills of central Sudan, the connection hit him like a thunderbolt.

Ian had come across a book called *The Last of the Nuba* by Leni Riefenstahl, the controversial German filmmaker and photographer. Riefenstahl had been accused of glorifying the Nazi regime in films that she made for Hitler during the 1930s, and her book of photographs of the Nuba people was also attacked for what some people believed was a racist, primitivistic portrayal of this ethnic group. At the time, however, Ian was unaware of the controversy over the book. He began reading other works about the Nuba and decided that they would be ideal subjects for his work. With the help of some local contacts in the Sudan, he made two short trips to the granite slopes of the Nuba Hills.

One hot morning Ian and his interpreter were visiting a Nuba tribal group called the Mesakin, asking the usual questions and making the usual drawings. As they approached a cluster of thatched huts, Ian noticed a collection of animal bones stuck between some boulders near the entrance to the compound. There were a few Mesakin men and women standing outside, so he asked them what they were. Cattle bones, they replied. Then Ian saw some more bones stuck between other boulders some distance away. He was informed that those were pig bones. Why were they not put in the same place? Ian asked. At that point two women and a young man invited him to come inside the compound for a drink of water and a chat. They cleared away the corn husks, ash, and broken bits of pottery on the packed mud floor of the compound's shady central court. Ian and his interpreter sat down with their backs against one of the thatched huts.

For the next three hours the Mesakin answered Ian's questions with a mixture of patient tolerance and occasional amazement that what they were telling him was not obvious. Cattle, they said, were tended by the men, while the women took care of the pigs, which were considered dirty. The bones could not be mixed together because women were considered impure, especially when they were menstruating. And when they were menstruating, women were not allowed to do any work or handle food. Unmarried men who tended cattle could not eat pig meat at any time, because otherwise their cattle might die. Mesakin men and women also ate from separate plates on opposite sides of the central courtyard, to avoid pollution between the two sexes.

Ian put down his notepad and listened as the two women and the man spun out an ever longer list of taboos and rules about what could and could not be done. When he finally said good-bye and emerged with blinking eyes into the hot sun, Ian felt dizzy and feverish. His entire world, all the assumptions he had been working with all these years, had fallen apart. The Mesakin didn't put their cattle bones in one place and their pig bones in another because doing it that way made them better adapted to their physical environment or helped them to cooperate or compete with other tribespeople. They did it because otherwise men and women would contaminate each other. Why did they believe that? Ian had no idea. One thing was clear: the culture that led to this behavior had to be understood on its own terms, as something that had a life of its own. An archaeologist who came along years later and dug up these cattle and pig bones wasn't going to have a clue why they were put in different places if he or she followed the precepts of the New Archaeology. Even as his old world was coming apart at the seams, Ian was beginning to see how a new one might be put together.

5 / Return to Çatalhöyük

"So Ian said…, 'I've got a brand-new plan for archaeology…We are going to change the world, we're going to change the whole approach to archaeology.'" That is how Michael Parker Pearson, one of Ian Hodder's former graduate students, recalled events many years later. In reality, Ian's revolt against the New Archaeology was long in gestation. It was inspired by a number of different developments, of which his epiphany among the Nuba of the Sudan was simply the most dramatic.

By the end of the 1970s the New Archaeology was no longer new. As more and more archaeologists adopted its basic tenets, the Binford-Clarke school of thought became known as "processualism" or "processual archaeology," because of its emphasis on understanding the processes of change in ancient societies. In the United States Binford's graduate students were fruitful and multiplied, spreading out to take university posts across the country and spawning their own disciples in turn. But the messianic fervor with which many American archaeologists embraced the new paradigm took a more subdued form in the United Kingdom, where the 1976 death of David Clarke had left Colin Renfrew, a brilliant but somewhat less charismatic figure, at the helm of the British movement.

As the twentieth anniversary of Binford's 1962 manifesto, "Archaeology as Anthropology," approached, there were increasing signs that the scientific rigor championed by the New Archaeology was not delivering on all of its promises. The New Archaeology's critics had a number of complaints. Perhaps most serious was that after all these years, its adherents had failed to discover any universal laws that would explain how and why cultural change took place. Archaeology—the only discipline with the ability to look at the long sweep of thousands or even millions of years of history and prehistory at a time—seemed in a unique position to shed light on the basic dynamics of human behavior. Binford had asserted that the elucidation of cultural laws would be the field's biggest contribution to anthropology. But he and his colleagues had not been able to come up with any such broad generalizations.

At the same time, many archaeologists were concluding that processualism's insistence on hypothesis testing as the only valid method of interpreting the archaeological record had too many limitations. The range of questions that archaeologists could even consider testing was usually restricted to narrowly defined issues of subsistence, economics, trade, and technology; as a result, the New Archaeologists tended to ignore religion and ideology, despite bountiful evidence that these more ethereal realms were central to the lives of prehistoric peoples. The year 1982 also marked Ian Hodder's formal coming out as a renegade from the New Archaeology. Ian's rebellion came in the form of two books published that year: *Symbols in Action,* a detailed report on his ethnoarchaeological work in Kenya, Zambia, and the Sudan; and *Symbolic and Structural Archaeology,* a compendium of papers by Ian's group of Cambridge graduate students and other like-minded contributors. In the first book, Ian offered his own diagnosis of what was ailing the New Archaeology; in the second volume, he and his collaborators made their first fledgling attempts to prescribe a cure.

Ever since he had walked out of that Nuba hut and into the African sunshine, Ian had been trying to figure out where the New Archaeology had gone wrong. In *Symbols in Action,* he put his finger on what he now concluded was the processualists' biggest mistake: they had failed to appreciate the complexity and richness of human culture. Whereas the culture historians had defined it as a shared body of ideas, values, and beliefs, Binford had insisted—following his University of Michigan mentor, the anthropologist Leslie White—that culture was humankind's "extrasomatic" means of adaptation to its environment.

Yet Ian's work in Africa had convinced him that the New Archaeologists, by focusing so narrowly on culture's adaptive functions, were overlooking the more profound meanings of cultural symbolism in human communities. The Nuba people, for example, discarded their pig and cattle bones in separate areas as part of an intricate social negotiation about the proper roles of men and women, all against the backdrop of deeply held beliefs about purity and pollution. An archaeologist who dug up these bones later and tried to figure out why they were kept separate could not even begin to guess the truth if he or she tried to interpret this practice in strictly adaptive or functional terms. Thus Ian argued that culture had to be viewed in an entirely different way: material culture, he wrote, "is meaningfully constituted," a phrase he would repeat many times in his subsequent writings. In other words, the bones, pottery, tools, figurines, and other artifacts that archaeologists dig up were once active elements in the living symbolic world of ancient peoples. These symbols, Ian concluded, do not passively reflect adaptive strategies; rather "they play an active part in forming and giving meaning to social behavior."

One striking illustration that symbols are active rather than passive came from Ian's interviews in a village in Zambia, where he had talked to three women who made pottery. The first was the wife of the headman (a sort of minor chief), who originally came from another village and had been taught to make pots by her mother. This woman's daughter-in-law also made pots, but she had learned the craft in yet another village before she married into the family. These two women decorated their pots the same way, with a distinctive pattern of red-painted triangles. The third woman, who was married to the brother of the headman, had learned to make pots by watching the other two. And yet her pots were entirely distinct: they were unpainted and their dimensions were different. At first Ian was at a loss to explain this. Why did the third woman, who had learned potting from the other women in the village, make them differently, while the first two women—who had learned potting in two different outside villages—make them the same way? On further investigation, Ian discovered that the headman and his brother did not get along at all; in fact, they had long harbored an intense antagonism. He concluded that the brother's wife made her pots differently as a way of expressing hostility to her husband's enemies, while the other two women made their pots the same way to express feelings of friendship and solidarity with each other.

In *Symbols in Action*, Ian took direct aim at Lewis Binford, criticizing, among other things, his ethnoarchaeological work among the Nunamiut peoples of Alaska. "Binford provides no evidence at all of the cultural and symbolic context within which the Nunamiut carry out their food processing activities," he wrote. The book made a big splash among archaeologists. "Ian Hodder was able to demonstrate that, in addition to its technological role, material culture could be used to disguise and invert social relations, as well as to reflect and reinforce them," commented Bruce Trigger of McGill University in Montreal, a noted historian of archaeology. Yet now that Ian had thrown down the gauntlet to the New Archaeology, the biggest question of all was, What did he propose to replace it with?

JUST AS LEWIS BINFORD had gathered together a congregation of devoted disciples to spread the processual word, so did graduate students eager to work with Ian Hodder flock to the Cambridge archaeology department's red-brick Edwardian building. They began arriving around 1978, soon after Ian was appointed to replace David Clarke. The students were attracted by Ian's work in Africa and by the opportunity to study material culture in a new and different way. Before long, Ian's coterie included a dozen budding archaeologists and anthropologists, many of whom would go on to become well established if not controversial names in British academia themselves. The tight-knit group met every Wednesday afternoon to discuss books that Ian had assigned them to read or that the students themselves brought in. Often, on Friday evenings, the students boarded a train for the rural village outside Cambridge where Ian and Françoise then lived with their two young sons,

Christophe and Grégoire, in a small cottage with no central heating. Ian would pick the students up at the station, and Françoise would cook a traditional French meal accompanied by a seemingly endless flow of French wine. The group debated philosophy and cultural theory until late into the night, whereupon Ian and Françoise would retire to their bedroom and the students would crash on the couches or on the floor until the sun started peeking through the cottage windows.

If there was one thing Ian still had in common with the New Archaeologists, it was the conviction that archaeology had to be guided by some sort of theoretical framework. But rather than reading the works preferred by Binford—logical positivist Carl Hempel, philosopher of science Karl Popper, or historian of science Thomas Kuhn—Ian and his students concentrated on books that often had a closer affinity with the food and drink Françoise served up: many were the works of French anthropologists, social theorists, and philosophers. The reading list included a number of works by Claude Lévi-Strauss including *Structural Anthropology* and *The Savage Mind,* which had shaken up anthropology in the 1950s and 1960s with their arguments that culture had to be understood in terms of hidden conceptual structures in the human mind. The group also devoured the works of sociologist Pierre Bourdieu, a former student of Lévi-Strauss; philosopher Michel Foucault, whose often obtuse writings explored the relationship between knowledge and power in modern societies; and philosopher Louis Althusser, a leader in the movement to rescue the valid insights of Karl Marx into the nature of capitalist society from the flood of Stalinist repression that had flowed from the distorted application of Marxist ideas.

The works that Ian and his students were reading represented varying and sometimes contradictory theories. Many of them fit into what might loosely be called a postmodern view of the world, which is characterized by skepticism about human progress and especially about positivist claims that the scientific method is the only valid route to knowledge. The group became convinced that these new ideas, if adopted by archaeologists, could open the door to understanding the *meanings* of the art and artifacts that excavators uncovered, rather than simply their *functions.*

The notion that they were about to turn a new page in the history of archaeology infused Ian's students with the same revolutionary fervor that had animated the processual archaeologists during the 1960s. The excitement was sometimes unbearable. One day Michael Parker Pearson was taking a shower in his small room at Cambridge's Kings College when he suddenly had what seemed at the time like a brilliant insight into how Marxism could make a contribution to archaeology. He burst out of the shower, out of the room, and ran stark naked to the apartment of his next-door neighbors, archaeology graduate students Paul Halstead and Glynis Jones. Glynis made Parker Pearson stand behind an armchair, his stocky body dripping wet, while he burbled forth his somewhat jumbled thoughts.

Ian certainly shared his students' enthusiasm about the new path they were taking, but he was embarrassed by the claim that they were breaking entirely new ground. The social and cultural theories that the group was embracing so eagerly had been around for a long time, in some cases for decades. Yet it was only now, in the late 1970s and early 1980s, that archaeologists were beginning to discover what to many anthropologists and sociologists was old news.

Not everyone was ready to herald this news, however, as illustrated by a celebrated skirmish in archaeology's culture wars. During a speaking tour of Great Britain in late 1980, which Renfrew had arranged, Binford came to Cambridge to give a lecture. Afterward he was invited to attend a seminar organized by Ian and a number of his graduate students. To Binford's apparent surprise, Michael Parker Pearson and another student named Daniel Miller got up and read prepared texts in which the New Archaeology, and Binford's work in particular, were subjected to sharp, no-holds-barred critiques. At one point Binford, furious, got up to leave. "This is horseshit!" one witness recalled him saying. Binford was persuaded to stay, although some archaeologists in the audience were surprised that the fuming American did not do more to defend himself; indeed, some people present felt that the students were attacking Binford for positions that he had modified or abandoned many years earlier.

Binford, in his 1983 book *In Pursuit of the Past*, related his own version of events: "This discussion began with two students reading prepared papers in which science, archaeology and my own writings were accused of a long list of deficiencies, misdemeanors, and even intellectual felonies (for instance, I was informed by Hodder that a serious deficiency of my Nunamiut work was the fact that I had not questioned the

Eskimos about their attitudes towards dirt!)." Binford went on to cite the incident at Cambridge as "an example of a common form of argument used by the social philosophers. First the victim is asked when he is going to stop beating his wife. In reply, he states that in fact he does not beat his wife; however, he does agree with the accusers that one should *not* beat one's wife."

Binford did not, however, relate what happened next. Renfrew had asked Paul Halstead, whose apartment at Kings College was fairly spacious, to host a party for Binford that evening. Neither Ian nor his students showed up, with the one exception of Daniel Miller, who naively believed that he could share a friendly drink with the big man despite their intellectual differences. Binford, on spotting him, obviously felt that Miller needed tutoring on the adaptive function of academic culture: "You'll find out what natural selection means when you try to get a job, buddy boy!" he barked at the startled student.

In 1982 Ian's group, together with other like-minded British and American archaeologists and anthropologists, published *Symbolic and Structural Archaeology*, the first manifesto of what soon came to be called post-processual archaeology. This umbrella term for the new movement actually encompassed a fairly wide variety of different views, but the contributors to the volume all shared an antipathy to what was seen as the "positivism" and "functionalism" of the New Archaeology. Ian, in a kickoff article provocatively entitled "Theoretical archaeology: a reactionary view," outlined his new vision for what he called a "contextual or cultural archaeology." This new approach, Ian declared, would combine the New Archaeology's emphasis on studying the processes of social change with the concerns of an earlier generation of archaeologists, such as V. Gordon Childe and Glyn Daniel, who had viewed archaeology primarily "as a historical discipline" and artifacts as "expressions of culturally framed ideas."

As for what a contextual or cultural archaeology would mean in practice, the volume included a few preliminary case studies in which the group tried to apply this new approach to the patterns of burial practices and pottery styles at selected Neolithic and Bronze Age sites, as well as to an interpretation of Paleolithic cave art. But while *Symbols in Action*, which Ian published the same year, had been greeted enthusiastically by many archaeologists, the reviews of *Symbolic and Structural Archae-*

ology were much more mixed. Some commentators clearly thought that archaeology would be better off without the insights of Ian Hodder and company. "The wholesale borrowing of anthropological theory and explanation in developing a general theory of material culture appears as Hodder's unstated aim," wrote Aram Yengoyan, a social anthropologist at the University of Michigan, in the *Proceedings of the Prehistoric Society*. "This is unfortunate, since some of the borrowed concepts are not only poor, but wrong, and it would be best if they were contained within social anthropology without contamination of archaeology."

As Ian and his followers continued to refine and publish their ideas over the next several years, the polemics between the processualists and post-processualists degenerated into an ever more strident shouting match between the two camps, of which Lewis Binford and Ian Hodder were now the undisputed ringleaders. The post-processualists continued to attack the processualists for their "positivism," which they believed had turned the scientific method into a magic fetish that would supposedly open the doors to all the knowledge worth knowing, while the processualists countered that their critics wanted to infect archaeology with a postmodern, "anything goes" cultural relativism that was not subject to testing or any other kind of objective verification.

Ian made a definitive attempt to clarify his position in a 1986 book called *Reading the Past*, his most comprehensive explanation of the aims of post-processual archaeology. Today the book, now in its third edition, is required reading in nearly all university courses in archaeological theory. After laying out in detail his critique of previous approaches, Ian explained that post-processual archaeology "does not espouse one approach or argue that archaeology should develop an agreed methodology." Instead, "it is characterized by debate and uncertainty about fundamental issues that may have been rarely questioned before in archaeology." On the other hand, Ian insisted, post-processual archaeology was not antiscience, even if it discounted the positivist approach of hypothesis testing. "The alternative is to move backwards and forwards between theory and data, trying to fit or accommodate one to the other in a clear and rigorous fashion, on the one hand being sensitive to the particularity of the data and on the other hand being critical about assumptions and theories."

When *Reading the Past* was published, the journal *American Antiq-*

uity invited Lewis Binford to review it. Ian was now on the receiving end of the kind of criticism he had leveled at Binford years before. "This is a little book with a little message being blown through a large horn with a loud noise," Binford wrote in the review's first sentence. After this warm-up, Binford went on to list the various ways in which Ian's book was "packed with contradictions, misrepresentations, and distortions" and the extent to which "the author totally misunderstands the challenges facing archaeologists."

Ian was beginning to realize that all of the polemics and theorizing were showing diminishing returns. The only way he was really going to convince the archaeological community that his ideas were valid was to apply them in the field—that is, to an actual archaeological excavation. As the debates raged during the 1980s, Ian had engaged in only one major excavation, a fairly conventional multiperiod dig at Haddenham, north of Cambridge. He needed to find a prehistoric site that was rich in symbolic expression but that also had well-preserved architecture and artifacts, so that he could interpret the symbolism within the context of the community's everyday life—something like that Neolithic settlement in Turkey with which James Mellaart had dazzled Ian and his classmates so many years before. As he sat musing in his office in the Cambridge archaeology department, Ian recalled the hum of the projector and the flash of goddesses and bulls on the screen as he had sat dreamy-eyed in the darkened lecture hall. Yes, he needed to find a site like Çatalhöyük.

THE YEAR 1982, when post-processual archaeology was officially launched, also marked a turning point in Ian's personal life. The balancing act required to manage two careers and raise two young boys had put too great a strain on his marriage to Françoise Hivernel. After seven years together, the couple separated, and in 1984 they were divorced. In January of the following year, Ian fell in love again. Her name was Christine. She was an archaeobotanist, expert in recovering tiny plant remains from ancient sites. Christine was American, tall and slim, with restless, watchful brown eyes. She was intense, even a bit high-strung. She was an assistant professor at the University of Minnesota in Minneapolis. All of that added up very well in Ian's book, but Christine had one more thing going for her: unlike Ian, she had actually been to Çatalhöyük.

Christine Hastorf was born on December 7, 1950, in Hanover, New Hampshire. Her father taught psychology at Dartmouth College; her mother, who had attended college at Mount Holyoke in Massachusetts, stayed home and took care of Christine and her older sister. Their house in Hanover was surrounded by forest on three sides. Christine's walk to school took her across grassy fields dotted with strawberry patches. Her paternal grandmother was an avid amateur naturalist who lived in New Jersey and covered her walls with large photographs of birds and wildflowers. During summer holidays, Christine would go off with her grandmother for weeks at a time to the Adirondack Mountains in upstate New York, where the two would travel from lake to shining lake trying to identify every bird, plant, and flower they came across.

When Christine was about eleven years old, her father was offered a position at Stanford University in Palo Alto, California. Her parents sold their home in Hanover and the family moved to a house with a big garden on the Stanford campus. Just before her sophomore year at a Palo Alto high school, Christine's father spent six months teaching in Europe. Her sister was packed off to a school in France's Loire Valley, while Christine was sent to an international boarding school in Vienna, Austria. Strolling among the seventeenth- and eighteenth-century buildings of Vienna, Christine first realized that old could be interesting.

Back in Palo Alto, Christine finished high school. As graduation approached, she thought about going back to Europe, but her parents insisted that she start the following year as a freshman at Stanford. Christine designed her own undergraduate program, an interdisciplinary course that mixed both the biological and social sciences. At first, archaeology was not on her radar, because at that time the subject was not taught at Stanford. But during a college trip to Rome, an archaeologist who was showing the group around the Roman Forum offered to take Christine on a tour of the National Etruscan Museum the following morning. The Etruscans, a mysterious people who occupied what is today Tuscany in north central Italy during the first millennium B.C., had left behind some of the most sophisticated art and design in the ancient world. As the archaeologist led Christine past the displays of terracotta vases, jewelry, and bronze sculpture, she made up her mind then and there what she wanted to do with her life.

Fortuitously, during Christine's senior year an archaeologist named Ezra Zubrow came to Stanford to teach. Zubrow was a former student of Lewis Binford. He was filled with the early enthusiasm of the New Archaeology. Christine got the top grade in his class. That summer of 1972, after graduation, she was one of seven students who followed Zubrow down to central Mexico, where he was surveying archaeological sites in the region of Guanajuato. Christine focused on the local ecology, recording the various species of plants in the survey area. Later she joined another dig in Italy. She took a job for a year with the U.S. Geological Survey and then took off again to travel around Europe with a school friend. During the spring of 1974 Christine and her friend spent a month in Turkey. Christine had read James Mellaart's 1967 book about Çatalhöyük and decided she must see the celebrated Neolithic site. When she arrived at the mound, which was now surrounded by a fence, a guard let her in and showed her around. She gazed at the badly eroded remains of Mellaart's excavation trenches and the traces of mudbrick houses that had melted away from exposure to years of rain and wind. The guard tried to hand her shards of pottery for souvenirs, but Christine—having vaguely heard something about the Dorak affair—politely refused.

Back in California, Christine made up her mind to go to graduate school and get her Ph.D. She was accepted at the University of California, Los Angeles (UCLA). Her first doctoral supervisor was Marija Gimbutas, the Lithuanian-born archaeologist whose contention that Çatalhöyük was a matriarchical center for goddess worship had done so much to boost the site's fame. Gimbutas was a charismatic and imposing woman—something like a goddess herself, Christine thought. During one of their early meetings, Christine announced to Gimbutas that she intended to excavate Çatalhöyük herself one day. Gimbutas responded with an indulgent smile.

Gimbutas was an old-school archaeologist, a culture historian of the most traditional sort. But by the mid-1970s, UCLA was a hotbed of the New Archaeology. Christine was exposed to the excitement of the new processual paradigm. Before long she was spending her summers working with Steven LeBlanc at Native American sites in New Mexico's

Mimbres Valley and making plans to join Timothy Earle's new project in the Upper Mantaro Valley of Peru. When Earle agreed to take over as her doctoral supervisor, Christine made an appointment to see Gimbutas and break the news. As she stood shuffling apologetically in front of Gimbutas's desk, the older woman drew herself upright in her chair and threw her shoulders back. "If you go work in Peru," Gimbutas thundered, "you will never get to Çatalhöyük!"

IAN AND CHRISTINE had first met in 1981, in Los Angeles, when Christine was still a graduate student at UCLA. Ian had come to the university to give a talk. Christine was too busy working in the archaeobotany laboratory to attend, but she did go along to a party afterward where the two were introduced by a mutual friend. She heard later from her colleagues in the department that Ian's lecture had been disappointing. Everyone was expecting him to speak about his new methodologies for spatial analysis, yet all he wanted to talk about was the symbolic meaning of material culture and something he called "contextual archaeology."

In January 1985 Ian and Christine met again. Christine, upon completing her Ph.D. a few years earlier, had been hired by the University of Minnesota. She was asked by her department to organize a conference in connection with a traveling exhibit of Mimbres Valley ceramics, of which the university housed the largest collection in the world. Christine decided to broaden the focus of the meeting into a general discussion of the meaning of stylistic differences in pottery, art, and other artifacts, a controversial subject that only a handful of archaeologists had written about. She invited several experts known for their interest in this area to come and speak. Among the invitees was Ian Hodder.

For Christine, organizing a conference meant doing everything: inviting the speakers, arranging housing, cooking the food for the after-conference dinners, and picking people up at the Minneapolis–St. Paul airport. Ian was arriving a couple of days early, but Christine was worried that she might not recognize him again. She borrowed a copy of *Symbols in Action* from a colleague and waved its distinctive orange cover at the disembarking passengers until one of them—a tall, slim man in his mid thirties wearing wire-rimmed glasses on his slightly upturned nose—gave her a shy, boyish smile and walked over. As the meeting got under way, Christine noticed that Ian always seemed to be hovering around. When it came time to drive the speakers back to their hotels, he invariably climbed into her car. And when Christine begged off from a group walk around Minneapolis's picturesque Lake of the Isles, saying she had to cook dinner for everyone, Ian volunteered to stay behind and help her in the kitchen. The pair eventually snuck out and had a drink together. By the time Ian returned to Europe, their love affair was under way.

Over the next two years Ian and Christine saw each other whenever they could, at conferences and during holiday breaks. In 1987 Ian took a sabbatical leave from Cambridge, which he arranged to spend at Stanford University's Center for Advanced Study in the Behavioral Sciences. The couple made plans to get married at Christine's parents' house that spring. A few weeks before the wedding, Ian and Christine traveled down to UCLA, where Ian had been invited to give a big public lecture. By then he had been thinking about Çatalhöyük quite a bit. The Institute of Archaeology in London had asked him to write a paper for its annual bulletin. Ian had attempted a "contextual interpretation" of the symbolism at Çatalhöyük. He found that he agreed with Mellaart's notion that the vulture beaks protruding from female breasts represented an opposition of life and death. But on reading Mellaart's excavation reports and his 1967 book, he found the evidence for Mother Goddess worship to be lacking. Ian sent a draft of the paper to Mellaart, who responded in a friendly way but insisted that his assertions about the goddess were based on solid data.

At UCLA Ian tried out some of these ideas on his audience, as well as some new interpretations of the Neolithic in Europe that he was writing up for a forthcoming book. No sooner had he finished his talk than a hand shot up. It was Marija Gimbutas. She objected bitterly to Ian's dismissal of the goddess, as well as to some of his statements about the symbolic meanings of stone axes found in European Neolithic graves. "It is perfectly obvious that these triangularly shaped axes represent the female genitalia," Gimbutas declared. Ian countered politely that the great majority of the axes had been found with male burials, but Gimbutas dismissed that argument with a disgusted wave of the hand.

Once married, Ian and Christine had to deal with a serious problem. He was based in Cambridge, and she in Minneapolis. For the time being, their trans-Atlantic relationship would have to continue as it was. But what if they could find a dig to work on together during the summers? Despite their shared interest in Çatalhöyük, it did not occur to them at first that they might really be able to dig there. More than twenty years had passed since the site was shut down in the murky aftermath of the Dorak affair. If it had been possible to renew the excavations, surely someone would have done so by now.

"There's lots of symbolism in Peru," Christine suggested. "Why don't you come work with me there?" No, Peru did not really appeal to him. What about Egypt? "No, no, not Egypt," Christine answered. The only site they were both interested in was Çatalhöyük. They knew that David French, who was into his third decade as director of the British Institute of Archaeology at Ankara, spent several weeks in England every year with his wife, Pamela. Why not invite him to lunch, they thought, and see what he says?

EVERY ARCHAEOLOGIST who worked with David French on the various excavations he directed in Turkey over the years knew the unspoken rule: you did not try to talk to him about Çatalhöyük. Ever since French had taken over from Michael Gough as the BIAA's director in 1968, one of his main jobs had been to restore the good reputation of British archaeology in Turkey in the wake of Mellaart's disastrous misadventures. He kept the institute's copy of *The Dorak Affair* in his office rather than in the library, and he did his best to keep the BIAA from becoming embroiled in any new controversies. The Turkish antiquities authorities had allowed him to finish his own dig at Can Hasan, but they had showed little enthusiasm for further Neolithic or Chalcolithic excavations. Instead the Turks asked the British to help them with a number of rescue digs at sites threatened with flooding by new dam projects.

After a number of delays and distractions due to their academic workloads, Ian and Christine finally got around to inviting David French to lunch. On a cold, gray day in January 1990, the three of them sat at an oak table by the windows of The Mill in Cambridge, an old pub that looks out over a boatyard on the River Cam. Meeting with French was a real treat. Not only was he a codiscoverer of Çatalhöyük, but, while working at Can Hasan, he had invented the flotation machine that Christine and many other archaeobotanists used to recover plant remains. Ian and Christine gingerly posed some general questions about excavating in Turkey. French could easily guess what they were after. He leaned back a little on the oak bench and said, "Well, you're probably thinking about Çatalhöyük, but of course that is untouchable." Ian and Christine shot quick glances at each other. "Oh yes, of course," they said in unison, "we know Çatalhöyük is out of the question."

French did offer to show them other Neolithic sites in Turkey that they might consider digging. As Ian and Christine walked away from The Mill after saying good-bye to French, they decided it would be a good idea to take him up on his suggestion. Even if digging at Çatalhöyük was not realistic, perhaps they might find another site that would suit their purposes. Ian got back in touch with French and arranged the trip for the following October. But when the time came, Christine was busy teaching in Minnesota and could not come with him. Ian went alone.

French picked Ian up at the Ankara airport, and the grand tour of Central Anatolia began. Their first stop was Aşikli Höyük in Cappadocia, the Neolithic mound that appeared to predate Çatalhöyük by a millennium. Ian Todd, Mellaart's assistant director, had first examined the site in 1964. Under normal circumstances Aşikli would have been Todd's site to dig, but he too had been a victim of the fallout from the Dorak affair and had ended up digging in Cyprus. Finally, in 1989, excavations had begun at Aşikli under the direction of Istanbul University archaeologist Ufuk Esin; after two seasons, the work was already producing critical new information about the origins of the Neolithic in Anatolia.

French and Hodder arrived in Konya in the evening and took rooms in a hotel. The following morning, October 3, 1990, Ian finally got to see Çatalhöyük. While French stayed below talking to the guard, Ian scurried excitedly over the mound, hardly believing that he was finally there. At the south end of the tell, where Mellaart had dug, everything was eroded and collapsed, and thick grass had overgrown much of the area. Yet despite the sorry state of Mellaart's old trenches, Ian had never seen such dense, complex stratigraphy, such amazing preservation of mud-brick walls, such an incredible opportunity to do the contextual archaeology he had been advocating for so many years. As he slowly descended the mound, he saw French looking up at him with a decidedly grumpy expression. But French had already pretty much resigned himself to Ian's desire to dig at Çatalhöyük. If Ian could get the Turks to agree, why not let him try?

Ian made plans to come back to Turkey and began making the rounds. The first thing he did was meet in Istanbul with Ufuk Esin and Mehmet Özdoğan, Turkey's preeminent Neolithic specialists. At that point Ian still assumed that Çatalhöyük lay off in the future. But Esin and Özdoğan wasted little time talking about other sites; to them it was obvious that Ian should pick up Mellaart's long-extinguished torch. Ian then went to Ankara and saw the director general of antiquities and other officials in the culture ministry. They were all mildly encouraging, although they stressed that Ian had to demonstrate that he could raise the money for the excavations before he would have any hope of getting approval. Ian had the impression that something wasn't quite right. He sensed a hidden resistance to his project. When he went to London to talk to officials in the British Academy about funding the dig, he got the same reaction.

Finally, during another trip to Ankara, he went to see Timothy Daunt, who at that time was the British ambassador to Turkey. Daunt had worked for the British foreign service in Turkey on and off since the 1960s, and he knew the Mellaarts quite well. "Have you got Mellaart's permission?" Daunt asked. "What?" said Ian, not understanding. Daunt explained that, Dorak or no Dorak, there were still a lot of people both in Turkey and in Great Britain who thought that Mellaart had been unfairly treated. Moreover, according to Turkish archaeological tradition, Çatalhöyük was still considered a British dig. It was up to the British to sort out amongst themselves who was going to excavate the site, even if Mellaart had been banned forever from coming back himself. And as long as Mellaart was still alive, no one else was going to dig Çatalhöyük without his blessing.

DESPITE DAVID FRENCH'S personal aversion toward all things Çatalhöyük, during his time as director the BIAA's London-based governing council made several attempts to get the excavations going again. The closest it came was in 1974, when, after several months of negotiations with the Turkish authorities, a working group appointed by the institute received tentative permission to reopen the dig. Kenneth Pearson, coauthor of *The Dorak Affair*, wrote up the news for the London *Sunday Times*. The council had even approached Colin Renfrew to ask if he would be interested in directing the excavations. Renfrew was reluctant to do so, however, in part because he sympathized with Mellaart's plight and also because he was busy with his own excavations in Greece. A week after the story broke, several BIAA members got the *Sunday Times* to publish a joint letter insisting that if Çatalhöyük was to be dug again, Mellaart should be the one in charge.

In the end, however, the plan had to be scuttled after the Turkish army invaded Cyprus in reaction to a coup on the island instigated by the mainland Greek government. For the time being, the Turks were too preoccupied with the resulting international crisis to concern themselves with a 9,000-year-old Neolithic village. During the 1980s another BIAA working group was put together, but it did not get very far.

As Ian sat in an armchair facing the Mellaarts in their Finsbury Park apartment, sipping the Turkish coffee that Arlette had prepared, he knew that he was asking a great deal. In reality, he was asking for everything. He explained to Mellaart that they could not dig the site jointly, nor could Mellaart's name be on the permit, but he hoped that he could count on Mellaart for informal advice and counsel.

Mellaart said nothing for several minutes. For more than twenty-five years he had hoped to get Çatalhöyük back one day. It was the site of his greatest glory and his greatest shame. The pain of finally letting it go was intense. But he was now sixty-six years old and about to retire from the Institute of Archaeology. It was too late for him, but perhaps not too late to see a new generation of archaeologists bring Çatalhöyük alive again.

Mellaart turned to Arlette. "What do you think, darling?" he asked. Arlette looked up, her hands folded tightly in her lap. "I think it would be okay."

Mellaart turned back to Ian and smiled. "We think it would be okay."

6 / On the Surface

JAMES CONOLLY was as excited as a young archaeologist could be. On a warm day in late August 1993, he was at London's Heathrow Airport about to board an airplane for Istanbul. It was the first leg of his journey to Çatalhöyük. That morning James had turned in his master's thesis to the Institute of Archaeology in London. His dissertation was an analysis of obsidian tools unearthed at Abu Hureyra in Syria. Abu Hureyra, a prehistoric village on the Euphrates River that had been excavated by a British team during the 1970s and 1980s, rivaled Çatalhöyük as one of the biggest Neolithic sites in the Near East. It had produced critical new information about the transition from hunting and gathering to agriculture. On the strength of James's study, his supervisor at the Institute, Andrew Garrard—the archaeologist who had introduced Ian Hodder to his first wife, Françoise Hivernel, so many years before—had recommended him to be the stone tool specialist on the new excavations Ian was launching at Çatalhöyük.

James knew the obsidian at Abu Hureyra backward and forward, but he had never been there, nor had he ever traveled to the Near East. He had based his dissertation on the collection of Abu Hureyra obsidian tools kept in the Pitt-Rivers Museum at the University of Oxford. Now he was flying to Turkey with Roger Matthews, the director of the British School of Archaeology in Iraq. Roger was a veteran of numerous archaeological digs in the Near East. He and his archaeologist wife, Wendy Matthews, had been the first to jump aboard when Ian began gathering his team together the previous year. Ian had asked Roger to be his field director at Çatalhöyük, that is, his second in command. James and Roger had never met before, but they found each other easily at the airport. James was twenty-four years old, tall and lanky, with a casually handsome face and light brown hair that fell over his forehead. Roger was thirty-nine, shorter, slim and spryly built. He was handsome too, with a high forehead and fine, angular features.

Ian had told James that there was not enough money in the excavation budget for him to fly from Istanbul to Ankara. He would have to take the overnight bus to the Turkish capital. James would then make his way to the BIAA and meet up with Ian and Christine, who were already there. Once the plane took off, James learned that Roger had a ticket for the onward flight to Ankara. James had no Turkish lira, so when the plane landed, Roger gave him some money and he made his way by taxi to the Istanbul bus station.

When James arrived at the BIAA early the next morning, half asleep and badly in need of a shower, Roger and Ian were already in top gear making arrangements for the trip down to Çatalhöyük. Christine was doing her best to help out, but she was also busy taking care of Nicky and Kyle, the twin boys she had given birth to in November 1991. Ian asked Roger and James to gather together the equipment they would need for the dig, which they began doing with the aid of David French. As French showed them where to find the institute's collection of trowels, shovels, and pickaxes, James excitedly fired question after question at the older man. French feigned a lack of interest in anything that had to do with Çatalhöyük. But he seemed happy to talk about the flotation machine he had invented at Can Hasan; Christine was planning to build a similar device to recover plant remains at Çatalhöyük.

With the BIAA's help, Ian had arranged to use a new building in Çumra—the town near Çatalhöyük where Mellaart, French, and Alan Hall had drunk toasts of raki to celebrate the site's discovery in 1958—as the team's initial headquarters until a dig house could be built next to the mound. The Çumra municipal authorities had constructed the multistoried concrete structure to house a new shopping center, but no shopkeepers had shown an interest in moving into it. The building was empty and needed furnishing. The British Embassy in Ankara had offered to let the team take its pick of some old furniture it had stored away. Roger hired a large van and a Turkish driver to carry the load down to Çumra. At the embassy Roger and James supervised while some of the embassy staff loaded an assortment of dusty, dilapidated sofas, desks, and carpets into the van. The embassy people seemed to view this as an opportunity to get rid of a lot of old junk. They kept putting items in the van that Roger and James had not asked for, including a decrepit wooden bar covered with brown Naugahyde. The bar was removed, but just before leaving, the men noticed that somehow it had been loaded back on again. Once again they had the bar taken off.

It turned out that the driver had a friend who for some reason had to come along on the trip. There was only room for three people in the van's front cab, so Roger and James flipped a coin to see who would go. James lost. He once again boarded a bus, this time for the four-hour trip to Konya, where he caught yet another bus for the bumpy ride to Çumra. Meanwhile Ian, Christine, the twins, and a Turkish graduate student named Adnan Baysal, who was doing his archaeology studies in England, piled into the institute's Land Rover and made their way down to Çumra separately.

Roger was the last to arrive. He was in the midst of one of his many attempts to give up smoking, but both the driver and his friend had puffed away on powerful Turkish cigarettes during the entire journey. Roger looked shattered and a bit sick. James helped him open the back doors of the van so they could begin unloading the furniture. They caught the bar just before it could fall out and land on their feet.

• • •

OVER THE NEXT few days more members of the team arrived. They included Roger's wife, Wendy Matthews; Tom Pollard, a recently graduated archaeology student from Cambridge University; Tom Strasser, an American who had done his doctoral work on the Neolithic period in Crete; and Naomi Hamilton, a Ph.D. student at the University of Edinburgh. Naomi had earlier studied for her master's degree with James Mellaart at the Institute of Archaeology. At that point Ian and Christine were the only ones who had actually seen Çatalhöyük. The others were beside themselves with anticipation that they were finally going to see the celebrated tell they had only read about in archaeology textbooks. But Ian's permit to work at the site did not begin until September 1. He was insistent that no one could go to Çatalhöyük until the season had officially begun and the representative from the Turkish General Directorate of Monuments and Museums, as the Antiquities Department was now called, had arrived. The rep, as this person would come to be called by the team, was required by law to be present on the site whenever the team was excavating. Given Çatalhöyük's scandal-ridden history, Ian was determined not to put a foot wrong. He even made Wendy, Naomi, and Christine wear headscarves when they went out on the streets of Çumra, a conservative town in this conservative region of Muslim Turkey.

Finally the day came. The entire group, including Nicky and Kyle, managed to squeeze into the Land Rover. Ian took the wheel. The gravel, potholed road to the mound, nine miles from Çumra, was not in much better shape than it had been thirty-five years before, when Mellaart, French, and Hall drove down it in Hall's Land Rover. But the surrounding landscape had changed a great deal. A massive irrigation program, including a network of deep canals, had transformed the region from a dusty outback into a major agricultural center of wheatfields, melon patches, and fruit trees. When they arrived at Çatalhöyük, everyone realized that the warning in the tourist guidebooks was true: there was not much to see, except for Mellaart's eroded trenches and spoil heaps, and here and there sections of fallen mud-brick walls. But nothing could dampen the intense excitement they all felt.

Roger recalled what Ian had written a few years earlier in his book *The Domestication of Europe*: "Çatalhöyük and I, we bring each other into existence." At the time, those musings had seemed rather abstract.

Now he understood exactly what Ian meant. The potential for what they might learn here was nearly limitless. And all of their lives would be forever changed by the experience.

ARCHAEOLOGISTS, as a rule, are very patient people. They have to be. Nowadays an excavator can't just show up at a site and start digging, the way that Mellaart did. The complex stratigraphic layers of a mound like Çatalhöyük must be peeled away slowly and meticulously, and with a lot of advance planning. In fact, Ian had no intention of actually excavating Çatalhöyük during the first two years. Instead the time would be spent probing the surface of the mound and exploring the ancient environment and prehistoric settlement patterns of the surrounding region.

Despite the feverish pace of Mellaart's four seasons at Çatalhöyük during the 1960s, he had excavated only about 3 percent of the thirty-two-acre tell, and that only at its south end. Ian wanted to begin his own dig in another area of the mound. He needed to know as much as possible about the entire Neolithic village so he could choose the best place to begin. Archaeological science had made enormous leaps since Mellaart's day; a great deal could be learned from surface studies. Indeed, Lewis Binford and his colleagues had pioneered the first systematic attempts at surface work in the 1960s, at the Native American site of Hatchery West in southern Illinois. During the 1980s Roger Matthews had helped direct an extensive surface study at the Sumerian city of Abu Salabikh in southern Iraq, a project run by Cambridge University archaeologist Nicholas Postgate. Ian was determined to make maximum use of these new techniques before plunging headlong into the depths of Çatalhöyük.

Ever since James Mellaart had given his blessing to the new project, Ian had been slowly descending from the lofty heights of theory and philosophy to the real world of archaeological fieldwork. His primary aim at Çatalhöyük remained the same: to understand the meaning of the art and symbolism by putting it into the rich context of the community's daily life, a goal that the site's excellent preservation seemed to put within reach. Yet while Ian's notion of contextual archaeology remained sharply antithetical to the hypothesis-testing approach of the New Archaeologists, in more recent years he had tried hard to shed the reputation of being antiscience. He had begun to embrace scientific methodology as the best route to the contextual information he sought.

As Ian recruited the members of his team, he looked for young, up-and-coming archaeologists who had trained on the latest techniques yet were still open-minded enough to tackle research questions that science alone could not answer. He also tried to find people who could work well together in a group. Although Ian had spent most of the previous decade writing and theorizing, he had done enough digging in his career to know that an excavation can sink or swim on the strength of its community dynamics. When dozens of archaeologists are cooped up together for weeks or months at a time, far from home, the slightest conflict has the potential to blow up into full-scale warfare.

Ian did not, however, insist that everyone on the dig had to be a card-carrying post-processualist. To do so would have been contrary to a central principle of his archaeological philosophy, something Ian called "multivocality." This meant that no one archaeologist, no matter how many degrees he or she had or how much experience in the field, could claim to have the magic key to understanding the past. Rather the archaeologist engaged in a complex and often frustrating process of interpretation, in which there were no open-and-shut answers; in searching for the best interpretation of what had happened in prehistory, an excavator had to be receptive to multiple points of view. Moreover, it would have been self-defeating for Ian to insist that the members of his team toe the post-processual line. Despite the major inroads that his rebellion against the New Archaeology had made by the early 1990s, especially in the United Kingdom, the majority of archaeologists still preferred to excavate rather than read Pierre Bourdieu and Michel Foucault.

In reopening Çatalhöyük, Ian also set more conventional goals for the project—goals that most other archaeologists, whether processualists or post-processualists, could endorse. One key question was how Çatalhöyük fit into the overall picture of the spread of farming after the first appearance of agriculture in the Levant, at least 2,000 years before Çatalhöyük was founded. When Mellaart excavated the site in the 1960s, it seemed to stand in splendid isolation on the Anatolian plateau, a shining beacon of Neolithic culture surrounded by barren wilderness. But in the years since, some important new digs—such as Ufuk Esin's excavations at Aşikli Höyük in Central Anatolia and

Mehmet Özdoğan's work at Çayönü in southeastern Turkey—had helped fill in the gaps in the chronological and cultural sequence as the Neolithic way of life spread from east to west. The renewed excavations at Çatalhöyük could shed light on the role that this enormous village, still one of the largest early farming communities ever discovered, had played during these crucial early stages in the development of human civilization.

More fundamentally, Çatalhöyük seemed likely to harbor important clues about the central unresolved mystery posed by the so-called Neolithic Revolution: why had it taken place at all? Why, after the end of the Ice Age more than 12,000 years ago, had human beings—who had contented themselves with hunting and gathering for the first few million years of their evolution—suddenly crammed themselves into villages when they could be comfortably spread across the landscape? Ever since V. Gordon Childe coined the term *Neolithic Revolution* in the 1920s, archaeologists had assumed that sedentary life was necessary for successful agriculture: farmers had to stay close to their crops and animals. In more recent years it had become clear that this was an explanation that didn't explain anything. For one thing, a number of excavations in the Near East had since demonstrated that sedentism—living in permanent or semipermanent houses or other structures—sometimes preceded agriculture by thousands of years. Nor did archaeologists agree about why people had turned to farming. Was it a conscious choice, part of a cultural transformation in the relationship between humans and nature, as some argued? Or were they forced into it by overpopulation or climatic changes that put a stress on available resources, making the survival of our species dependent on more efficient ways of producing food?

Çatalhöyük, even though it was a relative latecomer in the Neolithic sequence compared to sites like Jericho in Palestine or Abu Hureyra in Syria, could still help archaeologists figure out why the earliest farming communities had formed. By reconstructing the ancient environment around Çatalhöyük—including the climate, the nature of the landscape, and the plants and animals that were native to the region—Ian and his team hoped to uncover clues about what had attracted as many as 8,000 people to congregate in this relatively isolated spot by the Çarsamba River. If they could understand that, they might better understand why people wanted to live together rather than apart, with all the blessings and evils that this turning point in prehistory had brought to humanity.

Ian had a lot of good reasons for coming to Çatalhöyük. The Turkish authorities were happy for him to come, although they had reasons of their own for welcoming him so warmly. More than one million tourists visit Konya each year, to explore the famous Mevlana Museum or watch dance performances by the Whirling Dervishes, the mystical Muslim sect that was founded in this southern Anatolian city during the thirteenth century. Yet as long as the guidebooks continued to say that there was nothing to see at Çatalhöyük, tourism was unlikely to spread beyond the Konya city line. In his negotiations with the Turks to reopen the dig, Ian proposed to transform the eroded ruins of Çatalhöyük into a heritage site, complete with a multimedia museum, visitors' center, and conserved Neolithic houses among which visitors could stroll while imagining themselves living in the distant past.

Ian was ambitious, but he knew that carrying out all of these plans would take time—a lot of it. One evening, early in the 1993 season, Ian was at the wheel of the Land Rover as the team journeyed to Konya. They had been invited to a joint cultural event between Turkey and Uzbekistan, where the Whirling Dervishes were to dance and one of Uzbekistan's most famous folk singers—a beautiful young woman in a purple ball gown who ended up having a devastating effect on the male archaeologists—was scheduled to perform. The sun was just setting behind the western hills as they drove along. James Conolly asked Ian how long he thought the excavations at Çatalhöyük would go on. "About twenty-five years," Ian replied. Everyone gasped. It was the first time that Ian had revealed just how long-range his plans really were. Wendy, who was sitting in the front seat, looked at Ian's face silhouetted against the hills as he stared straight ahead at the road. She thought she saw his hands tighten on the steering wheel.

THE FIRST SEASON at Çatalhöyük was only thirty days long, from the first of September to the end of the month. The team worked on the site every day except Fridays. The Turkish workmen helping them—most of whom came from Küçükköy, the village of mud-brick houses next door to Çatalhöyük where Mellaart and his team had lived during the 1960s—had asked for Fridays off so they could pray at the local mosque. Each evening, after eating dinner together in the Çumra dig house, the team members would work late into the night, labeling and categorizing the piles of pottery, obsidian, animal bones, and pieces of broken figurines that had been collected from the surface of the mound during the day. They took occasional drink breaks at the British Embassy bar, which had been set up in a corner of the dining room and quickly became the focal point for the fledgling community's social gatherings. Since time was so short, Ian was determined that they should get as much done as possible. He insisted that everyone be on site at exactly seven o'clock each morning. The bleary-eyed archaeologists would pile into the Land Rover and Ian would take off down the road, adjusting his speed—faster or slower, as necessary—so that they would arrive right on time. At that hour little birds would sit in the road warming themselves in the sun. The faster Ian drove, the less likely it was that they would get out of the way in time. James Conolly and Tom Pollard would sit in the back of the vehicle and pass the time counting how many birds failed to do so. One day, when they were running very late, the body count was disturbingly high.

Once they arrived at the mound, everyone on the team knew his or her mission. Adnan Baysal, the Turkish graduate student, was the project's official translator: he was assigned to recruit the workmen and to help Ian and Roger talk to the government representative and other Turkish officials. Tom Pollard, along with Colin Shell, a lecturer at Cambridge, set out to map the three-dimensional topography of the mound using a state-of-the-art electronic surveying device called a total station. Tom and Colin also methodically walked over the tell with an instrument called a fluxgate magnetic gradiometer, which picks up small differences in the surface magnetic field due to differences in the iron content and density of underlying structures. This magnetic survey was critical to the effort to identify the location of mud-brick buildings that might be good candidates for later excavation.

The team was also joined by archaeologists Douglas Baird of the University of Liverpool and Trevor Watkins at the University of Edinburgh, who were launching a wide-ranging survey of other prehistoric sites in the Konya area, and Neil Roberts, a geographer from Loughborough University in Leicestershire, who was an expert in reconstructing ancient environments. Tom Strasser helped supervise the Turkish workmen as they gathered artifacts from the surface, while James Conolly analyzed the large number of obsidian and flint stone tools that turned up. Meanwhile Naomi Hamilton divided her time between helping Roger with the surface work and running the dig house in Çumra. Since Naomi was one of the few members of the team who could speak Turkish, which she had learned during a long stay in northern Cyprus, she often had to stay behind to look after the kitchen staff.

Christine Hastorf, who had started out as Ian's partner in the scheme to reopen Çatalhöyük, now found her role changing. In the beginning she and Ian had talked vaguely about codirecting the project. But Christine had a lot on her plate. She had just left the University of Minnesota for the University of California at Berkeley, an important career move. She and Ian, who was still based in Cambridge, were now living even more thousands of miles apart. Christine had the major responsibility for taking care of Nicky and Kyle, who lived with her most of the time. Shortly before she left Minnesota, during one of Ian's visits to the United States, the two had a talk in their Minneapolis home. "Oh, Ian, this isn't going to work," Christine said. "I don't think we are going to codirect this. I'll be your sidekick and do the archaeobotany." By then she knew Ian well enough to realize that being a codirector was not his style. Behind the shy smile and soft voice was a man who wanted to be in charge. So Christine looked after the twins and began working on the design of the flotation machines she would need once full-fledged excavation began.

Roger and Wendy Matthews came the closest of anyone on the team to actually excavating Çatalhöyük that year. As veterans of Near Eastern digs, they were the only ones who had real experience working with mud-brick architecture. Ian relied heavily on Roger and Wendy, without whom he would have been hard put to get things going at Çatalhöyük. Outside of a few weeks digging in Israel with Eric Higgs while still an undergraduate student, Ian had never worked in the Near East.

Wendy took charge of cleaning and recording what remained of Mellaart's excavations in the south of the mound. The idea was to learn as much as possible from the 1960s dig before the badly eroded sections fell into even worse shape. She also prepared the area for further excavation by correlating each building with those reported in Mellaart's preliminary reports in *Anatolian Studies.* Mellaart had left many of the mud-brick walls standing, some of which were up to seven feet high. There was little to keep them from falling down. In many cases they already had, exposing the fill of yet-to-be-excavated buildings next door. Wendy photographed each building in its original state, then painstakingly cleaned the walls and floors with a trowel, an artist's palette knife, or a plasterer's blade to reveal as many features as possible. She then drew and photographed each structure again. Archaeologists who had worked with Wendy on other digs in the Near East knew her meticulous style. They referred affectionately to her assortment of implements as "Wendy tools."

Wendy was not only an experienced digger; she was also a member of an avant-garde of archaeological specialists called micromorphologists. Micromorphology is a relatively new technique, one of an arsenal of sophisticated methods which together make up what is called high-definition archaeology. While archaeologists are trained to notice the tiniest details—a subtle change in the color of soil layers, for example, could signal an entirely new stratigraphic layer—there is only so much they can see with the naked eye. Micromorphologists literally put archaeological sites under the microscope, hoping to find evidence of past human activities that might otherwise be overlooked. This was the kind of detail that Ian wanted for his contextual approach to digging Çatalhöyük. As Wendy cleaned and recorded the buildings, she cut out a number of small blocks for later microscopic examination: samples of the mud bricks and mortar, to analyze the materials used to make them; samples from the house floors, to see if she could determine what kinds and sequences of activities—for example, cooking or obsidian working—had taken place in which parts of the buildings; and samples of burned plaster and fuel from ovens, which might help determine how often they were used and at what temperatures.

Meanwhile Roger took charge of the labor-intensive surface collection and surface scraping work. During the 1993 season, he and his crew plotted the entire mound into a pattern of grids measuring two meters by two meters. A total of 242 squares, representing a little less than 1 percent of the tell, was then selected for sampling. Roger, with the help of the Turkish workmen from Küçükköy and those archaeologists on the team who could be spared from other tasks, carefully cleared the dense vegetation in each square; the crew then scooped up exactly thirty-six liters of surface soil and sieved it through a wire mesh mounted in a wooden frame. The holes in the mesh were five millimeters in diameter, which allowed the team to catch all but the tiniest fragments of obsidian, pottery, and other artifacts. That first season, among other items, they retrieved 11,419 shards of pottery, 1,416 pieces of obsidian, 6,540 fragments of bone, and 118 bits of what was recorded as "charred remains."

For the surface scraping, a much larger area was plotted out in the north end of the tell. Once the vegetation had been cleared and all the artifacts collected, Roger and the crew began attacking the loose surface soil with pickaxes and shovels. When this layer had been removed, the team then scraped the earth with sharp, wide-bladed hoes that had been specially manufactured for the job by a local blacksmith. The tops of the Neolithic village's mud-brick walls were often found hidden as little as two inches beneath the surface, and seldom deeper than twenty inches. About thirty distinct buildings were exposed in this way, some of which seemed to be very well preserved. That bode well for the success of future excavations in the north area.

Roger loved this kind of work. Being outdoors with the sun shining on him, engaged in a strenuous physical activity that was at the same time intellectually stimulating—this was the main thing that had drawn him to archaeology in the first place. As he scraped the mound's surface with his sharp hoe, Roger thought about the last time he had carried out such a project: at Abu Salabikh in Iraq, the spectacular Sumerian city excavated by Nicholas Postgate. Roger wondered if he would ever see that country again.

ROGER AND WENDY MATTHEWS loved Iraq. They loved the openness and generosity of the Iraqi people and they loved living in Baghdad. As far as they were concerned, this sprawling city on the Tigris River was the most romantic spot on earth. It was there that they fell in love with each other. And as archaeologists, they couldn't find a better place to work than ancient Mesopotamia, where the Sumerians founded the world's first cities some 5,500 years ago. Had they not been forced to leave Baghdad during the 1991 Gulf War, their lives would probably have taken a much different course. Certainly they would not have become founding members of Ian Hodder's team at Çatalhöyük.

Roger Matthews was born in Cardiff, Wales, on August 21, 1954, the son of two English physicians who were living in the Welsh capital. When Roger was still young, the family moved to Aberdeen, Scotland, where they lived until he was thirteen years old; then they moved again when his father was hired by the University of Manchester. While still in Aberdeen, Roger had his first exposure to the excitement of archaeology. His best friend's father was an amateur archaeologist who participated in excavations and wrote articles about Scottish prehistory. Roger would sometimes watch him dig, holding his breath in suspense at what he was going to find next. Yet although Roger took a lot of history courses in school and had a keen interest in the past, when it came time to choose a career, he decided to go to law school. He lasted one year at the University of Leeds before dropping out, realizing he had no interest in the law. For the next several years Roger hung out in Leeds or worked in factories in the Manchester area. He embarked on a career as a cloth cutter in the apparel industry. In his spare time he read voraciously, especially poetry and history, and practiced playing the guitar.

When Roger was twenty-six years old, he decided it was time to get serious about his life. He checked out the courses on offer at the University of Manchester. He enrolled in the joint history and archaeology program. Roger had found what he was looking for. His first day at Manchester, he met Charles Burney, an eccentric but charismatic archaeologist who had taught at the university for many years. Burney loved to regale the students with stories about all the colorful archaeologists he had known over the years. He believed that you could not fully understand an archaeological excavation without a keen insight into the personality of the person who led it. As a young archaeologist during the 1950s, he had dug with Kathleen Kenyon at Jericho, where he met James Mellaart. Burney and Mellaart had become close friends. Later Burney had been appointed to the governing council of the British Institute of Archaeology at Ankara. He had been present at the fateful council meeting of October 28, 1966, when the BIAA—fed up with the sensationalist coverage of the Dorak affair in the Turkish press—unanimously voted to dissociate itself from Mellaart and stop sponsoring his work in Turkey. However, after some years of estrangement, Burney and Mellaart had reestablished their friendship.

Soon after graduating from Manchester, Roger made his first trip to Iraq. Burney was excavating a small Iron Age site near Mosul in the north of the country. The site was one of many in the region that were going to be flooded by the Tigris River once a dam project was completed. An eccentric British millionaire had somehow persuaded Burney to let him join the project. Burney asked Roger to drive the millionaire from England to Baghdad. With Roger driving the man's Mercedes most of the way, they made the journey to Baghdad in about ten days. At the end of the excavation season, Roger drove the millionaire back to England, with a stop in Istanbul to pick up a couple of his aristocratic friends. In the evenings, while the other three made their way around the bars of every city they stopped in, Roger would happily walk around and see the sights.

Roger had done so well at Manchester that he had no trouble getting into Cambridge. His doctoral supervisor was Nicholas Postgate, head of the dig at Abu Salabikh. Roger also spent a lot of his time attending the seminars that Ian Hodder and his graduate students held each week. He was present on one occasion in 1984 when Lewis Binford, visiting Cambridge at the invitation of Colin Renfrew, dropped in unannounced. One of the graduate students was giving a talk about the Celts of Iron Age Britain. When he finished, Binford launched into a ten-minute critique of the student's approach and pointed out how he could better tackle the subject from a processual point of view. Roger was fascinated by the discussion. In the end he decided that he was at least as interested in digging as in theorizing, so he was thrilled when Postgate agreed that he could do his doctoral work at Abu Salabikh, where he focused on the use of clay seals in ancient Mesopotamia. By the end of Roger's first season at Abu Salabikh, Postgate appointed him to be the dig's field director.

At that time British archaeologists were very active in Iraq. Their headquarters was the British School of Archaeology in Iraq, a sister institute to the BIAA in Ankara and the other British schools and institutes across the Near East. In 1986 Roger was appointed as the librarian and secretary of the Baghdad-based school. That same year the school took on a new visiting fellow named Wendy Knight. She had long blond hair, a tanned, freckled face, and a somewhat reserved manner. Roger thought she was beautiful. And he soon realized that beneath Wendy's cool exterior beat the heart of a passionate archaeologist.

Wendy was born on February 19, 1961, in Inverness, Scotland. Her father was an English officer in the Royal Air Force; her mother was a Scottish lass from Inverness. Every few years Wendy's father would be transferred to a different air base. She did most of her growing up in foreign countries: Yemen, Cyprus, and Germany, among other brief sojourns. It was in Cyprus, where she began attending secondary school, that Wendy got her first taste for archaeology. Her parents would often take Wendy and her younger brother and sister to see the island's abundant Greek and Roman ruins. One day they were visiting the classical ruins of ancient Amathus, perched dramatically on cliffs overlooking the island's south coast. As they strolled among the colorful mosaic floors and marble columns, Wendy's mother noticed her daughter closely examining a shard of pottery that she held in her hand. "That would be a good job for you!" she said.

In 1980 Wendy was accepted at the University of Edinburgh. She initially enrolled in the history program, but before the first week of classes, she met Douglas Baird, the archaeologist who would later help launch the survey of the Konya region as part of Ian Hodder's Çatalhöyük project. Douglas, who was a year or two ahead of Wendy at the university, was sitting at the student help desk. He told her that she could include archaeology as part of her curriculum. Wendy immediately decided to do so. During her third year, Trevor Watkins, the Edinburgh professor who codirected the Konya survey with Douglas Baird during its first years, asked Wendy if she wanted to work on his dig at Kharabeh Shattani in northern Iraq, a multiperiod settlement that had first been occupied about 5000 B.C. during the Halaf period and several thousand years later by the Assyrians. She jumped at the chance, and her own love affair with Iraq began.

No sooner had Wendy received her master's degree in Near Eastern archaeology from Edinburgh, in 1984, than she began looking for a way to get back to Iraq. She wrote to Nicholas Postgate asking if she could work with him at Abu Salabikh; Postgate wrote back saying that he needed a photographer and a cook but not another archaeologist. A pottery specialist she had met at Kharabeh Shattani, who was on the staff of the British school in Iraq, agreed to take Wendy on as her assistant. Before long Postgate had agreed to be Wendy's Ph.D. supervisor. She spent most of the second half of the 1980s working at Abu Salabikh, where she first learned to apply micromorphological techniques. Wendy's doctoral dissertation for Cambridge University, which she completed in 1992, was entitled "The micromorphology of occupational sequences and the use of space in a Sumerian city."

The British School of Archaeology in Iraq occupied a low-slung concrete building in the pleasant Baghdad neighborhood of Mansour. Soon after Wendy began her fellowship at the school, she and Roger began taking walks together in the neighborhood. The walks quickly took a romantic turn. In March 1988 the two were married in the garden of the British Embassy in Baghdad. That same month Roger was appointed the school's director. The couple spent two more happy years together in Baghdad, although this sojourn was often interrupted by Wendy's trips back to Cambridge to do laboratory work. Then, on August 2, 1990, Iraq invaded Kuwait. Wendy and Roger were on holiday in England at the time. The school's London-based council closed it down, awaiting further events. Left behind in the Baghdad apartment were a lot of the couple's personal belongings, including a wardrobe full of clothes and some of Roger's guitars. When the Gulf War began in early 1991, Roger and Wendy began to wonder if they would ever get back to Iraq. The council continued to pay Roger's salary for several years afterward, on the assumption that the school would eventually reopen. But it never did. The United Nations–approved sanctions against Iraq prohibited the British from spending money in the country. Under the circumstances few archaeologists were going to risk trying to start projects there.

Their life in Iraq was over. The couple took up residence in Cambridge, where Wendy finished writing her Ph.D. dissertation. Although the school was still paying Roger's salary, he cast around for other things to do. Roger began spending his spring months working at Tell Brak in northeastern Syria, a Mesopotamian site first excavated by Agatha Christie's archaeologist husband, Max Mallowan, during the 1930s. A new team, which reopened the site in the 1970s, had made a number of interesting discoveries about the complex societies that had occupied the tell between the fourth and second millennia B.C. Then one day

Nicholas Postgate mentioned to Roger and Wendy that Ian Hodder was going to hold a small meeting in Cambridge to discuss the possibility of launching new excavations at Çatalhöyük. Would they like to come along? Without hesitation they said yes. It sounded like just the kind of exciting new project they were looking for.

DURING THE 1993 SEASON at Çatalhöyük, the entire team had managed to squeeze into the BIAA's Land Rover for each day's trip from Çumra to the mound. By the following year, it no longer could. In 1994 several new members joined the group for that year's five-week season. They included Jonathan Last, one of Ian's graduate students, who had come to study the Neolithic pottery; Louise Martin, a zooarchaeologist—an expert in animal bones—who had just completed her doctoral work at Sheffield University with Paul Halstead, the former Cambridge student who had been treated to the spectacle of Michael Parker Pearson's naked body more than a decade earlier; and Nurcan Yalman, a Turkish graduate student who was planning to launch an ethnoarchaeological study of the mud-brick villages near Çatalhöyük, in a search for clues as to how the Neolithic occupants of the Konya Plain might have carried out their daily lives. Nurcan would be joined on this project by a British anthropologist named David Shankland, who had been serving as acting director of the BIAA since David French retired in 1993.

The ranks swelled even more in 1995, with the arrival of two archaeologists from the University of California at Berkeley: zooarchaeologist Nerissa Russell, who was teaming up with Louise Martin to study the animal bones, and Mirjana ("Mira") Stevanovic, a flamboyant and acerbic Serbian archaeologist with lots of experience excavating Neolithic houses in southeastern Europe. Nerissa and Mira had worked in Yugoslavia and Bulgaria with the feminist archaeologist Ruth Tringham, a charismatic figure at Berkeley who was thinking about bringing an entire team over from California to work at Çatalhöyük.

As Ian's core group of archaeologists steadily expanded, word began to spread far and wide that the long-dormant Neolithic mound was coming alive again. One day the team returned from a lunch break in Çumra to find a group of women holding hands and dancing in a circle on top of the mound. One of the site's Turkish guards, Mustafa

Tokyağsun, was standing by looking perplexed and helpless. The women, who wore long, flowery dresses, turned out to be members of a goddess-worshipping group from the San Francisco Bay Area. At their invitation, Ian and the other archaeologists joined them at a teahouse that evening in Çumra. The women brought along a large thermos filled with vodka, and some of them brought their husbands. The goddess worshippers and the archaeologists surreptitiously filled their tea glasses with vodka and cherry juice, and the discussion began. The group's leader soon launched into a critical attack on the new dig. "This place is sacred to women," she declared, "but archaeology is entirely dominated by men. You are bringing too much sexist baggage to these excavations." As a result, she insisted, the evidence that Çatalhöyük had been a matriarchical society where women were in charge was likely to be suppressed and buried.

Ian listened patiently—too patiently in the view of some other members of his team. Tom Strasser tried to counter these arguments, rattling off a long list of women who had been pioneers of Near Eastern archaeology: Dorothy Garrod, Kathleen Kenyon, and Marija Gimbutas, among others. The women nodded at the mention of Gimbutas. "She was the first to expose the conspiracy by male archaeologists to hide the truth," said one. Not everyone was taken aback by the women's arguments. Naomi Hamilton was happy to hear the archaeologists' assumptions challenged by outsiders. Although she came from an academic background herself, Naomi often felt that her colleagues spent too much time in their ivory towers. As for Ian, dismissing the goddess group's arguments out of hand went counter to that cornerstone of post-processual archaeology, the notion of multivocality. In fact, feminist archaeologists, concerned that the role of women in prehistory was being ignored by the New Archaeologists, had been among the first to embrace the post-processual movement during the 1980s. Ian had worked behind the scenes to encourage the 1991 publication of a now-classic collection of essays by feminist archaeologists, *Engendering Archaeology*, which included contributions by Christine Hastorf, Ruth Tringham, and Ian's former graduate student Henrietta Moore.

Despite persistent accusations from the processualists that Ian and his followers were embracing an "anything goes" postmodernist cultural relativism, in recent years Ian had come to accept that the stories archaeologists told about the past had to be rigorously consistent with the available evidence. While there was still plenty of room for imaginative interpretations—indeed, as Mellaart had demonstrated, possessing a vivid imagination was a major plus for any archaeologist trying to reconstruct the past—any flights of fancy had to be tethered to what the excavator was actually digging up. Ian politely told the visitors that the case for Mother Goddess worship at Çatalhöyük, let alone for matriarchal dominance, remained unproven. Indeed, this was one of the issues that the new excavations were hoping to tackle; as archaeologists, they would have to go with what the evidence told them. By the end of the evening the thermos bottle was empty, but the two sides were no closer to agreement.

As early as 1987, in the article he wrote for the Institute of Archaeology's bulletin about the symbolism at Çatalhöyük, Ian had begun expressing doubts about some of Mellaart's interpretations. By the third season of surface work, in 1995, the team had already collected enough evidence to conclude that what the archaeology textbooks said about Çatalhöyük, especially about its religious life and social organization, needed some modification. These tentative conclusions were based partly on the surface work that the team had itself carried out. Some of the new crew also reanalyzed Mellaart's preliminary reports in *Anatolian Studies* and reexamined the artifacts he had dug up, many of which were still stored in the vaults of the archaeology museums in Konya and Ankara. The overall results were compiled in a 1996 volume entitled *On the Surface,* the project's first formal publication—and its first attempt to distance itself from Mellaart's still very influential vision of what life at Çatalhöyük had been like.

Mellaart had drawn a distinction between buildings he called shrines or "sanctuaries," those which harbored the richest collections of wall paintings and sculpture, and relatively unadorned structures, which he considered to be ordinary domestic dwellings. The community's religious rites, he believed, must have been carried out by a select body of priests. And since at least a third of the buildings he excavated in the southwest corner of the mound appeared to be shrines, Mellaart decided that he must have been digging in what he called a priestly quarter of the settlement. While he was sometimes vague on the point, at times he heavily implied that the priests were women. If he was right, it would suggest that even in these early Neolithic days, matriarchy or not, Çatalhöyük was a hierarchical society with distinct social classes.

The new team came up with a different conclusion. Ian asked Tim Ritchey, a graduate student in computer studies at Cambridge, to go over all of Mellaart's reports and tabulate the details of each building he had excavated during the early 1960s. Ritchey entered every bit of available information into the computer: the number and type of platforms and benches, pillars, pits, basins, ovens, sculptures, and wall paintings, along with the sizes of the rooms and the number of artifacts found in each building. He then printed out all of the data—in the form of a series of bar graphs—on Microsoft Excel spreadsheets.

The graphs confirmed part of Mellaart's claim: some buildings were certainly more elaborate than others. But rather than a clear demarcation between shrines and ordinary houses, Ritchey found a continuity of styles. "The idea of 'shrine' versus non-'shrine' is seen to be a much more blurry concept both theoretically and methodologically," Ritchey concluded in his report in *On the Surface.* This finding, which argued against Mellaart's idea of a "priestly quarter" and indirectly against the notion of a social hierarchy, was also supported by the results of Roger Matthews's surface-scraping work in the northern end of the mound. Over the three seasons of surface work, Roger and his crew exposed a cluster of more than thirty Neolithic buildings, covering an area of nearly 2,000 square meters. Not only were these structures nearly identical to those Mellaart had found at the south end, but many of them had features similar to those found in the so-called shrines. In one building in the north area, for example, the scraping had revealed a huge pair of cattle horns apparently attached to a wall, as well as a number of figurines depicting humans and animals, including birds.

For Ian the evidence that most clinched the case against Mellaart's interpretation came from Wendy's micromorphology work, which suggested that domestic activities had taken place in some of the so-called shrines: in other words, people appeared to have been living in them. In one structure from Level VIII, which Mellaart had designated as a shrine because it had paintings of apparent hunting scenes on the walls and elaborately treated human burials under the floor, Wendy cut about half a dozen small blocks out of the floor and prepared them for examination under the microscope. In these sections, which were taken from an area of the building near a hearth or oven, Wendy was able to identify charred fragments of cereals, grasses, and hackberries as well as traces of animal dung that had been used as fuel, all of which were typical remains of everyday living in the Neolithic.

Wendy also found evidence that some buildings seemed to go through cycles in which they started out as domestic houses and then later became more shrinelike, perhaps after their inhabitants had abandoned them—for example, if an entire family line died out. This appeared to be the case in one building that was apparently not included in Mellaart's original excavations but had been exposed by erosion over the intervening years. Wendy identified this building as belonging to either occupation Level VI or Level V. Its earliest floors were made up of thick plaster layers interspersed with charred plant remains and burned pieces of animal bone, all consistent with domestic activities. The plaster layers were disrupted by a shallow pit, which Wendy thought was probably meant to hold a pot set in the floor; Mellaart had found pots sitting in similar depressions in a number of houses he excavated. At some point, however, the use of the building seemed to have changed. This shift coincided with the cutting of a human grave into the plaster floor, in which Wendy found several leg and toe bones. Wendy also found traces of red ochre that had apparently been sprinkled over the grave, a sign of ritual activity commonly found at Near Eastern sites. The later floor surfaces, which overlay this grave, were made up of much thinner and cleaner layers of plaster, on which Wendy could find no traces of charred plants or burned animal bones. And lying on top of the last plaster layer were the cores of three cattle horns, a cattle jaw, and the remains of some sort of plaster sculpture—features commonly found in Mellaart's "shrines."

In her report in *On the Surface*, Wendy described these findings in her typically dispassionate writing style, which belied the excitement she and Ian felt at what they thought was a potentially very important finding for understanding Çatalhöyük's social organization. "The coincidence of this change in microstratigraphy with the act of burial and use of red ochre," Wendy wrote, suggested that the purpose of this building had gone through a dramatic change, "perhaps from a residence to an ancestral shrine, after the death of human individuals, possibly the inhabitants."

The surface work had now given the team a much more representative picture of the entire mound. Yet there was still no evidence of public spaces—such as plazas or temples—where the members of the community might have come together *en masse*. In the volume's concluding chapter, Ian commented that "the site as a whole appears to consist of two main elements: houses, with varying degrees of elaboration of interior features, and open spaces, generally covered by spreads of rubbish." These open areas, which Mellaart had called "courtyards," appeared to serve as latrines and dumping areas for adjacent houses rather than social gathering spots. The new team began calling them "midden areas" instead. This broader view of the settlement also seemed to argue against Mellaart's contention that Çatalhöyük was the world's first city, a notion that had been popularized by Jane Jacobs in her 1969 book, *The Economy of Cities*. Again, Ian begged to differ: the evidence, he wrote, instead supported "an interpretation of the site as an elaborate village rather than as an urban settlement with differentiated functions."

If there were no clearly defined shrines or public places for religious gatherings at Çatalhöyük, what did Ian and his team have to say about the Mother Goddess? Mellaart thought he had unearthed plentiful evidence that just such a deity had been worshipped here. The statuette of the fat woman with pendulous breasts, seated on a throne with her arms on the heads of two leopards, bore some resemblance to figurines from much earlier Paleolithic sites, such as the 26,000-year-old "Venus" found at Dolní Věstonice in Moravia, as well as small sculptures found at many later Neolithic and Bronze Age sites in Anatolia and Europe. Mellaart, and most emphatically Marija Gimbutas, had argued—convincingly to many, although not all, archaeologists—that the people of Çatalhöyük had helped pass the torch of a long tradition of goddess worship.

On this somewhat delicate issue, the team was much more circumspect. Nevertheless, Naomi Hamilton, a feminist archaeologist with a keen interest in gender issues, agreed to tackle the difficult job of trying to track down the figurines Mellaart had found during his four seasons of excavation. Poring over Mellaart's reports, Naomi was able to find references to a total of 254 figurines and fragments of figurines. She went to see the small number of more spectacular statuettes on display at the museums in Konya and Ankara, and took detailed notes, but these represented a small fraction of the total. Most of the figurines lay in boxes and bags in the museum storerooms. In the end Naomi was able to find all but twenty-six of them. Yet her attempts to interpret what the figurines meant or how they had been used—which depended not only on their form but also on knowing the contexts in which they had been found—were frustrated by the fact that Mellaart had not recorded the precise locations of individual artifacts. Indeed, such meticulous record keeping was rare in Mellaart's day. However, certain patterns did emerge.

Naomi found that nearly half of the figurines represented animals of various sorts, although it was often hard to figure out which animal was depicted. Some did appear to resemble cattle or goats, and there were at least two birdlike figures. As for context, there was little reason to question Mellaart's contention that the fat woman with the leopards had been found in a grain bin, which he and others believed strengthened the interpretation that she represented a goddess associated with bounty and fertility. Mellaart had not recorded the exact location of most of the other "fat woman" figurines, which in any case represented a small minority of the total. Naomi was able to figure out, however, that this type of figurine did not show up any earlier than Level VI, and that most of the fat ladies came from Levels V or later. Thus if these particular figurines did represent goddesses, the goddess did not make her first appearance until the settlement at Çatalhöyük was already several hundred years old.

One of Naomi's most striking observations was that the great majority of figurines were not found within houses but in the midden areas, as if they had been thrown away. This might argue against the notion that the objects had a sacred, religious significance. Instead, Naomi suggested, at least some of them might have served as children's toys or pieces from some sort of prehistoric board game. Nor did the fact that a small number of the human figurines clearly represented dignified-looking fat women convince Naomi that they were meant to be goddesses. Another interpretation, she suggested, was that they symbolized femaleness itself rather than fertility. In a section of her report subtitled "Women's rites or women's rights?" Naomi argued that "it is equally feasible that they were concerned with sex-based gender roles and the consequent social conflict this doubtless created." In contrast to the "acceptable view" that "women tamely embraced a life of endless child-bearing," Naomi wrote, "the figurines may also be demonstrating their challenge to fulfill other roles in society—perhaps in debate over lineage, access to power, etc."

Such attempts to interpret prehistoric gender roles in the light of twentieth-century feminist studies of sex and gender seemed sure to provoke controversy among archaeologists. Naomi was careful not to go too far out on a limb. "My challenges to orthodoxy are not offered as proven, but as matters to consider. Further discoveries during the current excavations may be able to enlighten us in some of these areas, while others are likely to remain bones of theoretical contention," she concluded.

By the beginning of 1995 it seemed clear to Ian and his team that they had learned pretty much all they could about Çatalhöyük by remaining on the surface of the mound. It was time to start digging.

7 / At the Trowel's Edge

"OKAY, ROGER. Yes. Yes, I will think it over. Sorry. Thank you very much for calling. Good-bye."

Shahina Farid hung up the telephone. Roger Matthews had been on the other end of the line. Shahina's colleagues at the Newham Museum Archaeological Service in east London gathered around.

"Well?" one of them asked.

Shahina put her elbows on her desk and cradled her chin with both hands. Her dark brown hair flowed down over her dark brown arms.

"I think I just turned down a job digging at Çatalhöyük," Shahina said.

"What?" one of the archaeologists cried. "You must be crazy!" The others nodded emphatically in agreement.

What choice did she have? Roger's telephone call did not come at the best time. Shahina was in the middle of preparing a detailed report on one of the biggest digs she had ever worked on. The previous summer, in 1994, she had supervised a team of thirty archaeologists excavating a medieval abbey and cemetery in the Stratford district of London. The site was just below the spot where the £3.5 billion project to extend the London Underground's Jubilee Line from Green Park to Stratford was supposed to end. A fancy new tube station was being constructed, along with an £18.7 million train maintenance depot. The Jubilee extension passed through some of the most historic and archaeologically sensitive neighborhoods of the city. The Museum of London, which was in overall charge of a massive rescue archaeology project to record as many ancient ruins as possible before construction was completed, had awarded a subcontract to the Newham unit to carry out the Stratford dig.

Shahina and her crew were given two months to excavate the cemetery, which ultimately yielded 683 skeletons, many of them apparently monks who had lived in the abbey hundreds of years before. One body had been buried together with a pewter chalice. The archaeologists worked seven days a week, arriving at the site at six thirty in the morning and sometimes not leaving until ten o'clock at night. The Jubilee Line contractors continued to work on the rail line nearby. Shahina sometimes had screaming matches with the workmen if they got too close to the archaeological remains. Now, in these early days of 1995, Shahina and her colleagues at Newham were spending long hours at their desks, flipping through their recording sheets, cross-referencing their notes, and trying to prepare a comprehensive report about everything they had dug up. This was the part of archaeology Shahina could do without. She loved to dig; writing it all up was another matter.

Shahina was flattered that Roger had thought of her. She had met Roger and Wendy Matthews a few years earlier in Bahrain, an island Arab state in the Persian Gulf. She was supervising the excavation of a Bronze Age temple at Saar, a spectacular site with well-preserved streets and stone houses whose walls stood six feet high. Wendy had chosen Saar as one of several Middle Eastern sites for her micromorphology studies. The archaeologists working at Saar were fascinated by what Wendy was doing, but their enthusiasm sometimes waned when she actually got to work. Wendy would choose a particularly well preserved house—the team called this a Wendy House, after the large dollhouses popular with British children—and ask the excavators to divide it up into a grid pattern of one-meter squares. These were called Wendy squares. She would then get out her Wendy tools and begin taking small blocks from the squares for later examination under the microscope. The process took a lot of time. And dividing the Bronze Age houses into squares was not easy, because they were filled with Bahrain's fine desert sand.

One year Roger came out to visit Wendy and spend a week working at Saar. Wendy had chosen a house in Shahina's area to sample. Shahina was very busy that season collating the results of the temple excavation for a pending publication, so she asked Roger to take over supervising the Wendy House while she got on with her own work. Everyone on the site knew that Roger was the field director at Çatalhöyük. They had all studied Çatalhöyük in their university courses. It was one of those mythical sites all archaeologists dream of working at. That whole week the excavators took turns dropping half-serious hints: "Hey, Roger, have you got a job there for me?"

Now Roger had offered just such a job to Shahina. When she got home that evening from her office in Newham, she called him back. "Listen, I've been under a lot of pressure getting this publication done. I wasn't thinking straight. I would love to come out." Roger suggested that she come up to Cambridge as soon as she could to meet with him and Ian.

Shahina had heard of Ian Hodder, of course. She had a bachelor's degree in archaeology from the University of Liverpool. No one could study archaeology at the university level without learning something about the theoretical debates that still raged on both sides of the Atlantic. Yet Shahina had never taken an actual course in theoretical archaeology, nor had she read any of Ian's books. She was a professional excavator, not an academic. As far as she was concerned, theory was a waste of time. Instead of standing around at the edge of a trench talking about various interpretations for hours at a time, why not just get down in there and work it out with a trowel?

Roger met Shahina at the Cambridge train station and the two walked over to Darwin College, where they were to meet Ian for lunch. Shahina was surprised when she first saw Ian. Because he was so famous, she had assumed that he was an old man, but the slim, boyish-faced man facing her at the table was only in his mid-forties.

"Roger tells me you have a lot of experience digging skeletons," Ian began. The food on Ian's and Roger's plates gradually disappeared. An hour later Shahina had still barely touched her lunch as she answered question after question about her work in London and the digs she had worked on in the Near East, including her time in Turkey. Ian knew that Shahina had a lot of experience excavating mud-brick buildings. She had spent several seasons working with David French at his rescue excavation of Tille Höyük on the Euphrates River, a multiperiod site that was eventually flooded by the waters of the Atatürk Dam.

Ian and Roger explained that the surface work at Çatalhöyük was now winding up. Preliminary excavations were set to begin during the 1995 season. The men told Shahina that it was a good chance for her to get in on things at the beginning.

Ian and Roger were very impressed with the young woman who sat across the table from them. And from her lilting voice and the melodious intonations of her London accent, it was obvious that she was just as British as they were. Yet Shahina, whose parents were from Pakistan, sometimes felt suspended midway between two different worlds. She had grown up reasonably self-confident, yet this confusion over her identity had left her with some residual feelings of insecurity. So she was a little unsure about why Ian and Roger were asking her to come to Çatalhöyük. She knew that she was a competent excavator, but surely there were plenty of other archaeologists who could do the job just as well. What she didn't know was that Roger and Wendy had been raving about Shahina ever since they had met her in Bahrain. "She's a wonderful digger," they had told Ian. "She does the most beautiful drawings and records. She really is one in a thousand." Ian was intrigued, but he had some reservations. "What is her academic background?" he had asked. "What is her intellectual potential?" They weren't really sure how to answer that. But they did know that Shahina was very bright and enthusiastic. And when it came to knowing how to excavate, they said, she was one of the best in the business.

One of the best. Ian decided that was good enough for him.

SHAHINA FARID WAS BORN in London on October 20, 1962. Two years earlier her mother and father had emigrated to London from Pakistan, with Shahina's three older sisters. Her father had come to England to study for a Ph.D. in physics at University College London, but he soon found that the balancing act of trying to support a family and earning an advanced degree was too much to handle. Shahina's mother came from a large traditional family in Lahore. Had it been up to her, they might all have returned to Pakistan, but Shahina's father found that life in England suited him better. His family, which came from Hoshiarpur in the East Punjab, had also been large at one time. But now he was somewhat of a loner, possibly because a number of his older brothers and sisters had died when he was quite young, and when he was twelve years old, his mother had died in a fire in their house. So after he gave up his graduate studies, he began working in the London school system as a mathematics teacher.

Shahina and the youngest of her sisters attended the all-girls Parliament Hill School in the borough of Camden. Unlike many Pakistanis of his generation, Shahina's father believed that girls should get an education, although neither of her parents was keen to have their daughters mixing with the opposite sex. Shahina loved to draw and soon became very good at it. In 1972, when she was ten years old, Shahina had her first exposure to archaeology. The glittering exhibition of the funerary treasures of the Egyptian king Tutankhamen, which had been traveling the world since 1961, came to the British Museum for several months. Shahina visited with her classmates. Afterward her teacher assigned the class a project on Egyptian counting methods. The students learned how the Egyptians had counted their cows by putting a stone in a pot each time an animal entered the corral. Shahina was amazed that people were actually counting so many thousands of years ago. She also learned how to write King Tut's name in hieroglyphics.

At Parliament Hill School Shahina's favorite subject was Classical civilizations. She loved studying Greek art and mythology. In 1976 London's Royal Academy of Arts hosted a major exhibit about the destruction of Pompeii when Mount Vesuvius erupted in 79 A.D. Shahina's classics teacher took the students to see it. As she walked among the replicas of Pompeii's stone houses, Shahina could barely contain her astonishment. Why did they build their houses that particular way? Why did they arrange their furniture just so? Shahina realized that at some point, way back in the past, all of the things that people do today, and now take so much for granted, were once done for the first time.

By the time she was fifteen years old, Shahina—who by then was spending much of her spare time wandering around the British Museum on her own—had decided that she wanted to be an archaeologist. An older friend she had met at school, whose girlfriend was working at the Passmore Edwards Museum in east London, took her to visit the museum's archaeological unit. Shahina took one look at all of the technical drawings lying around and said to herself, "Oh no, I thought archaeology meant going into holes and digging! This is way too complicated. I'm never going to be able to do this!" Nevertheless, she got in touch with one of London's archaeology societies and began volunteering on Sundays to work on local excavations. Shahina's first dig was a multiperiod Roman and medieval site on the River Thames in Southwark, a district in south London. She loved putting on her Wellington boots and coming home covered with mud. Her mother thought she was going through a phase.

At the Southwark site an archaeologist named Eric taught Shahina how to use a trowel. One day, as the two were working together in the trench, Eric found a Roman die fashioned from bone. He dusted it off and held it in his open palm. "The last time someone rolled this die was more than fifteen hundred years ago," Eric declared. "I am going to roll it now." As the tiny cube bumped and bounced on the ground, Shahina's jaw dropped open. For one brief moment, with a flick of his wrist, Eric had bridged the impossible gap between the past and the present.

In 1982 Shahina enrolled in the archaeology course at the University of Liverpool. She chose Liverpool because the faculty members seemed very friendly and welcoming when she visited, unlike her experience at the University of Bristol, where an intimidating panel of lecturers seemed to be trying to trip her up with their questions. She also wanted to experience life away from home. Shahina realized right away that she was not cut out to be an academic. She did the best she could in her courses, but her real passion was for the summer fieldwork that the archaeology department required undergraduate students to carry out each year. One season she worked on an early Christian site on the Isle of Man, where she was supervised by an up-and-coming archaeologist named Mark Roberts. Roberts, whose team later discovered the oldest known human fossil in Great Britain at Boxgrove on the Sussex coast, was so impressed with Shahina's skill and enthusiasm that he recommended her as supervisor of the archaeological finds when she returned to the dig during the following Easter holiday.

During her final year at Liverpool, Shahina decided to specialize in Near Eastern archaeology. The university had some grant money available for students who wanted to travel abroad. With the exception of two family trips to Pakistan and a school trip to France, Shahina had not ventured out of England. She had read some articles about Turkey in travel magazines, so she wrote to the British Institute of Archaeology at Ankara asking if she could work with David French on his dig at Tille Höyük. She received a letter back from the institute's assistant director saying that it was too late to get her on the permit to work at Tille that year, but that they did need someone to draw the pottery shards in the institute's reference collection. Shahina had taken a course in archaeological illustration at the university, so she accepted.

The work was deadly boring, but she met a lot of colorful characters in Ankara. One of them was David French, who had now been the institute's director for nearly two decades. The other was Alan Hall, the Classical archaeologist who had discovered Çatalhöyük along with French and Mellaart. Hall, who was then teaching at Keele University in Staffordshire, often spent time in Ankara. He and French were still good friends. Shahina soon found Hall to be a delightful lunch and dinner companion. He would regale her with stories of the old days in Turkey, the discovery of Çatalhöyük, and James Mellaart's rise and fall. Hall sneaked French's copy of *The Dorak Affair* out of his office and gave it to Shahina to read. The following year Shahina applied to work at Tille in time to get on the permit. She earned a reputation among her fellow archaeologists as a loyal team player, someone who could always be counted on to sense her coworkers' moods and help everyone pull together when the going got rough. David French and her other supervisors realized that she was a "natural" excavator, often able to work out complex stratigraphic relationships that eluded more experienced diggers.

For the next five years Shahina spent her summers working at Tille and the rest of the year on short-term contracts with the Museum of London, working on rescue digs in the city. Some days she would come home to her parents' house, where she still lived, her boots and clothes caked with mud. Her father would ask her when she was going to get a real job.

Development in London was booming during the late 1980s, and there were a lot of important rescue sites that needed excavating. With every new dig, Shahina was given more responsibility. She helped excavate the Roman baths at Huggin Hill, the charred remains of Queen Boudica's torching of London during her revolt against the Romans, and medieval houses where she found beautifully preserved wooden bowls and spoons. At the end of the day, happy and reeking from the aromas of the city's underground stratigraphy, Shahina would make her way home on the London tube, where the other passengers would give her plenty of room.

In the early 1990s the London building boom came to an end. Many archaeologists working for the Museum of London were laid off, including Shahina. She decided to apply for a job at the Passmore Edwards Museum, the archaeological unit that had run the first excavation she ever worked on, the one where her colleague Eric had rolled that Roman die. There was a lot of rivalry among archaeological units in London. When she was at the Museum of London, her colleagues had derisively referred to the Passmore Edwards unit as "Pissmore Backwards." Shahina swallowed her pride and was happy to accept a job there when it was offered to her. A short time later the museum closed, and the archaeological unit was taken over by the borough of Newham. It was there, at what was now called the Newham Museum Archaeological Service, that Shahina was working when Roger called her about coming to Çatalhöyük.

WHEN SHAHINA ARRIVED at Çatalhöyük for the beginning of the 1995 season, she was in for a number of surprises. For one thing, all of the archaeological specialists—archaeobotanists, zooarchaeologists, anthropologists, lithics analysts, pottery experts, micromorphologists, geophysicists, and paleoecologists—had arrived as well. Shahina had never worked on a dig where the specialists stayed for more than a fraction of the season, let alone spent up to two months working alongside the excavators. Usually the diggers bagged and labeled the samples of human and animal bones, stone tools, and so forth, and the specialists either collected them at the end of the season or received them in their laboratories as tidy Federal Express packages.

But Ian had decided that what he called contextual archaeology required a constant flow of information between the excavators and the specialists. How could Louise Martin or Nerissa ("Rissa") Russell make educated guesses about the possibly symbolic meaning of a cattle horn or sheep's tibia unless they had a chance to see exactly where it had been deposited on the floor of a mud-brick house? And telling James Conolly that a hoard of black obsidian had been found buried next to an oven was not nearly as informative as allowing him to watch with his own eyes as the sparkling slivers were unearthed. Nor was the contextual process supposed to be a one-way street: the feedback that Shahina and her fellow excavators received from the specialists about what they were finding could help them understand what kind of archaeological remains they were digging up and how they should be excavating them. When one day, for example, Shahina found an unusual cluster of strange organic material in a human burial, Peter Andrews of the human remains team—who also happened to be an expert in owl physiology—was able to tell her that it consisted of regurgitated owl pellets and that she should carefully plot and record how the pellets had been deposited.

Shahina had assumed that Ian and Roger would bring out a whole crew of full-time, professional diggers like herself, but she was the only one of that special breed present that year. All the others either had academic positions or were Turkish students working on archaeology degrees. While many of them had years of excavating experience just like she did, archaeologically they spoke a different language, one that Shahina often did not understand.

Lewis Binford and the processual archaeologists had their share of catchphrases and buzzwords: "Culture is man's extrasomatic means of adaptation," "hypothesis testing," "Middle-Range Theory," and so forth. Likewise Ian and the post-processualists had their own specialized jargon: "Material culture is meaningfully constituted," "multivocality," and "context," among other bits of lingo. Recently Ian had added another concept to his list of post-processual principles: "reflexivity." This meant that it wasn't enough for the archaeologist to simply draw, photograph, or write down what he or she was digging up in the hopes that an objective account of the past would somehow emerge from the data. Rather the excavator had to adopt a thoughtful, self-critical approach to what he or she was doing down there in the trench. "Interpretation," Ian contended, begins "at the trowel's edge."

Binford and the New Archaeologists had themselves acknowledged that the very act of digging—exactly what the excavator chose to dig, how, and in what order—was heavily influenced by the prior theories and assumptions that the archaeologist brought into the trench. If, for example, an excavator came to Çatalhöyük having read Mellaart and Marija Gimbutas beforehand, he might be tempted to interpret every female figurine as yet more evidence for Mother Goddess worship and a matriarchal organization of society. And as Binford had argued in his debate with the prehistorian Glynn Isaac, an archaeologist who assumed that early humans were great hunters might misinterpret a collection of gazelle bones as evidence of a glorious Great Hunt rather than recognizing them as the gnawed scraps left behind by hungry hyenas. For the New Archaeologists the best way to stave off the temptations of subjectivity was to adopt the most rigorous possible scientific methodology; for Ian and the post-processualists, the answer lay in self-critical and self-aware contemplation. At every moment the excavator had to be reflecting on what she was doing and why.

To help foster this reflexive process, Ian invited a team of filmmakers and film students from Karlsruhe in Germany to make daily videos of the archaeologists as they tried to explain what they were doing and what preliminary interpretations they were coming up with at the "trowel's edge." Ian had decided to begin simultaneous excavations in two different parts of the long, pear-shaped mound. He assigned Roger to begin digging a particularly well preserved building in the center of the scraped area at the northern end. The previous seasons' surface scraping had revealed that this structure, which was now designated as Building 1, had relatively intact, well-plastered mud-brick walls. Yet in one corner of the building they could see the ashy traces of an oven, which suggested that at least some of the remaining walls did not stand very high. This meant that Roger's crew should be able to get down to the plaster floors of the building fairly quickly, where the most valuable clues to the daily activities of the villagers might be found.

Meanwhile Shahina was put in charge of reopening excavations in the southwestern section of the mound, where Mellaart had dug back in the 1960s. Ian asked her to open up a trench 20 meters by 20 meters where Mellaart had begun his deep sounding in 1965, a sounding he was forced to abandon when Turkish authorities banned him from the site. The idea was to excavate down to the deeper occupation levels Mellaart had not yet reached. The ultimate goal was to reveal the buildings and any other remains left by the very first residents of Çatalhöyük. First Shahina would have to make her way through Mellaart's backfill, that is, the earth that he had used to bury and protect his excavations in hopes that he would be back one day.

The mound had lain dormant for three decades since Mellaart's departure. The video crew was there to record what should have been those first glorious moments as the new excavations got officially under way. Instead it captured the nervous uncertainty—and, sometimes evident in Ian's quavering voice, the sheer terror—of finally breaking into Çatalhöyük's hallowed soil. In one video clip Ian, Shahina, and Roger stand on top of the "Mellaart area." Shahina is wearing a blue-and-white checked shirt and a long white headscarf; Ian and Roger sport nearly identical straw hats with black hatbands. The sun is shining brightly, and the sound of shoveling is heard just off camera.

> SHAHINA: "We're scraping back the area, our twenty-by-twenty trench, to locate one of Mellaart's trenches, the deep *sondage* he dug in 'sixty-five. It should be here somewhere, and this scraping should define it, but so far we've not found it." Shahina laughs nervously. "We've got a wall coming up there," she says, pointing to a spot behind her, "and one is just coming up where the men are working now." The camera pans over to where the Turkish workmen are exposing the top of a mud-brick wall with their shovels. "What we will probably do is carry on cleaning back northwards. We can start cleaning out some of the walls. And as the walls are defined, we'll start recording, but continue to clean back."
>
> IAN: "Well, I, uh, we're having a bit of a disagreement about what we're actually standing on here, and what's been cleaned off here," he says, pointing behind him. "Because it looks very much like the stuff that we clean off in an untouched house, Neolithic house."

Ian looks down at a sheaf of papers he is holding in his hands. "But looking at Mellaart's plans, we've . . . I reckon that we're standing here where he dug down to his very lowest, to his deep sounding. But we clearly can't see it here. And so there's something gone wrong, either in our ability to identify, or with these plans, or something, so we are rather at a loss to know where we are."

SHAHINA: "Or we're standing right on it. This hollow here," she says, pointing to a shallow depression right next to them, "is the only indication of anything that's backfill, unless it's a room."

IAN: "But I think if you filled up a room with something that's come out of another room, and it's been there for thirty years, it would end up looking very similar to the Neolithic deposit."

SHAHINA: "Well, what I think is, yes, that could be, but the deposit looks very unbroken."

ROGER: "It is, it's a very intact, compact deposit. It looks original to me."

SHAHINA: "Yeah. Unless he was shoveling out, and literally just shoveling out, and the lumps might stay intact. But we'll see. We will find it." She laughs again, this time with more confidence. "We *will* find it!"

A few days later, the exact location of Mellaart's deep sounding was still a mystery. Ian was becoming increasingly frustrated.

SHAHINA: "We're back on, over areas eight and one, still looking for the deep sounding. We originally scraped it to see if we could—we scraped the area to see if we could find the walls and the backfill, but that didn't work. We did define a backfill layer, so we've started digging into it now, and hopefully that will start showing up some walls."

IAN: "Yeah, we sort of slightly changed strategy. We started off coming back from a visible wall and going very slowly and carefully. But I'm increasingly worried about the overall timescale

> here. Because the idea of using this area at all was to get down to very early levels very quickly . . . Maybe we would be better digging somewhere else. The idea of digging here was that we could use his excavation to get to the early levels quickly. But as it turns out there is an enormous amount of stuff that he backfilled, so that the idea is being slightly compromised by that. We might end up spending ages and ages and ages removing Mellaart's old earth."

Six weeks later, as the 1995 season came to an end, Shahina still had not found the exact location of Mellaart's deep sounding. Yet she and her crew had made considerable progress. They removed most of Mellaart's backfill and exposed the remains of the structures that he had excavated up to 1965. Most of these buildings corresponded to Levels VII and VIII in Mellaart's original scheme for labeling Çatalhöyük's dozen or more stratigraphic levels, in which the deeper—that is, older—occupation layers were given the highest numbers. The area encompassed all or part of eight buildings that Mellaart had designated as shrines, as well as ten "houses" and a "courtyard." There was still time left to do a little bit of new excavating before the season was over. Shahina found that the walls of one house were heavily scorched by fire, although it was not clear whether the burning was accidental or deliberate.

While most of the buildings excavated by Mellaart as far down as Level VI had their own individual walls, some of the deeper houses had shared party walls and were linked together by crawl holes. This was a possible indication that the occupants of each house had desired more privacy and isolation over time, or perhaps that they had become more self-sufficient. Finally Shahina's efforts were rewarded with her first glimpse of Çatalhöyük's celebrated artwork: the plaster wall of one "shrine" bore red painting depicting an abstract trellislike pattern and a motif that looked like a rosette or a sunburst.

If Ian was in a hurry to get to the bottom of things in the Mellaart area, his strategy for Building 1 was just the opposite—at least in principle. Mellaart had excavated nearly two hundred buildings over the four seasons he worked at Çatalhöyük. In 1995 Roger and his crew—which was made up mostly of Turkish and British archaeology students—spent several weeks working in this one structure, with no intention of trying to finish it this first year. This building was to be excavated slowly, and in exquisite detail. It would be a showcase for Ian's concept of contextual archaeology.

The previous years' surface scraping had revealed that the Neolithic inhabitants of Building 1 had divided it into three rooms. The rooms, defined by partial internal walls made of mudbricks, were designated as Spaces 70, 71, and 72. (The numbering sequence was part of the overall scheme for identifying the thirty or so buildings in the north area and their internal subdivisions.) Roger and Ian decided to begin excavation in Space 70, a long, narrow room that ran along the western wall of the structure. In its far corner they could already see the telltale deposits of ash, charcoal, and plaster that indicated the presence of an oven or hearth—or, as Ian preferred to call it, using a more neutral term invented by Nicholas Postgate, a "fire installation." It seemed clear that in this corner of the room, at least, they were already close to the floor.

For the excavators, reaching the floor was the ultimate goal: the building would then be "excavated." Their job was to carefully dig out the assorted materials with which the Neolithic villagers had filled and packed their old houses before they built new ones on top, such as crushed bricks and plaster, animal bones, and ash. The plastered walls and any internal features, including ovens, benches, plastered walls, and so forth, would be exposed in all their glory. A large amount of the fill was sieved through a four-millimeter wire mesh to catch any small fragments of bone, jewelry, or other artifacts; other fill samples were put in large bags and taken down to the flotation machine to catch any tiny plant remains.

For Wendy Matthews, reaching the floor was just the beginning. Just as a forensic scientist combs the carpet of a hotel room for every possible clue to how that dead body came to be lying on it, Wendy's brand of high-definition archaeology—and its promise of providing detailed clues about the kinds of activities carried out in the rooms—required the taking of dozens of samples for later microscopic examination and chemical, physical, and mineralogical analysis. As the days passed and Roger and his team got close to the bottom of Space 70, they did not wait until the floor was actually exposed before beginning to take samples. When the excavators were one or two inches from the often uneven plaster surface, they scooped out roughly 250 grams of floor deposits at every fifty-centimeter interval, dropping them into paper envelopes or wrapping them in aluminum foil. Sometimes it was difficult to distinguish debris that had apparently fallen onto the plaster when the Neolithic occupants were dismantling the timbered roof, such as charred wood or thatch, from materials that they had left lying directly on the floor. At times the excavators would find the roofing material lying right on top of clusters of acorns or lentils. Wendy's solution to this problem was to cut out a number of small blocks made up of the plaster floor and the material above it, which she could later examine under the microscope.

To help make the sampling more precise, Roger and the students divided Space 70 into a grid of half-meter squares. The grid system had been pioneered back in the 1930s by Mortimer Wheeler and other archaeologists who realized the importance of recording the horizontal as well as the vertical arrangement of features and artifacts in an excavation trench. Roger used the tried-and-true method of stretching long pieces of string across the trench and tying them securely to metal pegs arranged around its edges, thus forming a taut gridwork. But the excavators soon found that trying to dig within half-meter squares cramped their style and slowed down the pace of excavation too much. It is also made it difficult to see and record some of the more intricate stratigraphic relationships. They eventually opted for larger, one-meter squares, and at times—for example, when they were excavating complex features such as the oven or craw holes—they abandoned the grid system entirely.

Even at this early stage the inherent conflict between Ian's contextual approach and the need to make visible progress had begun to rear its head. At times Roger and Wendy would have tense words with each other about just what the priorities should be. Later, in his report on the 1995 season in Building 1, Roger captured the conflict in a more dispassionate tone: "At all stages of the excavations we keenly felt the need to maintain a careful balance between, on the one hand, the requirements of a rigorous sampling programme of excavated deposits and, on the other, the desire to excavate at a reasonable pace in order to produce enough evidence at the gross scale."

Striking the right balance was critical to the success of Ian's project. For example, Mellaart, during his 1960s excavations, had noticed that the Neolithic villagers often made changes in the layout of their houses during the buildings' lifetimes of eighty years or so. Yet in his haste to get to the wall paintings and sculptures, he seldom recorded these changes. Nevertheless, they were of great interest to Ian and his team for the hints they might give of how the inhabitants made use of the fairly small spaces they lived in, how they organized their daily routines, and how and why they had eventually abandoned their houses. By the end of the 1995 season, thanks to the project's more meticulous style of excavation, Roger was able to determine that Space 70 had gone through at least two phases over the years that it was occupied. During the first phase, the room was entered through a crawl hole from the adjacent Space 71, which was a much larger room. The southwest corner of Space 70 harbored an oven or "fire installation" enclosed in a thin shell made of clay, and a rectangular plastered platform ran along part of the opposite wall.

At some time during the life of Space 70, the room was ravaged by a major fire. The floor was heavily burned as well as some of the adjacent walls. On some parts of the floor the burn marks seemed to form parallel stripes, as if the plaster had been seared by roof timbers that had caught fire and then fallen onto it. Some time later the room was rebuilt, with some important changes; it was now subdivided with some sort of narrow wall or bench, on both sides of which lay large cattle bones. A chunk of cattle horn protruded from the face of the north wall. The oven in the southwest corner, however, was rebuilt in the same place; it was plastered over and a new installation constructed directly on top of it. Finally, around the time that all of Building 1 was abandoned, Space 70 was destroyed. The walls were knocked down and the room set on fire again, this time apparently deliberately, leaving a pile of burnt brick, timber, and wall plaster.

There was at least one other interesting set of findings during the 1995 season. As Roger and Shahina excavated their respective areas at the north and south ends of the mound, a lot of animal bones began to turn up, either as larger pieces that the diggers put in plastic bags or as smaller fragments recovered from the sieving of building fills and midden deposits. These were collected by Louise and Rissa. By the end of the season, they had accumulated 547 bone fragments from Building 1 and 2,941 pieces from an apparent midden deposit that Shahina had excavated in the Mellaart area; in addition, more than 5,000 fragments were recovered from Mellaart's old backfill, which Shahina and her crew had removed before beginning their own excavation. Most of these bones were so fragmented that only a minority of them included enough joint ends or tell-tale bumps and ridges to allow Louise and Rissa to determine what kinds of animals they came from. Yet one thing seemed clear: the most common species so far were sheep and goat, with the number of bones from cattle and other animals, such as horses, pigs, and dogs, trailing far behind.

Louise and Rissa had come to Çatalhöyük to answer a number of questions posed by the animal remains. They wanted to know which animals were used as food, which were most commonly eaten and under what circumstances, as well as which were used to make clothes and other products like bone tools or jewelry such as rings and pendants. They also wanted to explore the role of feasting and other ceremonial use of animals. Finally, they wanted to tackle a key issue at Çatalhöyük and in Neolithic archaeology generally: which species were domesticated and which were wild.

The faunal expert who analyzed the animal bones from Mellaart's 1960s excavations, Dexter Perkins, concluded that the cattle at Çatalhöyük were domesticated and had made up a major part of the community's economy. He went even further and declared that Anatolia, and Çatalhöyük specifically, had been one of the earliest centers of cattle domestication in the Near East, a claim that was still often cited in the archaeological literature. Perkins based his conclusion mostly on the range of sizes he found when he measured the cattle bones. Over many decades of research, zooarchaeologists have found that the wild ancestors of today's domesticated cattle, sheep, goats, and other animals were usually larger than their domesticated descendants. But they have also come to realize that bone size is only a rough guide. For example, the distinction between domestic and wild animals is much more difficult to detect when the bones come from prehistoric periods soon after the domestication process occurred.

Yet one piece of cattle bone, found in Mellaart's backfill, impressed them. It was part of a humerus, the upper part of the animal's forelimb. When Louise and Rissa measured it, they found that it was larger than any cattle humerus ever recorded from Çatalhöyük during Mellaart's excavations. How many other similarly large bones might be waiting to be found? The pair was not ready to challenge Perkins' conclusions at this early stage, and certainly not based on this one specimen, which for the moment simply extended the range of cattle bone sizes at Çatalhöyük. The discovery did make them wonder, however, if the story of cattle domestication at Çatalhöyük was as clear-cut as previous generations of archaeologists had assumed.

Of course, it was still early days for Ian's dig. This first short excavation season had barely scratched the surface of the mound. It had raised many more questions than it answered. The widespread episodes of burning within the buildings, which Mellaart had also found in some Level VI structures during his own excavations, remained very difficult to explain. Were houses deliberately set on fire as part of the cycle of abandonment and rebuilding? Or was the risk of accidental fires so great that buildings went up in smoke on a regular basis? And if there really was little difference between houses and shrines, as the team was inclined to believe, what did that say about social organization and religious practices at Çatalhöyük? Was religion a private, household affair rather than a widespread community activity? Did Mellaart's "priests" exist at all, and if so, to whom did they turn for spiritial guidance—the Mother Goddess, or some as yet unidentified deity or deities?

As far as Ian was concerned, the results of the relatively short 1995 season, preliminary though they were, demonstrated that there was a great deal to be learned by bringing a combination of modern science and reflexive methodology to bear on the mysteries of Çatalhöyük. The skeptics who had rolled their eyes when Ian Hodder, archaeological theoretician *par excellence*, managed to get his hands on this very real and very famous site would have to reconsider. James Mellaart had certainly paved the way, and in spectacular fashion, but he would not have the last word about Çatalhöyük.

THE 1995 SEASON ENDED on September 30. This date came five days after the thirtieth anniversary of Mellaart's ejection from Çatalhöyük by the Turkish authorities. No one thought of honoring this particular anniversary, but soon there was another occasion to celebrate: Mellaart's seventieth birthday, which fell on November 14. Several of the British members of the team, including Ian, Shahina, Roger and Wendy, Louise Martin, James Conolly, Jonathan Last, and Naomi Hamilton, trooped over to the Mellaarts' apartment in London's Finsbury Park. Ian brought a birthday cake with a large frosted image of the Mother Goddess on the top, which Wendy had designed. Arlette served up a buffet Turkish lunch, which they all washed down with wine, whiskey, and strong Turkish tea.

Naomi took one look at the goddess on the cake and laughed. She and some of the other archaeologists had earlier questioned whether this particular image—a vague figure with outstretched arms and legs that Mellaart had found sculpted on a number of plaster walls—was a woman or a man, or perhaps even some animal like a bear. Nevertheless, this same image had already found its way onto the letterhead of the Çatalhöyük Research Project, as Ian's dig was officially called. Nor did anyone think Mellaart's birthday was the proper occasion to get into polemics about the Mother Goddess or any of the other issues on which the team was already forming divergent opinions. After all, had Mellaart not given his blessing for them to dig, none of them would be working at Çatalhöyük right now.

Instead the group sat around the living room while Ian showed slides of that season's excavations. Mellaart looked at the slides politely. When the lights came back on, he jumped up from his stuffed leather chair and began pacing the floor excitedly, holding forth about the discoveries he had made at Çatalhöyük thirty years before. Occasionally he would disappear into his study for a few minutes and reemerge with faded drawings of wall paintings and plaster sculptures that the artists on his dig had drawn on thin tracing paper. Ian, Louise, and Naomi, all of whom had been students at the Institute of Archaeology, exchanged smiling glances as they recalled the vivid slide shows that Mellaart himself used to give in the institute's darkened auditorium.

It was clear to Ian and the others that Mellaart was not particularly impressed with what they had accomplished so far. Yet as he sat listening to Mellaart's reminiscences, Ian was already hatching his plans for the following year. The last three seasons had been just a warm-up. In 1996 he would descend on Çatalhöyük with one of the largest armies of archaeologists ever assembled.

8 / Dear Diary

THE 1996 SEASON began on August 1. The team moved out of its headquarters in downtown Çumra and into the new dig house at the northern edge of the Çatalhöyük mound. The dig house, designed to be a single-story complex of dormitories and laboratories arranged around a central gravel courtyard, was still under construction, and there was dirt and dust everywhere. Ian had landed a $190,000 development grant from the European Union, one of his first big fund-raising coups, part of which he used to help fund the building project. The dilapidated sofas from the British Embassy in Ankara were arrayed on the veranda, and the Naugahyde-covered bar—now even the worse for wear—was parked out behind the buildings. The community of archaeologists now had two social gathering spots: the veranda, where the main drink was Turkish beer, and the bar out back, where the harder stuff was served.

The team needed the increased space. Ian had recruited more than a hundred excavators and specialists to work on the site in 1996. Nearly sixty archaeologists flocked to Çatalhöyük from the United Kingdom, the United States, Germany, Greece, Spain, Canada, and South Africa, joining about twenty Turkish archaeologists and archaeology students from Istanbul, Ankara, and Konya. In addition some two dozen Turkish workers from Küçükköy and other local villages were hired to help the excavators in the trenches, prepare and serve meals in the kitchen and dining room, and keep the dig house as clean as possible.

As the season got under way, the film crew from Karlsruhe returned to continue its video recording. And Ian had thought up yet another way to enhance the excavation's reflexivity. He asked Roger, Shahina, and other excavation team leaders to use the project's computers to keep an online diary of what they were doing as well as what they were thinking and observing as the dig unfolded. The idea behind these "excavator diaries" was to add some richness and depth to the dry data sheets and two-dimensional drawings with which archaeologists conventionally record their findings. And since each digger usually concentrated on his or her small part of the building under excavation, the diaries could be used to tie together their individual observations into an overall narrative, one that would make sense to someone trying to get the bigger picture.

The diaries also became vehicles for letting off steam from the pressure-cooker atmosphere of the dig. The archaeologists slept in bunk beds, with up to eight people squeezed into each of the small dormitory rooms. Working space was at a premium because most of the laboratories were not yet built. The population density was at least as high as that of the Neolithic villagers who had packed themselves into Çatalhöyük's mud-brick houses thousands of years before. For many of the archaeologists, particularly those who had worked on the site during previous seasons, the new situation represented somewhat of a culture shock. Some of them decided to escape the dormitories. A tent city soon sprang up around the margins of the dig house.

Except for the Friday break, when the archaeologists could venture into Çumra, Konya, or wherever else they could get to and back from within one day, there were few opportunities to escape from Çatalhöyük. The entire team was pretty much stuck on the site day and night, with little to entertain them. Since the diary entries were available online for everyone to read, peeking voyeuristically into other peoples' musings soon became a favorite pastime.

As the 1996 campaign began, Roger and Shahina again took up their commands in the north and south areas of the mound. Roger's plan was simple: entirely excavate Building 1 by the end of the season, including the floors and any human burials underneath. This seemed a reasonable goal; after all, James Mellaart had dug at the blazing pace of about one building per day during the 1960s. As in the previous year, Roger's crew was primarily made up of Turkish and British students with various degrees of experience. There was one important addition to the north area team: Gavin Lucas, one of Ian's former graduate students at Cambridge. Gavin had earned a Ph.D., but he had also worked as a professional excavator for the Cambridge Archaeological Unit, the university's rescue archaeology outfit. Like Roger, Gavin had a lot of digging experience, and also like Roger, he had the kind of intellectual engagement in the process of excavation at Çatalhöyük that Ian was looking for.

In the south area, Shahina had also convinced Ian to recruit some reinforcements. She was joined by two ace professional excavators from the Cambridge Archaeological Unit, Mary Alexander and Roderick ("Roddy") Regan, as well as Naomi Hamilton. The goal in the south area remained the same—to get down to the lower levels of Neolithic occupation. Meanwhile, just east of Shahina's area, where the mound rose up to form a flat peak, a new team made up of Greek archaeologists was expected to begin excavating in September, to explore these later occupation levels. This team would be led by Kostas Kotsakis, an expert in the Neolithic period in Greece from the University of Thessaloniki. Kostas had long been interested in how farming and Neolithic culture had spread from the Near East to Greece, the first major step in the so-called Neolithic Revolution's conquest of Europe. By excavating in the summit area, as his section of Çatalhöyük was dubbed, Kostas was hoping to find evidence for the origins of the Greek Neolithic here in next-door Anatolia.

Roger got off to a good start, largely because the specially constructed wood and canvas shelter used to cover Building 1 during the 1995 excavations had protected it well from the elements. Shahina, who was excavating in a much larger area, was not so lucky. She had protected her trenches against the harsh Anatolian winter with big sheets of canvas held down by sandbags, but she hadn't counted on the rapid growth of vegetation that had spread over the site during the spring. In her diary entry for August 4, she laments,

> Work in Mellaart's area of excavation started today by clearing the overgrowth that had erupted across the areas of excavation since last season. Erosion in the area had been expected but the overgrowth was a surprise and had damaged considerably the horizons at which we'd left off. In future we'll have to cover areas with sacking and backfill, not canvas because it rots.

By the end of the first week of work, things were going better for Shahina and her crew, although the dig as a whole still had some growing pains. Ian reported on some of them in his diary entry for August 9.

> There have been some initial difficulties which are gradually being sorted out. Of particular importance is that the specialists realised that during the first few days of sieving the workmen were insufficiently trained and recovery was very poor . . . Also, it has been taking a long time for people to learn the recording systems . . . I feel that there is insufficient circuitry at the moment between the diggers and the specialists. Still, we have all these things in mind and will work on them in seminars etc . . . Roger's area is being dug in a very different way from the Mellaart area, largely because he is dealing with deposits near floors, whereas most of the Mellaart contexts are midden-like in one way or another . . . One of the most interesting aspects of the northern (Roger) area is the endless subdivision of Building 1—is this why the area had to be abandoned?

Ian's diary entries were intermittent that season, in large part because he was often away in Ankara or Istanbul. Ian was one of the few archaeologists at Çatalhöyük who was not stuck at the site day and night. Someone had to raise the large sums of money required to keep a dig on this scale going, and that someone was him.

• • •

THE TURKISH AUTHORITIES had laid down two conditions when they agreed to give Ian an excavation permit to reopen Çatalhöyük. First, he had to be prepared to protect any wall paintings, sculptures, or other fragile features and artifacts that he uncovered. Second, he had to come up with enough money to support a program of full-scale excavations. Given the site's murky history, the last thing the Turks wanted was for Çatalhöyük to be reopened to a lot of fanfare and then shut down again for lack of funds. On the conservation side, Ian had recruited a team of conservators from the University of Pennsylvania led by Frank Matero, one of the best in that archaeological specialty. And the $190,000 development grant from the European Union, along with a five-year, £250,000 grant from Cambridge University's Isaac Newton Trust, had convinced Turkish officials that Ian did have the ability to raise money. Yet when it came to paying for the actual fieldwork, he had just squeaked by the first three seasons. He managed to convince the BIAA, the British Academy in London, and the University of Cambridge to contribute modest amounts, but just that.

Ian's ambitious plans for 1996 were going to cost nearly $200,000. Only a handful of digs around the world could boast that kind of funding. To support his excavations at the Philistine site of Ashkelon on Israel's Mediterranean coast, Harvard University archaeologist Lawrence Stager had found a generous benefactor in Wall Street financier Leon Levy, one of the richest men in America. But if Stager had been lucky enough to seduce a sugar daddy into funding his dig in the biblical Holy Land, it was not immediately obvious to Ian which of the world's wealthy industrialists had a secret passion for the Anatolian Neolithic. Nevertheless, he knew where the big money was. After some hesitation, he decided to go for it: corporate sponsorship.

Ian concluded that such sponsorship was the best, and perhaps the only, option for making his Çatalhöyük dreams come true. There were two basic issues: first, whether or not it was ethical for an archaeologist to take corporate money in the first place; and second, whether the sponsors would try to call the shots about how he dug the site. Ian decided that there was nothing unethical, and certainly nothing new, about taking money from big business. These days, most excavations in Europe and the United States are rescue digs, funded by the developers whose sites overlie archaeological ruins and who are obliged by antiquities laws, civic pride, or both to protect these ancient remains. Ian did, however, resolve not to take money from tobacco companies or any other sources that clashed with his personal ethics or made him uncomfortable. While he did have some qualms about the subtle and not-so-subtle expectations that some sponsors might have in exchange for their money, he decided that it was better to have the problem and try to deal with it than to make drastic cutbacks in the project.

Ian set up a charitable body, the Çatalhöyük Research Trust; as patrons, he recruited Colin Renfrew, who was now director of the McDonald Institute for Archaeological Research at Cambridge and a member of the House of Lords, and Sir David Attenborough, the legendary naturalist and BBC broadcaster. Having a lord and a knight on board lent the project an air of gentility and respectability. The British Embassy in Ankara supplied Ian with a list of the hundreds of British companies doing business in Turkey. He checked into the nineteenth-century Büyük Londra (Great London) Hotel in Istanbul, the city where most of the companies had their headquarters, and sat down next to the telephone. A half hour later he was still staring at the phone, battling his natural shyness. Finally he got up his courage. For two days Ian stayed closeted in his room, ringing the switchboards of one company after another.

"Hello, this is Ian Hodder from Cambridge University," he would say to the often befuddled secretaries and junior executives who came on the line. "I am directing the new excavations at Çatalhöyük. Yes, it is in Turkey. Near Konya."

Some of the calls led to meetings, although the great majority did not. Then Ian had a lucky break. He got an appointment with the director for Turkish operations of Visa International, the credit card people. It so happened that the director was fascinated by archaeology. Even better, the head of the Istanbul-based public relations firm that Visa had hired to represent it in Turkey, a very sophisticated and persuasive woman, was an archaeology fanatic. After some negotiation, the two convinced Visa executives at the company's San Francisco headquarters to sign on as the principal sponsor for the 1996 season. Ian had given them a good argument to use: the obsidian found at Çatalhöyük and other sites in Anatolia had been traded all over the Near East during the Neolithic period. These shiny black flakes and blades, Ian said, could be considered the first credit cards.

Emboldened by this first big success, Ian became more aggressive in his search for funds. He went to see Ömer Koç, a young scion of the rich and powerful Koç family, founder of the Koç Group—the largest conglomerate in Turkey. Ömer Koç persuaded the executives of KoçBank, one of the group's major holdings, to sign on as well. With just a little imagination, Ian had pointed out, the hoards of obsidian hidden away under the floors of Çatalhöyük's mud-brick houses could be seen as the first bank accounts. By the time the 1996 season began, a number of other sponsors were also on board: the Turkish food processing company Merko, the pharmaceutical giant Glaxo Wellcome, as well as British Airways and Shell. Each company had its own motivation for supporting the dig. For the Turkish companies, Çatalhöyük was the wellspring of "Anatolian civilization," even though the Turks had not occupied Anatolia en masse until after they had defeated the Byzantine Empire in 1071 A.D.—about 7,500 years after Çatalhöyük was abandoned. In the case of the British and other foreign outfits, their primary aim was to be seen as good corporate citizens concerned with Turkey, its people and history.

Back at Çatalhöyük Ian's archaeologists were happy to hear how well his fund-raising was going, but they were less happy about some of the public relations that went along with it. All of the sponsors wanted to visit the dig. Hardly a week went by that Ian was not leading a group of VIPs up and down the mound. One day James Conolly was in his laboratory with the season's collection of obsidian spread out before him on a table. In walked Ian with a representative of Visa International and a company photographer. "I was just explaining," Ian said, giving James a sheepish smile, "that Anatolian obsidian could be considered to be the first credit card. I thought perhaps you could tell them more about it." James decided to ignore this cue. Instead he showed the visitors the different types of obsidian tools found at Çatalhöyük. They could be categorized as either flakes—a technology widespread in the earlier Neolithic of the Near East—or more finely worked blades, typical of later sites. James told them that nearly every mud-brick house had its own obsidian cache, which was usually buried under the floor near the oven. Just such a cache had been found in Building 1 that season. Most of the obsidian pieces were flakes, but it appeared that in later phases of the building, blades became more numerous. In the Mellaart area

James had detected a shift from flake to blade technology at about Level VI, a possible indication that this occupation layer heralded some sort of change in the community's lifestyle. He pointed out that Jonathan Last, in his analysis of the pottery, had also noticed a shift in ceramic style and technology beginning at about Level VI. This level also coincided with the widespread fires that Mellaart had reported during his own excavations.

James was always happy to talk about obsidian, but he didn't like being under pressure to impress the sponsors. Indeed, many of the archaeologists felt that Ian was pandering to the sponsors with his line about credit cards, and Ian himself later admitted that he had been embarrassed by it. After that episode, when James knew ahead of time that visitors were coming, he would often turn off the laboratory lights, lock the door, and lie down on the floor until the danger had passed.

Ian, for his part, often worried that the sponsors would not feel that they were getting their money's worth. Çatalhöyük was a world-famous archaeological site, yet the photographs most people had seen of the settlement had come from Mellaart's excavations. They depicted wall paintings of vultures, Mother Goddess sculptures, and vast panoramas of exposed Neolithic buildings. The new excavations were uncovering lots of new information about how the Neolithic villagers had lived, but when the news media and sponsor representatives came around, what did Ian's contextual approach have to show? One building in the north area, Mellaart's partially reexcavated trenches in the south, and a team of Greeks who—given the long-standing tensions between Greece and Turkey—were doing their best to keep a low profile. At times Ian wondered if he was on the right track. On September 3 he confided his concerns to his diary:

> Feeling unbelievably frustrated today about the rate of progress. When you stand back from all the detail, we have three weeks to go in effect and very little to show for the £120,000 we must have spent this season. I sometimes wonder whether modern archaeology is possible—there is such an enormous disjunction between the scientific requirements and expectations and the public (or private) purse. The only people who will pay for all the detail are, eg, the British Academy which can only give us £7,000! The people

> with big money want so much more than microdetail—eg reconstructed rooms, museums and car parks. To do that we need to move earth. But we aren't . . . Even Kostas asked me today if they were going too slow in the Summit area—what can I say? Yes from the point of view of raising money and being able to continue here; no from the point of view of science and not destroying sensitive floors. I feel hopelessly frustrated and cannot see a way out. Perhaps I should only bring a team of Roddys and Marys in future?

Ian was having a bad day. On the other hand, from Roger's point of view deep in the trench of Building 1, the excavations were proceeding pretty much according to plan. Just two weeks earlier he had summed up the situation as he saw it in the north area:

> Overall I think we have every reason to be happy with the progress so far and we can now be reasonably confident of completing the excavation of Building 1 in all its phases this season . . . This morning I recovered a fine stone mace-head, pierced right through—it probably rolled off the roof one Neolithic night . . . I have now drawn up a plan for the excavation through the upper floors—this will be done in meter squares . . . This will provide us with [a] wealth of sections through the floors and interwoven deposits and will enable Wendy to take blocks for thin-section analysis from all interesting points. I hope this operation will not be too time-consuming. I think Building 1 will be the most thoroughly and meticulously excavated building in the history of Near Eastern archaeology.

A week later Roger's optimism was rewarded when he reached the plaster floor in several parts of Building 1. Three days after that, his crew uncovered its first human burials. Roger recorded the event in his diary that evening:

> Thursday's big news was the discovery of human remains in the pit, just where it cuts the platform. We have at least two skulls, one with lower jaw attached . . . It is exciting to come face to face, liter-

ally, with the inhabitants of the place after such a long and patient chase after them. If only those jaws could move and the true story emerge!

EACH NIGHT BEFORE going to sleep in the room she shared with several other women, Shahina set her alarm for five thirty A.M. She lay in bed, thinking and half-dozing, until six, when she finally got up. She went into the kitchen and made herself a mug of black coffee, and then sat down on the edge of the veranda, as far as possible from everyone else. From time to time she would gaze up at the mound, thinking about what had to be done that day. Everyone knew not to talk to her until she finished her coffee.

Shahina was not a morning person. On the Friday day off, she slept as late as she could, sometimes not emerging until lunchtime, if then. But the morning was her favorite time to dig. At seven A.M. Shahina, Roddy, and Mary would march up the dusty trail that led from the dig house to the Mellaart area, pull out their trowels, and take up their places in the trench. Unlike Building 1, Shahina's area was too large to be covered with a protective shelter, but at this time of the day the sun was still low in the sky, its yellow rays just peeking over the Konya Plain. The three archaeologists had now dug deeply enough into their respective rooms that Shahina could not see Roddy and Mary behind the mud-brick walls that separated her from them. But she could hear the gentle grating of their trowels as they worked their way slowly through the building fill. To Shahina the soft, rhythmic scraping of a trowel was one of the most soothing sounds she knew.

As she troweled away Shahina looked for the subtle changes in colors and textures that told her she was near an oven, or that some small event, such as the depositing of some burnt ash or the disposal of a pile of sheep bones, had taken place here thousands of years ago. Sometimes she had to clean a fairly large area with her trowel before she could see it. Then, suddenly, a brown stratum would gave way to a fine layer of ashy gray, or to the telltale yellowish red staining that signaled she was near a bone. To Shahina, digging through these stratigraphic layers was like turning the pages of a book. It was her job to read and understand it.

Every small detail was exciting to her. If she came cross a small pit dug into the plaster floor, she wondered who had dug it and why. As she cleaned and exposed the mud bricks that made up the walls of a house, she tried to imagine the person who had made the bricks, mixing up the clay and straw according to some special Neolithic recipe and laying the blocks out in the sun to dry. Was it a man or a woman? What did they wear? Did they sing while they worked? If so, what song, in what language? Would she find the mason's skeleton buried beneath the plaster floor on which she now stood?

The answer to this last question, Shahina knew, was probably yes. Wendy's preliminary micromorphology studies of the mud bricks had already shown that there was a lot of variation from building to building in their sizes and in their composition: that is, the types and proportions of sediments, clay, straw, bone fragments, and other ingredients differed markedly. Wendy and Ian had concluded that each house must have been constructed by its own inhabitants. There were no centralized building contractors at Çatalhöyük who could be called upon to do it for them. If only a handful of skilled masons had built all of the houses, one would expect a lot more uniformity among the bricks.

Since Shahina was digging from top to bottom, she was reading the story in the reverse order from that in which it had actually unfolded. As long as she carefully recorded and drew everything she saw on her recording sheets, she could put the events together in the right order at the end. Sometimes she had to wait a season or two to know how it all turned out. The delay created a tension that required all the patience she had. If the clay shell of a domed oven began poking up through the deposits, she knew she would not be able to find out what had been burned in it until all of the fill surrounding it—perhaps a ton or more of earth—had been carefully dug out. Only then, when she had reached the plaster floor, did she have the satisfaction of seeing the oven released from time's grip.

Over thousands of years the fill had become packed and compressed until it had the consistency of a very solid cheese—but not so solid that it did not yield easily to the trowel's edge. If Shahina was sure that the deposits she was digging were homogeneous and hid only the tiniest of artifacts, she could in good conscience stand up, stretch out, and attack them with a shovel or a mattock until they had loosened up a bit. She would put the fill in a bucket for dry sieving and then go back to her troweling.

Interpretation at the trowel's edge. Shahina chuckled to herself. True, Ian had come up with a good phrase to describe the archaeological process. But wasn't this what she and other field archaeologists had always done, even if they didn't have a name for it? At every moment the archaeologist had to make decisions: was this bit here important or not, should she go in this direction or that, should she excavate this skeleton herself or call down for one of the human remains specialists to come and do it? Each of these judgments required that she make some assumptions about the context of what she was digging up, that she make at least a preliminary interpretation of what she was seeing.

Shahina's reveries were interrupted by the insistent ringing of a bell down at the dig house. She looked at her watch. It was nine thirty, time for breakfast.

CHRISTINE HASTORF was back, after a year's absence. Christine had not come to Çatalhöyük for the 1995 season. Her teaching load at Berkeley, her ongoing archaeobotanical work in South America, and the responsibility of caring for Nicky and Kyle had been more than enough to keep her busy that year. Ian had replaced her temporarily with an archaeobotanist from the Institute of Archaeology in London, Ann Butler, who built the project's first flotation machine with the help of a local village blacksmith.

The basic principle behind flotation is simple: charred plant remains, such as seeds and fragments of husks, tend to float in water, while most everything else found on an archaeological site, including pottery fragments, silt, and clay particles, does not. Before the invention of the flotation machine, botanists working on archaeological sites would throw handfuls of sediments into buckets of water and wait for the denser particles to settle—an inefficient and tiresome procedure. Hans Helbaek, the pioneering Near Eastern archaeobotanist who had examined the plant remains from Mellaart's excavations of Çatalhöyük during the 1960s, had to rely on this relatively primitive method. But the rise of the

New Archaeology with its emphasis on scientific techniques—as well as on such challenging questions as the origins of agriculture—spurred a search for more systematic ways of retrieving plant remains from archaeological sites. Most important, archaeobotanists had to sample large amounts of soil if they were to get a truly representative picture of which plant species were present and whether they were domesticated or wild.

Archaeologists working in the Near East usually credit the invention of the flotation machine to David French, who built a prototype at Can Hasan in 1969. There are rival claims, however. Many American archaeologists would date the beginnings of modern flotation methods to a 1968 article in *American Antiquity* by Stuart Struever, an archaeologist at Northwestern University in Illinois, in which he describes the use of galvanized steel washtubs, wire mesh, and various chemical procedures to capture the plant remains left by early Native Americans. The advantage of French's machine, however, was that it used a generator-driven electric pump to propel a constant flow of water through an array of flotation and settling tanks. The process began when a bucket of freshly excavated soil was poured into the first tank. As the water circulated through the machine, the floating plant material—called the "light residue"—was gently carried away and captured in an array of increasingly fine sieves. The plant remains were then transferred to cloth bags and set out in the sun to dry. Meanwhile, the "heavy residue" settled to the bottom of the tanks, where it was caught in nylon meshes. The result was a much cleaner separation of the two fractions and a very high recovery rate of the plant remains.

In later years Gordon Hillman of the Institute of Archaeology, the dean of British archaeobotanists, improved upon French's design. It was Hillman's version of the machine, called "the Ankara," which was now being pressed into service at Çatalhöyük. Ian had decided that he wanted a large sample of soil from every excavation unit—that is, every distinctive archaeological feature—put through the flotation machine. In 1995 Roger's and Shahina's teams collected about two hundred buckets containing sixty liters of soil each from the north and south areas of the mound. But by the end of that season, Ann had been able to process only about ninety of the buckets through her one flotation machine. When Christine arrived in 1996, she built a second, much larger machine with a souped-up motor to help handle the load. The day it arrived on site, on the back of a flatbed truck, everyone rushed out to see it: they had never seen a flotation machine that big before. With the two machines rumbling loudly all day long behind the dig house, Christine and her team of archaeobotanists were able to float almost seven hundred soil samples during the 1996 season.

In addition to Christine, two other archaeobotanists helped make up that year's team: Maria Mangafa of the University of Thessaloniki, who had come to Çatalhöyük with Kostas Kotsakis, and Julie Near, one of Christine's graduate students at Berkeley. Julie, a tall, pretty American with long red hair, had studied for her master's degree with Gordon Hillman at the Institute of Archaeology. She then signed on to do her Ph.D. with Ruth Tringham at Berkeley. In 1995 Ruth had begun a new excavation at the Neolithic site of Podgoritsa in Bulgaria, which she was codirecting with another British archaeologist and a Bulgarian colleague who had been assigned by the Institute of Archaeology in Sofia to work with them. Rissa Russell was also working at the Bulgarian site, as was Mira Stevanovic, the Serbian-American archaeologist from Belgrade with whom Ruth had dug for many years in the former Yugoslavia. But that excavation quickly turned into a disaster. When the team had a major disagreement with the Bulgarian codirector over how the site was to be dug, Ruth decided to pull out, swearing up and down that she was never going to direct an excavation again. Julie, left without a doctoral project, was eventually rescued by Christine, who agreed to help supervise her Ph.D. on the botanical material at Çatalhöyük.

The search for the origins of agriculture, where it arose and why, had long been a hot topic among Near Eastern archaeologists. At first Christine was not sure how much new information the excavations at Çatalhöyük would add to the debate. The settlement had been established at least a millennium or two later than the very first farming villages, such as Jericho or Abu Hureyra. The archaeobotanical team at Abu Hureyra, which Gordon Hillman had led, was able to trace some of the first steps in the domestication of wild plant species. While it was clear from Hans Helbaek's work at Çatalhöyük during the 1960s that a variety of wild fruits and nuts were consumed by its inhabitants, he concluded that many of the agricultural products found there—including at least three varieties of wheat, barley, peas, and bitter vetch—were already under intense cultivation.

Çatalhöyük had at least two other things going for it, archaeobotanically speaking. First, as Helbaek had earlier discovered, the fires that seemed to sweep frequently through the village had charred many of the plant remains, turning them into almost pure carbon. This protected them from attack by bacteria and chemical breakdown and helped preserve their original shapes so that they could be identified under a microscope. Second, recent research by plant geneticists strongly suggested that the original habitat of the wild ancestors of several domesticated crops had been in southeastern Anatolia. A DNA fingerprinting study of einkorn wheat carried out by scientists from Norway, Germany, and Italy and published in the journal *Science* traced the wild species to the Karacadag Mountains of southeastern Turkey. At the very least, Çatalhöyük could provide new clues about how agriculture had spread within the Near East as well as on to Greece and the rest of Europe.

Christine was eager to see what contributions Çatalhöyük might make to this already crowded research field, yet her primary motivations for working at the site lay elsewhere. One of them was purely practical: from the beginning Christine and Ian had seen working together at Çatalhöyük as a way for their family to be together during the summers. Also, while working in South America, she had increasingly shifted the focus of her research away from traditionally processualist questions, such as subsistence patterns and food technology, and concentrated more on plant use as a possible indicator of social relations among early peoples—including the relationships between men and women.

Christine had never considered herself to be a feminist archaeologist. The turning point came when she was asked to contribute a paper to *Engendering Archaeology*, the 1991 collection of essays that had made feminist archaeology a force to be contended with. Ruth Tringham, in a contribution entitled "Households with Faces," described her attempts to understand the social organization of individual households at the Neolithic site of Opovo in Serbia, where she had worked with Rissa and Mira prior to the Bulgarian misadventure. Among other things, Ruth argued that archaeologists had to try to imagine prehistoric villagers as real people rather than "faceless blobs" if they were to understand the respective roles of men and women in ancient times.

Christine's paper, which was based on her work in Peru, stood out because it presented actual archaeological data that pointed to differing male and female roles. In collaboration with her former Ph.D. supervisor, Timothy Earle, Christine had been studying the Sausa people, whose ancestors had lived in the Mantaro Valley for thousands of years. The valley is replete with food plants, especially maize, tubers, and legumes. Through a combination of ethnoarchaeological studies of living Sausas, excavations of their ancient dwellings, and chemical isotope analyses of skeletons from ancient burials—which gave an indication of what people had been eating—Christine was able to demonstrate that a shift in gender roles had probably taken place after the Incas conquered the valley in about 1460 A.D.

Prior to the Inca invasion, it appeared that Sausa women had been responsible for food preparation, which they carried out mostly but not exclusively next to hearths or ovens; thus some plant remains were found on patios and other parts of the houses. After the Inca invasion, however, plant remains were rarely found in areas of the house not closely associated with cooking. Moreover, the isotope measurements from male and female skeletons suggested that in pre-Inca times men and women had consumed equal amounts of maize. The corn has long been used to make a beer called *chicha*, which is drunk especially during ritual or political activities. After the conquest men appeared to be consuming much more maize than women. Christine concluded from this assorted evidence that women, despite being responsible for food preparation, had probably participated fairly equally in social life with men before the Incas came. Afterward they were more or less relegated to the kitchen and possibly were no longer included in ritual and political gatherings.

Christine was hoping that Ian's emphasis at Çatalhöyük on high-definition, contextual archaeology would allow her to carry out research into gender roles and social relationships at the site. She was also interested in the balance between the wild and domesticated foods consumed at Çatalhöyük, and what this might say about how the villagers viewed their relationship with the nature around them. The team would have to get much further along in the excavations before she could seriously tackle such challenging questions. Nevertheless, thanks to the intense sampling strategy and the high-powered flotation machines, the first two seasons had turned up some important new findings.

As might be expected, many of the plants and cereals recovered were similar to what Hans Helbaek had turned up during the 1960s.

Grains and husks of domesticated einkorn and emmer wheat were plentiful, as were well-preserved barley and peas. There were many wild fruits, especially hackberries, which Christine thought may have been used to make some sort of juice or possibly even an early fermented wine. Her team also found a significant number of charred tubers and rhizomes. The tubers, mainly bulrushes from the genus *Scirpus*, were particularly interesting because they tend to grow in marshy, wetland environments. The Çatalhöyük team was keenly interested in knowing what kind of environment had surrounded the settlement during Neolithic times. The Konya plateau is semiarid today, with limited rainfall, but the presence of *Scirpus* could provide evidence that it was once much wetter.

The team also recovered some large caches of acorns and lentils, plants which had shown up much less often during the Mellaart excavations. Along one wall of Building 1, Roger's crew had uncovered a large storage bin, about one meter long and a half meter wide, that was filled to a depth of two inches with charred lentils. Lentils are usually cultivated in dryland conditions, as are wheat and barley, and acorn-producing oak trees prefer higher ground as well. For the moment these contradictory indications of Çatalhöyük's ecology were difficult to reconcile: were the farmers' fields next to the settlement mound, as had always been assumed for most Neolithic villages, and the wetlands farther away? Or was it the opposite? It was difficult to believe that the settlers would build their homes right in the middle of a marsh, but the possibility could not be dismissed. As the churning and bubbling of the flotation machines delivered up the long-hidden secrets of their ancient diet, one thing was becoming clear: out here on the vast expanses of the Konya Plain, Neolithic life had been bountiful.

WITH THE EXCAVATIONS going at full steam, the specialists had plenty of artifacts to study. Naomi, for one, was keeping plenty busy. During the 1996 season Shahina's team found sixty-two figurines depicting humans and animals in the Mellaart area, mostly in midden areas. Small fragments of twelve more figurines were unearthed by Roger and company in Building 1. Now that human burials were beginning to crop up under the floors of Building 1, Ian assigned Naomi to record the various grave goods—bead necklaces, pendants, and bracelets—that adorned some, but not all, of the skeletons. Meanwhile Jonathan Last was making his way through the several hundred shards of pottery found in the north, Mellaart, and summit areas, while Louise and Rissa typed away on their laptop computers, recording 11,634 animal bone fragments during the 1996 season.

Louise Martin and Rissa Russell had never met before they started working together at Çatalhöyük. Louise, the British member of the faunal team, was thirty-three years old in 1996, outgoing, talkative, and enthusiastic about everything she did. She was tall, wore glasses, and greeted everyone with a bright smile. Rissa, the American, was about to turn thirty-nine years old. She was quiet and introverted, with a reserved, observant manner that seldom revealed what she was thinking or feeling. Louise had finished her Ph.D. work with Paul Halstead at the University of Sheffield in 1994 and almost immediately afterward had landed a position at the Institute of Archaeology in London. Rissa, who had earned her Ph.D. with Ruth Tringham at Berkeley in 1993 and had much more archaeology experience than Louise, had not yet found a permanent job.

Despite these seeming differences in their personalities and career tracks, Louise and Rissa got along well and worked together closely as team. When it came to analyzing the animal bones, they were usually of one mind. As their database got larger, their suspicions that something was wrong with the conclusions that Dexter Perkins, the zooarchaeologist who analyzed Mellaart's faunal remains, had reached about Çatalhöyük's animals continued to grow. Perkins had claimed that cattle were by far the dominant species at the site. But with a sample size now large enough to be meaningful, and more thorough collection methods, the pair had found just the opposite in the new excavations. In both the north and Mellaart areas, sheep and goats together made up about 63 percent of all the bones, whereas cattle accounted for only 13 percent in the north area and 11 percent in the Mellaart area.

In their report on the 1996 season, the two bluntly flagged their concerns: "It is likely that zooarchaeological findings from the 1960s excavations at the site are potentially severely flawed, at least in terms of taxonomic abundance," Louise and Rissa wrote. "It seems most likely that the previously recorded predominance of cattle was simply an artifact of the haphazard collection of large pieces of bone."

About once each week, as part of the ongoing effort to foster reflexivity, Ian or one of the other archaeologists would lead an evening seminar in the dining room. Some of the seminars dealt with technical or methodological issues, such as recording techniques or ways to prepare cattle bone samples for DNA analysis; others, which most of the team members found much more stimulating, focused on topical issues such as Neolithic burial practices, the Mother Goddess, or the overall aims of the project. About midway through the season, Ruth Tringham, who was visiting for several days, led a session on "storytelling" in archaeology. Ruth argued, as she had in her paper in *Engendering Archaeology*, that it was the archaeologist's job to go beyond the dry data and create "narratives" about the past. Roger found this discussion particularly thought-provoking, as he recorded in his diary the next day:

> Interesting discussion last night about archaeology and storytelling—ie putting flesh on the bare bones. It's something we are duty bound to do but the question is how. I have always felt that excavation directors should be scientific novelists.

Ruth had come to Çatalhöyük at Ian's invitation. Ian wanted her to bring a team to the site from Berkeley, but Ruth, after the disastrous experience in Bulgaria, decided to take a good look at what was going on before she made any commitments. Ruth liked what she saw, and on the last day of her visit during the 1996 season, she agreed to come out the following year together with Mira Stevanovic and other Berkeley colleagues. Ruth was not exactly taking back her vow never to lead a dig again. One of the things that attracted her to Çatalhöyük was that Ian would take care of all the bureaucratic hassles, such as excavation permits and the like; while she did have to raise her own funds, once Ruth arrived at Çatalhöyük, all she would have to do was excavate. With her usual flamboyance, Ruth declared that her squad of excavators would be known as the Berkeley Archaeologists at Çatal Höyük, or BACH team. To many of the other archaeologists, the notion that the American team at Çatalhöyük would be led by a Brit and a Serb was highly amusing. But everyone agreed that it was a terrific opportunity to open up yet more territory in the north area and possibly even decipher the relationships among the buildings in this part of the mound.

Most evenings, before finally going to sleep, the archaeologists gathered for an hour or two on the dig house veranda to chat and drink Efes beer, Turkey's national brew. Efes was the Turkish name for Ephesus, the vast Classical city on the Aegean coast whose well-preserved ruins draw hundreds of thousands of tourists each year. One of the biggest Efes breweries in Turkey was just down the road toward Konya. The team at Çatalhöyük had become regular customers. Sometimes the beer drinking would be accompanied by musical entertainment, especially if Roger was in the mood to break out the guitar he had brought with him from Cambridge. Roger had a varied repertoire that included Jimi Hendrix, the Beatles, and an occasional folk song. Rissa was one of his most avid listeners, particularly when he played Donovan's "Catch the Wind," one of her favorite songs. The past few years had been tough ones for Rissa. She was married to an anthropologist and had two young children, but her future was very much up in the air. The academic job market was very tight; despite earning her Ph.D. three years earlier, she had not yet found a permanent position. On a warm, moonlit Çatalhöyük night, Roger's singing was just what she needed to forget about all that for a while.

AROUND THE TIME that the twenty-first human skeleton was found beneath the floors of Building 1, Roger began to wonder if his goal of completely excavating the structure by the end of the 1996 season was realistic. In addition to himself, Gavin, and Wendy, who was pitching in with some of the drawing and recording, a half-dozen British and Turkish archaeology students were working full-time in the cramped building. There were only two weeks left in the season, but the burials just kept on coming. Two-thirds of the skeletons were those of children or babies, which suggested a high rate of child mortality. Some were intact, or nearly so, such as the fully articulated but headless skeleton of an adult and two of the babies; in other burials, however, especially those of older children, the bones tended to be disarticulated and scattered about. So far only adults had appeared beneath the eastern half of the building, while the children were concentrated in the west.

Given the certainty of finding human burials, Ian had recruited two highly respected experts from the Natural History Museum in London, Theya Molleson and Peter Andrews, to lead the physical anthropology team at Çatalhöyük. Theya had recently completed a major study of 162 human skeletons excavated at Abu Hureyra during the 1970s. She found that while the people of this early farming community had been in generally good health—except for their teeth, which were in terrible shape from eating coarse grains—they had numerous bone deformities, which suggested they had carried heavy loads, beginning when they were still children. Peter's specialty was early human evolution. Together with paleoanthropologist Chris Stringer of the Natural History Museum, he had been one of the first to argue that modern humans originated in Africa about 150,000 years ago, a controversial claim at the time but one that today represents the majority view among anthropologists.

The sheer number of burials came as a surprise to everyone. While Mellaart had found more than forty skeletons in one of his mud-brick buildings, most of them had many fewer bodies than that, and some had none at all. There were so many skeletons that Theya and Peter would not be able to study more than a few of them this season, but they already knew quite a bit about the people of Çatalhöyük. While awaiting the beginning of full-fledged excavations, the two had received permission from Turkish authorities to export an assortment of lower jaws and teeth unearthed during the Mellaart excavations to London. In the laboratories of the Natural History Museum, Theya and Peter X-rayed the bones and teeth and examined them with a scanning electron microscope for signs of microwear, the tiny marks and scratches that can tell anthropologists what ancient people might have been eating. There were two interesting findings. First, the tiny pits found on the surfaces of all teeth were relatively wide, indicating that fairly large chunks of food were being chewed. And second, there were very few scratches on the teeth, meaning that whatever they were eating did not have to be chewed for very long. This suggested that cereals, except for those that had perhaps been boiled in water, did not make up the majority of the diet. Their preliminary conclusion was that the people had lived mainly on tubers and pulses such as peas or lentils.

To test this hypothesis further, Theya and Peter decided to analyze the teeth and bones for twenty-two different trace elements using a technique called induced coupled plasma spectrometry, or ICP for short. The interpretation of ICP results is tricky, because it often depends on determining the ratios or correlations between two or more elements rather than the absolute amount of any one element. Moreover, the bones and teeth uncovered in some sections of Mellaart's excavations gave different values than others, an indication that the diet might have varied over time and from household to household. For example, the bones and teeth from one building in Level VII had higher-than-average levels of zinc, which could indicate a diet rich in meat or fish. While most of the other samples had somewhat lower concentrations of zinc, a strong correlation between the zinc and strontium levels combined with a weak correlation of zinc and iron levels suggested that most people in the village were eating plant foods rather than meat. Overall, the ICP results convinced Theya and Peter that they were on the right track. "The results give tentative support to an earlier analysis on the microwear of the teeth that a non-abrasive diet was being eaten by the individuals tested from Çatalhöyük," they wrote in their report in *On the Surface*. "Despite the evidence for grain preparation at the site the most likely diet was one of pulses and tubers."

Once again the evidence was showing that the Neolithic villagers had an ample food supply, although the high infant and child mortality remained to be explained. The burials under the house floors, which seemed to anchor each family or household to its chosen place within the community through the chains of ancestry, suggested that once the people of Çatalhöyük had settled here, they had no intention of moving anytime soon. Indeed, as Mellaart's excavations had demonstrated, they would build and rebuild their houses one atop the other over hundreds of years, as if rooted to the spot. But why? It was one thing to settle into a landscape where cattle, sheep, and goats grazed happily, where wheat, barley, and lentils were easily grown, and where wild tubers and fruits were everywhere for the plucking. It was another thing entirely for everyone to smash themselves together into a meshwork of mud-brick houses when there was plenty of space for everyone to spread out. Over the years since Mellaart dug here, some archaeologists had suggested that the inhabitants had huddled together for defensive purposes. As far as the new team was concerned, however, that explanation did not wash: there were few artifacts at Çatalhöyük that could have been much use as weapons; nor did the skeletons show any evidence of injuries from warfare.

So why, around 10,000 years ago, did people all over the Near East start living together in close-knit communities? For the past seventy years archaeologists and other experts had been struggling to answer that very question.

9 / The Neolithic Revolution

At seven one foggy Friday morning, a dozen sleepy archaeologists boarded an aging bus and plopped themselves onto its worn cloth seats. The bus pulled out of the Çatalhöyük dig house's gravel courtyard and rumbled toward Konya, the first leg of its journey to Cappadocia. Cappadocia, in east Central Anatolia, is one of Turkey's most popular tourist areas. A rugged land of volcanic mountains, oak forests, and swift rivers, it was occupied in later antiquity by the Persians and the Romans. Eager as the Çatalhöyük archaeologists were to have a change of scene from the flatlands of the Konya Plain, this was not really a tourist trip. Rather it was a journey into the past. The bus was on its way to Aşikli Höyük, the Neolithic village excavated by Istanbul University archaeologist Ufuk Esin and her colleagues between 1989 and the mid-1990s. The calibrated radiocarbon dates from Aşikli indicated that this community, which is about a third of the size of Çatalhöyük in area, was established about 8400 B.C. and abandoned about 7500 B.C.—right around the time that Çatalhöyük is now thought to have been founded.

Did the settlers at Çatalhöyük originally live at Aşikli, about 90 miles to the east as the crow flies? Most archaeologists who study the Anatolian Neolithic consider this to be a distinct possibility, although alternative scenarios have been proposed. Çatalhöyük's settlers could also have come from Neolithic Can Hasan, about thirty-five miles to the southeast, which was excavated by David French during the 1960s; or from the Neolithic occupation layers that James Mellaart unearthed during the 1950s at Hacilar, about 240 miles to the west; or even from several smaller, nearby communities that might have converged at Çatalhöyük to form this supernova in the Neolithic galaxy. If this last scenario is correct, one such candidate community might be found at the cliffside site of Pinarbaşi, just 18 miles southeast of Çatalhöyük, which was discovered by David French in the 1970s. In 1993, during the first year of their Konya Plain survey, Douglas Baird of the University of Liverpool and Trevor Watkins of the University of Edinburgh took another look at Pinarbaşi and detected several prehistoric occupation layers, including some that predated Çatalhöyük. The following year Watkins began a modest excavation at Pinarbaşi to see if any evidence of cultural continuity with Çatalhöyük could be found. But it was still too early to draw any definite conclusions.

The fog began to lift, and the flat landscape gave way to grassy hills. The volcanic mountains loomed ever closer. At the farming town of Aksaray, the archaeologists stopped for breakfast at a restaurant on the dusty main street. Everyone soon became much more talkative. After a little shopping for fruit and nuts in Aksaray's central market, they boarded the bus again and rode the last 15 miles to the mound of Aşikli, which overlooks a lazy stretch of the Melendiz River. They were met there by Mihriban Özbaşaran, a vivacious archaeologist from the University of Istanbul who had worked at Aşikli with Ufuk Esin. The excavations at Aşikli had recently been completed. Mihriban was now shifting her attention to an enigmatic Neolithic site about a quarter of a mile west of the main mound. The Aşikli team had discovered this site, called Musular, in 1993 during a survey of the area. Its most dramatic feature was a series of strange stone alignments whose purpose Mihriban was reluctant to speculate about. One stratigraphic level at Musular had yielded a radiocarbon date that fell right between the abandonment of Aşikli and the founding of Çatalhöyük. Archaeologists working in Anatolia were watching Mihriban's excavations at this new site very closely.

Ian Todd, who was James Mellaart's assistant director at Çatalhöyük during the 1960s, had carried out an extensive surface survey of Aşikli in 1964. He collected more than 6,000 pieces of obsidian from the top of the Aşikli mound during his survey, an extraordinary number for any Neolithic site. A few years later Colin Renfrew and his colleagues reported that the volcanoes of Cappadocia were the source of the obsidian found not only at most Anatolian sites but also at Jericho and many other Neolithic villages in the eastern Mediterranean area. And the obsidian from the later excavations at Abu Hureyra in Syria, which James Conolly studied for his master's degree, also came from Cappadocia. It appeared that the people of Aşikli were living almost right on top of one of the most sought-after raw materials in the Near East.

Like Çatalhöyük, Aşikli was made up mostly of mud-brick buildings with plastered walls, although certain structures were reinforced with stones—a building material readily available in volcanic Cappadocia but not on the Konya Plain. Ufuk Esin's team had found several dozen burials under the floors of the houses, another indication of possible cultural continuity between the two sites. But one of the most striking findings at Aşikli was the uniformity of the houses over time. Like the people of Çatalhöyük, the inhabitants of Aşikli had rebuilt their houses one atop the other during the settlement's nine-hundred-year lifespan. Toward the end of the excavations, the team had dug a deep sounding at one edge of the mound, revealing in one scoop at least a half dozen of the estimated ten occupation levels at the site. Whereas the excavations at Çatalhöyük had shown that its inhabitants felt relatively free to change the locations of their ovens, platforms, and other features over time, the deep sounding at Aşikli revealed a stunning conservatism: in every house, at every level, the ovens had been constructed in exactly the same place. Ian Hodder, during an earlier visit to Aşikli, had found it astounding that a community a thousand years older than Çatalhöyük would be more highly structured rather than less so.

In another departure from Çatalhöyük, where the excavations so far had failed to reveal any central public buildings or spaces, the Aşikli team had uncovered several larger buildings with red painted floors, buildings separated from the residential area by a street or alleyway. Esin concluded that these buildings might represent temples or other ritual centers of some sort. Nevertheless, no wall paintings or sculptures have been found at Aşikli, although a small number of animal figurines and beads made of agate or stone did show up. Perhaps the most important distinction between the two sites, however, was in the findings of the archaeobotanists and zooarchaeologists who studied the plant and animal remains at Aşikli. At Çatalhöyük there was little question that farming provided a major portion of the villagers' daily diet. It also seemed very likely that they had herded sheep and goats, even if Louise and Rissa were starting to have some questions about whether or not the cattle were domesticated. But while the later stratigraphic levels at Aşikli showed evidence that wheat and barley had begun to be cultivated, throughout the life of the site the settlers relied heavily on wild plants and fruits, as well as on wild cattle and possibly wild sheep and goats as well. They were primarily hunter-gatherers who for some reason had settled down in one spot and stayed there for hundreds of years; only later had they begun to experiment with cultivation. Had the people of Aşikli formed their community even before the Neolithic Revolution was fully under way? If so, what had brought them together?

SOMETIMES IT TAKES a revolutionary to spot a revolution. With his 1925 book *The Dawn of European Civilization,* the Australian-born British archaeologist Vere Gordon Childe launched a career as one of the twentieth century's most original and influential prehistorians. Politically Childe was a Marxist, although archaeologists have long debated to what extent his Marxism actually influenced his theories about the past. Mortimer Wheeler concluded that it colored rather than shaped Childe's interpretations, although others have pointed out that his commitment to the Marxist principle of historical materialism predisposed him to see a series of stages in human cultural evolution.

At the very least, Childe's left-wing sympathies seem to have influenced his somewhat eccentric behavior. He strolled the streets of Edinburgh, where he was appointed to the university's chair of archaeology in 1927, wearing a wide-brimmed Australian hat, a cheap mackintosh, and worn, baggy trousers that he claimed to have purchased in Belgrade. Agatha Christie's husband, the archaeologist Max Mallowan, once commented that Childe's small face, which was garnished with thick-rimmed glasses and a scruffy mustache, was so ugly that it was painful to look at; this appearance, and Childe's tall, awkward frame, may have contributed to his modest, self-effacing manner. Yet he loved to play the provocateur. When he checked into a fancy hotel, during one of his many travels in Europe or the United States, he would immediately demand a copy of the Communist newspaper *The Daily Worker,* and his public speeches were often peppered with quotations from Joseph Stalin.

Childe's extensive travels, including many visits to the Soviet Union, gave him an overview of European and Near Eastern archaeology greater than that of most other prehistorians of his time. "He had an acute visual memory, allowing him to spot similarities among artifacts in far distant regions that went unnoticed by regional specialists," wrote Canadian archaeologist Bruce Trigger in his 1980 biography of Childe. As early as 1928 Childe, in his book *The Most Ancient East,* concluded from the patterns he saw in the archaeological record that prehistory in Asia and Europe had been altered by two major upheavals: the Neolithic Revolution, marked by the beginnings of agriculture, about 10,000 years ago, and the Urban Revolution, around 5,000 years ago, when the first cities sprang up in the fertile valleys of Mesopotamia, Egypt, and the Indian subcontinent. The Neolithic, Childe later wrote, "was an economic revolution—the greatest in human history after the mastery of fire. It opened up a richer and more reliable supply of food, brought now within man's own control and capable of almost unlimited expansion by his unaided efforts."

The phrase "Neolithic Revolution," which was Childe's invention, is still widely used by archaeologists, even though some argue that the development of agriculture should be seen as a gradual evolutionary process rather than a sudden cataclysm. But the word Neolithic ("New Stone Age"), as well as the term for the earlier and much longer epoch of human prehistory, the *Paleolithic* ("Old Stone Age"), was coined during the nineteenth century by John Lubbock, also known as Lord Avebury. The Paleolithic era dates from the first human use of stone tools, which make their first appearance in the archaeological record of Africa around

2.5 million years ago—a date that coincides with the earliest fossils of *Homo habilis,* the first species of the genus *Homo.* While some archaeologists and anthropologists have postulated that earlier "revolutions" had taken place over the course of the Paleolithic—for example, the explosion of symbolic representation during the Upper Paleolithic period in Europe, beginning about 40,000 years ago, as manifested by cave paintings and other works of art and sculpture—most would agree that the transition between the Paleolithic and the Neolithic periods was the most essential turning point in human cultural development.

"The Neolithic of the Near East was not a simple shift in subsistence pattern from hunting-gathering to farming and domestication, but more significantly—a period of major social, economic, and technological innovation," wrote Mehmet Özdoğan, the doyen of Anatolian Neolithic specialists. Childe himself believed that the later Urban Revolution, heralded by the rise of cities and the true beginnings of modern civilization, was made possible by the agricultural surpluses amassed over several thousand years by Neolithic farmers.

In 1946 Childe left Edinburgh to become the first full-time director of the Institute of Archaeology in London, where by all accounts he was very popular among the students and faculty. He retired from the institute in 1956. The following year, while hiking on a clifftop in Australia's Blue Mountains, Childe either fell or jumped to his death, at the age of sixty-five years. Most of his friends and colleagues, who knew that he had been despondent over ill health and a fear that his intellectually productive days were over, assumed that Childe had committed suicide. In his will he left the royalties from his many books to the institute, which installed a bust of Childe in its library soon after it occupied its new quarters in London's Gordon Square in 1958. He also left a huge intellectual legacy to modern archaeological thought, even if many of his ideas are now considered outdated. Finally, Childe left archaeologists pondering the question that he had been the first to raise, but which no one since has been able to fully answer: why had the Neolithic Revolution, arguably the most important single event in the history of humankind, taken place at all?

• • •

NOWADAYS OUR NEWSPAPERS and magazines are full of articles about the perils of global warming. Had newspapers existed 25,000 years ago, however, the headlines would have been much different: "Global Cooling Hits Earth, read all about it!" Another in a long series of ice ages was on its way. Prehistoric humans had seen it all before: colder, warmer, colder, warmer. The most reasonable explanation for all these climate shifts, the experts now believe, lies with periodic variations in the earth's orbit around the sun. These variations influence how much sunlight our planet is exposed to. According to astronomical calculations, if we ever do get a handle on global warming and let nature take its course, we can expect to endure another ice age about 25,000 years from now.

Some scientists believe that being whipsawed around by dramatic climate changes provided the evolutionary impetus for humans to grow big brains, which in turn gave us the smarts we needed to adapt to anything Mother Nature could throw at us. The leading proponent of this hypothesis, human origins researcher Richard Potts at the Smithsonian Institution in Washington, D.C., calls this process "variability selection": humans evolved to adapt not to any one environmental niche or set of conditions but to change itself. If correct, this idea may also explain why our own species, *Homo sapiens,* was able to survive the constant series of climatic upheavals, while the Neandertals—who were very well adapted to the cold but not necessarily to warmer weather—went completely extinct sometime between 25,000 and 30,000 years ago, just before the next onset of the cold weather they apparently thrived in. By 18,000 years ago, at what is somewhat hopefully termed the Last Glacial Maximum, North America and northern Europe were covered by ice sheets nearly three miles thick. Southern Europe, which lay beyond the glacier's edge, was a sparsely vegetated tundra where nary a tree could be seen. Conditions were a little better in Japan and the eastern United States, however, where forests somehow survived the worst ravages of the Ice Age.

Archaeologists use the terms *Paleolithic* and *Neolithic* to refer to earlier and later epochs of human prehistory, which can be distinguished by the types of artifacts they left behind, especially the types of stone tools they used. These periods correspond to phases of human activity. Geologists use the terms Pleistocene and Holocene to refer to the last

1.8 million years of our planet's natural history. We still live in the Holocene period. The earliest Holocene, which began about 11,500 years ago and marks the official end of the last ice age, coincides closely with the first known human experiments in the domestication of plants in the Near East—that is, with the beginning of the Neolithic Revolution. Archaeologists and other experts have long assumed that this is no coincidence and that one has a lot to do with the other—for example, that the warmer conditions of the Holocene made agriculture possible, necessary, desirable, or some combination of these or other factors.

The connection between the Holocene and the Neolithic certainly did not escape the attention of V. Gordon Childe, who proffered an explanation for the origins of agriculture that has come to be known as the Oasis Theory. Childe searched for the roots of his revolution in the material, real-world changes in climate and environment that prehistoric humans were exposed to at the time. Childe spelled out his theory, which was heavily influenced by the earlier work of the American geologist Raphael Pumpelly, in his 1936 book *Man Makes Himself.* Like Pumpelly, he assumed that the beginning of the Holocene had been marked by much drier climatic conditions than those of the icy late Pleistocene. Childe proposed that the increasing dessication had forced both people and animals to gather together next to permanent water sources such as rivers and oases, and the humans ended up taming the animals so that they could eat them without first having to give chase. Childe was much vaguer on the question of how plants came to be domesticated, even though he did believe, as most experts still do, that plant cultivation preceded animal herding in the Near East.

Childe's hypothesis, elegant as it may have been, was based on very little empirical evidence, and it later fell out of favor, especially after geologists and botanists determined that conditions in the early Holocene of the Near East had been generally wetter rather than drier. A number of other explanations have been proposed since, which fall generally into two categories: those that tend more or less toward environmental and ecological determinism, holding the climatic changes of the early Holocene and the stress of population growth responsible for propelling prehistoric humans to adapt by inventing agriculture, and those that focus on social and cultural factors, thus awarding the credit for the Neolithic Revolution to the conscious or unconscious actions of the humans who, in this view, made it happen. Neither type of explanation excludes the other, because all social and cultural activity takes place within a given set of environmental conditions, while at the same time humans are capable of making at least some choices about how they respond to their environments. Yet, as might be expected, the environmental and ecological hypotheses have been most eagerly pushed by processual or New Archaeologists, while an emphasis on social and cultural factors is favored by post-processual archaeologists.

The first major challenge to Childe's Oasis Theory came from archaeologists Robert and Linda Braidwood of the University of Chicago, who excavated the Neolithic site of Jarmo in Iraq during the late 1940s and early 1950s. The Braidwoods were searching for evidence of the first food-producing societies. They assembled a multidisciplinary team of experts at Jarmo, including Hans Helbaek of the Danish National Museum, the archaeobotanist who would later work at Çatalhöyük and many other Near Eastern sites; University of Illinois zoologist Charles Reed; and University of Minnesota geologist Herbert E. Wright Jr. They were also able to take advantage of the brand-new technique of radiocarbon dating, which was just coming into regular use in the 1950s. The excavations at Jarmo turned up the earliest evidence then known for domesticated wheat and barley, which the Braidwood team dated to about 8,500 years ago. And when the political upheavals in Iraq during the mid-1950s forced the Braidwoods to leave the country, they began working at an even older site, 9,000-year-old Tepe Sarab in western Iran, which also showed evidence of being an early farming village. (Later calibrations of radiocarbon dating would push these dates back at least a thousand years.)

The excavations at Jarmo and Tepe Sarab posed a big problem for the Oasis Theory: both sites were located in the foothills of the Zagros Mountains, rather than near lowland oases or river valleys as predicted by Childe's model. This location made much more sense to the Braidwoods, because many of the wild ancestors of today's domesticated plants and animals flourished in the hills of the so-called Fertile Crescent of the Near East. This alternative model soon came to be known as the hilly flanks theory. One of the new theory's implications, the Braidwoods believed, was that environmental or climatic explanations for the Neolithic Revolution were not sufficient in and of themselves, particularly since agriculture had apparently arisen independently in several parts of the world, such as China and the Americas. "The multiple occurrence of the agricultural revolution suggests that it was a highly probable outcome of the prior cultural evolution of mankind and a peculiar combination of environmental circumstances," Robert Braidwood wrote in the September 1960 issue of *Scientific American.* "It is in the record of culture, therefore, that the origin of agriculture must be sought." At least one cultural development essential to agriculture, Braidwood suggested, was the mental process whereby humans "settled in" to ecological niches, with the result that prehistoric humans would have a more intimate knowledge of, and relationship to, the plants and animals they would later domesticate.

The hilly flanks model was popular for a number of years, although few archaeologists of the time took up Braidwood's invitation to search for the cultural origins of the Neolithic Revolution. Instead the scientific approaches that he and his wife had pioneered at Jarmo helped inspire the rise of the scientifically oriented New Archaeologists, who soon relegated cultural factors to a minor role in their own attempts to explain the origins of agriculture. And since solving the mystery of the Neolithic Revolution was considered to be one of the biggest and most exciting challenges that archaeologists faced, no one was surprised when the big man himself, Lewis Binford, stepped up to the plate to take a crack at it. Binford's key contribution was a 1968 paper entitled "Post-Pleistocene Adaptations." After a lengthy description of the Childe and Braidwood models, Binford dismissed both of them in favor of yet a third explanation that later came to be known as the marginality or edge hypothesis.

The key ingredient missing in the older recipes for the Neolithic Revolution, Binford argued, was population pressure. Binford was heavily influenced by the views of University of Chicago anthropologist Marshall Sahlins, who argued on the basis of ethnographic studies of modern-day hunter-gatherers that the rise of agriculture was not such an enviable development as boosters of progress might have us believe. Sahlins maintained that hunter-gatherers, rather than being poor, starving brutes who needed to be rescued from famine by the blessings of civilization, were actually so well off that they represented "the original affluent society"—a reference to the influential 1958 book *The Affluent*

Society by the American economist John Kenneth Galbraith. They were also, Sahlins added somewhat tongue-in-cheek, the first practioners of Zen philosophy: "Adopting the Zen strategy, a people can enjoy an unparalleled material plenty—with a low standard of living. That, I think, describes the hunters."

Binford, following upon this idea of hunter-gatherer affluence, proposed that preagricultural peoples living the good life would live it where it was best, in those optimal ecological zones where the most plentiful supplies of wild plants and animals could be found. Along with the good life came more and healthier babies, leading to population growth and demographic stress, which in turned forced some of those living in the best areas to move out to their margins. As the numbers of people living in the margins increased, Binford argued, they began to domesticate plants and animals so that they could have food supplies as rich as those found naturally in the more bountiful center. Binford's early disciple, Kent Flannery, suggested that the first cultivation of plants might have represented an attempt by people living on the edges of the optimal zones to produce crops of cereals as dense as the naturally occurring wild stands within the zones. Flannery also expanded upon Binford's original hypothesis by proposing that the Neolithic Revolution had been preceded by a "broad spectrum revolution," in which prehistoric humans began eating a much wider variety of plants and animals than they had previously.

Binford had little time for cultural explanations of the Neolithic Revolution, including Braidwood's notion of humans "settling in" to their landscape. In a later survey of ideas about the origins of agriculture, Binford ridiculed Braidwood's proposal as suggesting that "man 'settled in' to his environment, like a chicken getting comfortable on the nest, and then—one must suppose—had great thoughts!"

The debate over the Neolithic Revolution has taken a number of additional twists and turns, particularly as processual and post-processual archaeologists, in trying to explain it, have argued over the primacy of environmental or cultural factors. The Neolithic Revolution marked a dramatic shift in technological, social, economic, ideological, and religious practices, not all of which happened at the same time or in the same place; moreover, the relationship among these different aspects of the revolution is not at all clear. To a large extent the debate among archaeologists reflects a more profound division over just what constitutes a proper explanation for any given set of archaeological findings. In the parlance of philosophers, the field is suffering from a chronic epistemological crisis: how do we know whether or not we know something, and how do we know that we know that we know?

The task of archaeologists attempting to explain the Neolithic Revolution is at least twofold: they must explain the origins of agriculture, the domestication of plants and animals, and they must explain why people squeezed themselves into sedentary villages, that is, why they chose to live together in large social units rather than dispersed across the landscape. For many decades after Childe coined the term, archaeologists tended to regard these two key components of the Neolithic Revolution as two sides of the same coin: humans had to settle in one spot if they wanted to tend to their fields and flocks, and conversely, the desire for a reliable food supply encouraged people to congregate together. Even Childe had cautioned that these two concepts should be kept separate. "The adoption of cultivation must not be confused with the adoption of a sedentary life," he wrote in *Man Makes Himself*. Childe went on to cite several cases where the one had existed without the other, including the nineteenth-century tribes of hunters and fishermen who lived in permanent wooden houses on the Pacific coast of Canada, and the Cro-Magnons of Ice Age France who occupied the same caves over many generations.

Despite Childe's warning, however—and perhaps because agriculture, as a technological innovation, is somewhat easier to get a handle on than the far murkier question of why humans would want to live together rather than apart—most archaeologists have tended to focus their work on why farming arose when and where it did. The mysteries of sedentism were relegated to a much lower place on the research agenda. Yet more recent archaeological excavations in the Near East, combined with the ongoing refinement of radiocarbon dating methods, have confirmed that sedentary life preceded agriculture by at least 2,000 years and probably much more. The first cereals were cultivated around 11,000 years ago, but there are at least tentative signs of sedentary behavior going back to the Upper Paleolithic, more than 20,000 years ago, and true sedentism appears to have arisen in the Near East just after 13,000 years ago, before the Holocene officially began. Meanwhile research in the New World has opened an even greater time gap between plant domestication and sedentism, although in the reverse direction: archaeobotanists working in Mexico, Panama, and Ecuador have recently found evidence that humans began domesticating squashes some 10,000 years ago, about 5,000 years *before* they began to settle in permanent villages.

In recent years a number of leading prehistorians have focused their attention on a mysterious group of prehistoric peoples called the Natufians, who thrived in modern-day Israel, Palestine, and Jordan about 12,500 years ago. The Natufians lived in villages, built houses, stored food, and buried their dead either under their dwellings or nearby; in other words, they did many of the things once thought to be the exclusive province of Neolithic peoples. But they were not farmers. They hunted wild animals and ate wild plants. Many archaeologists believe that the Natufians were the first truly sedentary peoples. And agriculture had nothing to do with it.

> THROUGH GAPS IN the leafy trees [he] sees five or six dwellings aligned along the woodland slope. They are cut into the earth itself, having subterranean floors and low drystone walls that support roofs of brushwood and hide . . . Just inside the entrance [of one dwelling] there is a spread of ash where a fire had burned the previous night to keep the biting insects at bay. Another hearth now glows in the center of the floor; a man squats alongside and plucks a brace of partridges . . . A few young people . . . are repairing bows and arrows . . . Stone pestles and mortars, wicker baskets and wooden bowls, are stacked around the walls.

This is the scene witnessed by an imaginary time traveler—a character created by British archaeologist Steven Mithen for his 2003 book *After the Ice*—during a furtive visit to 'Ain Mallaha, a 12,000-year-old Natufian village next to Lake Huleh in the Jordan Valley. Yet the building Mithen describes is not imaginary. It is Dwelling 131, excavated at 'Ain Mallaha by French archaeologist Jean Perrot in 1954. Mithen's description is based closely on the archaeological remains that Perrot found there. The people of 'Ain Mallaha used their pestles and mortars to grind wild grain and cereals, and their bows and arrows to hunt the wild gazelle that then roamed the Levant in huge numbers.

The credit for discovering the Natufians goes to the British archaeologist Dorothy Garrod, the first woman professor at Cambridge University and a major contributor to our present-day understanding of Levantine prehistory. During the 1920s and 1930s, Garrod excavated a cave at Wadi en-Natuf in the Judean Desert, where she found a stratigraphic layer that predated the earliest known Neolithic settlements. It was characterized by a unique assortment of small, crescent-shaped stone tools, sickle blades made of flint, fishhooks, and bone tools. She named this newly recognized culture after the site where it was first found. Based on the artifacts Garrod unearthed, she assumed that the Natufians were early farmers, although it is now clear that she was wrong. Soon afterward Garrod and others discovered a number of other Natufian sites. The earliest occupation levels that Kathleen Kenyon identified at Jericho, at the end of her 1950s excavations, turned out to be the remains of Natufian settlers. Kenyon concluded that Jericho was first frequented by hunter-gatherers who built a small shrine at the site's natural spring.

The Natufians posed a serious quandary for the conventional wisdom about a close link between agriculture and settled life. It took a lot of research before the extent of the problem became clear. Some archaeologists questioned whether just building houses qualified the Natufians as truly sedentary, even if some of the dwellings did seem to be fairly permanent affairs. The debate occasionally centered on questions of terminology: if the houses were permanent but the people only occupied them part of the year, did that count? Other commentators questioned whether archaeologists were really capable of determining from their excavations whether particular sites were sedentary or not. In a 1989 article in the *Journal of Mediterranean Archaeology*, Phillip Edwards, an archaeologist at the University of Sydney in New South Wales, Australia, went down the long list of normal criteria—including settlement size, the shapes of buildings, the existence of storage facilities, and the seasonality of plants and animals found at Natufian sites—and concluded that none of them was sufficient to justify certainty.

Even if the Natufians were truly sedentary, were they the first prehistoric peoples to settle down? Paleolithic hunter-gatherers often established base camps, either out in the open or in caves, and there is evidence going back at least 2 million years that early humans liked to return again and again to the same spot. In 1954 the celebrated Czech archaeologist Bohuslav Klíma reported his discovery of hutlike structures, apparently constructed from timbers, stones, and animal hides, at 25,000-year-old Dolní Věstonice, a spectacular Upper Paleolithic site where prehistoric peoples hunted mammoths and fashioned figurines of animals and humans. A more controversial claim, made by French prehistorian Henry de Lumley, would put the earliest known huts (or at least tents) at 380,000-year-old Terra Amata, a Lower Paleolithic hunters' camp near Nice.

No one has claimed that any of these earlier sites, despite habitual occupation, were truly sedentary. One quite recent discovery suggests strongly that sedentism was a gradual development in human prehistory rather than an all-or-nothing affair. During the late 1980s a long drought in Israel caused a drastic drop in the water level of the Sea of Galilee. At the end of the decade the remains of a small camp—later radiocarbon dated to 23,000 calibrated years ago—began to emerge on the southwestern shore. When it was excavated by archaeologists from the University of Haifa and the Hebrew University in Jerusalem, the site, called Ohalo II, revealed the well-preserved remains of three huts made from brush plants, as well as a human burial and several hearths. The huts, which had been burned, were largely constructed from thick branches of tamarisk, willow, and oak trees, and then covered with thinner branches, grasses, and leaves. Their exceptional preservation was due to a lucky combination of the burning, which preserves plant remains, and the fact that they were submerged under water for so many thousands of years. Moreover, more than a hundred plant species have been identified at the site, from all four seasons of the year—suggesting, the excavators say, that Ohalo II was occupied year-round.

As for the Natufians, evidence that they too occupied their villages year-round has steadily accumulated in recent years. One of the most elegant studies was carried out by biological anthropologist Daniel Lieberman at Harvard University. Lieberman analyzed the teeth of gazelle found in Natufian layers (dated between 12,500 and 10,000 years ago) at the prehistoric site of Hayonim Cave in Israel, which was excavated by his former doctoral supervisor, Harvard archaeologist Ofer Bar-Yosef. (Although the Natufians lived in the cave, they were indeed architects:

Bar-Yosef, who has done as much as anybody in recent years to put the Natufians on the archaeological map, excavated six circular stone structures inside.) Lieberman looked at the growth patterns of a bonelike tissue called cementum, which is continuously deposited around the roots of mammalian teeth. However, in gazelles and many other animals, the rate of cementum deposition depends upon the season. During the warmer months of April to October, the rate is much higher than during the colder months of November to March. As a result, the teeth develop cementum growth bands of varying thicknesses, which can provide clues to when the gazelles were killed.

Out of thirteen well-preserved gazelle teeth from the Natufian layers at Hayonim, the cementum bands showed that eight animals had been killed sometime between April and October while five had been killed between November and March. That is, the gazelles had apparently been hunted year-round. In contrast, eight gazelle teeth from an earlier, pre-Natufian, layer at Hayonim, dated between 17,000 and 14,000 years ago, all turned out to be those of animals killed between November and March, an indicator that those animals were only hunted part of the year. When Lieberman extended his study to other Natufian sites in the Levant, the results came out the same.

Thus has the hammer of scientific evidence broken one link after another in the chain that once bound sedentism and agriculture together. Moreover, since sedentism apparently came first, settled human life cannot be considered simply a byproduct of the agricultural revolution. What, then, brought people together? Over the past two decades a small group of archaeologists and anthropologists has begun offering alternative explanations to this most profound of human mysteries. Four names stand out in particular: Barbara Bender, Jacques Cauvin, Peter Wilson, and Ian Hodder.

10 / The Domesticated Human

Do HUMAN BEINGS live together in large communities because they have to or because they want to? By "have to," of course, we could be referring to biological drives or instincts, economic or environmental necessity, or cultural pressures. Yet as humans, we know that we are capable of making exceptions to most every rule: the occasional desert island survivor or cave-dwelling hermit proves to us that we can shun society if we really "have to" or really "want to." And if we "want to" live in communities, does that mean that we do so of our own free will? Or have biological instincts, economic necessity, or cultural pressures made us think and feel that we "want to" when, like it or not, we really "have to"? Over the past several decades, archaeologists and anthropologists trying to explain sedentism and the Neolithic Revolution have swung back and forth between opposing types of explanations. As things stand today, they are roughly divided into two camps: some stress environmental factors, especially the role of the climatic changes at the end of the Pleistocene era and the beginning of the Holocene, while others prefer to focus on cultural and social factors, especially symbolism and religion. For better or worse, only a handful of researchers have tried to make biology and human evolution part of the story.

In 1968 Lewis Binford proposed, in his article "Post-Pleistocene Adaptations," that population pressures had pushed some prehistoric hunter-gatherers to the "margins" of food-rich zones, where they adopted farming so that they could eat as well as the people living in the centers of nature's bounty. Over the following decade, processual explanations dominated debates about the Neolithic Revolution. One of the most widely read and discussed works during this period was anthropologist Mark Nathan Cohen's 1977 book, *The Food Crisis in Prehistory: Overpopulation and the Origins of Agriculture,* which maintained that long-standing population pressures were behind the development of both sedentism and agriculture.

The first significant challenge to the New Archaeologists' hegemony over the debate came in 1978, when Barbara Bender, a Marxist archaeologist at University College London, published an article in the journal *World Archaeology* entitled "Gatherer-Hunter to Farmer: A Social Perspective." Bender rejected the notion that pre-Neolithic peoples were buffeted around helplessly by outside environmental, economic, and demographic pressures, responding blindly as any other animal species might do. This point of view, she charged, revealed a "strong techno-environmental bias" on the part of processual archaeologists, which Bender declared to be "unacceptable"—especially as an explanation of sedentism—because it left out social and cultural factors. She took particular issue with Cohen's thesis, arguing, among other things, that there was no archaeological evidence for population explosions in areas where food had been most plentiful.

In formulating her alternative view, Bender cited the work of anthropologists, including Claude Lévi-Strauss and Marshall Sahlins, demonstrating that present-day hunter-gatherers have extensive and complex social systems. Sahlins' contention that prehistoric hunter-gatherers must have represented the original "affluent society," and his skepticism about the advantages of farming, had earlier helped to inspire Binford's own hypothesis. But Bender argued that Binford and the New Archaeologists had overlooked the social complexity and sophistication that Upper Paleolithic peoples must have achieved over the long course of human evolution. Most likely, she wrote, they lived in bands or tribes and engaged in long-distance trade of valued items, such as obsidian and mollusk shells, which are found at both Upper Paleolithic and Natufian sites across the Near East. All this social activity, Bender suggested, would have been accompanied by the rise of social institutions and authority figures—leaders—to pull the bands and tribes together as well as arbitrate conflicts and disputes. "Leadership plays a vital role," Bender declared. "The leader both draws people to him and acts as a mediating focus for different units within the group. The leader both promotes and permits sedentism."

As for the development of agriculture, Bender dealt with it only briefly, assuming that increasing sedentism would logically result in increased local exploitation of resources and the invention of farming. But she did launch a preemptive strike against anticipated criticisms from processualist archaeologists that evidence about the kind of social and cultural factors she was emphasizing would be difficult to dig up, quoting the respected University of Chicago Near Eastern expert Robert Adams on the dangers of a narrow approach to hypothesis testing: "We should not be constrained by what we conceive to be the limitations of our data in our formulation of hypotheses; frequently this simply sets up a vicious circle."

Bender, as a Marxist archaeologist, focused on leaders, followers, and social institutions in proposing an alternative to what she saw as the New Archaeology's deterministic approach to the Neolithic Revolution. But her critique, and the wide attention it attracted among archaeologists, also demonstrated a growing willingness to consider factors much less tangible and testable than environment and demographics. Could it be, for example, that people came together because they shared not only the desire to eat and survive, but also the same view of the world, the same religious beliefs, the same deities—such as the goddess and the bull?

EVERY ONCE IN A WHILE someone will invent an idea so original and persuasive that even those who don't agree fall under its influence. Such was the power of the novel explanation for the Neolithic Revolution that French prehistorian Jacques Cauvin first put forward during the 1970s. In the early part of that decade Cauvin, together with the Dutch archaeologist Maurits van Loon, excavated the tell of Mureybet in northern Syria, which included both Natufian and Neolithic occupation layers. Cauvin was struck by the finding that the transition from the Natufian to the Neolithic period was marked by two important changes. First, the round houses typical of the Natufian eventually gave way to rectangular structures in the Neolithic, an indication that ideas about architecture were undergoing some sort of transformation. But even more dramatically, right at the transition point between the Natufian and the Neolithic—about 10,000 B.C.—the excavators discovered the skulls of huge wild bulls (aurochs), complete with horns, buried under the floors of the houses or embedded inside benches made of clay. The team also found the horns of aurochs, the extinct wild ancestor of domestic cattle, embedded in the walls of houses throughout the site's Neolithic period.

Slightly later in the stratigraphic sequence at Mureybet, between 9500 and 9000 B.C., the excavators uncovered a number of female figurines. Many of the statuettes had obvious breasts, although some were more vague and schematic in their form. And when Cauvin checked out what was happening at other ongoing or recently concluded excavations in the Near East, he saw the same pattern. The apparently sudden appearance of bull skulls and female figurines at the end of the Natufian could mean only one thing, Cauvin concluded: the Neolithic Revolution had been preceded by a "revolution of symbols," a change in collective psychology, that led to new beliefs about the world. And these new beliefs, Cauvin argued, were expressed through religious icons that at first took the form of what he called the woman and the bull.

Cauvin felt that the bull imagery was unmistakable, but he was cautious about concluding that the female figurines of the very early Neolithic period, schematic as they sometimes were, necessarily represented full-fledged goddesses. Yet he had little doubt that this was the case at later settlements such as Çatalhöyük, which was founded about 7500 B.C. "There we can perceive that this 'woman' is truly a goddess," Cauvin wrote in his book *The Birth of the Gods and the Origins of Agricul-*

ture, the most comprehensive exposition of his theory. In the celebrated figurine found by James Mellaart in a grain bin, which depicted an obese woman apparently sitting on a throne with her arms on the heads of two leopards, Cauvin saw "all the traits of the Mother-Goddess who dominated the oriental pantheon right up to the time of the male-dominated monotheism of Israel." And like Mellaart, who at Çatalhöyük had noted the juxtaposition of the goddess with wild animals such as leopards and vultures, Cauvin concluded that Neolithic peoples had regarded the goddess as the mistress of both birth and death—themes which, he pointed out, still resonate in modern human psychology. "The ambiguity of the symbol, where birth and death are joined, is readily decipherable for us who bear the 'terrible mother' in the deepest strata of our unconscious," Cauvin declared.

As for the symbolism of the bull, Cauvin saw little ambiguity: the animal represented the darker, male side of the human spirit. From Çatalhöyük to Minoan Crete to the bull-fighting rings of modern Spain, Cauvin saw the clear tracks of a masculine god that took the form sometimes of a human and sometimes of an animal. Cauvin wrote that "the culture recognizes something of itself in the animal and projects on to it some subliminal dimension of its collective psychology." He added, "The idea that the image of the wild bull signifies a brute force, instinctive and violent, is spontaneous in us and is without doubt universal."

Cauvin argued that the symbolic and religious dimensions of the Neolithic Revolution were much more fundamental than its technological aspects. He pointed out that the Natufians at Mureybet and other Near East sites had sickles for harvesting wild cereals and grains, grinding stones on which to pound the seeds and stems, and woodworking tools that were nearly identical in form to the hoes that Neolithic farmers would later use on the soil. "Until the much later invention of the plough and animal traction, the people of the Neolithic had no new tool to invent in order to pursue their strategy of farming production," Cauvin maintained, arguing that "everything they needed already existed in the Natufian culture, and sometimes even earlier, among the hunter-gatherers of the advanced Paleolithic."

Likewise he took a new look at the finding, at Mureybet and many other sites in the Near East, that the round houses of the Natufian gave way to rectangular structures as the Neolithic Revolution progressed. In

1972 Kent Flannery of the University of Michigan, an early disciple of Lewis Binford, published an influential paper interpreting this architectural evolution in terms of changes in social and family structures. Flannery concluded, from the archaeological evidence as well as anthropological studies of existing cultures in Africa and the Americas, that the circular huts were too small to accommodate an entire family. Rather they must have housed marital couples who were part of large, extended family structures that stored most of their food and other supplies in storage facilities outside the huts and shared communally most of what they had. Later on, once the Neolithic was well under way, these extended families clustered into nuclear families, which stored their food inside the house and kept it largely to themselves. Unlike the circular structures, the rectangular form, as a matter of simple geometry, allowed for subdivision into rooms and the creation of interior storage areas. Among the many implications, of course, is that notions of private property had their origin in the Neolithic.

Cauvin, along with some other archaeologists, took issue with various aspects of Flannery's argument, arguing among other things that it was not firmly based on the archaeological evidence. More important, Cauvin felt that Flannery's explanation was too mundane in light of the tumultuous revolution of symbols he saw unfolding in the Near East during the transition to agriculture. "Geometric forms have a deep significance in the human mind," Cauvin declared in *The Birth of the Gods and the Origins of Agriculture.* The symmetries of nature, such as those seen in stars, flowers, and the crystals of minerals, represent a universal and abstract "language," separate from the practical activities that people carry out in their daily lives. Cauvin, citing philosophers and historians of religion, argued that in this universal language, the circle or the sphere signifies "both that which transcends man and remains beyond his reach," such as "the sun, the cosmic totality, 'God.'" The rectangle, however, is rare or nonexistent in nature. It "requires human initiative for its existence . . . The square and the rectangle denote then the manifest, the concrete, that which has been realized."

In other words, Cauvin concluded, the Neolithic Revolution signaled an entirely new "mental attitude," a dramatically altered relationship between human beings and the natural world in which they lived—even if, on a regular basis, they felt the need to call upon gods and goddesses to help them through the travails of this new mode of existence. "Till then spectators of the natural cycles of reproduction in the living world, Neolithic societies now took it on themselves to intervene as active producers."

When Jacques Cauvin died in 2001, archaeologists were still actively debating his theories; specifically, just how well did his argument that a symbolic revolution had preceded the Neolithic fit with the growing archaeological record? Yet long before, Cauvin's insistence that ideology, religion, and psychology were paramount over technology, economy, and demographics had struck a chord with at least one archaeologist. During the late 1980s Ian Hodder, who was then struggling with the implications of his own rebellion against the New Archaeology, came across Cauvin's work. The argument that humans had undergone some sort of transformation on the eve of the Neolithic seemed convincing to Ian, but it also seemed that this transformation had yet another dimension to it, one that reflected the domestication of plants and animals, the taming of the wild nature that prehistoric peoples faced on a daily basis. Could it be that humans had to tame themselves before they could domesticate anything else? And if so, where else could this human domestication have taken place, other than inside the very houses they were now building?

In 1987 Ian took a sabbatical from Cambridge University. He spent six months of it at the Center for Advanced Study in the Behavioral Sciences at Stanford University in California. While there he performed two of his life's most important acts. First, he married Christine Hastorf. Second, he began writing the book that moved him yet another step closer to excavating Çatalhöyük. With *The Domestication of Europe*, Ian jumped right into the middle of the debates over the Neolithic Revolution.

Earlier that year Ian had written an analysis of the symbolism at Çatalhöyük for the annual bulletin of the Institute of Archaeology in London. Like Cauvin, he was struck by the powerful juxtapositions represented in the art. Women were associated with vultures, the skulls of bulls were brought into the house, and the dead were buried under the floors. While rereading Mellaart's reports and recalling the vivid slides

Mellaart had shown in the institute's lecture hall nearly twenty years before, Ian was also reminded of his later epiphany in the Nuba hut, when he had walked out of the sunlight and into a strange interior world decorated with depictions of women's breasts and the jaws of various animals.

As an early farming site, Çatalhöyük was supposed to be all about the domestication of plants and animals. The faunal expert working with Mellaart, Dexter Perkins, had concluded that the cattle actually underwent domestication during the life of the settlement, and archaeobotanist Hans Helbaek had found some fourteen domesticated crops in the site's upper levels. Why, then, were there so many paintings of wild deer hunts and men taunting huge bulls? Why not have some nice pastoral scenes of men and women in the fields hoeing and harvesting, or of shepherds tending their flocks? In his article for the bulletin, Ian, as had Bender and Cauvin before him, argued that previous processual explanations for the Neolithic Revolution were not adequate.

"Most theories for the origins of agriculture have not successfully explained the originality and creativity of the acts involved," Ian wrote, adding that "one is always left wondering why solutions other than agriculture were not adopted." He cited Cauvin's contention that symbolic and cultural factors must have been the prime movers:

> Cauvin . . . notes that, in the Near East, bull symbolism occurs prior to cattle domestication. He suggests that a large aurochs, as well as representing half a ton of meat on the hoof, was above all a dangerous force, appropriate for representing and evoking a thousand irrational fears and insecurities . . . Great emotional and psychological forces create new solutions as individuals try to deal with their fears . . . The driving force is not the need to tame the external world, but the need to tame the world within us . . . The taming of the wild is thus intimately connected to the ability to change society and also to control it.

In *The Domestication of Europe*, Ian expanded these initial ideas into a full-fledged model of his own. During the research for the book, he got a lot of help from the Stanford library, as well as from Ruth Tringham, who was just an hour's drive up the freeway at Berkeley. Ruth, who had excavated extensively at Neolithic sites in Serbia together with Mira Stevanovic, had her brain thoroughly picked by Ian, who ended up devoting two full chapters to Southeast Europe—a pivotal crossroads in the Neolithic's spread from the Near East to all of Europe. After an introductory chapter restating his analysis of the Çatalhöyük symbolism, Ian went on to review the evidence from across Europe, beginning with the celebrated site of Lepenski Vir, in the Djerdap Gorge of the Danube River in eastern Serbia, which was excavated in the late 1960s by the Yugoslav archaeologist Dragoslav Srejović. Lepenski Vir was first settled by hunter-gatherers and fishermen about 12,000 B.C., and later occupied by farmers. The earliest occupation of the site could be roughly compared with the Natufian occupation in the Levant. Srejović had uncovered trapezoidally shaped houses whose hearths were always at the eastern, more open end, toward the Danube. Beneath the floors near the hearths, Srejović found human burials, along with various structures he interpreted as altars and carved boulders that depicted everything from abstract designs to human heads that sometimes looked like fish.

Ian, following Srejović's own interpretations, concluded that representations of the dead dominated the houses at Lepenski Vir. "As at Çatalhöyük, death at Lepenski Vir is closely associated with the wild. Stag antlers occur in the graves and as 'offerings' behind the hearths. . . . The boulder art links humans, death and fish. The . . . wild resources exploited at Lepenski Vir . . . seem closely associated with the main symbolic metaphor used within the house—death."

As Ian moved across Europe from east to west and south to north, reviewing the archaeological data, he saw the same juxtaposition of houses, death, and the wild nearly everywhere. Some of the most striking examples came from the so-called linear tombs—called variously "long mounds" and "long barrows"—of central Europe and Scandanavia, which served as burial places during the later Neolithic period. Ian was able to demonstrate that after about 3300 B.C. the forms of these structures were increasingly patterned after the rectangular wooden houses that people inhabited during their lifetimes. In some cases the long houses and long mounds were so similar that archaeologists had a hard time telling them apart. Ian listed six points of similarity between them, including the placement of their entrances, the alignment of their axes, and the division of space within them.

Convinced that he had identified a dichotomy between the domestic and the wild in the Neolithic, Ian coined two key terms to characterize these opposing spheres. The house, and all of the activities that went on within it, he chose to call the *domus,* after the Latin root for the words "domestic" and "domesticated." A rough translation of the term, he suggested, would be the "home." Everything outside the house he called the *agrios,* after the Greek word for "wild" or "savage." (The Latin root is *ager,* which means "field"; the word *agriculture* thus literally means "the cultivation of a field.") In using these Latin and Greek terms, Ian hoped to invest the concepts of the domestic and the wild with the deeper symbolic meanings he believed they had during the Neolithic.

Ian suggested that the domus had its roots in the very first experiments with the building of huts and shelters in the Upper Paleolithic period and became well established by the time of the Natufians. "I expect that the house was always a safe haven, providing warmth and security, the focus of a child's early life, and the center of production," he wrote. A primary consequence of settling down, he argued, was that hunter-gatherers increasingly had to sacrifice immediate rewards to the needs of the larger group. The Natufians, for example, clearly stored food within their communities, a subsistence strategy that required everyone to have confidence in the rules, regulations, and social structures that dictated who was entitled to what, and when. The house became what Ian called the "central metaphor" for this social process:

> In early societies, the house would have evoked certain emotions including security and the social and cultural as opposed to the wild and natural...In the Natufian if not earlier, a creative link was made which was to have lasting and expanding consequences...The household is a production unit and it is through that production that the larger social unit is to be constructed. But it is also a conceptual unit opposed to the wild, the dangerous and the unsocial.

In other words, the house, in its larger significance as the domus, became the locus where people were domesticated and took their places within the larger community. The idea that humans had to take themselves in hand before they could form civilized societies was not new. Back in the nineteenth century the Victorian-era British economist Walter Bagehot had written, "Man, being the strongest of all animals, differs from the rest; he was obliged to be his own domesticator; he had to tame himself." But Ian gave the idea a new twist: the primary way that humans domesticated themselves, he argued, was by bringing the wild into the house and taming it. At Çatalhöyük, that meant burying the dead beneath the floors and mounting the skulls of wild bulls on the walls; in the Neolithic of Europe, it meant that the house and the burial place took on the same form. "The domus became the conceptual and practical locus for the transformation of the wild into the cultural," Ian concluded.

At the same time that Ian was at Stanford writing *The Domestication of Europe*, on the other side of the Pacific Ocean an anthropologist named Peter Wilson was writing his own book. Wilson, a professor at the University of Otago in New Zealand, was well known for his 1980 book *Man, the Promising Primate*, a sweeping review of human evolution. In 1988, two years before Ian's volume appeared, Wilson published a new book entitled *The Domestication of the Human Species*. Ian did not see Wilson's book until after his own was published, and vice versa. The two men, independently, were pursuing very similar themes, and both of their books would end up having a big impact on the way that both archaeologists and anthropologists thought about the Neolithic.

Like Ian Hodder, Wilson began by assuming that sedentism had preceded the invention of agriculture and that the house, as he put it, was "a dominant cultural symbol and a central rallying point and context for social organization and activity." Wilson traced the roots of human sedentism back to our evolutionary heritage as primates, and particularly the highly developed visual abilities of members of the primate order. "The primate emphasis on visual perception and visual display contributes to the more detailed, nuanced, and direct expression of mood, intention, and feeling than seems to be the case among other species. This in turn contributes to the more intense and varied emotional and intellectual lives lived by primates, particularly humans. Primates . . . live as much to keep each other company as to live simply in each others' company." Once humans developed language and began to speak, Wilson wrote, their ability to express themselves to each other vastly increased.

Wilson relied heavily on field studies of today's hunter-gatherers for his insights into the differences between their way of life and that of Neolithic farmers. He argued that the ties that bound Paleolithic hunter-gatherers together were "personal" rather than formalized, institutionalized, or governed by rules. "Neither extreme competition nor extreme cooperation have any place in hunter/gatherer social psychology," Wilson wrote, "because they require formal structure and rules, which are incompatible with a way of life that rides with the environment instead of attempting to control it." In domesticated society, on the other hand, "the sense of place, of belonging and of owning, becomes the key to a person's legitimacy and relation to others."

In one of his most provocative statements, Wilson argued that the organization of Neolithic peoples into nuclear families, and the apparent strong ties of kinship, were more a by-product of the desire for a sense of place than a direct cause of it: "In effect, kinship and especially descent, by virtue of their emphasis on generation, genealogy, and ancestors, contribute in a most important way to the creation of a sense of permanence, one of the primary aspirations of Neolithic life. The pivotal juncture of domestication, architecture, and kinship comes in the tomb, which is architecturally . . . and ideologically the focus, the center point, of many domesticated societies."

By the early 1990s the arguments against what Barbara Bender called the "techno-environmental bias" of processual models for the Neolithic Revolution had received a thorough hearing among archaeologists and anthropologists. Many were now convinced that symbolic, ideological, and psychological factors, while not necessarily the entire story, did indeed have to be taken into account. In the meantime the processualists were not just sitting around and watching the paradigm shift. They were doing serious research of their own into the causes of the Neolithic. Now, bolstered by new findings about the vagaries of early Holocene climates, they came up with an alternative model. The world of the Natufians had not been turned upside down by the goddess and the bull, the processualists declared, but by something called the Younger Dryas. No, the Younger Dryas was not the son or daughter of yet another Neolithic deity. It was a cold, sharp, downturn in the weather that made the Natufians reach for their animal skins and invent agriculture in a big hurry.

ABOUT 15,000 YEARS AGO life started looking pretty good for the hunter-gatherers of the Near East. The Last Glacial Maximum, the height of the Ice Age, was well behind them. The weather was getting both warmer and wetter. The mostly treeless steppe, where silvery wormwoods, shrubby chenopods, and stands of tall grasses once extended as far as the eye could see, began yielding to woodlands of oak, terebinth, almond, maple, and hawthorn. The same weather conditions triggered massive increases in the growth of the wild cereal plants that were native to the region. Archaeobotanist Gordon Hillman of the Institute of Archaeology in London, in a 1996 paper detailing the latest research into the ecology of this period, envisaged "a vast expanse of wild einkorn [wheat]" and "huge dense stands [of] wild barley and wild annual rye." The hunting was good too: dense herds of gazelles grazed just beyond the edges of the woodlands, and bands of docile fallow deer roamed among the trees.

These beneficent conditions would seem excellent for any people who wanted to settle down and partake of the bounty around them. And according to the archaeological record, that is exactly what happened. About 12,500 years ago in the Levant, the Natufians founded their first villages at 'Ain Mallaha, Jericho, the Hayonim Cave, and many other sites. Further inland, a similar culture of sedentary hunter-gatherers took root at Abu Hureyra on the Euphrates River in Syria. Yet this apparent Garden of Eden was short-lived. Just as the Natufians were settling in, the warming trend suddenly reversed.

Experts in reconstructing ancient environments had first spotted this new cold spell back in the 1950s, in the pollen record of northern Europe. Pollen analysis, or palynology, is a powerful technique for determining past climatic conditions, because—as any gardener knows—most plants and trees are fussy about things like temperature, sunlight, and water. Over thousands of years pollen grains and spores are often trapped and preserved in lake muds, peat bogs, or other sediments, leaving a stratified record of past vegetation histories. By coring into these sediments, identifying the pollen, and radiocarbon dating these stratigraphic layers, the palynologist can determine what was growing when. At the same time, some plants that do not produce much pollen can be identified in the cores from the fossil traces—called macrofossils—that they leave behind.

In northern Europe, pollen analysis had shown that the region was largely covered with tundra vegetation during the last ice age. As temperatures rose and the glaciers began to melt, the tundra gave way to birch and pine woodlands. But then, about 11,000 years ago, temperatures suddenly dropped, glaciers began to reform, and the woodland frontier moved southward, allowing the tundra—which was largely identified from macrofossils of the cold-adapted mountain avens, *Dryas octopetala*—to reestablish itself. Later research demonstrated that the Younger Dryas was not restricted to northern Europe; it was a worldwide phenomenon, and it has been identified in cores taken through the ice of Greenland. The Younger Dryas lasted about one thousand years, and represented a return to almost full glacial conditions.

For the first several decades after the discovery of the Younger Dryas in Europe, researchers working in the Near East were not sure how great its effect had been there, largely because of the small number of pollen cores that had been taken. Among those who made early attempts to reconstruct climatic conditions in the region was geographer Neil Roberts, who studied fluctuations in lake levels in Anatolia; but Roberts, who would later head the climate reconstruction team at Çatalhöyük, was only able to chart a fairly general cooling trend, which was not enough to pinpoint the Younger Dryas with any precision.

In 1992, however, Gordon Hillman, along with archaeologist Andrew Moore, who had led the excavations at Abu Hureyra, published a paper in *American Antiquity* reviewing the most recent research into Near Eastern climatic conditions. The paper shed new light on what the Natufians may have been up against. Moore and Hillman focused on two new lines of evidence: a new pollen analysis from the basin of Lake Huleh in northern Israel, which was carried out by Uri Baruch of the Hebrew University in Jerusalem and Sytze Bottema of the Biological-Archaeological Institute in Groningen, the Netherlands, and a study of plant food remains at Abu Hureyra, which had been first occupied by hunter-gatherers between about 11,500 to 10,000 years ago. The Lake Huleh study demonstrated that the ratio of tree pollen to that of grasses and steppe plants steadily increased in the postglacial period, until about 11,500 years ago, when it began to decrease again, reaching a low point about 10,650 years ago. Baruch and Bottema concluded that this millennium-long reversal represented proof that the Younger Dryas had indeed hit the Near East, and at roughly the same time as it hit Europe.

Meanwhile, at Abu Hureyra, Hillman and his team of archaeobotanists, who used flotation techniques to recover enormous amounts of ancient plant remains, had identified three different phases during the hunter-gatherer occupation of the site. The first phase, about 11,500 to 11,000 years ago, was marked by findings of fruit stones and seeds of hackberries, plums, and pears, along with wild einkorn wheat and wild rye. Then, around 11,000 years ago, there is an abrupt change: the tree fruits disappear, although there is an increase in wild cereals, as well as grasses and the seeds of the white-flowered asphodel plant, a member of the lily family. Finally, at around 10,600 years ago, there is an even more dramatic change in the plant profile. The asphodel seeds disappear and the wild cereals decline markedly. At the same time there is an increase of legumes such as clovers and medicks. These plants, Moore and Hillman suggested, "require careful detoxification" and thus should be regarded as " 'fallback foods,' which would generally have served as staples only when major plant foods were becoming scarcer." The botanical record at Abu Hureyra showed that things only got worse until about 10,000 years ago, when hunter-gatherer occupation of the site ended and, after a short gap, Neolithic farmers took over.

The Younger Dryas had hit right in the middle of the Natufian period in the Levant and its equivalent hunter-gatherer phase in Syria. The effects on food supplies were devastating. How had these early settlers survived? To Moore and Hillman, as well as many other archaeologists, the answer was very clear: they had invented agriculture. The Younger Dryas, they concluded, had "acted as a powerful incentive for the peoples of the Levant to develop new modes of subsistence." If nature could not provide an adequate supply of wild plants, then prehistoric humans would just have to do it themselves. But before they took this fateful step—which, after all, did not take place overnight—the Natufians made one last effort to adjust to the new situation they faced. During the so-called Late Natufian stage, they became less sedentary, largely abandoning their huts and villages for a more nomadic existence, possibly to follow the herds of gazelle, which were still plentiful on the steppe-lands that were now rapidly encroaching on the forests of oak and fruit trees. Then the Natufians disappeared from the archaeological record. Whether or not they later reappeared as Neolithic farmers, no one has been able to determine.

Moore and Hillman did not claim that the Younger Dryas was the only factor leading to the Neolithic Revolution, although they were convinced that it had been at least a "significant catalyst" in getting the revolution under way. The rise of sedentism, along with population growth, probably also contributed to this great next leap in human development, they suggested. But processual archaeologists still had little time for symbolic revolutions as causative explanations for the Neolithic.

ABOUT ONCE OR TWICE each year I sat Ian down for what I called a philosophical discussion about archaeology. On one such summer evening we were sitting on the Çatalhöyük veranda, drinking Efes beer and swatting mosquitoes.

"Ian, I've got a problem with all of these explanations," I said. "I don't think anybody in this debate has really explained sedentism. Your ideas about human domestication, and Peter Wilson's very similar take on things, seem to describe what was happening, what changes people were going through. But they don't explain why it all happened in the first place. I could make the same criticism of your domus model that you recently made of Jacques Cauvin's ideas."

Not long before our discussion, Ian had contributed a paper to a special issue of the *Cambridge Archaeological Journal* that featured the comments of a number of leading archaeologists on Cauvin's ideas. The occasion was the translation of Cauvin's book *The Birth of the Gods and the Origins of Agriculture* from French to English by Trevor Watkins, the University of Edinburgh archaeologist who had worked on the Çatalhöyük regional survey and led the first excavations at Pinarbaşi. Ian had pointed out that Cauvin gave no reason for the revolution of symbols, the mental shift that made the Neolithic Revolution possible. Ian wrote that he now preferred a model in which there had been a "long drawn-out domestication process with no clear beginning."

"I think that a lot of the domus stuff still works," Ian now said. "But there is a lot that doesn't. I think what I got wrong was the timing: the domus was a fairly late development. All sorts of things happened before that. Look at Ohalo II, on the Sea of Galilee, twenty thousand years ago, where you really have sedentary occupation, burials, houses, and it's all enormously early. But at first, agriculture is not a huge benefit to hunter-gatherers. Then later it does become significantly beneficial. Lately I have been thinking that the whole thing involves a process of what some people call material engagement. You become more entangled in material things, in material culture. You want to build a house, you want to make it out of clay, so you have to go get the clay. There are various social rites involved in getting the clay, and so you have a mushrooming of entanglements, not only in the material world but in the social and ritual world. And that whole process has a snowballing effect, a positive feedback effect. You end up being more sedentary and more tied by the material world to a particular place; you have to store food and other things nearby. And that creates the conditions for agriculture. Then there are a whole series of other changes going on, cognitive and symbolic changes, psychological changes. In fact what you create is an ability to change the world around you."

"But even if it was a long, drawn-out process," I said, "don't we have to try to trace it back somehow? For example, what about this cognitive shift you mentioned? Is that some sort of change in hardwiring, in the human brain?"

"No, not hardwired," Ian said. "It seems to me that this shift occurs through ritual, communal ritual. Look at the findings from Göbekli Tepe in southeast Turkey, the very early site where German archaeologists have found enormous carved pillars, some sorts of monuments, back around 9300 B.C. But they say there is no domestic architecture there that early. That's two thousand years before Çatalhöyük. You see similar things at Jericho in the Levant and Çayönü in southeast Turkey, with its skull cult. The focus is on ceremonial ritual centers. It's as if the communal is created first, and then the domus emerges out of that. Somehow it is the ceremonial that pulls people together, and that is something that does go back all the way into the Paleolithic."

"Don't we also have to look at the biological side of things?" I asked. "Remember that Peter Wilson, in *The Domestication of the Human*

Species, traced the whole thing back to the sociability and communication among primates. He seemed to see these traits as the evolutionary backdrop to human sociability and community. If we are going to talk about the Paleolithic, why not trace it back all the way? Even if the biological drive for community takes a cultural form, could it be that this sociability itself is hardwired? Maybe the cultural stuff is just the details, and the biology is the real scaffolding that holds everything together."

With that last suggestion I knew that I was being provocative. But Ian kept his cool.

"Then how do you explain the relative lack of it in the earlier Paleolithic?" he asked. "How do you explain why it didn't become expressed for so many hundreds of thousands of years? You are looking for a single cause, a single factor, and I don't think that works."

THE BIG MERCEDES bus pulled out of the Konya bus station and headed toward the highway to Ankara. The air conditioning was working, but I had still taken the precaution of asking for a seat on the left, or west, side of the bus, to keep the morning sun from blazing in my face. As we cruised north along the dry, flat Konya Plain, I thought about what Ian had said. Yes, perhaps it was a mistake to search for one overriding principle that would explain why people wanted to live together rather than apart. And yet, it really did seem that there was some driving force behind our choice to pull together as humans and live in communities, despite the often considerable disadvantages in terms of overcrowding, social strife, violence, and warfare. Otherwise why, over the past 10,000 or so years, have we continued doing it on an ever-grander scale, building not just villages but towns and cities, all the while inventing new ways to be connected to each other—the Internet, cell phones, and the Goddess knows what next.

I pulled out my notebook and pen and started to write: "From Tree Branch to Traffic Jam, a 10-Step Program." As a reporter for the journal *Science*, I had spent many years covering not only archaeology but also human evolution. Could I come up with a story that would trace the roots of sedentism and human community back to our very origins?

Step 1: The rise of the primates. Today there are well over 200 living species, which can be loosely characterized as lemurs, lorises, tarsiers, monkeys, apes, and humans. Some 350 extinct species are known from the fossil record, but primatologists consider this to be just a small fraction of the estimated 5,000 or more extinct species thought to have lived on earth dating back at least 60 million years. All living primates share certain characteristics that few other mammals have: their brains are bigger relative to body weight than those of most other mammals, they have exceptionally well developed visual abilities, and their hands and feet have five highly flexible digits, with one larger toe and often an opposable thumb. They also, unique among mammals, have Meissner's corpuscles, special nerve endings that make their hands and feet exquisitely sensitive to touch. And of all the living primates, apes and humans have the most Meissner's corpuscles.

Step 2: The primates go ape. The primates were fruitful and multiplied, spreading all over Africa, Europe, and Asia. Their manual dexterity and sensitive hands and feet made them well adapted to life in the trees. Then, sometime after 24 million years ago, a new type of primate shows up in the fossil record, most notably in Kenya and Uganda. It has a larger brain; its eye sockets are closer together and face fully forward, no doubt enhancing its binocular vision; and it has more flexible joints and no tail. This is the ancestor of modern apes such as chimpanzees, gorillas, orangutans, and humans. It still does very well in the trees, but it can also forage on the forest floor.

Step 3: The chimps and humans split. About 8 million years ago the evolutionary line leading to gorillas branched off, and sometime between 5 to 7 million years ago the chimp and human lines went their separate ways. Despite some important fossil discoveries in recent years, however, no one yet has found a fossil representing that last common ancestor of chimps and humans, although many researchers believe that it probably looked and acted like today's chimps. But which chimp? There are two species, the so-called common chimpanzee and the bonobo (formerly called the pygmy chimpanzee). Both are extremely sociable. But the societies of the common chimpanzee are male-dominated and often plagued by intergroup warfare; the bonobos, sometimes called the "make love, not war" ape, are female-dominant and peaceful, and they spend a lot of time having sex. Primatologists are still arguing about which is the better model for the first human ancestor—or is it perhaps a combination of both?

Step 4: Will the first bipedal hominid please stand up? Around 5 million years ago our ancestors began to walk on two feet. There are almost as many explanations for this as there are anthropologists studying the question. One theory, proposed in 1981 by C. Owen Lovejoy of Kent State University in Ohio and still often cited, puts the emphasis on male-female relationships and mating patterns. Bipedality, Lovejoy argued, freed the hands and allowed both hominid parents to gather more food for their kids. That meant that more of their offspring survived. (It also meant, later on, that the hands were free to invent stone tools.) This was a real departure, because in most primate species the male is not very involved in parenting, if at all. The evolution of "male parental investment," Lovejoy argued, led to monogamous mating behavior in early hominids and ultimately to the nuclear family.

Step 5: Our brains get bigger. The first hominids had fairly small brains, as did australopithecines like Lucy, as did the first members of the human species, *Homo habilis.* Seriously impressive brain expansion did not begin until about 2 million years ago with *Homo erectus,* that is, after 3 million years of hominid evolution had gone by. So what did we need those big brains for? Surely not for figuring out inventive new ways to pick fruits and dig termites out of trees. In 1993 psychologist Robin Dunbar and anthropologist Leslie Aiello proposed in the journal *Current Anthropology* that the tendency of early humans to live in increasingly large social groups was the driving force behind both brain expansion and the development of language. In an earlier study Dunbar had plotted brain size against group size among living primates and found that there was a close correlation: the bigger the group, the bigger the brain. Moreover, Dunbar demonstrated that the bigger the primate group size, the more time the animals spent in grooming, which is the glue of primate social life (and which no doubt makes those Meissner's corpuscles come in handy). The main purpose of a big brain, Dunbar and Aiello concluded, was to keep track of all those other social beings, who was who and who was doing what with whom. And since one can only groom so many other primates in the course of a day, the evolution of language allowed us to stroke each other with words instead of fingers.

Step 6: Humans get modern. Once we had evolved big brains, the world was our oyster. *Homo erectus* began to move out of its original home in Africa and colonize the world. Soon early humans were spread throughout Asia and Europe. As our social networks grew ever wider, our brains expanded even more, until—around 150,000 to 200,000 years ago—a new species of humans arose, probably in Africa. This was *Homo sapiens*, or the "modern" human. The moderns proceeded to take over all the niches previously occupied by earlier humans, until they were the only human species left. At the same time, the first convincingly symbolic expressions began to leave their traces in the archaeological record, in the form of etchings on pieces of bone, occasional beads, and ritualistic human burials. And many human evolution experts think that true human language—that is, the highly inventive, rapid-fire speech that we know today—actually dates from the advent of *Homo sapiens*, a species which, if nothing else, is incredibly social and communicative. As soon as humans could talk, it became much easier to transmit their cultures down to future generations. Indeed, psychologist Michael Tomasello has proposed that culture is continually enriched over time by a ratchet effect: that is, each generation starts off with all of the wisdom accumulated by all the previous generations without having to learn everything all over again.

Step 7: The Upper Paleolithic. Now symbolic expression is in full swing, with magnificent works of cave art, human and animal figurines, and beautifully carved bone tools. But some archaeologists and anthropologists believe that this pivotal point in human development, which began about 40,000 years ago, was also marked by a great intensification of the social networks that had been the hallmark of human behavior since the human-chimp split. In the course of successive ice ages, long-distance networks were essential to human survival. And they made human sociability a two-sided coin: on the one hand, they allowed and encouraged the existence of even more complex human social groups; at the same time they made possible what Harvard University anthropologist Richard Wrangham and his colleagues have called the "release from proximity"—the ability to maintain close relationships with other people even if they are far away and even if we seldom, or even never, see them. Humans are the only primates that do this. As the British archaeologist Clive Gamble put it, the closeness of the bond has nothing to do with proximity: "You may see your sister once a year at Christmas and the bus-driver every day on your way to work."

Step 8: Settling down with the Natufians. By 12,500 years ago, the Ice Age is well over, and, if Gordon Hillman's vision of vast fields of wild wheat and barley is correct, the Near East is a veritable Garden of Eden. The clear evidence of huts and other structures at much earlier sites such as Dolní Věstonice and Ohalo II demonstrates that building houses was something prehistoric humans had learned to do long before—no big deal. Now that environmental conditions are finally right, 5 million years of human ultrasociability find their expression at Jericho, 'Ain Mallaha, and the Hayonim Cave. It was just a matter of time before

Step 9: The Neolithic Revolution. The Younger Dryas may well have triggered the invention of agriculture, or given enough time surrounded by wild plants and animals, people may eventually have invented it without prodding. But why? If Marshall Sahlins was right, and hunter-gatherers—the original affluent society—were really better off than farmers, then the reasons for agriculture must be found elsewhere. Could it be that farming allowed people to continue to live together? That is what Sahlins himself implied in *Stone Age Economics:* "Agriculture not only raised society above the distribution of natural food resources, it allowed Neolithic communities to maintain high degrees of social order where the requirements of human existence were absent from the natural order . . . Culture went from triumph to triumph . . . until it proved it could support human life in outer space—where even gravity and oxygen were naturally lacking."

Of course, we could have stopped at Step 9. But we didn't. We just kept on going, becoming more and more sociable and more and more entangled in each others' lives, until, beginning about 5,000 years ago:

Step 10: The Urban Revolution. Cities, writing, entrenched social classes, organized warfare, advanced technology, traffic jams. Full-blown civilization.

I put down my pen and looked out the window. We were on the outskirts of Ankara. The highway was thick with cars and trucks, and the sky thick with pollution. In the course of a four-hour bus ride and ten easy steps, I had made it from tree branches to traffic jams. I had not, of course, necessarily solved the mysteries of sedentism and human communities. I had simply written a story, picking and choosing the evidence and points of view that best fit with my idea. Yet that fact that we did not stop at Step 9, the Neolithic Revolution, nor at any previous step—our human insistence on taking this whole process to its very limits—made me think that the answer might well be traceable back to our primate origins. If so, then it might be said that biology made us want to live together, the environment allowed us to do it, and culture—well, culture would be how we went about doing it, and why we've always done it in style.

11 / Fault Lines and Homecomings

NURCAN YALMAN, like most of the Turkish archaeology students who joined the Çatalhöyük team, was not from the Konya area. Konya was at the heart of a region of Turkey known for religious, social, and political conservatism, where independent-minded women like Nurcan did not easily prosper. Her father was from Istanbul and her mother from Izmir, two of Turkey's more cosmopolitan cities. Nurcan was born in 1969 in Ankara, Turkey's modern capital, where her father was then working as a prosecutor. She was the youngest of four sisters. The oldest sister went on to become a judge, the next one a sociologist, and the next a lawyer. Nurcan wanted to be an astronaut. But her teachers told her that was quite impossible in Turkey: the country had no astronauts, nor was it likely to any time soon. So Nurcan spent most of her high school years living in an imaginary world, dreaming of being in space.

Then one of her teachers showed the class a Japanese documentary film about the Silk Road, the ancient trade route that linked the east coast of China with the Mediterranean, a distance of some 4,000 miles. Now, instead of dreaming about space, Nurcan dreamed about mountains and deserts. She spent her time sketching landscapes and listening to the haunting music from the film's soundtrack, which had been composed by the Japanese musician Kitaro. As soon as she graduated from high school, she applied to Istanbul University, where she found her way into the archaeology laboratory of Mehmet Özdoğan, Turkey's leading expert on the Neolithic. Özdoğan, together with archaeologist Ufuk Esin, had been early supporters of Ian Hodder's quest to reopen Çatalhöyük. When Özdoğan asked Nurcan if she wanted to wash pottery shards, she felt blessed and chosen. Surely she was destined to be an archaeologist. So she asked him to take her on his upcoming excavations at Çayönü, an early Neolithic site in southeast Turkey that predated Çatalhöyük. Çayönü had been excavated during the 1960s and 1970s by the American archaeologist Robert Braidwood and his Turkish collaborator Halet Çambel; Özdoğan was now in charge of the dig. Özdoğan readily agreed, but Nurcan's normally liberal-minded parents had a fit at the idea of their daughter's going off to such a remote part of the country. Nurcan screamed and cried for several days until they gave in.

The following year Nurcan joined David French's rescue excavation at Tille Höyük on the Euphrates River, where Shahina Farid had also worked for many years. Nurcan, who was petite, dark-haired, and strikingly beautiful, created a sensation among the male archaeologists. She loved the picturesque village of Tille, where the archaeologists lived during the excavations. To her the people seemed the kindest, most wonderful people she had ever met. When the excavations were completed and the villagers were forced to move before Tille was covered over by the waters of the Atatürk Dam, Nurcan was inconsolable. "I cried for two years," she said later.

Nurcan's experiences with the Tille villagers convinced her that she really wanted to be an ethnoarchaeologist—an archaeologist who studies present-day cultures to gain insights into past behaviors. Yet hardly anyone was doing ethnoarchaeology in Turkey. When the excavations at Çatalhöyük started up, Özdoğan told her to go see Ian Hodder. Nurcan visited Ian during the 1994 season. He agreed to let her carry out an ethnoarchaeology project in the villages around Çatalhöyük. Nurcan thought that Ian was just being kind, but when she returned the following year, she saw that he was serious. Together with David Shankland, an anthropologist who had also been serving as acting director of the British Institute of Archaeology at Ankara since David French's 1993 retirement, Nurcan began visiting local villages and talking with the people to see what insights she could gather about how they built their own mud-brick houses and how they found their raw materials. When she was not busy doing that, Nurcan found herself pressed into service as a translator or as an extra hand in Building 1, where Roger Matthews was always chronically short of excavators.

While Nurcan was growing up in Ankara, Mavili Tokyağsun was growing up next door to Çatalhöyük, in the village of Küçükköy. Mavili was born in the village during the summer of 1973, although she does not know the exact date. The villagers do not keep track of time that closely. However, her mother later told her that the zucchini flowers were blooming when she was born. So each summer, when the zucchinis bloom again, Mavili celebrates her birthday. As a young girl Mavili had dreams of traveling abroad, but in her conservative village, girls seldom even go to school. She had to content herself with long walks into the local hills to feed the family's sheep and goats.

In the early 1990s Mavili married a young man from the village, but the marriage did not work out. In 1994, heavily pregnant with her son, Ferdi, Mavili left her husband. She later divorced him. In some Turkish villages, especially in eastern Turkey, her family might have killed her for doing that, as a matter of honor. But Mavili's brothers, Mustafa and Hasan, took her side and protected her. Nevertheless, as the village's only divorcée, Mavili—whose dark eyes and mischievous smile would normally make her one of the most attractive women in Küçükköy—seemed unlikely to find another husband. She spent a summer after the divorce working in a hotel in Ula, a small town near Turkey's heavily touristed Mediterranean coast. But Mavili's one chance at travel was short-lived. She was a single mother with a small child. She soon returned to the village, where her mother could help her take care of Ferdi.

Meanwhile Mustafa and Hasan had begun working as guards at Çatalhöyük. Other villagers were hired as workmen or for other tasks.

While the team was still living in Çumra, Mavili was asked to prepare the lunches, which she cooked at her house in Küçükköy and brought onto the site each day. When the dig house opened for business, in 1996, Mavili was taken on as one of the house staff, working in the kitchen and helping to keep the place clean. Mavili was happy as a lark. Her dreams of travel had not come true, but now people from all over the world came to her.

EVERYONE WHO CONVERGED on Çatalhöyük had their own reason for being there, their own special role to play. For Ian Hodder, Çatalhöyük was his one big chance to prove that his post-processual rebellion against the New Archaeology was more than just theoretical pie in the sky. For Roger Matthews, Shahina Farid, Roddy Regan, Mary Alexander, and the other excavators, it was the chance of a lifetime to dig at one of the Near East's most famous and exciting sites. For Wendy Matthews, Nerissa Russell, Louise Martin, Christine Hastorf, Julie Near, and other specialists on the dig, Çatalhöyük was a laboratory for cutting-edge archaeological science. Everyone on the dig shared the common goal of making Çatalhöyük one of the best studied and recorded archaeological sites ever. The archaeologists worked long hours, sometimes seeming to compete for who was going to be the last one to stop and go to bed. As the 1996 season went on, everyone was getting more tired and more stressed out. The situation was ripe for drama and conflict.

It soon became clear that the priorities of the excavators and specialists were not always entirely compatible. Indeed, during the 1995 season, the first signs had arisen of conflict between the excavators, who wanted to dig at a reasonable speed, and the specialists, whose need for systematic sample taking tended to slow things down. The conflict also reflected Ian's constant struggle to reconcile the expectations of the sponsors and the public for dramatic results with the principles of high-definition, contextual archaeology. It also tracked the different world-views of contract excavators and university-based archaeologists, and the long-standing feeling among professional diggers that their highly skilled work was not sufficiently valued by the academics. In 1996 these tensions broke into the open, splintering the community of archaeologists into two camps and threatening the future of the dig.

In late August Shahina and her crew had noticed what seemed to be a sharp fault line in a wall separating two spaces in one of the south area buildings. A whole section of mud bricks had shifted, along with the corresponding part of the house's floor. The team debated whether this shift represented an ancient earthquake or whether it was just the result of a slumping of the structure over the millennia. Carolyn Hamilton, a social anthropologist from the University of Witwatersrand in Johannesburg, South Africa, who had come to Çatalhöyük for a month to observe the archaeologists at work, immediately adopted the phrase "fault lines" to describe the conflicts she saw brewing among the team. Earlier in the season Shahina's excavator diary had already begun reflecting the frustrations she was feeling. "Please no more samples!" she pleaded in her entry of August 10. Wendy Matthews, whose micromorphology studies required the most intensive sampling—and who frequently organized the taking of samples for chemical analysis and other tests—was often the focus of resentment. Some days later Shahina complained in her diary that Wendy had been "adamant" about taking two samples from a plaster wall, even though Ian had suggested that they could get away with only one.

The excavators were especially resentful about the "specialist tours" that Ian had organized to help foster ongoing reflexivity about the excavation process. Every day the specialists would troop up to the trenches, pens and notebooks in hand, to exchange ideas and interpretations with the diggers. To the specialists these expeditions were an opportunity to put their work in context, and also to take a refreshing break from the grind of processing samples in the lab. But to the excavators these encounters were often premature and sometimes highly annoying, especially when they resulted in requests for yet more samples. Carolyn Hamilton, whose curious inquiries into the conflicts made her both a confidante and a shoulder to cry on for both sides of the argument, later described what she saw as the source of the excavators' frustrations: "Laboratory staff demands on field staff were deemed by the latter to be intolerable," Hamilton wrote. "Every time the excavators recognized a new unit, they were obliged to plan it, take spot heights, fill out a unit sheet, take a [flotation] sample from the center of the unit, an archive sample, and on occasion an average sample, a residue sample, pot sample, a photograph and a host of other possibilities."

Roddy Regan, a burly, red-haired Scot from Edinburgh with ten years of digging experience in Great Britain and Italy, did little to hide his increasing impatience with the specialists. He would often tease Wendy as she took her samples, pointedly leaning on his large mattock—which the other excavators sometimes called Big Pick—while she worked away with her intricate Wendy tools. As the season wore on, Roddy began showing up at evening seminars clutching a beer in his hand and ready to debate the specialists on whatever happened to be the topic of the day. At one seminar Roddy and Wendy got into an argument over how close to the floors of the mud-brick buildings the excavators should dig before they called the specialists in. Wendy complained that the diggers were not leaving enough of the floor deposits to analyze. "How do we know it's a floor until we get down to it?" Roddy demanded. The argument summed up the entire conflict: the excavators felt that they had been trained to dig and didn't need the specialists to tell them how to do it; the specialists felt that the excavators were minimizing the specialists' contributions to the project and treating them as interfering nuisances.

Soon afterward Roddy went to Ian and told him that he was going to quit. This was a wake-up call to Ian that something had to be done to resolve the dispute. Many members of the team suspected that, up until then, Ian had seen the conflict between excavators and specialists as some sort of creative tension that would ultimately work to the overall benefit of the excavation. But creating tension was the opposite of what Ian really wanted. He was trying to put his ideas about contextual archaeology into practice, which required a close integration between the excavators and the specialists so that the gap between raw data and interpretation could be bridged. He had hoped to retrain both excavators and specialists, who were used to working in their separate domains, to come together and do archaeology differently.

Instead the distance between the two groups had only grown. "For me the major worry was that the whole idea of feedback and interaction seemed threatened," Ian wrote in his diary. He concluded that "the emphasis had shifted too much in favor of the lab people and their endless questions and specialisms." Ian called a meeting of all the diggers in which he gave them permission to decline requests from the specialists if the requests would compromise the digging schedule. Ian also proposed that the excavators contribute a paper about their perspectives at the upcoming Theoretical Archaeology Group (TAG) meeting in Liverpool in December.

The TAG meeting was an annual event where archaeologists debated the field's multitudinous theoretical issues. Ian had originally decreed that all of the presentations by the Çatalhöyük team should be authored collectively, without naming individuals. He decided to make an exception in the case of the excavators, who would now be named on the papers and given a separate voice. Ian did not seem to realize that this move was sure to exacerbate the divisions between excavators and specialists, which were already near the breaking point. Some of the laboratory staff felt that Ian was taking sides by inviting only the excavators to present their side of the story. They also resented being pigeonholed as "specialists." Most of them also had years of excavation experience, even if they were academic archaeologists rather than contract archaeologists.

Around this time Louise Martin had to leave Çatalhöyük and return to London to teach at the Institute of Archaeology. Rissa Russell, who had not been been contributing to the excavator diaries on the project's computers, now decided to begin a private diary, in part to keep Louise informed of events. "Why are the excavators . . . the only ones to have a voice at TAG?" Rissa asked her diary in late September. The specialists were particularly concerned when Shahina and the other excavators videotaped what was supposed to be a "typical" specialist tour in a way that the lab people suspected was designed to ridicule them. The specialists assumed that the video was to be shown at TAG, although, in fact, Shahina and the others had only intended it as a practice exercise. Rissa, as an American, thought that the best approach might be to air her feelings openly. That day at lunch she and Wendy took up the issue with Shahina. Shahina, insulted that they would think she was out to ridicule them, stalked out of the room, leaving the other two on the verge of tears. When Ian later scolded Rissa and Wendy for upsetting Shahina, they both figured that this would be their last season at Çatalhöyük.

Then, over the following days, everyone pulled back from the brink. Ian finally realized that the excavator-specialist conflict was jeopardizing the future of the excavations. As dig director, it was his responsibility to set things right and pull the splintered community back together. Ian began making the rounds, meeting with people individually and in groups and trying to get them to air their feelings about what had happened. For Ian, whose shyness and emotional reticence made it difficult for him to talk about his own feelings, getting others to talk about theirs was one of the hardest things he ever had to do.

The healing process now took hold. Roddy, satisfied that the excavators' concerns had been heard, decided not to quit after all. And the specialists were reassured that Ian was not going to take sides. When the excavators' video was shown in Liverpool that December, it was much more conciliatory than the specialists had expected. The video featured Shahina, Roddy, and Mary Alexander standing in one of the south area trenches and voicing their concerns about the specialists' demands, including their feelings that, as diggers, their work had not been valued as much as that of the laboratory staff. But they also praised Wendy by name for her contributions to the excavations and concluded that in future years it would be easier to strike a balance between the dig's conflicting priorities. Despite the swirl of differing egos, personalities, and agendas, the archaeologists at Çatalhöyük had resisted the temptation to let the dispute destroy the project. The bonds that held their fledging community together had frayed, but they had not broken. Everyone later agreed that the team emerged stronger and more united in its common goal: to understand what had brought Çatalhöyük's Neolithic community together, so many thousands of years before.

THIRTY-ONE YEARS had now passed since James and Arlette Mellaart had last set foot on Çatalhöyük. The Turkish authorities had never lifted the ban they had imposed in 1965. While the Mellaarts had occasionally visited Istanbul, where their son, Alan, lived, the great Neolithic mound had remained off limits. At the end of the 1995 season Ian, Shahina, and several other members of the team celebrated Mellaart's seventieth birthday by taking a goddess-adorned cake to his London apartment. Soon afterward Ian began to feel that it was time to offer Mellaart a more substantial gift: a visit to the new excavations. Ian had a number of reasons for wanting to arrange this. For one thing, it would fulfill the pledge he had made to Mellaart, when the senior archaeologist gave his blessing to the reopening of Çatalhöyük, that he would serve as a consultant on the dig, even if only informally. Indeed, both Ian and Shahina were eager to get Mellaart's help in finding the exact location of the old deep sounding in the south area of the mound, as well as with filling in other details of the 1960s excavations. Ian also felt that he and Mellaart needed to perform the symbolic passing of the torch, a ritual that could only take place on Çatalhöyük's hallowed soil. For Mellaart, it might represent a cleansing ritual that could help erase the stain on his reputation, a homecoming that would reunite him with the site of his life's greatest achievement.

Before Ian could invite Mellaart to Çatalhöyük, he needed to get the Turkish authorities to lift the ban. During a visit to Ankara, Ian went to see Engin Özgen, the director general for monuments and museums. Özgen, a Classical archaeologist who had studied for his Ph.D. at the University of Pennsylvania during the 1970s, had earlier given Ian a great deal of help in cutting through bureaucratic red tape to get the Çatalhöyük excavations going again. He was a lively, barrel-chested man with twinkling eyes, black hair, and a black goatee. He spoke English well and loved to play jazz on a stereo he kept in his office. As Ian laid out his arguments, Özgen stroked the goatee with his thick fingers, responding occasionally with a smile and a nod. When Ian was done, the director general thought for several minutes before finally speaking. "As you know, this is a very sensitive issue. Personally I have no objection to it. But I cannot give you an answer before consulting with my colleagues in the culture ministry. The minister himself may have to make the final decision."

The Turks had not forgotten Mellaart, nor the Dorak affair. He had never excavated another site, but as the ancient mound languished on the Konya Plain, undug and neglected, Mellaart had done everything he could to keep its memory—and his own reputation—alive. Arlette's photographs of wall paintings and goddess sculptures soon became staple illustrations for textbook discussions of the Neolithic period. And from his exile at the Institute of Archaeology in London, Mellaart continued to be a formidable presence in Near Eastern archaeology. His 1967 book, *Çatal Hüyük: A Neolithic Town in Anatolia*, was an instant classic, required reading for any student of the prehistory of Anatolia. Mellaart published several more books during the 1970s, including *The Archaeology of Ancient Turkey* and *The Neolithic of the Near East*; many archaeologists still consider the latter volume, although now out of date, to be the most comprehensive survey of the Neolithic period ever published.

Çatalhöyük was James Mellaart, and James Mellaart was Çatalhöyük. That state of affairs might have endured indefinitely, had he been content—in his books and lectures—to stick to the findings published in his first reports in *Anatolian Studies* and in the 1967 volume. But around the mid-1980s Mellaart began showing brightly colored sketches of what he called "reconstructed" Çatalhöyük wall paintings to students taking his Anatolian prehistory classes. These drawings depicted highly detailed scenes of erupting volcanoes, goddesses surrounded by vultures and leopards, and intricate patterns that seemed to resemble those on the handwoven Turkish carpets called kilims. Most of them were much more elaborate than anything Mellaart had previously published from Çatalhöyük, either as drawings or photographs. He explained to the students that they were the result of years of painstaking reconstruction of plaster fragments that had fallen from the walls of Çatalhöyük's mud-brick buildings.

As word got around the institute about Mellaart's new claims, many eyebrows were raised, but no one immediately challenged what he was saying in the classroom. Mellaart, who had now been on the faculty for more than two decades, was nearing retirement. His imaginative flamboyance had long been indulged by the institute's faculty and directors. Indeed, the current director, prehistorian John Evans, was an old friend of Mellaart's. But in early 1987 Mellaart began posting some of the reconstructions on the bulletin board next to his office on the third floor. Anatolian experts outside the institute soon heard about the new paintings, which had never been reported in the archaeological literature. Two of them approached John Evans to complain: Dominique Collon, an archaeologist at the British Museum, who also happened to be the niece of Mellaart's old boss at the BIAA, Seton Lloyd; and David Hawkins of the School of Oriental and African Studies in London. Hawkins, who had also known Mellaart for many decades, had a particularly keen memory of Çatalhöyük. He and another archaeologist had arrived at Mellaart's excavations the evening in September 1965 that the Beycesultan workmen were accused of stealing artifacts. The next morning, when the two had woken up, the workmen were gone.

At the insistence of Collon and Hawkins, Evans agreed to convene a seminar at which Mellaart would be asked to back up his claims about the paintings. Mellaart's talk was scheduled for two P.M. on June 11, 1987, in a small seminar room on the second floor. A few days before, a flyer announcing the seminar appeared on the institute's bulletin boards. No one who was involved could recall who prepared the flyer, nor who posted it. As the appointed hour approached, the crowd of students, faculty, and visitors in the second floor hallway grew so dense that the seminar had to be moved to the large ground-floor lecture hall. As Mellaart danced around the stage, flashing slide after slide on the large screen behind him and obviously relishing all the attention, the audience became increasingly restless. Finally the projector was switched off and the questions began. One of the first hands to go up belonged to Edith Porada, a professor of Near Eastern art at Columbia University in New York. Porada, who had been Dominique Collon's Ph.D. supervisor, happened to be visiting London at the time. "Do you really expect us to believe all this?" she asked.

Then Collon, who had carefully prepared her questions beforehand, began going down the list on her notepad. How, she asked, could Mellaart explain the discrepancies between his original reports in *Anatolian Studies* and what he was saying now? Mellaart was now claiming that there were paintings on certain plastered walls which he had previously reported had no paintings at all. Moreover, Collon went on, he was now reporting having found colors of paint—especially a striking shade of blue—that were absent from any of the earlier reported paintings, which were rendered in red and black. Mellaart stuck to his guns. The question-and-answer period ended in a stalemate. As the crowd filed out of the lecture hall, Collon and Hawkins looked at each other dejectedly. The only thing left to do, they decided, was to go to the local pub and have a stiff drink.

But the matter did not end there. Two years later Mellaart's claims surfaced again, this time before a much larger public. In 1989 Mellaart teamed up with two well-known experts on Turkish carpets to publish a lavishly illustrated, four-volume work entitled *The Goddess from Anatolia*, which featured illustrations of forty-four of the "reconstructed" Çatalhöyük paintings. Many of these paintings depicted intricate patterns, again similar to those found on Turkish kilims. These claims were not entirely new. Mellaart had long maintained that there was a connection between the geometric designs depicted in some of the Çatalhöyük paintings and the colorful kilims sold all over Turkey today. Indeed, he had reported a number of these paintings in his 1960s publications. In his 1967 book, for example, he declared that "it seems now likely that kilims have been woven in Anatolia since the late seventh millennium B.C. or for at least the last eight thousand years." At a talk before the IV International Conference on Oriental Carpets, held in London in 1983, Mellaart had electrified the audience with a slide show of Çatalhöyük wall art.

The publication of *The Goddess from Anatolia* also electrified the kilim market. "Kilims that had been a 'hard sell' at $2,000 were fetching prices in the vicinity of $50,000 or more," remarked Murray Eiland III, an Oxford University archaeologist and carpet scholar, in a commentary in the journal *Antiquity*. But while some rug dealers were thrilled, others—along with a large number of archaeologists—were scandalized by what they saw as the lack of evidence for Mellaart's claims. Dominique Collon made her own doubts known in an article in the September 1990 issue of the leading carpet magazine *Hali*, which earlier that year had given prominent coverage to a talk Mellaart gave at the Anatolian Kilim Symposium in Basel, Switzerland. Collon recalled Mellaart's explanations at the Institute of Archaeology seminar in 1987, in which he said that the original tracings of the plaster fragments had been destroyed in the fire that burned down Arlette's wooden *yali* on the Bosphorus in 1976. Mellaart said that he had assumed that the reconstructions he had made from these tracings were also destroyed but that during the early 1980s they had turned up again in his London office. "This would explain the total lack of any surviving corroborative evidence for these paintings," Collon remarked, before going on to detail what she termed the "numerous discrepancies" between what Mellaart had originally published and what he was saying now.

Some rug dealers, worried about the credibility of the scholarship that underlay the aura and the market value of Turkish kilims, also took public issue with Mellaart. Marla Mallett, a reputable rug dealer based in Atlanta, Georgia, undertook an even more detailed critique of Mellaart's claims. In two lengthy articles in *Oriental Rug Review*, Mallett reported on her wall to wall review of the findings Mellaart had published in his 1960s reports. Like Collon, Mallett concluded that Mellaart was now claiming the existence of paintings on walls that previously had been said to have none. She also noted that none of the participants in the original dig at Çatalhöyük who were still alive had any memory of seeing the original plaster fragments from which Mellaart had reconstructed the paintings.

Most of the critics had been reasonably polite and respectful of Mellaart's previous accomplishments and original reports, which no one questioned. Few came straight out and accused Mellaart of deliberately fabricating the reconstructed paintings, preferring instead to suggest that Mellaart had let his imagination run away with him. But Harvard University archaeologist Carl Lamberg-Karlovsky, responding to an earlier positive review of *The Goddess from Anatolia* by Marija Gimbutas, did not mince his words. "Bluntly put, there is no objective reason to believe that these 'new' wall paintings at Çatal Hüyük exist," he wrote in the spring 1992 issue of *Review of Archaeology*. Lamberg-Karlovsky, after pointing out that he had known and admired Mellaart for many years—"he introduced me to the existence of Scotch malt"—concluded sadly that a "competent scholar and a most important archaeological site have been badly discredited."

Yet Mellaart stuck to his claims. In an article in the February 1991 issue of *Hali*, entitled "James Mellaart Answers His Critics," he tackled most of the points made by his doubters. Mellaart wrote that the fairly intact paintings reported in his previous publications—that is, those which had remained on the plaster walls and were photographed or drawn in situ—represented only "a minority of the whole." Meanwhile, he said, "extreme care" had been taken to record the plaster fragments, "which did not respond well to photography in their often worn, partly burned or smoke-stained state." Mellaart repeated his earlier explanation that the "drawings, tracings, notes on color, etc., made in the field, together with color slides and black-and-white photographs of the better pieces," had been destroyed in the fire in the house on the Bosphorus. As for why he was now reporting paintings on walls that previously he had said were blank, Mellaart argued that the earlier publications had only reported those paintings found intact on the walls, "not those found afterwards below the floors, in patches above them, or discarded when renovations took place."

Mellaart also complained that his critics did not understand the preliminary nature of his original reports. "These disputed paintings were not mentioned . . . either because they had not been reconstituted from fragments at the time, or because further excavation was required to establish their place in the sequence of successive paintings," he wrote, and concluded with a warning that in the future archaeologists will "have to put disclaimers on preliminary reports or cease to produce them, with disastrous consequences for research and the exchange of information." Mellaart ended his article with a comment about the Dorak affair, which Collon and many other critics had mentioned in the context of evaluating Mellaart's credibility. In response to this resurrection of Dorak, he quoted a lengthy section from the report to the directors of the British Institute of Archaeology at Ankara by Kathleen Kenyon's committee of inquiry into the Dorak affair, in which Mellaart was fully exonerated.

IAN HODDER, at the time he decided to invite Mellaart to visit Çatalhöyük, was well aware of all this recent history, but he had decided that he did not want to get involved in it. He was sincerely grateful to Mellaart for giving his blessing to the reopening of Çatalhöyük. He had no desire to engage in polemics against him, nor did he feel he needed to. Those who felt strongly one way or the other on the matter had already expressed themselves publicly. From time to time some archaeologists working at Çatalhöyük would argue that something had to be done to distance the new team from Mellaart's claims, out of concern that the general public—not to mention other archaeologists—would be confused about what had been found at the site. Ian told them that he did not object to anyone else doing this, either by publishing an article or in some other public forum. But he made it clear that he was not going to do it himself.

Engin Özgen finally got back to Ian to say that Mellaart's visit to Çatalhöyük had been approved. There were, however, a number of conditions. It must be made clear to everyone that this was a private visit, at Ian's personal invitation. The Turkish news media must not be told about it. The visit had to be brief, a day or two at most, and Mellaart could not stay overnight at the site. When Ian called Mellaart to give him the news, he and Arlette were delighted. They made plans to come to Çatalhöyük in September, toward the end of the 1996 season. On September 15 they arrived in Konya by bus from Ankara. Ian put them up in Konya's best hotel. The next morning he went to pick them up in the Land Rover. As Ian and the Mellaarts arrived in the dig house courtyard, a crowd of archaeologists gathered around excitedly, as if greeting a celebrity. Mellaart bounced out of the Land Rover, his face beaming, while Arlette looked on with a satisfied smile. The couple were whisked to the most comfortable chairs on the veranda, where they were served Turkish tea. Mellaart immediately began holding forth about the old days at Çatalhöyük and how many buildings he had dug in just four seasons.

Ian then took the Mellaarts on a tour of the excavations. The first stop was Building 1, where Roger and his crew were busy digging. "What a grotty building!" Mellaart exclaimed. "This is obviously a domestic house, not a shrine." Ian and Roger looked at each other glumly. Ian pointed to a horn of a large bull that was sticking out of one of the mud-brick walls, but Mellaart did not seem impressed. As the group reached the south end of the mound, however, Mellaart became much more animated. He recognized the outlines of the trenches he had dug forty years before. Shahina watched him approach, ready with the question she had been waiting two years to ask him: where was the deep sounding?

Without hesitating, Mellaart pointed to a spot right next to the north end of the building that he had designated Shrine 8. "Right under there," he said. Mellaart then noticed Roddy Regan, who was standing nearby, leaning on Big Pick. Mellaart lit up. "I'm glad to see that people are still using those things!" he said approvingly.

James and Arlette stayed for lunch in the dining room, where Ian had arranged for a bottle of whiskey—one of Mellaart's favorite beverages—to be placed on every table. There were speeches and toasts, and then more speeches and more toasts. Arlette's eyes glistened with tears. Mellaart chatted away, basking in the glow of his homecoming. At one point he leaned over to Ian and said that it was just possible that Building 1 was a shrine after all.

The next day the Mellaarts, Ian, Christine, and the twins, Nicky and Kyle, piled into the Land Rover for a day trip to Aşikli Höyük, where they had a picnic by the river while the boys played and swam. That

James and Arlette Mellaart in the early years of their marriage. Arlette loyally followed Mellaart on the ups, and then the downs, of his controversial archaeological career, including his ejection from Turkey after the mysterious "Dorak Affair."
Courtesy of James and Arlette Mellaart

Ian Hodder came to Çatalhöyük to prove that his rebellion against traditional archaeological approaches was more than just theoretical pie-in-the-sky. Despite major achievements at the site, his new methods continue to be controversial.
Courtesy of Tim Ready/Science Museum of Minnesota

Nearly a hundred archaeologists and other experts flock to work at Çatalhöyük each year. The 1998 team poses in front of the site's dig house. *Courtesy of Çatalhöyük Research Project*

The people of Çatalhöyük were among the world's first farmers. These bins in Building 5, fashioned from clay, were probably used to store lentils, wheat, and barley. *Courtesy of Çatalhöyük Research Project*

Excavations in the south end of Çatalhöyük's huge mound. The Neolithic settlers built their houses one atop the other, always leaving a portion of the mud-brick walls to serve as new foundations. *Courtesy of Çatalhöyük Research Project*

The “American” team at Çatalhöyük, which was given its own building to dig, is led by British archaeologist Ruth Tringham (foreground), a professor at the University of California, Berkeley. *Courtesy of Çatalhöyük Research Project*

The Neolithic settlers partitioned their houses into smaller spaces, and apparently followed strict rules about what kinds of activities took place in each. A number of human skeletons was found in the spaces behind the mud-brick wall labeled “feature 1026.” *Courtesy of Çatalhöyük Research Project*

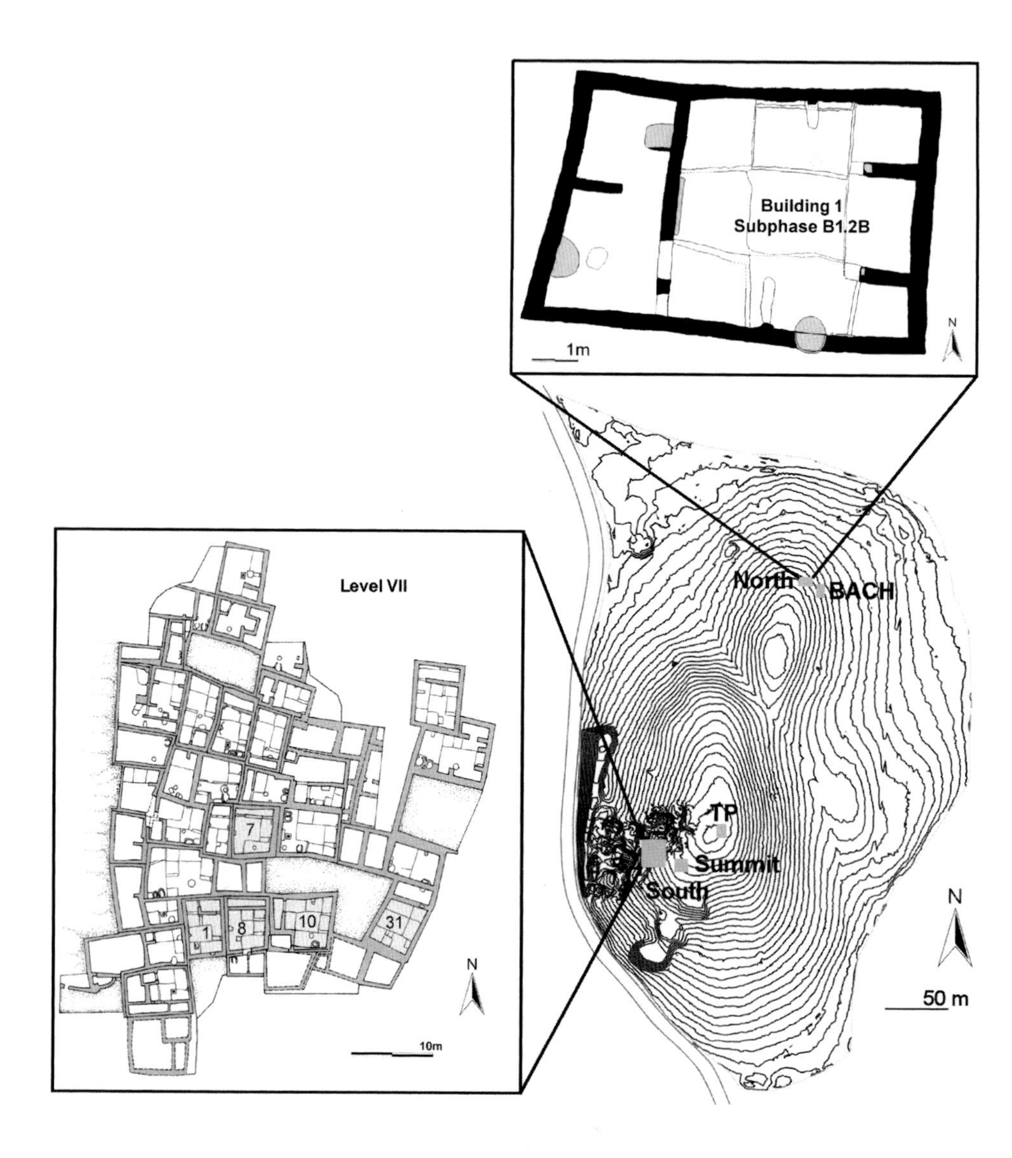

Çatalhöyük's 32-acre mound (contour map at right) was discovered in 1958 by James Mellaart, who excavated it during the 1960s. In the early 1990s, a new team led by Ian Hodder reopened the site. The Hodder team excavated numerous houses in the vicinity of Mellaart's original excavation trenches at the south end of the mound (inset left) while conducting meticulous digs of two newly discovered buildings at the north end: Building 1 (inset upper right), and a second building excavated by the Berkeley Archaeologists at Çatal Höyük (BACH team). In addition, Greek and Polish teams excavated the summit and TP (Team Poznan) areas, respectively.
Courtesy of Çatalhöyük Research Project

Michael Ashley, one of the Berkeley team's Wonder Twins, high above the excavations in the "Goddess Pavilion."
Courtesy of Çatalhöyük Research Project

Building 5 in the north area, which was revealed after Building 1 was completely excavated. This house, one of the best preserved in the Near East, was later put on public display.
Courtesy of Çatalhöyük Research Project

Çatalhöyük's settlers built their houses from mud-bricks made of clay, ash and straw, which were put out in the sun to dry. They used thick mortar to hold the bricks together.
Courtesy of Çatalhöyük Research Project

Cattle seemed to have important symbolic significance to the people of Çatalhöyük. Archaeologists including Ruth Tringham (left), Louise Martin (hand on chin), and Julie Near (right) examine a large pair of horns embedded in a plaster platform. *Courtesy of Tim Ready/Science Museum of Minnesota*

After nearly six months of digging during the 1999 Long Season, Craig Cessford (left) and Jez Taylor reached the very bottom of the mound. The grayish material is marl from a large lake that once covered the Konya Plain. *Courtesy of Çatalhöyük Research Project*

During his 1960s excavations, James Mellaart's team uncovered this wall-length mural of a red bull. Mellaart assumed that the cattle at Çatalhöyük were domesticated, but the Hodder team came to a startlingly different conclusion.
© Arlette Mellaart. Reprinted by permission.

Mellaart found the earliest known wooden implements during his excavations at Çatalhöyük, including this 9,000 year old wooden bowl.
© Arlette Mellaart. Reprinted by permission

This pot was unearthed during recent excavations of Çatalhöyük's West Mound, which was occupied during the Copper Age.
Courtesy of Çatalhöyük Research Project

The people of Çatalhöyük were expert artisans, producing tools made from black obsidian (left), gray flint, and animal bone, as well as clay figurines depicting animals and humans (center).
Courtesy of Çatalhöyük Research Project

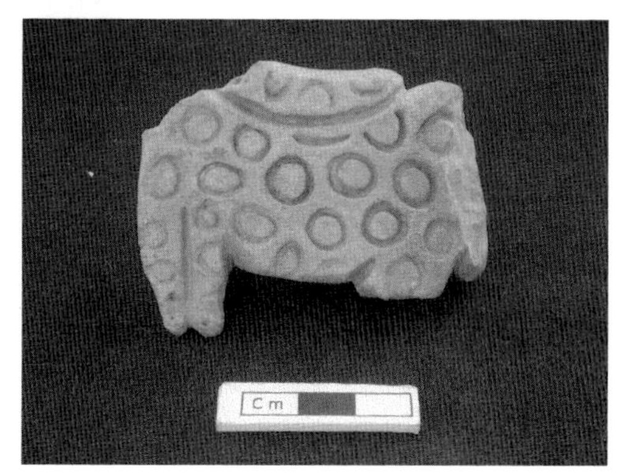

Archaeologists have found dozens of "stamp seals" at Çatalhöyük, including this one in the shape of an elephant. Their purpose during the Neolithic is not clear, although in later periods similar stamp seals were apparently used to stamp items of private property.
Courtesy of Çatalhöyük Research Project

Is it a dog or a cow? The majority of clay figurines found at Çatalhöyük are very schematic. Archaeologists debate whether they were religious objects, children's toys, or game pieces.
Courtesy of Çatalhöyük Research Project

This "Mother Goddess" style figurine, carved from stone, was found in a human burial during the 2004 excavation season.
Courtesy of Çatalhöyük Research Project

Babies received special treatment when they died, and were often placed in reed baskets before burial. Child mortality was very high, probably reflecting the crowded conditions in the settlement and the hardships of the early farming life.
Courtesy of Çatalhöyük Research Project

The people of Çatalhöyük buried their dead under the plastered floors of their houses. Mellaart thought that the bodies were first put outside the settlement so that the vultures could eat their flesh, but the Hodder team has found little evidence for this idea.
Courtesy of Çatalhöyük Research Project

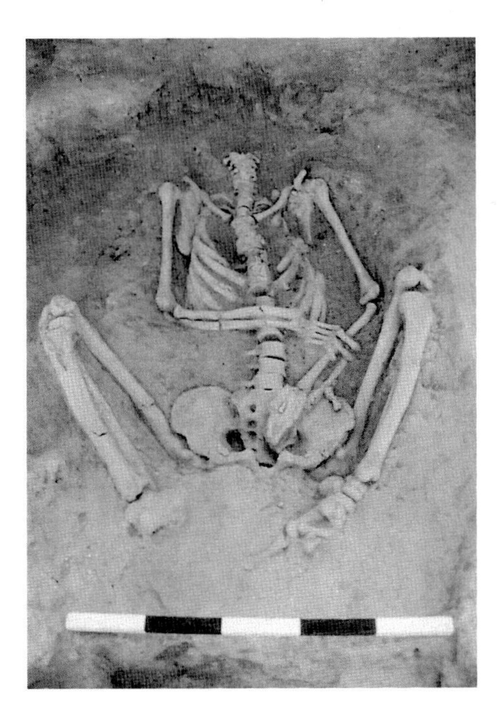

A small number of bodies, possibly those of especially revered elders, were buried after their heads had been removed. The "skull cult" at Çatalhöyük had its roots in a tradition that became widespread throughout the Near East beginning about 11,000 years ago.
Courtesy of Çatalhöyük Research Project

Archaeologists must take special care when excavating skeletons, removing them bone by bone. Here the middle burial has been carefully removed, leaving the outer two. *Courtesy of Çatalhöyük Research Project*

Building 1 in the north area had more than 60 burials under its plaster floors. There were so many bodies that the Neolithic settlers had a difficult time finding space for all of them. *Courtesy of Çatalhöyük Research Project*

Roger and Wendy Matthews spent a number of years excavating in Iraq before they were forced to leave the country during the first Gulf War. They were the first to answer Ian Hodder's call for archaeologists to come and dig at Çatalhöyük.
Courtesy of Roger and Wendy Matthews.

Shahina Farid, whose reputation as one of the best diggers in the business brought her to Ian Hodder's attention, rose through the ranks to become Hodder's number two at Çatalhöyük.
Courtesy of Tim Ready/Science Museum of Minnesota

Craig Cessford, who was put in charge of excavating Buildings 1 and 5 and played a key role during the 1999 Long Season, later coordinated the radiocarbon dating of the site—which demonstrated that Çatalhöyük was founded 9,500 years ago.
Courtesy of Tim Ready/Science Museum of Minnesota

American Nerissa ("Rissa") Russell worked with Ruth Tringham in the former Yugoslavia and Bulgaria before teaming up with Louise Martin to lead the project's animal bone team. She is particularly interested in ritual feasting, for which there is plentiful evidence at Çatalhöyük.
Courtesy of Michael Balter

Ruth Tringham, a flamboyant feminist archaeologist from London, came to Çatalhöyük after two decades of digging at Neolithic sites in the former Yugoslavia. One of her chief goals was to put "faces" on the settlement's people.
Courtesy of Tim Ready/Science Museum of Minnesota

Christine Hastorf, the wife of Ian Hodder, thought she was going to co-direct the dig with her husband —but ended up being content to lead its archaeobotany team.
Courtesy of Tim Ready/Science Museum of Minnesota

Louise Martin, co-leader of the zooarchaeology team, has been in the animal bone business since she was 18 years old. When Ian Hodder telephoned to ask her to work at Çatalhöyük right after she received her Ph.D., Louise thought someone was playing a joke on her.
Courtesy of Tim Ready/Science Museum of Minnesota

American Julie Near landed on Çatalhöyük's archaeobotany team after the collapse of Ruth Tringham's ill-fated dig in Bulgaria. She also rose to prominence as co-organizer of the dig's colorful Thursday night costume parties.
Courtesy of Tim Ready/Science Museum of Minnesota

John Swogger is the dig's archaeological illustrator, and co-organizer with Julie Near of its Thursday night costume parties.
Courtesy of Tim Ready/Science Museum of Minnesota

Naomi Hamilton studied with James Mellaart in London, but her studies of the figurines at Çatalhöyük led her to conclude that Mellaart was wrong when he claimed that the Neolithic settlers had worshipped a Mother Goddess.
Courtesy of Tim Ready/Science Museum of Minnesota

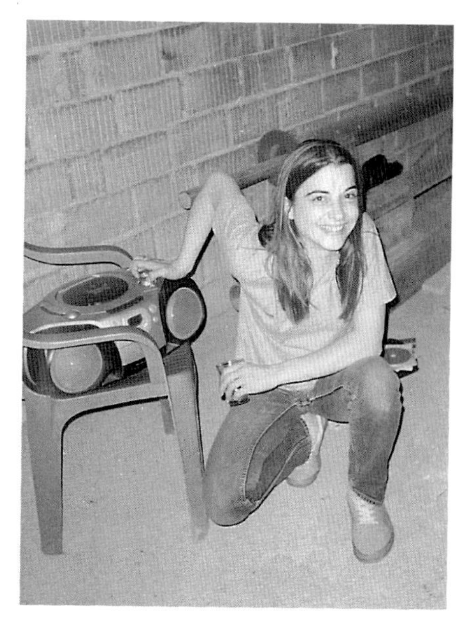

Eleni Asouti, from Athens, is the dig's charcoal expert. Her career at Çatalhöyük was almost cut short after a downturn in Turkish-Greek relations.
Courtesy of Michael balter

Turkish archaeologist Burcu Tung found a female figurine with a wild seed in its back. The discovery inspired some of Ian Hodder's conclusions about the meaning of the art at Çatalhöyük.
Courtest of Michael Balter

Ayfer Bartu met Ian Hodder when he needed Turkish lessons, and later became the dig's resident social anthropologist and "cultural broker." One of her jobs was to smooth Ian's relations with Turkish authorities.
Courtesy of Tim Ready/Science Museum of Minnesota

Başak Boz, who studied physical anthropology in Ankara and London, excavates a human burial bone by bone. Her studies of the teeth of the Neolithic residents helped figure out what they ate.
Courtesy of Tim Ready/Science Museum of Minnesota

Mirjana ("Mira") Stevanovic, an archaeologist from Belgrade, had to become an arson investigator to figure out why Neolithic people burned down their own houses.
Courtesy of Tim Ready/Science Museum of Minnesota

Ian Hodder is best known as an archaeological theoretician rather than a hands-on excavator. But it is his job to explain the site's intricate stratigraphy when visitors come to call.
Courtesy of Çatalhöyük Research Project

Beginning with the 2003 season, Ian Hodder's team modified its previous meticulous excavation strategy and began to dig a much larger area of the mound. The new approach has already led to a number of important discoveries.
Courtesy of Jason Quinlan.

evening Ian took the Mellaarts to the bus station in Konya for the return journey to Ankara. Ian and Mellaart shook hands warmly. "Come back any time," Ian said. "Thank you," Mellaart replied. "Thank you for everything."

The torch had been passed.

ENGIN ÖZGEN had made it clear that the press should not be told about Mellaart's visit. On the other hand, since 1996 was the first full excavation season, Ian and some of his major funders thought that the end of the season would be a good time to invite the news media to visit. A major "press day" was set for September 25, organized by the Visa card people and their Istanbul-based public relations company. It was to be followed two days later by an official inauguration of the dig house, to which the European Union ambassador to Turkey and the Turkish culture minister were invited. After a long and tense season, the archaeologists were looking forward to showing off what they had accomplished—even if they were annoyed that press day had been scheduled for the very end, when they were busy getting ready to leave. They were also looking forward to the evening of dinner and dancing at a nice restaurant in Konya that had been organized for the evening of press day. The team spent several days making preparations for the events, which mainly consisted of tidying up the natural messiness of an archaeological dig and arranging some of the most interesting finds for display.

Some sixty print and television journalists showed up for press day. Ian and the Visa representatives held a news conference, which was followed by a tour of the excavations in the north and south areas of the mound. Meanwhile the specialists stood by in their labs, ready to show and tell what they had been doing. A number of artifacts were put out, including some of Naomi's figurines, Rissa's bone rings and jewelry, and a nice assortment of obsidian blades that James had laid out neatly on a lab table. The reporters seemed particularly interested in a small stone bead that Naomi had put on display. It had been intricately incised with some sort of design. Ian explained that this artifact had been found on the surface of the mound during one of the previous seasons. It probably dated from a later era, possibly Byzantine. As for the incision, Ian joked that he thought it looked like a helicopter.

Then disaster struck. Sometime during the afternoon, the stone bead disappeared. After a frantic search, the Turkish police were called. They showed up accompanied by gendarmes wearing camouflage uniforms and toting machine guns. The gendarmes blocked access into and out of the site for several hours and strip-searched all of the journalists. The police, after examining the videotapes of the television crews, were able to determine that the theft must have taken place sometime between 2:50 and 3:10 P.M. As Rissa characterized events in her diary late that night, "Everyone freaks out; parallels with Mellaart too chilling." Ian's emotions were running the gamut from angry to sad and back again. Over the past four years of work at Çatalhöyük, not one item—not even a pencil or a piece of paper—had ever been stolen. Now the dig was in danger of being shut down over a stone bead that had little or no commercial value and wasn't even Neolithic.

As a wave of panic and depression spread throughout the team, Rissa—who had a store of *palinka*, a Hungarian apricot brandy, which she had picked up during a recent conference in Budapest—began distributing drinks to those most in need. Meanwhile the archaeologists were ordered to stay in their labs while the police and gendarmes carried out their investigation. To Julie Near, who watched everything through the dig house window, it all seemed like a bad television movie—and one that was likely to end badly for her. She had lost one thesis project when Ruth Tringham's and Mira Stevanovic's Bulgarian excavations ended in fiasco, and now she seemed about to lose Çatalhöyük. Julie was sure she would never get her Ph.D. All she wanted to do was find someplace to curl up and have a good cry, perhaps behind the flotation machine.

Finally, as evening wore on, the police announced that everyone was free to leave. The archaeologists and some of the journalists piled into the chartered bus that had been waiting to take them to the restaurant in Konya. "Excellent therapy, much wine, get back at 2:00 A.M.," Rissa told her diary.

The stone bead was never found. As might be expected, the Turkish news media—nearly all of which had been present to witness events first-hand—had a field day with the story. The Islamic fundamentalist press suggested that foreigners could not be trusted to carry out excavations in Turkey, while some of the Istanbul newspapers theorized that the whole episode had been orchestrated by the country's political right wing. As for the incision on the Byzantine bead, some newspapers reported, in all seriousness, Ian's joking hypothesis that it represented a helicopter—which would have pushed back the earliest known date for manned flight to about 1,500 years before the Wright brothers. To Ian's great distress, all of the hoped-for publicity—at least, positive publicity—that Visa was expecting to get from the press day went down the drain. He was worried that Visa would stop sponsoring the dig and that other sponsors—including another bank that was thinking about signing up—would abandon the project as well. If, that is, the project was allowed to continue at all.

The next day the police returned to question Naomi and the other archaeologists who had been working in the lab where the stone bead was on display. To Ian's relief, the Visa officials reassured him of their continued support, although he did get word that the culture minister had decided not to attend the inauguration of the dig house on September 27. The European Union ambassador to Turkey did show up, along with Mehmet Akif Işik—the new director general who had recently replaced Engin Özgen—the governor of the Konya region, the mayor of Çumra, an assortment of minor officials, and the machine gun–toting gendarmes. Işik took Ian aside and told him that if the investigation showed that Ian had been negligent, the dig would have to be shut down. All they could do was hope for the best.

As THE END OF THE 1996 season approached, Roger Matthews found himself facing a tough decision—whether or not to return to Çatalhöyük the following year. In 1995 David Shankland, the acting director of the BIAA, left Turkey to take a teaching position in Wales. The BIAA's governing council had asked Roger to take over as acting director while it launched a search for a permanent replacement for French, who had held the post for twenty-five years. In the fall of 1995 he and Wendy moved from Cambridge to Ankara. While their feelings about Turkey never reached the intensity of the love affair they had with Iraq, Roger and Wendy liked living in Ankara, a sophisticated, cosmopolitan city. Most important, they were back in the Near East, the region they had both chosen to specialize in. Roger and Wendy still harbored some hopes of returning to Iraq, although that possibility looked less likely as the years wore on. When the BIAA council announced that it intended to fill the position permanently as of September 1996, Roger decided to apply for the job himself.

It came down to a choice between Roger and one other candidate. Despite Roger's proven record in the Near East and Turkey, his connection with Çatalhöyük made some members of the council hesitate. After all these years, and despite Ian's successful reopening of the excavations, the site symbolized the one big black mark in the institute's history. But the council was reassured by the fact that Roger was planning to leave the project and launch his own research elsewhere in Turkey. In the spring of 1996, shortly before the Çatalhöyük excavation season began, Roger learned that he had been chosen.

Roger told Ian that he probably would not return as field director in 1997. His duties as permanent BIAA director would begin as soon as the season ended. It was hard to see how he could juggle that and being Ian's number two at Çatalhöyük as well. Ian asked him to reconsider. But as the long, tense season wore on, Roger's resolve to leave grew stronger. He had been feeling increasingly frustrated and out of place on the dig. The traumatic conflict between the specialists and diggers had left him questioning whether Ian's meticulous, highly contextual approach to excavating Çatalhöyük was really paying off in new information—whether it was worth all the time and trouble. From time to time Ian had voiced similar doubts in his excavation diary. Early in September, upon returning to Çatalhöyük after a few days in Ankara, Roger announced in his own diary that after twelve years of digging in the Near East he was going to quit excavating and focus exclusively on survey projects:

> We truly have lost our innocence as diggers and can no longer pretend, as Jimmy must have been able to, that digging a Neolithic house is a simple matter, the work of a few hours in the field. Perhaps we have become dominated by our specialists who make increasingly stringent and laborious demands upon the time and material resources of the project for often a small return in the way of useful information or interpretation.

A week later, after attending a planning meeting for the Çatalhöyük team's contribution to the Theoretical Archaeology Group meeting in Liverpool, Roger made his feelings even more explicit:

> I came away from it quite depressed . . . I realize now that I am a positivist and a processualist, because I am interested in the processes of the past and I am not interested in understanding the subjective, culture-specific roots of my own standpoint, beyond being aware that they exist. I am interested in just being me and finding out about the past for myself and others and in using the scanty fragments as a basis for imagining the multiple universes of the past, which the evidence can never entirely substantiate but does not contradict . . . I feel up one day, then down for five days . . . Up days coincide with shifting earth, down days coincide with overlong specialist tours or endless discussions about the point of it all.

If Roger had any second thoughts about returning to Çatalhöyük, they were put to rest the last week of the season, when it became clear that he and his team could not possibly finish excavating Building 1 that year. "We have been defeated by the sheer quantity of burials," Roger wrote on September 28, his last diary entry. The body count was now up to thirty-seven, with many more to come. But at the end Roger made it clear he had no regrets about what he had accomplished in Building 1. "We have plotted in great detail how that structure went through a complex and quirky evolution to end up as a more compartmentalized and more modest building, suffering the effects of an intense fire in the process. We have also recovered a tremendous assemblage of human remains which will no doubt receive much future study. In all, the digging has been good."

SEPTEMBER 27, the day that the new dig house was inaugurated, was Rissa's thirty-ninth birthday. The great celestial machine had prepared a special gift: a total lunar eclipse, scheduled to begin just after three A.M. Rissa, Roger, Wendy, and Julie had arranged to watch it together from the top of the mound. They met in front of the dig house at the appointed hour, armed with blankets and Rissa's *palinka.* The full moon bathed the mound in a soft, silvery light, making it easy for them to find the trail leading to the summit. They found a reasonably level patch of ground and lay down on their blankets, eyes fixed on the sky. The days were still hot, but the nights had become cool. Julie, exhausted from the stresses and strains of the season, struggled to stay awake. She could hear the sounds of insects rustling in the grass near her ears and feel the cool breeze on her face.

Julie began to wonder what the Neolithic inhabitants of Çatalhöyük would have seen from the top of the mound at night. Doug Baird's survey of the Konya Plain had raised the possibility that there were other, smaller settlements in the vicinity. Would the people of Çatalhöyük have seen the fires from these distant villages? For that matter, what did a lunar eclipse mean to them? Would they have been frightened, excited, calm? What did they think the moon was, and how would they explain the eclipse to their children? Who would gather to watch? Everyone in the village, or just a chosen few? Julie had no answers to these questions, but just thinking about them made the people of Çatalhöyük, and the lives that they had lived so many thousands of years before, more real to her than ever before. They were still mere shadows, but somehow they were there on the mound—there with her and her friends.

Just then the eclipse reached totality, as the earth passed before the sun and cast its full shadow on the moon. The moon's silvery glimmer turned to dark orange. To Julie it looked like a tangerine that someone had hung in the sky with a string. It was all she could do to stop herself from reaching out and trying to grasp it. After another hour the moon's bright edge reemerged. The four archaeologists went back down to the dig house to try to get a little more sleep before the workday began.

That evening everyone gathered behind the dig house to celebrate Rissa's birthday. Rissa did not normally advertise her birthday widely, but after all the team had been through this season, she felt it needed an excuse for a good party. While the fences between the excavators and specialists had been largely mended by now, Rissa knew that there was nothing like a community ritual to bring people together.

The kitchen staff baked a cake, and Rissa brought out the last of her Hungarian brandy and salami to share around. Roddy built a big bonfire and Roger brought his guitar. The whole group sat around the fire, singing and talking. Roddy surprised everyone with a soulful rendition of the Scottish folksong "Peggy Gordon," the plaintive lament of a brokenhearted lover. Even Ian and Christine, never big partygoers, joined in for a while. As it got close to one A.M., Roger said that he was going to play one more song. He told Rissa that she could pick her favorite. Rissa knew that Roger was leaving the dig. She thought that this might be the last time she would ever hear him play.

"Would you play 'Catch the Wind'?" Rissa asked. Roger hitched the guitar up on his leg and began to sing.

TWO DAYS LATER the season ended. Ian had heard, through informal channels, that the director general had already decided that he had not been negligent in the matter of the stolen bead. While he still had to make an official report about the episode, it was unlikely that the dig's future was in danger. Relieved at this news, Ian spent much of the fall raising funds for the 1997 season. He also had to decide who was going to replace Roger as field director. He wanted someone who was a skillful excavator, who was well liked and respected, and who was also intellectually engaged in the excavation and its goals.

He picked Shahina.

12 / Burning Down the House

ROGER MATTHEWS HAD left Çatalhöyük, but he still had to write up his report on the 1996 season. While the excavations of Building 1 were not completed, his crew had dug close enough to its foundations to allow some tentative conclusions. After all his hard work over the past years, Roger had no intention of leaving all the fun of interpreting the building to his successors. His legacy to the dig, Roger decided, would be a preliminary analysis of Building 1 and what this house might have meant to the lives of its inhabitants. It was an opportunity to stretch his interpretive imagination as an archaeologist, without, he hoped, going beyond what the evidence from the dig could support.

After two seasons of excavations, much of the complex history of Building 1 had been revealed. As was usually the case with a stratified site, the excavations represented a journey backward in time. During the roughly one hundred years of its lifetime, the structure, and presumably the lives of its residents, had gone through many changes. Roger could now see that the life cycle of Building 1 had consisted of at least four phases. During the first phase the Neolithic builders had cleared an area for the building, possibly by leveling an earlier structure that once stood underneath—a structure the excavators might hope to discover later on. They then constructed the outer mud-brick walls, forming an architectural shell that remained intact during the building's entire lifetime. After laying down a layer of finely packed ashy rubbish, the builders fabricated an interior wall that divided the house into one larger room, which the excavators called Space 71, and a smaller room, Space 70. The ashy layer was plastered over, forming the building's very first floor. Ovens, hearths, and other features were installed, and the inhabitants then moved in and began their lives in the building. Roger noted that at this early stage in its life, Building 1 greatly resembled an elaborate structure in Level VI of the south area, which Mellaart had designated as Shrine 10. This might explain why Mellaart, during his visit to the site, was so insistent that this building was a regular house and not a "shrine": he did not see the earliest phase of the building.

During Phase 2 the residents carried out some remodeling. They bricked over a smaller oven and built a much larger one on top of it, constructed a storage bin along the south wall of Space 71, and placed a grinding stone into a shallow basin in front of it. On a platform on the east end of Space 71, the inhabitants installed some sort of plastered sculpture that included the skull and horns of a large cow. At the end of Phase 2, Roger reported, "a violent fire raged through the [south] parts of the building, blackening all floor and wall surfaces and searing into the walls to redden the bricks themselves." Roger had detected some evidence of this conflagration during the 1995 season. It now seemed likely that the fire, violent as it had been, was deliberately set and carefully controlled. The northern half of the building was not touched, but the southern half—which the residents never cleaned of its burned rubble—was not reoccupied. During Phase 3 new walls were built across Spaces 70 and 71 to divide the northern half of the building from the ruined south half, and the northern half was even further subdivided with smaller walls.

Phase 4 marked the abandonment of Building 1. It was filled with rubbish and left to the ages, its dozens of buried skeletons a monument to the generations who had once lived there. However, it did not go entirely undisturbed: sometime after it was abandoned, someone dug a pit into the rubble filling Space 71, just adjacent to its west wall, and removed a wall sculpture. The traces of the sculpture were clearly visible from scars in the plaster surface where it had once been attached. On the floor just below, apparently as an offering, Roger's team found a deposit of bones, bone tools, and pieces of obsidian.

Roger took it as a given that, in Neolithic times just as today, a house is more than just a container to live in. "The basic assumption," he wrote, "is that the layout and decoration of the Çatalhöyük buildings are richly laden with symbolic significance, involving concerns with birth and death, ancestry and descent, male and female, domestic and wild, and so on." In his attempt to decipher these symbolic meanings, Roger relied heavily on the results from Wendy Matthews's micromorphology work. Over the course of the season Wendy had taken more than fifty samples from the walls and the floors, including small blocks of plaster that she embedded in resin and then cut into large thin sections for examination under the microscope. Just as the macro-excavations had demonstrated that the inhabitants were constantly moving ovens, grinding stones, and other features from one place to another, the micromorphology revealed that they often dug into the floors to change the relative levels of different parts of the building. For example, a section of floor in the southeast corner of Space 71, right next to where the bottom of a ladder leading to the roof had been placed, had been plastered and replastered some forty-eight times during the lifetime of the house.

The interior walls of the house seemed to divide it into north and south sections, which were markedly different. Even within individual rooms, all of the "domestic" activities, such as cooking and grinding of grain and cereals, took place in the south, while the sculptures, paintings, and other decorations were restricted to the north. Again, Wendy's work suggested that these sections of the house were regarded very differently. The floors in the south had fewer plaster layers, which were coarser and thicker and covered with accumulations of organic material and burned materials from hearts and ovens. The northern floors and platforms, in contrast, were made up of many layers of fine, clean white plaster, and they seemed to have been kept scrupulously clean for most of the life of the house.

Roger adopted the view, still common among archaeologists, that women carried out most domestic labor in prehistoric societies. Thus the interior walls may have divided the building into "female and male zones," Roger suggested. This might also explain, he wrote, why the ladders that led into the houses from the roof were always on the south side, "just as entry to the physical world is via the female."

If the south end of the house represented women, life, and birth, in contrast all of the burials were restricted to the north and east of Building 1. Roger speculated that a traumatic death in the family—that of the "main female" of the house—may have explained why the entire southern half of the building was burned, apparently deliberately. With the female zone destroyed, the family huddled in the northern half, where a lone widower remained head of the clan. Now, in the last phases of the building's life history, the demarcation between domestic and decorated suddenly broke down. "There is now significant decoration along the new [south] zone in the form of animal parts set into the faces of the new dividing walls both in Space 70 and Space 71," Roger noted, adding that this finding supported "the idea of a single sex/male survivor living in the remnant of the house." To drive the point home, Roger pointed out yet another change that took place after the fire: "In contrast to the immaculately clean swept floors of earlier phases, the new floors have much more rubbish on them and are less well kept, perhaps a sign of a not too house-proud elderly male." Roger also found support for this interpretation under Wendy's microscope: the plaster floors of this later phase were irregular, poorly constructed, and imbedded with thick layers of ash. For whatever reason, Roger concluded, the standards of this once proudly maintained household had fallen to an all-time low.

In this imaginative reconstruction of the life of Building 1, Roger, who by the end of the 1996 season had concluded that he was a processual and not a post-processual archaeologist, still went further than many hypothesis-testing Hempelians might have dared. He had attempted to breathe some life into its Neolithic inhabitants. Yet the people who lived in this house remained distant, ill-defined, and faceless, and their motivations for burning down half of their house were still murky. The following season Çatalhöyük would welcome a new team of excavators whose leaders had spent much of their careers poking through the ashes of Neolithic fires and trying to put faces on Neolithic people: Ruth Tringham, Mirjana Stevanovic, and the Berkeley Archaeologists at Çatal Höyük were on their way.

RUTH TRINGHAM WAS BORN on October 14, 1940, in Aspley Guise, a village in Bedfordshire. Her parents were native Londoners, but the outbreak of World War II, and especially the German blitz bombing of the city that began in September 1940, convinced Ruth's mother and father that the family, which included her two older brothers, was safer out in the countryside. The family saw out the war in Aspley Guise, where Ruth attended the village school. When the war ended, they moved backed to London, settling in the district of Wembley Park. Before Ruth was born, her father had tried his hand at pig farming, but that didn't last. He was now in advertising.

When Ruth was nine years old, at her parents' urging she took up the violin, the beginning of a lifelong love affair with music. A few years later the family moved to Hampstead Village, a relatively well-off district of north London. Despite their middle-class existence, Ruth's parents were ardent socialists. The bookshelves were lined with history books. The dinner table buzzed with political discussions. Ruth's mother, a schoolteacher, was involved in local politics. The famous Marxist archaeologist V. Gordon Childe lived in Hampstead at that time, and sometimes she and her mother would see him eating at an Indian restaurant on South End Road where they also often ate. Ruth was always afraid that her mother would go over to Childe's table and try to talk to him, but to her relief her mother never did.

Ruth attended South Hampstead High School, where she loved learning Latin and ancient Greek. Thanks to her precociously tall, lanky frame, she also began to excel at sports. But her greatest pleasure came on the weekends, when she would take the underground to London's Natural History Museum for meetings of the museum's Natural History Club. Among the people she met there was Theya Molleson, who later would codirect the human remains team at Çatalhöyük. Ruth spent one holiday with the club on Alderney in the Channel Islands, helping to excavate a castle and learning English and Irish folk songs from the archaeologists working there. Ruth loved the social life on the excavation. She learned to play the guitar and drink hard cider, both of which made her very popular.

By the time Ruth graduated from high school, she had made up her mind to be an archaeologist. Her mother encouraged her to go to the University of Edinburgh, where Childe had been professor of prehistoric archaeology for two decades before taking over as director of the London Institute of Archaeology in 1946. Childe's successor at Edinburgh, Stuart Piggott, was a renowned prehistorian who had excavated at Stonehenge and other Neolithic sites in Britain. Piggott was happy to take Ruth under his wing. Around the time Ruth left for Edinburgh, her parents underwent a bitter separation. With her family divided, Ruth no longer felt she had a home to return to. Instead she spent every summer and holiday digging. The first couple of years she worked at a number of sites that Piggott and his colleagues were excavating in Great Britain, including the Neolithic tomb of Wayland's Smithy in Oxfordshire and a field school in Cornwall, where one of her supervisors was the future New Archaeologist David Clarke.

On one occasion James Mellaart came to Edinburgh to give a lecture about his new excavations at Çatalhöyük. Piggott introduced him to the audience, saying that these discoveries were sure to revolutionize our understanding of the spread of agriculture into Europe. Ruth, whose own interest in the Neolithic was by now well established, was extremely impressed by this claim.

In 1962, during Ruth's third year as an undergraduate at Edinburgh, she was handed an opportunity that would set her on the road to archaeological fame. Piggott knew some colleagues in Prague, who put Ruth in touch with an archaeologist named Bohumil Soudsky at Prague's Charles University. Soudsky was excavating a large Neolithic site near Prague called Bylany. At 6,000 years old, it was one of the earliest farming settlements in Central Europe, with some twenty phases of occupation levels—each composed of a cluster of a half dozen or more houses. And since it was behind the Iron Curtain, few Western archaeologists had ever seen it.

The Cold War, with its severe limitations on East-West research collaborations, had greatly inhibited progress in understanding the Neolithic Revolution's spread from the Near East, where it had begun with the first cultivation of wheat and barley, to Europe, where it eventually culminated in great Neolithic monuments such as Stonehenge in England and the standing stones at Carnac on France's Brittany coast. While there was limited evidence that some Neolithic peoples had traveled along the Mediterranean coast from east to west, Central and Eastern Europe were clearly the major crossroads for this continent-wide transformation from hunting and gathering to farming.

Archaeologists had recently established that farming first leapt from Anatolia to Greece about 7000 B.C., as evidenced by early Neolithic sites such as Nea Nikomedeia in Greek Macedonia, a village of rectangular, timber-framed houses where excavators found a cache of female figurines. From Greece the agricultural way of life, which certainly did not recognize modern borders, made its way over the Balkans, sweeping (or crawling, as some archaeologists would maintain) north and west through modern-day Bulgaria, Yugoslavia, Hungary, Romania, Czechoslovakia, and Poland. The proof: hundreds of well-preserved Neolithic settlements throughout Eastern and Central Europe, many of which have yet to be properly excavated. V. Gordon Childe, who had a keen interest in Russian and Eastern European archaeology, did a great deal to bring these cultures to the attention of western archaeologists. After Childe's death in 1957, few researchers followed his lead. That left western archaeologists, who normally worked either in the Near East or Western Europe, reasonably informed about the beginning and the end of the Neolithic story but almost totally in the dark about the middle of it.

For Ruth, Bylany was the first stepping-stone to a career as an expert in the Neolithic of Eastern Europe. She began traveling to other Iron Curtain countries, visiting sites, making contacts, and digging here and there with the local archaeologists. Ruth eventually wrote her senior thesis on the region's Neolithic clay figurines. When she began work on her Ph.D.—a comparison of the Neolithic of Central and Southeast Europe—both Piggott and Soudsky served as her doctoral supervisors.

Ruth was one of Piggott's favorite students, but she had competition for his affections. In 1966 Bruce Chatwin, who was then taking his first fledgling steps toward a stellar career as a novelist and travel writer, decided that he wanted to be an archaeologist. Piggott agreed to take him on. Ruth, who thought that Chatwin was a bit of a dilettante, was considerably annoyed. Her irritation with Chatwin only intensified when the Citroën van she bought from him conked out within the first year after purchase. Things got even worse when Ruth, having organized an archaeological tour of Russia for herself and Piggott, learned that Piggott had invited Chatwin along—and Chatwin, in his turn, had invited his friend George Ortiz, a millionaire art collector. One evening they were invited for dinner at the home of Vladimir Masson, director of Leningrad's Archaeological Institute, where a great deal of alcohol was consumed. As Nicholas Shakespeare described events in his biography of Bruce Chatwin, "Tringham was sick in the bathroom while Bruce, with Masson slumped under it, stood on the table," reciting a Shakespearean sonnet to Masson's wife. Chatwin, in his own account of the episode in his last book, *What Am I Doing Here*, referred to Ruth only as "a lady Marxist archaeological student from Hampstead."

Chatwin did not stay the course as an archaeologist; as a result, the fields of literature, and perhaps archaeology, too, are now much better off. But there was no stopping Ruth Tringham. After receiving her Ph.D. from Edinburgh, she spent a postdoctoral year in Leningrad with Masson, where she began specializing in the microwear on stone tools, that is, the microscopic marks that help archaeologists determine how the tools were used and on what materials. At that time, microwear studies were in their infancy. Ruth quickly developed a reputation as an expert in this new field. The specialty marked a departure from the culture history tradition in which she had been trained. Stuart Piggott had made his reputation excavating Avebury, Stonehenge, and other Neolithic and Bronze Age megalithic monuments in south central England. This work led him to identify what he and others called the Wessex culture, noted for the rich grave goods of its burials. But as a microwear maven, Ruth was now propelled into the ranks of the New Archaeologists. Excavation directors began inviting her to analyze the microwear on their stone artifacts. Ruth received invitations to work on digs in Yugoslavia and Greece—in the latter case, from Colin Renfrew, who was codirecting, along with Marija Gimbutas, excavations at the prehistoric mound of Sitagroi in Greek Macedonia. During the 1969 season Renfrew and Gimbutas discovered a large timber-framed house, dated about 3100 B.C., which had been extensively burned, although the circumstances of the fire were not clear.

Also in 1969, Ruth was hired by University College London to teach in a special program devoted to the study of material culture. At first Ruth found teaching scary and often felt that she was just one step ahead of the students. She was rather more confident of her skills as a volleyball player. Ruth, who had loved sports since she was a teenager, was now a star player on her local amateur women's team, which eventually became the best in England. After a year teaching in London, she got a call from the British prehistorian Glyn Daniel, who had recommended her for a position teaching European archaeology at Harvard University. Ruth's first reaction was that America was no place for a British socialist. But since Harvard was paying her travel expenses, she agreed to go for the interview. Her visit was hosted by Carl Lamberg-Karlovsky, the celebrated archaeologist who would later have so much to say about James Mellaart's "reconstructed" paintings. Ruth was seduced by the enthusiasm that Harvard showed for her syntheses of Eastern European prehistory, as well as by the salary the university was offering: $10,500 per year, which in 1970 was a fortune compared to the £1500 she had been receiving in London. The position was supposed to start at the beginning of September, but Ruth showed up three weeks late, telling Harvard vaguely that she had had a "prior engagement." The prior engagement was that Ruth had agreed to captain the English team in the European women's volleyball championships.

Once she was settled in at Harvard, Ruth's colleagues urged her to launch her own excavation project. She decided to look for an early Neolithic site in Yugoslavia, where she had lots of contacts from her years working in Southeastern Europe. She spent several summers in the country trying to get a project going, which, at that time in East-West relationships, turned out to be more complicated than she had anticipated. She finally succeeded in getting permission to dig at a late Neolithic site called Selevac in Serbia's Morava Valley. Armed with a grant from the U.S. National Science Foundation, and in collaboration with colleagues in Belgrade, she was finally able to get excavations under way in 1976. Selevac was a key site of the so-called Vinča culture, named after a celebrated Neolithic tell near Belgrade that had first been excavated early in the twentieth century. Selevac was a huge site, covering 131 acres, which was founded some 6,000 years ago and occupied for 500 years. It had lots of houses constructed from wattle and daub—closely placed timbers covered with thick layers of clay to keep the warmth in and the weather out. Many of the houses had been burned, although whether by accident or deliberately was not at first clear.

A lot of archaeologists worked with Ruth at Selevac, including two very talented students. One was Rissa Russell, then an undergraduate at Harvard, who took on the job of analyzing the bone tools at the site for her senior thesis. The other was Mira Stevanovic from Belgrade.

AT THE TIME Ruth arrived at Selevac, she had lots of expertise analyzing stone tool microwear. Her excavation experience, on the other hand, was much less impressive. At times she had difficulties recognizing a hearth or an oven on the floor of a Neolithic house. Ruth would later tell people that Mira taught her how to dig like a real archaeologist, and that she taught Mira how to think like a real anthropologist. (Ruth also taught Mira how to drive.) Ruth was eleven years older than Mira, and much senior academically: at the time they met, Mira was still an undergraduate student. But Ruth soon began thinking of Mira as a partner rather than an underling. One thing the two women had in common was flamboyance. Ruth's flamboyance was kinetic: her tall frame bobbed and swayed with energy, enthusiasm, and ideas. Mira's flamboyance was more mannered: a nonchalant toss of her red hair, an ironic smile, and a French cigarette in a long holder were her trademarks.

Mira was born in Belgrade on December 25, 1951, during the bad old days of the Cold War. Her parents were civil servants and members of the Yugoslav Communist Party, although they were not ideologues: the only thing they tried to indoctrinate Mira and her younger brother about was the importance of social equality. The family lived first in the Belgrade suburbs and later in the city. During the summers and holidays, Mira would spend time in the village where her father had grown up. There she got to know the eighty or so members of her father's *zadruga*, or extended family. The *zadruga* kept rituals and customs that dated back to medieval times, such as covering all the mirrors in the house when someone died or working collectively on the annual harvest. Mira was keenly aware of belonging to this larger community.

After graduating from high school, Mira entered Belgrade University. She started off studying economics but soon found it deadly boring. Some friends in the archaeology program urged her to join them, so she switched over. The first excavation she worked on was a mediocre Iron Age site near Belgrade, where the archaeologist in charge did not let her do much. Mira began to wonder if archaeology was really as exciting as her friends had made it out to be. Then, during her second year in the department, she got the chance to dig at Gomolava, a huge, multiperiod double tell on the Sava River with stratigraphy ranging from the Neolithic to the medieval period. Her excavation talents were quickly recognized: Mira became a core member of the Gomolava team, and while she was still a student, both the Archaeological Institute in Belgrade and the National Museum paid her a salary for her work there. During the five years Mira spent digging at Gomolava, she concentrated mostly on the Neolithic houses, which became her specialty. Mira's interest in Neolithic architecture was also influenced by her future husband, an architect named Vladimir, whom she met at Gomolava.

Later on Mira dug for two seasons at Vinča itself, where excavations had been renewed. She then came to Selevac when Ruth began digging at this Vinča culture site in 1976. Ruth and Mira immediately hit it off and soon became good friends. Indeed, a lot of the women archaeologists working at Selevac came under Ruth's influence. Her high energy level contrasted markedly with the phlegmatic temperaments of many of the male archaeologists they had worked with in Yugoslavia. Yet Ruth and Mira did not always agree about archaeological questions. Mira had a practical, commonsense approach to excavation, while Ruth was into big ideas and big questions about the past. Ruth told Mira that she should question all of her assumptions about prehistory. The two would sometimes get into heated arguments.

Ruth and Mira did share a keen interest in Neolithic architecture, as well as a burning curiosity about why so many houses at so many sites in Southeastern Europe—including Gomolava and Selevac—had been destroyed by fires. At that time the most popular explanation was inspired by Marija Gimbutas, for whom all of prehistory was a dramatic pageantry of invasions and conquests. The villages, Gimbutas believed, had been destroyed by raiders from the east, who stamped out Europe's peaceful, Mother Goddess–worshipping matriarchies and replaced them with patriarchical warrior cultures. Other archaeologists suggested that the fires might be signs of local unrest, while still others suggested that they were accidental, caused by the spontaneous combustion of grain stores or by hearth or oven fires that got out of control.

Ruth and Mira dug Selevac from 1976 to 1979, using conventional excavation methods. They learned a lot about the site, but their techniques were not fine-tuned enough to determine definitively how and why the houses had been burned. Yet they had a hunch that the traditional legends about the prehistoric settlement, which the local villagers had recounted to them, were not correct. Later Ruth repeated in an article the story she had been told about Selevac: "Once there was a great place there, with houses that were so close together a cat could jump from one roof to another. One day, the whole village was burned and destroyed in a great fire and the people moved away." In contrast, in her final report on the excavations, Ruth concluded, "Our model . . . leads us to favor intuitively the idea that the houses . . . were burned deliberately at the end of the household cycle."

Already, at Selevac, Ruth and Mira were beginning to think of Neolithic houses as having symbolically meaningful life cycles. They were not simply built and then abandoned or rebuilt when they fell into a bad state: rather houses, like their inhabitants, were born, lived, and died. To determine whether or not this theory was valid, they needed to find another site that they could dig in a new way, using an excavation strategy that focused on the detailed changes that each house had gone through over time. It took a while, but finally they found one. It was a Vinča settlement called Opovo, a late Neolithic site on the Tamis River in northeastern Yugoslavia that had been founded about 4700 B.C. and abandoned some two hundred years later. At Opovo they would find the answer they were looking for.

MIRJANA STEVANOVIC, arson investigator. By the time she and Ruth had completed their seven seasons of excavations at Opovo, in 1989,

Mira probably could have landed a job investigating criminally suspicious blazes for any fire department or insurance company. Instead she earned a Ph.D. from the University of California at Berkeley.

A decade earlier Ruth had left Harvard for Berkeley. Harvard University had a long-standing, albeit unwritten, tradition of not giving tenure to its junior faculty. Ruth, despite her growing international reputation, was no exception. But her microwear work had attracted the attention of Berkeley anthropology professor J. Desmond Clark, a giant in African archaeology and one of the world's leading experts in stone tools. What Clark did not know was that by the time Ruth came to Berkeley, she was fast losing interest in microwear. Ruth later believed that Clark, who died in February 2002 at the age of eighty-five, never forgave her for what he saw as a betrayal. Her work at Selevac had opened her eyes to a whole new world beyond the microscopic scratches on stone tools, as informative as they could be about the lives of the people who had made and used them. Now she focused her attention on the houses these people had lived and died in. At Opovo Ruth's big ideas about house life cycles and Mira's excavation skills formed a perfect complement. By the time the excavations were over, Mira had some good ideas of her own, and Ruth was good at digging. In addition Ruth had convinced Mira that she needed the intellectual stimulation of a Berkeley graduate school education. The year before the Opovo dig ended, Mira was accepted by the university's anthropology department; she and Vladimir moved to a modest house in the Berkeley hills overlooking the campus, which they remodeled into a stunning work of modern architecture.

Ruth and Mira realized that they could never solve the mystery of the house fires if they stuck to traditional digging methods, especially those commonly used in Yugoslavia and elsewhere in Eastern Europe. Together with Bogdan Brukner, who had directed the excavations at Neolithic Gomolava, they set about designing a novel excavation strategy at Opovo, based on what they had learned at Gomolava and Selevac. Instead of concentrating on clearing the floors of the Opovo houses and the site's portable artifacts, Mira carefully recorded the rubble of the collapsed roofs and walls that had fallen in the course of the fires, as well as the rubble in between the buildings. She also took careful note of the materials used to build the wattle-and-daub houses, especially the relative proportions of wood and clay. And after interviewing arson investigators, thoroughly grounding herself in their technical literature, and performing a number of her own experiments, Mira learned how to determine the temperatures at which clay had been burned from such qualities as its color and the degree of vitrification, or glassiness. She also learned how to pinpoint a fire's ignition point, using a critical investigative technique by which arson experts determine where and how a fire started.

When Ruth and Mira finished the dig and mapped all of this data onto detailed diagrams of the four main houses they had excavated at Opovo, there was only one possible conclusion: the fires had been deliberately set. The evidence was overwhelming: the stratigraphic relationships among the houses showed that each of the blazes had occurred at a different time in the history of the settlement, and the rubble between the houses showed little or no sign of burning. Clearly there had been no villagewide conflagrations. Moreover, the temperatures at which the clay had been burned, especially at the ignition points, were so high—800 degrees centigrade or more—that they could only have been maintained by constantly adding fuel to the fires.

At Berkeley Mira gobbled up the anthropological education that Ruth had insisted upon. She read all the literature she could get her hands on about the symbolic meaning of houses, including the works of anthropologists Claude Lévi-Strauss, Pierre Bourdieu, Marshall Sahlins, and Henrietta Moore, as well as Ian Hodder's book *The Domestication of Europe* and Peter Wilson's *The Domestication of the Human Species.* Now, armed with a powerful theoretical framework, a formidable pile of data from Opovo, and the insights from countless discussions with Ruth, Mira was ready to make her own statements about the symbolic universe of Neolithic people as they made the transformation from a hunter-gatherer existence to a life of settled human domestication. In a major paper in the *Journal of Anthropological Archaeology*, based in part on her Ph.D. thesis, Mira pointed out that the habit of house burning was not restricted to the Neolithic Vinča culture sites in Serbia but had been widespread in neighboring Bulgaria, Romania, Hungary, and the Ukraine. In Bulgaria, for example, it was a regular social practice at nearly every Neolithic site between about 5800 B.C. and 3900 B.C. Indeed, Ruth had first noted this phenomenon during the 1960s, during her Ph.D. research into the Neolithic in Southeastern Europe; in their 1990 report on the Selevac excavations, Ruth and Mira had coined the term "Burned House Horizon" to describe this seemingly ubiquitous finding.

Mira argued that what might seem a destructive act at first glance was really a way of constructing continuity between generations of people and family lineages. "The Neolithic house was brought to closure by burning," Mira wrote. "It was shut off from the active/utilitarian life. At the same time, it is preserved by that same fire." Indeed, the firing of clay, the major building material of wattle-and-daub houses, was the best way to preserve it, as the villagers must have known from their pottery making. The families in question, however, were unlikely to be the small nuclear clusters common in western societies today; rather, Mira suggested, they were probably much more similar to the extended *zadruga* that she herself had grown up in. Moreover, Mira said, the house was much more than a building or shelter, and even more than just a "home" to Neolithic peoples and their extended families. By being burned down, "the house as a *place* gains visibility in a much wider sense." The existence of this place, Mira concluded, "would have been known to the people who built a new house on top of it . . . with an aim to incorporate symbolically and structurally the old house into the new one."

Until then Mira had never dug outside of Yugoslavia, but she certainly had heard of Çatalhöyük, and she was vaguely aware from her reading that Mellaart had found burning horizons at the site, especially in Level VI. To archaeologists working at Neolithic sites in Southeastern Europe, Çatalhöyük was a mythical place, always mentioned with a tone of reverence. In 1993, while Mira was still working on her Ph.D. thesis, Ian Hodder came to Berkeley to teach as a visiting professor and to spend some time with Christine and the twins. Mira attended one of Ian's lectures, in which he briefly mentioned his plans to reopen excavations at Çatalhöyük. Mira could not believe her ears. After all the years she and Ruth had spent exploring the Neolithic Revolution in Yugoslavia, here was a chance to trace the whole process back in time, to get closer to the origins of houses and households. After the lecture she went straight to Ian's office and told him that she wanted to join the project. Ruth, however, had other things going on; she was not quite ready to drop everything and head to Turkey. But as far as archaeological theory went, she was more than ready for a place like Çatalhöyük. While Mira was becoming a real anthropologist, Ruth had been making her own archaeological journey.

RUTH'S MICROWEAR WORK, which clinched her early reputation, had been as scientific and processual as processual archaeology could be. Now, through her work at Selevac and Opovo, she had left microwear behind for the hot new area of "household archaeology," which by the early 1980s had become a very fashionable topic. Ruth was invited to speak at a number of conferences and to contribute to several edited volumes on the subject. Yet her archaeological methodology, including the arson investigation that she and Mira carried out at Opovo, remained empirical and science-based. She was still doing the kind of excavations that any New Archaeologist would be proud to carry out.

All that changed in 1988, when Ruth was asked to attend the Women and Production in Prehistory conference at the Wedge Plantation in South Carolina's low country. The Wedge conference, as it is now known among feminist archaeologists, was organized by anthropologists Margaret Conkey and Joan Gero and resulted in the landmark volume *Engendering Archaeology*. Conkey and Gero had invited a number of archaeological and anthropological theorists to give talks, but they also wanted contributors—such as Christine Hastorf and Ruth Tringham—who had actual empirical data to present. In her published paper in *Engendering Archaeology*, called "Households with Faces," Ruth dramatically claimed that she was dragged "kicking and screaming" to the meeting, where, in the end, she had an "aha" experience. The relevation, she wrote, came during an interchange with Henrietta Moore—Ian Hodder's former graduate student, now an anthropologist at the London School of Economics—while the participants were discussing Ruth's presentation on the household archaeology of Southeastern Europe. "How do you envisage these households?" Moore asked.

"You mean how do I imagine their composition?" thinking: Oh, heavens, she wants me to imagine their kinship structure, but I am interested in what households *did* not what they comprised . . .

Henrietta said, "No, how do you envisage them going about their daily actions?"

You can imagine, I felt quite defensive. "Archaeologists don't do that. We don't go around envisaging people leading cows to pasture and gossiping around the household chores."

"Yes, but what *if* you were allowed to do it; just relax; no one will tell. Now, just tell us how you see them. What do they look like?"

"Well," I said, "there's a house, and cows, and pigs, and garbage . . ."

"Yes, but the people, tell us about the people."

"Well . . . ," I said. And then I realized what I saw. "I see," I said, "a lot of faceless blobs."

Ruth understood what Henrietta was trying to get her to see, and what had been wrong with the processual approach she had taken to archaeology all these years. Until you can put faces on the prehistoric people whose lives you are digging up, she realized, you cannot tell the men and the women apart—not just biologically and sexually, but their relationships with each other and the roles that they play in society. And until you can tell the men and women apart, you cannot reconstruct the human past as something that happened to, or was actively created by, real people. "My wish to retain respectability and credibility as a scientific archaeologist was stronger than my motivation to consider gender relations," Ruth confessed. "Why have archaeologists produced a prehistory of genderless, faceless blobs?"

Ruth thought she knew why. The New Archaeology, she decided, with its emphasis on empirical data gathering and hypothesis testing, had frowned on too much use of the imagination in reconstructing prehistory, largely for fear of going too far beyond the bounds of objectivity and discrediting the entire discipline. Of course, the ability of archaeologists to literally put "faces" on prehistoric people, despite occasional successes such as the meticulous analyses that Christine Hastorf had conducted in Peru, was frustratingly limited. However, as Ruth wrote in an article she published later after several years of work at Çatalhöyük, archaeologists should not "throw up their hands in despair" at this state of affairs; rather, she argued, they should accept and embrace the need to engage in a "self-critical celebration of the ambiguity of archaeological data."

Ruth flung herself headlong into the post-processual camp. She felt liberated to say and write what she was really thinking, to let her archaeological imagination run free.

13 / "Always Momentary, Fluid and Flexible"

With Roger Matthews in Ankara running the British Institute of Archaeology, the Çatalhöyük team leaders moved up in the pecking order as the 1997 season began. Ian, as project director, was still in overall charge. Shahina, who now replaced Roger as Çatalhöyük field director, was Ian's number two. She also continued to lead the excavation team in the south area. Meanwhile Gavin Lucas, who had been Roger's second in command in Building 1, took over as head of that team. And Ruth, as head of the Berkeley Archaeologists at Çatal Höyük (BACH), arrived to direct the excavation of Building 3, a large mudbrick structure just east of Building 1 that had been identified during the surface scraping a few years earlier. Ruth was in overall charge of the BACH project, but she and Mira would share the duties of excavation field director.

Gavin Lucas had been one of Ian's most recent graduate students, receiving his Ph.D. from Cambridge University in 1995. His father was in the British foreign service. After Gavin's birth in Malaysia, he spent much of his childhood in the West Indies. From the age of seventeen he began digging with the Museum of London as a volunteer. Like many on the Çatalhöyük team, he earned his B.A. at the Institute of Archaeology in London, where he took James Mellaart's courses on the Neolithic of the Near East. While working on his Ph.D. thesis, he also excavated with the Cambridge County Council's archaeology unit. Gavin was working on a book about excavation methodologies and trying to figure out what to do next when Ian asked him to join the 1996 excavation team.

The human burials under the floors of Building 1 had slowed excavation to a crawl in 1996. The situation was not a whole lot better in 1997. "Two new, articulated inhumations. Oh joy." Such was the frustration that Gavin expressed in his excavator diary for August 16, although the physical anthropologists on the human remains team were thrilled to have such a large number of bodies to study. Gavin did have a nice moment two days later, however, when he found five bone rings on the left hand of one of the skeletons. The burials kept coming until about two weeks before the end of the season. Then Gavin's team was finally able to deal with something that the excavators had first had intimations of in 1995: a series of paintings on a plaster wall of Building 1, the first major artworks that the project had uncovered.

By the end of Mellaart's third season in 1963, he had excavated well over a hundred buildings, moving tons of earth as he plowed through the site looking for yet more paintings and sculptures. Ian Hodder's team, over the same number of seasons, had now excavated one complete building in the north area; in the south area, Shahina's crew was still exploring the remains of four buildings and several additional rooms that had been left partly excavated during Mellaart's dig. The slow pace was a deliberate part of Ian's contextual, high-definition approach to digging Çatalhöyük. But his strategy meant that the chances of quickly finding the kind of spectacular art that had made the site so famous, and which would impress funders and the news media, were markedly reduced. Of course, in both the north and south areas, the team had found the horn cores of large cattle imbedded in some of the walls as well as the probable remains of entire plastered skulls that had once been mounted there, along with traces of other plaster wall sculptures. But these features had not been very well preserved; the archaeologists knew that something interesting had once existed, but exactly what was not always clear.

The paintings in Building 1 did not depict goddesses, bulls, or vultures, but rather geometrical designs similar to many that Mellaart himself had found. Yet that did not make them any less satisfying or enjoyable for the excavators. Mellaart's strategy, when a painting was spotted—usually because red or black paint was seen peeping from the top of a mud-brick wall—had been to excavate away the layers of plaster until the most intact or interesting artwork was exposed, and then to remove the entire painting, plaster, mud-brick backing, and all. Little or none of the painting's context, other than which wall it had been on, was recorded. In contrast, Gavin and his crew set about to record as much as they possibly could about the works of art they uncovered. When the season was over and Gavin had a chance to go over all of the recording sheets and drawings, a fuller picture of the art history of this particular wall emerged.

The paintings were above a plaster platform where a large number of burials had been unearthed. The Neolithic residents had completely replastered this wall between eighteen and twenty-two times; at least ten of these layers had some evidence of having been painted, mostly during the first half of the building's life. Due to poor preservation of some of the layers, it was possible to trace the paintings extensively on only about five of them. The first few layers of wall plaster, corresponding to the early years of the building's life cycle, were not painted. Layer 6, however, had been decorated with a pattern of red and white rectangles; layer 10 was a red ladder design, as was layer 11; and the last layer was simply painted red all over. But layer 7 was very dramatic: there was a large, complex, red and black geometrical pattern, very similar to the sort of thing that Mellaart had seen in a number of buildings. The sequence of paintings illustrated a point that Mellaart had occasionally made in his own writings about Çatalhöyük and that was increasingly clear to the Hodder team: the walls of the buildings were not painted all the time. For many years at a stretch, they were blank. Did the paintings correspond to particular events in the life of the house and its inhabitants, such as births, deaths, or marriages?

Answering this question was one of the major goals of the project and a cornerstone of any post-processual approach to excavation—figuring out what the symbolism meant. The excavations in Building 1 had shown Ian, Shahina, and the rest of the team that making these connections was going to be more difficult than they had hoped. As Gavin noted in his report on the 1997 season, "Because the wall plaster was left to the very end, their removal was performed with, in effect, *no stratigraphic control;* this means that, for example, tying in the painted plasters to floors can be done only approximately and inferentially."

The team had been forced to make some hard choices in excavating Building 1. The Neolithic residents had applied the layers of wall and floor plaster at the same time, which meant that the only way to trace the paintings and, say, the order of burials under the floors was by working closely at the corners where the floors and walls met. This sometimes conflicted, however, with the need to divide the floors up into one-meter squares to accommodate Wendy's micromorphology samples. Moreover, since the inhabitants of the building had spent a lot of time walking back and forth, the floors were unevenly worn, making it hard to trace long patches. To make matters even worse, at the end of the building's life cycle, its people had vigorously cleaned the floors in preparation for its ritual destruction, destroying some layers. Finally, because wall plaster is fragile and begins to dry out as soon as it is exposed, Frank Matero and the dig's other conservators had advised the team to leave some unexcavated deposits against the walls until the very end and then expose all the plaster at once.

In short, the excavators, faced with this somewhat unexpected situation, had amassed a lot of data from the floors of Building 1, and a lot of details about its artworks—but the relationship between the two remained murky. They would have to do better next time. Shahina and Ian had a lot of discussions over the next few years about how to solve this problem.

RUTH TRINGHAM and the BACH team arrived in characteristically grand style. Ian had arranged for the donation of a very strong and elaborate tent shelter to shield Building 3 from the sun and the elements. When the shelter arrived, it immediately became clear that erecting it was going to be more difficult that anyone had imagined. To keep it from toppling over in the strong Anatolian winds, the supports had to be anchored into the ground. A cement truck was called to pour concrete into the numerous oil drums aligned around the building. Everything seemed to be going well until the team got to the part in the instructions which said they needed a crane to raise the shelter up. Work stopped while a crane was called for. Finally, several days later, the job had been done.

Ruth now declared that the shelter and all of its dominion would heretofore be known as the Goddess Pavilion. At the end of the working day, everyone trooped over to the BACH area for its official inauguration. Champagne and baklava were served. Two of the students had molded a goddess figure around a bottle of Johnny Walker Red Label whiskey, using a combination of napkins, mud, and Scotch tape. Rissa stepped forward with some offerings to the goddess. She described them later in her diary: "Fruits of the earth (domestic, apples and pears), flowers of the fields (wild), remains of creatures of the sea (a fossil coral), the earth (a string of snail shells), and the sky (an owl feather)."

That first season turned out pretty well for the BACH team. It started off by cleaning and scraping the area that had been defined in 1994 during the original surface work, which had revealed six separate spaces. The same six spaces now appeared again, three of which were small "cells" at one end of the building. One of the spaces showed signs of intense burning. The first two weeks were spent excavating some late Roman and Byzantine burials that were cut into the building fill. Although the mound was Neolithic from top to bottom, as Mellaart, French, and Hall had discovered back in 1958, a number of later graves had penetrated into the prehistoric buildings. They could not, however, be treated as filthy Roman muck; they had to be carefully excavated and recorded. In her report on the season Ruth pointed out that the existence of the graves was not surprising, since there was a large settlement dated to the Roman and Byzantine eras near the mound. "It seems an interesting direction for research to use the positioning of the graves as a means to understanding how much was known about the Neolithic architecture and how much was visible and in what way meaningful to the diggers of the Roman/Byzantine graves," Ruth wrote.

One of the most exciting finds of the season was the remains of an apparent collapsed roof, made up of layers of plaster and clay, covering part of one of the spaces. The clay layers varied in color from burned red to charred black. Ruth speculated that the discoloration of the clay might indicate that "domestic activities," such as cooking, took place on top of the roofs at Çatalhöyük. But the slow pace of the excavation meant that the roof could not be completely excavated until the following season. From a more conventional point of view, however, the most spectacular discovery took place on that season's press day, when Mira uncovered a beautiful flint dagger with a bone handle carved in the shape of an animal head—possibly a boar—just as a group of dignitaries was being escorted into the Goddess Pavilion. A similar dagger, found by Mellaart, is on display at the Museum of Anatolian Civilizations in Ankara.

SHAHINA WAS NOW doing double duty at Çatalhöyük. She still had all the responsibilities of supervising the excavation of the south area, plus she was now in day-to-day charge of the entire dig. She went from relatively happy excavator to detail-burdened administrator in the course of one season. Ian was often away, and in any case he hated dealing with daily problems, especially anything that had to do with personnel matters. It had taken all of Ian's inner resources to step in and solve the excavator-specialist conflict of the previous season. Shahina, although she was a partisan in the debate on the side of the excavators, emerged from that episode commanding a lot of new respect from almost everyone on the dig. As she took on new responsibilities, she also took on a new confidence. The insecure young excavator who could not understand why Ian and Roger wanted her to come to Çatalhöyük had proved herself to be a skilled mediator, a keen reader of people and their feelings at any given moment.

At times, however, Shahina felt like she was the den mother of a Cub Scout troop. Keeping more than a hundred independent-minded and often unruly archaeologists in line was often an impossible task. Unless she continually cracked the whip, the standards of cleanliness and civilized conduct at Çatalhöyük would occasionally plummet to dangerous lows. The men were usually the worst offenders, although not always. Shahina was joined in her vigilance by some of the women on the dig, who were equally offended by displays of thoughtlessness. Before long, handwritten signs began to appear throughout the dig house:

> DO NOT USE YOUR DRINKING GLASS AS A SHAVING CUP.
> ALWAYS THROW TOILET PAPER INTO THE BIN PROVIDED AND NOT INTO THE TOILET.
> TURN OFF THE BLOODY MODEM AFTER USE.
> ALWAYS PUT ANOTHER BEER IN THE REFRIGERATOR WHEN YOU TAKE OUT A COLD ONE.

The beer consumed at Çatalhöyük was, of course, the Turkish national brew, Efes. The company's local brewery, not far away on the road to Konya, had a leisure area for its employees, including a big swimming pool where the team sometimes unwound on the Fridays off. One member of the team pointed out that the general mood and stress level could be determined scientifically by monitoring fluctuations in beer consumption from week to week. This would be easy to do because all of the purchase statistics were computerized.

Shahina's day was not entirely taken up with administration. She still got to dig in the south area a fair bit of the time. Mary Alexander had decided not to return for the 1997 season, but Roddy Regan had come back, to Shahina's great relief. Naomi Hamilton moved over to Building 1, but Jonathan Last—who did not have enough pottery to keep him busy full-time—spent a lot of the season working with Shahina's team. In addition to the Turkish students from previous years, the south team was also joined by two newcomers: Burcu Tung, a student and diplomat's daughter from Ankara, whose excellent English meant that she was often called away for translation duties; and Craig Cessford, a Scottish archaeologist who had previously excavated for the Museum of London Archaeology Service and the Cambridge County unit, where Gavin had also worked.

By now Shahina and her colleagues had got well past the stage where they were cleaning up Mellaart's old trenches. A number of new features, including ovens or hearths, the remains of wall decorations, and pits apparently related to the ritual dismantlement of the buildings began to appear. One interesting find was a crawl hole or "doorway" in a wall between two rooms, something not often seen at Çatalhöyük. And

Shahina soon had her own share of burials under the floors, including several infants and a double burial of two adolescents.

But while a great deal of progress had been made, by the end of the season Shahina, who was now responsible for so much of what went on at Çatalhöyük, was feeling very frustrated about how some aspects of the dig were going. She confided these concerns to her diary of September 15:

> It's been too long since I last entered my diary and too much has happened to recap on specifics so I might just ramble on for a bit. I have to say losing some diary entries was demoralising [e]specially as time is so tight. The power problem has been a real setback which needs serious attention for next season, then there aren't always laptops available when the inclination is there, but most of all I think we need more people, and more competent people would make life a lot easier. For every student we ought to have a professional; if it's our duty here to teach students, then they need one-to-one teaching in the field . . . The final 10-day countdown and we're all panicking, well, I certainly am. I really need to get those southern walls down this year as they're not going to survive another year. We've been held up in so many areas by piddly complicated deposits, it's taken me well on three weeks to dig the fire installation 82 in space 109. It turned out to be a lot more complicated than originally thought, lots of small deposits, relining, modifications, raking out—events all made more difficult by being riddled by animal burrows.

Just before the end of the season, however, Shahina had an experience that made it all worthwhile. The video team from Karlsruhe, Germany, had hired a hot-air balloon so that they could film the site from on high. Ian was supposed to ride along, but at the last minute he had to leave early to return to Cambridge, so Shahina got to take his place. The event was scheduled for Friday morning, which was normally Shahina's day to sleep late. The night before, the wind had kicked up, and it was still blowing fairly hard at five A.M. the next day. Shahina sat with the crew in the dig house kitchen, waiting to see if the ride was a go or whether she would go back to bed.

After a couple of hours the wind died down. They drove out to the field where the balloon was tethered, climbed into the basket, and up they went. The wheatfields and irrigation channels of the Konya Plain spread out before them, and the tiled roofs of Küçükköy's mud-brick houses glimmered in the early morning sun. The dirt road that James Mellaart, David French, and Alan Hall had driven down nearly forty years before snaked through the trees to the long, tear-shaped East Mound of Çatalhöyük. The modest tent covering Building 1, and next to it the ostentatious white shelter of the Goddess Pavilion, stood proudly on the north end of the tell. Across what had once been a channel of the Çarsamba River was the smaller West Mound, which the East Mounders may have moved to during the Chalcolithic period.

Shahina's rapture was suddenly interrupted by the microphone that was now thrust in her face by the Karlsruhe team and the video camera that glared at her. She had to talk intelligently about everything they were seeing. Then it was time to come down. It was over all too quickly.

IAN HODDER had come to Çatalhöyük to prove that post-processual archaeology was not merely a brief theoretical fashion but a whole new way of digging up the past. With five seasons of work now behind him, he decided that it was time to go public about how his dig differed from previous ones and what he was trying to accomplish at the site. The 1996 *On the Surface* volume had dealt only with the preliminary preexcavation work, which, as Ian himself admitted in its introduction, had broken relatively little new methodological ground. Now he chose the journal *Antiquity* as his forum. The title of his article, in the September 1997 issue, was characteristically provocative: " 'Always Momentary, Fluid and Flexible': Towards a Reflexive Excavation Methodology."

Ian took issue with what he saw as a still-dominant habit in archaeology, the separation of data recording and description of finds—the so-called objective side of the field—from the interpretative, supposedly subjective side. "How we excavate a site is generally determined by our prior interpretation of the site," Ian wrote. Thus decisions are constantly being made about priorities, depending on the importance that the archaeologist gives to different parts of, say, a building that is under excavation. "A 'floor' context is excavated more intensively than one interpreted as 'fill,' with 100% water-screening only being used in the 'floor' context," Ian argued, posing the question, "How can it be maintained that subjective data interpretation should only occur after objective data description and collection?"

Ian proceeded to list various ways in which the dig at Çatalhöyük was encouraging "interpretation at the trowel's edge": having the specialists working on site to take part in initial interpretation along with the excavators, using computers to get information and feedback to excavators while the dig is under way, the writing of excavator diaries to record what the archaeologists were thinking as they excavated and recorded their data, and video recording of group discussions in the trenches, among other things. Ian also argued that the excavation team had to take into account the views of "outside" groups that have vested interests in what goes on at Çatalhöyük, such as the Turkish government, goddess worshippers, and even carpet scholars, some of whom look to the site as the source for the design of Turkish kilims.

In raising this issue, Ian made direct reference to an issue facing all archaeologists today: who owns the past? Whether it be the Kennewick Man from Washington state, whose 9,300-year-old bones have been fought over by archaeologists and Native Americans since their discovery in 1996, or archaeological finds in the Holy Land, which both Israelis and Palestinians claim as evidence for their rights to this small territory, the past conditions, informs, and sometimes even determines the present. "Within the global communities fascinated by some aspect or another of Çatalhöyük," Ian concluded, "where does one draw the line between those within and without the 'team'? Is not the better solution to make the line as permeable as possible while being responsible for the protection of certain rights? Is it not better to accept openly that even in the construction of archaeological data, interpretation is desired?"

As Ian well knew, that kind of talk was like waving a red flag in front of archaeologists who insisted on strict standards of rationality and objectivity. For a response, *Antiquity* opened its pages to Fekri Hassan, a well-respected Egyptologist at the Institute of Archaeology in London. After a few perfunctory acknowledgments of Ian's contributions to archaeology, Hassan launched a blistering attack on what he saw as "an ethos that celebrates capricious diversity." The job of the ethical archaeologist, Hassan insisted, "is to uphold the mandate of reason when we are overwhelmed by prejudicial emotions and engulfed by dogmatic beliefs, to abide by canons of knowledge that allow us to discern subjective errors, to evaluate the accuracy of our statements, and to assess the confidence we can assign to our judgement." Hassan argued that the viewpoints of outside "interest groups" are irrelevant to archaeological work. "Whether a group wishes to believe in a mother goddess or not, or that another looks to Çatalhöyük for the origins of kilim design, has nothing to do with whether I should use stratified or systematic sampling, or whether an expert colleague finds a bone fragment to be from a deer or pig."

In closing, Hassan took a potshot at Ian's strategy of raising money from corporate sponsors, a criticism often voiced privately among archaeologists but rarely expressed in print: "His advocacy for Information Technology in archaeological excavations is meritorious, but most archaeologists do not command substantial budgets provided by capitalist industries."

For Ian the debate, as he admitted in a later lengthy response to Fekri's response, provided "the nostalgic pleasure of revisiting [the] old battlefields" of the processual/post-processual wars of the previous decade. Ian questioned "whose reason" Fekri's plea for rationality was intended to uphold, and who had chosen and trained the academic archaeologists who now evaluated whether statements and facts were accurate. "We cannot assume an authority," Ian concluded, "we have to argue for it. We cannot simply police the boundaries of the academy and of the discipline against particularist world views. We have increasingly to argue our case in the temporal flows of a diverse global community."

If what Ian was saying was true, there were few digs in the world where it was more true than Çatalhöyük, with its long and controversial history. Just the previous year the site's permeable boundaries had been penetrated by the Turkish police after the episode of the stolen bead—an unsettling reminder that the team was able to work there only with the blessing of the Turkish government, which had its own motivations and priorities where the dig was concerned. Ian relied heavily on the excavation's Turkish speakers, as well as Shahina Farid's and Naomi Hamilton's knowledge of the language, to communicate with the large number of government representatives, Turkish officials, suppliers, and building contractors whose good graces were essential to keeping the dig running smoothly. Now he realized that he needed to gain greater fluency in the language himself.

During a three-week trip to Berkeley to visit Christine and the boys, Ian mentioned to Meg Conkey, the Berkeley anthropologist who had coedited *Engendering Archaeology*, that he was looking for someone to tutor him in Turkish. Meg told him about Ayfer Bartu, a Turkish graduate student who was working on her doctorate with another anthropologist at Berkeley, Laura Nader, the sister of consumer advocate and sometime presidential candidate Ralph Nader. Ian rang Ayfer up, and she agreed to give him lessons. That telephone call marked the beginning of an important friendship; it also cued the entry of yet another key player onto the dramatic stage that was Çatalhöyük.

AYFER BARTU was born on November 24, 1967, in Ankara. Her parents were living in Bursa at the time, a picturesque city across the Sea of Marmara from Istanbul, but her mother was visiting one of Ayfer's aunts in Ankara when her baby was born prematurely. Everyone was sure that Ayfer was going to die, but she had other plans.

Ayfer's mother, a housewife, was from a small village near Izmit, the city that was devastated when an earthquake measuring 7.4 on the Richter scale killed more than 15,000 people in August 1999. Her father was from Istanbul, but his job as a manager for one of Turkey's state banks had taken the family to Bursa. Since Ayfer's premature birth, her mother had been very protective of her: she wouldn't even let her daughter learn to ride a bicycle. But Ayfer's parents greatly valued education. At age eleven Ayfer was sent off to Istanbul to be a boarding student at Robert College, a famous private school founded in the nineteenth century by an American benefactor. The college stood on the quiet, wooded hills overlooking the Bosphorus. At Robert College, where all classes were taught in English except for Turkish literature, Ayfer got an excellent education. She also spent a lot of time visiting another one of her aunts, a left-wing political activist who lived in Istanbul, and a friend and neighbor of her aunt's, Mina Urgan, a well-known Turkish writer.

Ayfer spent all of her secondary school years at the college. She did not get brilliant grades, but they were good enough to get her into the psychology program at the University of the Bosphorus, which had once been part of Robert College but was now independent. Ayfer liked psychology, but her passion for studying really took off when she took an introductory course in sociology. She loved the emphasis on social and political issues—many of her older cousins had been involved in the Turkish student movements of the 1960s and 1970s—and so she decided to do a double major in sociology and psychology. She received her bachelor's degree in 1990. By then Ayfer was ready for a change. She had never been outside Turkey. She felt that she was overdue for some traveling. What better excuse to leave than to find a Ph.D. program somewhere? She went to see the head of the university's sociology department, who had received his doctorate from the University of California at Berkeley some years before. He told Ayfer that she should go someplace where the weather was nice, like Berkeley. "Where is Berkeley?" Ayfer asked.

Ayfer typed out three statements of purpose on Mina's old typewriter. One said that she wanted to do nothing in her life other than sociology; another claimed that she was hopelessly passionate about psychology; and the third implied that her life would be over if she could not do anthropology. She sent them off to the appropriate academic departments at eight American universities and was accepted by three, including the Berkeley anthropology department. The department assigned Laura Nader, who specialized in the anthropology of the law, to be her advisor. But Ayfer's own interests soon gravitated to the field of "heritage tourism," a booming international phenomenon. The U.S. National Trust for Historic Preservation defines heritage tourism as "traveling to experience the places, artifacts and activities that authentically represent the stories and people of the past and present." While Laura Nader remained her advisor, Ayfer began working closely with Nelson Graburn—another member of the department whose own research focused on how heritage tourism serves as a way for people to express their cultural identity—as well as other similarly interested faculty members.

After several years at Berkeley, Ayfer began to miss Turkey. She decided to base her doctoral project on heritage tourism in Istanbul and returned to the country for about a year to do her fieldwork. She called her Ph.D. thesis "Reading the Past: The Politics of Heritage in Contemporary Istanbul." Her choice of title was completely coincidental. At that time she had never heard of Ian Hodder or read his 1986 book *Reading the Past*, the primary manifesto of post-processual archaeology. Shortly after Ayfer had given Ian his first Turkish lesson, in spring of 1996, she was talking to a friend in Berkeley's architecture department about current events in Turkey. The subject came around to archaeology.

"There is a lot happening right now," the friend said. "Even Ian Hodder is digging in Turkey."

Ayfer laughed. "Who is Ian Hodder anyway?" she asked. "I've just been giving him Turkish lessons!"

As an architecture student, Ayfer's friend had read all about Çatalhöyük, a textbook case of some of the best-preserved prehistoric buildings in the world.

Later that year Ayfer met up with Ian in Istanbul and showed him some of the sites she had studied for her Ph.D. dissertation. Then, back in Berkeley, she learned that Ruth Tringham was planning to take a team out to Çatalhöyük for the 1997 season. At that time Ayfer was fairly indifferent to archaeology. She had seen so many Roman and Hellenistic sites in Turkey that she found them boring. But she and Ruth began to talk about how Ayfer could launch a heritage tourism project at Çatalhöyük, a site that in one way or another was claimed by so many different "interest groups." When Ruth discussed the idea with Ian, he got very excited. Ayfer was put on the team.

At Çatalhöyük Ayfer began interviewing everyone she could find who had a relationship of one sort or another with the site. She got to know the people in Küçükköy and Çumra who worked in the kitchen and helped the excavators in the field; she talked to a fashion designer in Istanbul who had made Çatalhöyük the theme of her latest collection; she accompanied goddess worshippers as they climbed to the top of the mound to commune with the Great Mother.

Before long, however, Ayfer found her role changing. She continued to do her research, but she increasingly became what she now calls the site's "cultural broker." As a Turk with an intimate knowledge of Western cultures, Ayfer was in a unique position to bridge the gap between the largely British-American team and the Turkish society in which it worked. And a gap there was. As Ayfer began to accompany Ian on his visits to various officials, it became clear to her that Ian needed help reading between the lines of what was being said, as well as with understanding the differences in body language between the British and the Turks. While as a general rule the British do not speak as directly as the average American, they are much more direct than the average Turk. This was especially true when it came to discussing money, something that Ian had to do often as he arranged for various goods and services for the dig. At first Ian tended to broach the subject quickly, only to be told, "Oh, we will talk about that later." Ayfer taught him that it was necessary to engage in preliminary chitchat before he got to the matter at hand. Ian learned to wait for Ayfer's signal, telling him that he could now begin discussing business.

Ayfer often went with Ian to see the mayor of Çumra, Recep Konuk, who was one of the biggest local supporters of the dig. The mayor, a tall, powerfully built man with jet black hair, had given Ian a great deal of aid in the early years of the excavations. He had helped to secure the use of the building in Çumra where the team first lived and worked, and he had arranged supplies of various equipment and materials. This was a big surprise to Ayfer and other left-leaning Turks who visited the dig, because Mayor Konuk was a member of the right-wing, ultranationalist MHP—the Nationalist Movement Party. The MHP was opposed to Turkey's entry into the European Union, hostile to foreign involvement in the country, and religiously conservative. Some members of the party would refuse to shake hands with female members of the Çatalhöyük team. But it seemed that Konuk had reasons of his own for supporting the dig, especially when, in 1996, he proposed to government authorities in Ankara that a Çatalhöyük museum be built in Çumra. Soon it became clear that the mayor relished the possibility of the increased tourism in the region that the excavations could bring, as well as the enhanced media attention and political prestige that it brought to him personally.

Around the same time, Mayor Konuk decided to rename the town's annual agricultural festival the Çumra Çatalhöyük Festival. The team was invited to make a slide presentation about the excavations, after which the mayor handed out prizes for the winning tomatoes and melons. Ian was called up to the stage and given a plaque. Indeed, it seemed that Konuk had taken a shine to Ian. Whenever Ian would visit his office, the mayor would grab hold of him and shake him, saying, "I like this guy, I really like him!" At first Ian, whose shy and reserved manner had never left him, would freeze up, but over time he got used to the mayor's ebullience.

One day Ian and Ayfer attended a meeting that included Mayor Konuk and a number of other officials from the town. Ian sat next to Konuk, who began shaking him back and forth in his chair. The mayor, who did not speak English, turned to Ayfer:

> MAYOR: I know you've told him how much I like him before. But please tell him that I like him so much, I want to wrestle with him!
>
> IAN: What did he say?
>
> AYFER: He says he wants to wrestle with you.
>
> IAN (BLUSHING): Right now?

On another occasion a local official was visiting Çatalhöyük when some goddess worshippers came through on a tour. Ian knew that the frequent presence of the goddess contingents was a sensitive point for Turkish authorities in this religiously conservative area. The Turkish press had occasionally made an issue of it. Ian's language skills were now somewhat better, so he decided to ask the official directly what he thought about these women coming to Çatalhöyük. But what he actually said, in perfectly grammatical Turkish, was "Do you love all the women?"

The official was a little taken aback at first. Ian, realizing that he had got something wrong, glanced at Ayfer. "Don't look at me!" Ayfer said.

The official recovered his composure. "It doesn't matter to us," he said. "Man or woman, we love everyone."

14 / The Long Season

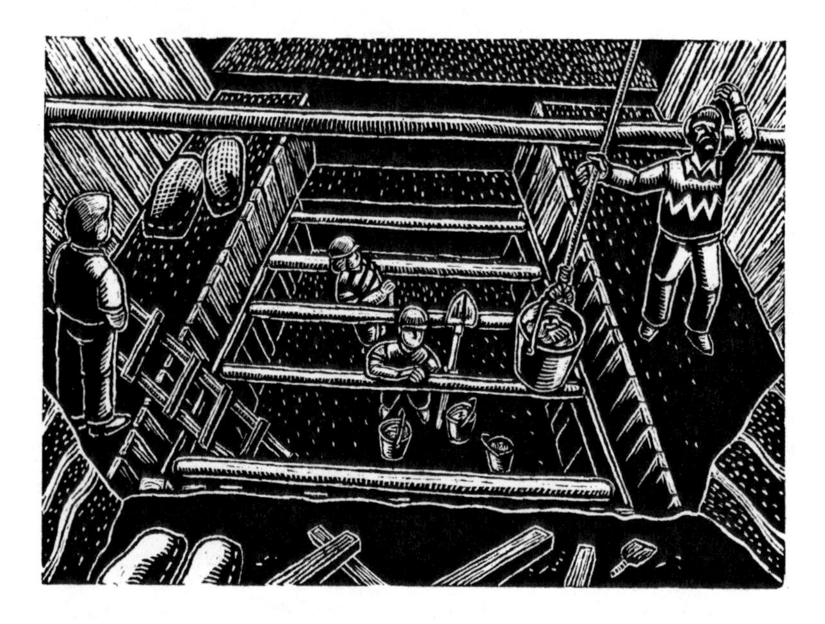

IN 1998, Gavin Lucas left the Çatalhöyük project to start his own excavation in Iceland. His legacy to the dig was completing the excavation of Building 1, except for some remaining walls and the fill from whatever structure might lie beneath it. Gavin also reexamined Roger Matthews's preliminary interpretations of the different phases of occupation in the building and concluded that its life cycle could be further subdivided into a total of seven detectable phases.

Gavin was replaced by Craig Cessford, the Scottish archaeologist who had made his debut at Çatalhöyük the previous year. Craig was short and a little stocky, with a shy manner and a dry, often devastating sense of humor. Three days into the season, Craig presented his own offering to the project: the first glimpse of the mud-brick walls of Building 5, as the house underneath Building 1 was now designated. As the season progressed, the beautiful preservation of this building became increasingly clear. It had four well-defined rooms, including one large central space and three somewhat smaller spaces. The plaster on the south wall of the central room showed the clear scars of the ladder by which its inhabitants had entered and exited. One of the smaller rooms had seven storage bins made of clay and plaster, and there was a small hole in the wall between the central room and an adjacent space, possibly for passing food back and forth to the main room from a kitchen area. In many rooms the large pits left by the wooden timbers that supported the building's walls and roof were clearly visible. Building 5 was, in short, one of the best-preserved Neolithic buildings ever found in the Near East.

As Craig excavated each day in this wonderful building, he assumed that it was only serendipity that had put him in charge of the Building 5 crew instead of his continuing to work with Shahina in the south area. "I have risen to the dizzy heights of supervising the North area," Craig wrote in his excavator diary. "Lots of extra responsibility and stress but no extra advantages or money. I would have been more happy to come back as a humble excavator and work on my oven and the rest of spaces 150/151 but thanks to Gavin giving up the on-going saga that is Çatalhöyük to dig in the land of the Sagas (here only 1 week and already I'm making appalling puns) and Chad having Rhodesia confused for Rhodes by the Turkish Embassy (can this rumor really be true?) I get to be third choice to run the North area."

"Chad" was Adrian Chadwick, a graduate student at Sheffield University who had excavated at Çatalhöyük in 1997. Chadwick's visa application at Çatalhöyük had indeed been denied. Every once in a while the Turkish authorities would strike someone off the project's excavation permit without explanation. The Greek team led by Kostas Kotsakis, after working at Çatalhöyük in 1996 and 1997, was not allowed back in 1998, an apparent casualty of a downturn in Turkish-Greek relations. In other cases, such as Chadwick's, the reasons remained a mystery.

Craig's suspicions that he had been chosen to supervise Building 5 by default did not reflect accurately his considerable skills as an excavator. Craig was born on December 24, 1969, in Edinburgh. He grew up in a small medieval market town called Jedburgh in Scotland's Borders region, south of Edinburgh. The family, which included Craig's younger sister, lived at the edge of Jedburgh, which was situated in a picturesque rural area. Craig did well in school, but until his last year in high school he did not think much about what he wanted to do in life, although he did have a long-standing interest in both history and archaeology. He had often visited local digs—there were plenty of medieval castles and Roman ruins in the Borders area—although he had never worked on one.

Craig decided to apply to the University of Newcastle, just over the border in England. He went to the university's open day and heard a talk by John Chapman, a well-known expert in the Neolithic of Southeastern Europe. Chapman was the first archaeologist Craig had ever talked to. He liked what he heard, and Chapman agreed to accept him into the archaeology program. Craig was the first member of his family to go to university.

To get some excavation experience, he spent that summer digging with the Raunds Area Project, a large, multisite rescue dig in Northamptonshire County. Like so many archaeologists, Craig loved the physical experience of excavation and the sense of achievement and discovery. Once he started his university courses, Craig found that his favorite archaeological period was the Anglo-Saxon epoch, which he much preferred to prehistory. Prehistoric sites in the United Kingdom tend to be poorly preserved. The kind of preservation seen at big tell sites like Çatalhöyük does not show up in Britain until the Roman period.

Craig dug at several other sites over the next several years, including a spectacular Roman town at Caerwent in southeastern Wales. In 1988, while excavating a postmedieval farm and a mill building at Roadford Reservoir in Devon, Craig met Anja Wolle, another student at Newcastle University. Anja was majoring in archaeology and minoring in computer science. She was German but had grown up in Brussels, where her mother and father had worked since the 1960s. Before long the two were a couple. Craig finished his bachelor's degree at Newcastle and went on to get his master's degree. At that point Anja decided to move to the University of Southampton to do her own master's degree. The pair moved to the city and spent five years there. Craig worked on short-term contracts on various rescue digs in southern England and then for eighteen months for the Museum of London Archaeology Service (MOLAS). While with MOLAS he worked on a big, very well preserved

Anglo-Saxon settlement at the Royal Opera House in Covent Garden. Meanwhile Anja, who had finished her master's degree, was hired by the Çatalhöyük project right after the 1996 season ended to run its computer operations. She asked Ian if Craig could join the project too. Craig and Ian had a half-hour chat in Ian's Cambridge office. Ian, in his usual distracted way, never got around to telling Craig that he had been accepted as a member of the Çatalhöyük team; Craig had to ask Anja to find out for him.

Now Craig was in charge of Building 5, a spectacular Neolithic house. But his joy was short-lived. Craig had already begun to worry about the fate of the Building 5 excavations when Ian made it clear that he wanted the building looking good for that year's press day. As the day approached, Frank Matero and his conservation team began spending a lot of time in the building, patching cracks in the mud-brick walls and stabilizing fragile plaster layers with chemical preservatives. "Hopefully we can work around him," Craig told his diary on August 9. "I am more concerned about what this means in terms of what I will be allowed to dig in Building 5. I am worried that we will reveal a nice palimpsest but will not be able to gain much real understanding and that we may also damage the building as an entity by excavating a few bits and destroying some evidence by partial excavation."

What Craig did not know at the time was that Ian had agreed to a request by the Turkish authorities that a building be put on public display for a period of five years. Ian had chosen Building 5. This meant that the building could not be entirely excavated; most of the walls, floors, and other features would have to be left in place. As the end of the 1998 season approached, Craig resigned himself to the situation: "In terms of progress I think that we have achieved quite a lot," he recorded in his diary for September 7. "We removed the walls of Building 1, examined the deposits and other buildings this revealed, removed a lot of infilling, revealed Building 5, dug a small selection of deposits from Building 5 and made a good start at understanding and interpreting the building. It is extremely frustrating that it will be a long time until Building 5 is excavated."

To some extent Ian shared Craig's frustration. The natural instinct of the archaeologist is to excavate a site completely, to understand it as thoroughly as possible. But archaeology is a destructive process. Excavating a Neolithic building means taking it apart piece by piece and layer by layer, until all that is left is the data on the archaeologist's recording sheets and the artifacts recovered, such as pottery, obsidian, and bone tools. The animal bones go to the faunal lab, the charcoal and burnt seeds to the botany lab, and the human remains to the anthropology lab. And in the case of a Neolithic tell like Çatalhöyük, which has more than a dozen occupation layers covering about a thousand years of prehistory, the only way to get a good look at the bottom levels is to take off the top ones.

On the other hand, a world-famous site like Çatalhöyük belongs to all of humanity. The Turkish authorities, as well as the corporate sponsors, had up to now been remarkably patient about Ian's slow digging pace and the minimal number of iconic, Mellaart-style goddesses and bulls to show off. By putting Building 5 on display, the team had fulfilled its responsibility to make Çatalhöyük more accessible to the public. Five years after the new excavations had begun, more than 90 percent of the mound was still untouched. There were still twenty years left to go in Ian's long-range plan. And just as Mellaart had left most of the site to Ian, it was likely that Ian would leave a large part of it for future generations of archaeologists to excavate.

Frank Matero and his team finished the conservation of the building, a wooden viewing platform was built around three sides of the structure, and numbered information panels were installed on the guardrails to explain what all the features were. The visitors to Çatalhöyük, whose numbers were increasing each year, could now enjoy a rare glimpse into the private home of a 9,000-year-old Neolithic family.

BY THE 1998 SEASON life at Çatalhöyük had settled into somewhat of a routine. The archaeologists now knew each other well enough to be able to resolve conflicts before they got out of hand. The tensions between excavators and specialists, which had nearly wrecked the dig in 1996, had not entirely disappeared, but they became manageable. After a number of discussions, the team decided to limit the almost daily specialist tours that had so annoyed the excavators and recast them as "priority tours." The specialists and excavators now chose particular excavation units—usually corresponding to spaces or features—which would be the subject of special analyses in which everyone would be involved. The priority tours took place less frequently and were focused on specific questions. With time the barriers between people began to fall. A greater sense of community took hold among the team members.

The Neolithic community that had lived here 9,000 years earlier may well have been held together by shared religious or ideological beliefs, expressed in the art on the walls and in community rituals—although a key tenet of post-processual archaeology was not to assume that everyone in prehistory had the same ideas about everything. With the archaeologists working at Çatalhöyük, such a uniformity in viewpoint was hardly possible. In 1998 the team was made up of more than ninety people from eight different countries: Turkey, the United States, the United Kingdom, Germany, the former Yugoslavia, Denmark, Sweden, and South Africa. What held the community of archaeologists together was a common goal—excavating Çatalhöyük—and common rituals, ceremonies, and symbols. From the very beginning of the Hodder dig, the most visible symbol had been the Mother Goddess. Of course, most of the archaeologists questioned the claims that James Mellaart and Marija Gimbutas had made about goddess worship at Çatalhöyük. No one on the team was a practicing goddess worshipper, or at least no one admitted to being such. Yet the goddess was everywhere. Her image was on the dig house, on Mellaart's birthday cake, on the project's official stationery, on the Çatalhöyük Web site, on the official visitor's guide to the excavations. At one level, it was all a joke, but all jokes have their serious meanings, and all jokes have the effect of bringing people together, if only in laughter.

One Thursday evening during the 1997 season, Julie Near decided to organize a barbecue. Since Friday was the only day off, Thursday was the one night that people could stay up late without worrying about how they would feel the next day. Julie, a vivacious American, felt that the team had gotten into a bad funk. Everyone was working very hard, and the dig's social life seemed to be suffering. A party seemed just the thing to liven things up. The barbecue was held in the courtyard of the dig house. There was music and dancing around a fire, and plenty of food and drink. The event was such a big success that the team decided to have a barbecue every Thursday night.

In 1998 Ian hired John Swogger, a talented American artist from New Hampshire, to be the team's archaeological illustrator. Julie and John teamed up to become the core organizing committee for the barbecues. One big problem was where to get the large amount of fuel required for the obligatory ritual fires. They took a cue from the Neolithic inhabitants of Çatalhöyük and decided to use dried animal dung. Each party was preceded by organized forays into the surrounding fields to find the stuff. Christine Hastorf got excited about the possible scientific spin-off. She put one of her students to work doing experiments to see how the dung burned, at what temperatures, what it looked like before and after, and so on. Then one week, on a whim, a few people showed up to the party dressed as Gypsies, apparently to express the idea that the archaeologists were like a band of nomads on the isolated Konya Plain. The Çatalhöyük costume theme party, a Thursday night ritual ever since, was born.

The old British Embassy bar, which had been a ritual gathering point when the team lived in Çumra, was retrieved from storage and set up next to a shed behind the dig house. It was in bad shape but still functional. Each week Julie and John would announce the theme ahead of time: the Masked Ball, Wild West Night, Çatalhöyük Wild Animals, Christmas in September, Turkish Night, Beaver-Moose Piñata, and so on. At first they were afraid that they would be the only ones to show up in costume, because no one seemed to be doing anything to prepare. It turned out that most people were spending Thursday afternoon secretly getting ready, eager to outdo the others with the most elaborate and imaginative costume. For Çatalhöyük Theme Night, for example, the Hodder twins, Nicky and Kyle, came as a double-headed figurine from the Mellaart excavations (a large flour sack with eyeholes for two), Julie dressed up as a wall painting, and Ruth, to no one's surprise, came as the Mother Goddess.

Despite the late-night parties, the team also got more organized about how to spend the Friday days off. Minibus trips were organized into Konya, to the Efes Brewery swimming pool, and occasionally farther afield to other archaeological sites such as Aşikli Höyük and Musular in Cappadocia. One Friday Louise and Rissa joined a minibus going to the Kara Dağ, a huge volcanic formation forty miles southeast of Çatalhöyük that rises more than 1,000 meters above the Konya Plain. The site of Pinarbaşi, where Edinburgh University archaeologist Trevor Watkins had recently been searching for the possible origins of the people who settled Çatalhöyük, is nestled in some hills just north of it. The minibus chugged up the side of the Kara Dağ, occasionally stopping so that local village men could pour water over its overheating radiator. Eventually they reached the village of Binbirkilise ("A Thousand and One Churches"), where the group stopped to look around.

One of the village women called the archaeologists over to have a drink of *ayran*, Turkish buttermilk. They sat on her porch, smiling politely and trying to communicate, although not with much success. Afterward Louise and Rissa wandered past the village into some fields where melons, onions, and tomatoes were growing. It was a rare moment of respite from the frenetic pace of the dig.

If the 1998 season marked a new sense of calm and community among the Çatalhöyük archaeologists, it also brought a sense of security to Rissa. Her long search for a job was over. She had recently been hired into a tenure track position by Cornell University, in Ithaca, New York. As if to celebrate the news, Roger Matthews showed up for a visit around midday on a Thursday. He had brought his guitar with him. At that evening's barbecue, as Roger played "Catch the Wind," Rissa thought back to her birthday two years before, when her career was looking bleak and she thought that she might never hear him play again.

SUDDENLY the calm was shattered. Ian's news fell on the team like a bombshell. Recent monitoring of the water table in the immediate vicinity of Çatalhöyük showed that it had dropped precipitously just within the past year. The intense irrigation of sugar beet and melon fields in the region had taken its toll. The drop meant that the deepest Neolithic levels of the mound, where high moisture levels might have been expected to preserve organic remains such as wood implements, baskets, and textiles, could be drying out. The team had to get to the bottom of the mound, and it had to get there fast.

In 1970 a team of paleoecologists working in the Konya area had measured the water table near Çatalhöyük and found that it was less than a meter from the surface. The current paleoecology team, led by geographer Neil Roberts, knew that the water table had dropped dramatically since then. But as recently as 1997, excavations by Neil's team in the area just north of the mound itself—which had been undertaken with the aim of looking at the off-site activities of the Neolithic settlement—had suggested that the lower levels might still be waterlogged. It now appeared that this was no longer true.

Ian told the team that both he and the Turkish government were seeking funding for an eight-month excavation season in 1999, including a possible loan from the World Bank. Eight months was nearly four times the normal season length. The aim would be to dig a deep sounding down to the lowest levels of Neolithic occupation. This would allow Turkish authorities to evaluate how much danger there really was to the site and what changes might be necessary in irrigation policy. From an archaeological point of view, the sounding would give the team a chance to learn about the earliest days of the settlement before the best evidence was destroyed. A core group of professional excavators and specialists would come out for the entire time. Ian gave the specialists less than a week to decide whether they were on board for the entire season or if they wanted to recommend people to fill in for them.

Çatalhöyük, the most ambitious research excavation in the Near East, was about to become a rescue dig. The whole plan was going to cost a lot of money. Ian got busy working the telephones.

THE LONG SEASON, as it was called by the Çatalhöyük team, officially began on April 1, 1999. The Konya Plain, dry and brown in the summer, was a lush green, dotted with pink flowers. The mountains in the distance were covered with snow. The days were nice, but nights were cold, sometimes below freezing. Shahina showed up looking lean, mean, and mentally prepared. She had cut her long hair very short. She was joined by seventeen other excavators and specialists who had likewise agreed to stick it out for the duration. Two more diggers would come out a little later in the spring, making the core group an even twenty. The rest of the Çatalhöyük team would come out in July or August as usual. In between seasons Ian and Shahina had discussed whether they should arrange for psychological counseling once the longtimers got back home. No specific plans were made, but Shahina agreed to be on the lookout for telltale signs of burnout.

The World Bank loan was not approved, but Ian raised over $500,000 from other sources, about half from corporate sponsors and the rest from British and American foundations and research councils. This was not enough to dig for a full eight months, so the length of the season was reduced to six months. But the goal remained the same: to get down to the bottom of the mound by the end of the season, or in archaeological lingo, to "reach natural." The shorter schedule made the pressure even greater. The excavators included Shahina, Craig Cessford, Jonathan Last, Nurcan Yalman, Adnan Baysal, and several other professional diggers who had either worked at Çatalhöyük before or whom Shahina knew to be levelheaded and mature enough to take the stress.

Finding specialists who could come out for the entire time was more difficult. Neither Louise nor Rissa, with their academic jobs, could do it. Rissa recruited a Canadian zooarchaeologist named Sheelagh Frame, who had just finished her Ph.D. at Berkeley with Ruth Tringham. The archaeobotany was handled by Andy Fairbairn, a graduate student at the Institute of Archaeology in London, and his wife, an Australian archaeobotanist named Amanda Kennedy. The human remains were covered by Başak Boz, a Turkish anthropology graduate student. And since James Conolly had decided to make 1998 his last season, another lithics expert, Tristan Carter from the Institute of Archaeology in London, made the long trip to Çatalhöyük. As for the pottery, which the team expected would diminish in quantity as the dig reached the so-called aceramic levels before pottery was used or invented, Jonathan Last took off his excavator's hat in the evenings and became the pottery specialist.

In between seasons Ian and Shahina had mapped out the strategy for 1999 very carefully. The idea was to open up a sounding nine meters by nine meters wide where Mellaart had dug his own deep sounding in the 1960s and which Shahina had excavated further, and then to go down the five meters they estimated would be necessary to reach natural. For safety purposes, they would step in the sounding so that the walls would not collapse on top of them, and end up with a space at the bottom that was about five meters by five meters wide. This would allow them to excavate a variety of different buildings, spaces, and midden areas. But less than two weeks into the season, the first crisis hit. Turkish authorities in Ankara had decided that no Neolithic walls could be removed. Not only did this rule compromise the safety of the team, but it made the strategy they had worked out impossible. On April 12 a difficult meeting was held with the director general of museums and monuments in Ankara, a meeting attended by Ian, Ayfer, and Roger Matthews in his capacity as director of the BIAA. The upshot was a change in the excavation plan. They would now excavate through the three buildings that Mellaart had designated Shrines 1, 8, and 10. In theory no walls would be removed or fully exposed, meaning that no artworks would be revealed; that was okay with Shahina, but she was concerned that the relationships between the floors they excavated and the walls would be lost, as had happened in Building 1.

The team got busy digging. Mellaart, during one of his visits to Çatalhöyük (he had come back again in 1998) had told the archaeologists that while digging his own deep sounding he had found some inscribed clay tablets. He said he had put them in a biscuit tin and left them at the bottom to preserve them from the elements. The excavators declared that the biscuit tin would be their Holy Grail for the season. Craig drew up a plan of Mellaart's deep sounding and organized a tongue-in-cheek competition: everyone put an X where they thought the tin would be found.

Mellaart had defined more than a dozen occupation levels at Çatalhöyük, which he numbered 0 to XII in Roman numerals. The higher the number, the earlier the level. Thanks to the work that Shahina's team had done in the south area since 1995, they were now able to start roughly at Level X, although the exact level varied from building to building. Mellaart had earlier given Ian a diagram of his own deep sounding with his depth measurements. The Konya Plain was about 1,000 meters above sea level. According to Mellaart's measurements, Level XII was 998 meters above sea level and the floors of Level X were at 1003 meters. If this was correct, it would mean they had at least five meters to dig through. When they got closer to the bottom, they would take a core down through the stratigraphic layers to see how deep they really had to go.

In mid May the grave of an infant was found in an area where Charlie Newman, a professional excavator who had dug in London and Oxford, was working. The baby had been laid to rest on a reed mat, of which only the impression was left. Two bracelets made of teardrop-shaped bone beads were found around its ankles, and its wrists bore bracelets made of bone and stone colored blue, black, and white. Red ochre had been sprinkled over the burial. Ian and Shahina decided to remove it as a whole skeleton, rather than bone by bone as usual, and have it put on display in the Konya archaeological museum. This made Charlie very happy, as it was one of the few skeletons found at Çatalhöyük to be treated this way. "The excavated skeleton is, in my opinion, very beautiful," Charlie wrote in his excavator diary. "There has been great care taken over the burial of the infant. These artifacts seem to be too large to have actually been used in life. Maybe they were gifts at the time of birth from relatives, things which the child would use when it was a little older."

Early in June an unusual grave of an adult was uncovered. The body was on its back, its legs bent and pushed to the side. There was a wooden plank covering its chest. A film crew from the BBC recorded the events as Başak excavated it. The skeleton turned out to be headless.

A few days later, in a layer roughly equivalent to Mellaart's Level XI, the team found a fine layer of organic deposits. Wendy Matthews was called in and immediately said that they were penning deposits, that is, dung from animals that had been kept inside a building or a courtyard. This strongly suggested that animals were right on the site in the early days of the settlement.

As June wore on, the core team realized that it was getting tired. The regular season people were due to start showing up in just a couple of weeks. The team would expand from twenty people to nearly a hundred practically overnight. The Long Season crew began to feel like it was about to be invaded. "I feel really drained" Craig told his diary on June 17. "I am also worried about the three-ring circus that the project normally turns into when everyone is here." Craig was also worried that the height measurements might be wrong. If natural was six meters below where they started rather than five, they might not make it before the season was over.

They were now just about halfway through the Long Season. The core team decided to take a few days of holiday before the rest of the people arrived. All twenty of them took off together for the Mediterranean coast.

ELENI ASOUTI did not come to Çatalhöyük to make a political statement. She came to study the site's charcoal remains. They would provide important new information about what types of trees and other plants the Neolithic people used for fuel and other purposes and where in the landscape they went to get them. In a perfect world the fact that Eleni was Greek and that Çatalhöyük was in Turkey would have been irrelevant. Unlike Kostas Kotsakis, the leader of the Greek team at Çatalhöyük, she was not trying to trace the links between the two regions in prehistoric times. The peoples of the Neolithic did not have national borders, nor did the natural world in which they lived. Eleni was an environmental archaeologist, devoted to understanding how humans in past societies interacted with other animals and plants to form an integrated ecosystem. But modern geopolitics forced Eleni to jump over a national border to work in Turkey. And when she got there, she felt more at home than she could ever have imagined.

Kostas had not brought a Greek team to Çatalhöyük to make a political statement either. He had come to trace the roots of the Greek Neolithic back to their origins in Anatolia. As a graduate student at the University of Thessaloniki during the late 1970s and early 1980s, Kostas studied the pottery at the Neolithic site of Sesklo in Thessaly, where the earliest occupation layers dated to about 6500 B.C.—right around the time that Çatalhöyük was abandoned. Sesklo and similarly ancient sites in Greece represented some of the first Neolithic settlements in Europe. Kostas was familiar with the work of Ruth Tringham, John Chapman, and other archaeologists who had worked in Southeastern Europe, where the Neolithic Revolution had spread quickly after its initial landfall in Greece.

Kostas had known Ian Hodder since the late 1980s, when he had spent a year in Cambridge. Sometime in 1995 Ian called and asked if he wanted to bring a team to Çatalhöyük beginning with the 1996 season. Kostas was excited about the idea, although he was not sure if Turkish authorities would grant permission. Relations between Greece and Turkey, never great at the best of times, were particularly strained. There had been recent clashes between Greeks and Turks on the Green Line in Cyprus. In early 1996 Greece and Turkey came to the brink of war over the so-called Imia-Kardak affair, a chain of events that had begun on Christmas Day 1995 when a Turkish freighter ran aground in the Dodecanese Islands. Kostas also knew that the Konya region was very conservative politically. He decided the best approach was to make it clear that he was not coming to Turkey as a representative of Greece but as an archaeologist interested in the Anatolian Neolithic.

For the first two years, that strategy worked well. During the 1996 and 1997 seasons, Kostas and his team excavated in what was called the summit area, corresponding to some of the later occupation layers at Çatalhöyük—the ones that might most be expected to bear cultural similarities to the early Neolithic of Greece. The mayor of Çumra welcomed the Greeks warmly, declaring that they were honored guests. Then, in 1998, the Greek team's visas were denied. No explanation was given, but Kostas assumed that it was because of politics. Diplomacy between Greece and Turkey was a complicated dance, not immediately readable, and the consequences of tensions one year might not be felt until later on. Whatever the reason, for two years no Greek archaeologist worked at Çatalhöyük—until, one day in 1999, a slim young woman with an intense passion for archaeology showed up at the site. The place was never quite the same again.

Eleni Asouti was born on January 25, 1972, in Athens. Her father worked for Olympic Airways, a job that took him and the family all over Greece. The family, which eventually included Eleni's two sisters and one brother, usually lived in the countryside just outside the cities her father was based in. Compared to many other children, Eleni had a lot of freedom to roam around the landscape. From the age of about nine years, she became a voracious reader. The first book she remembers reading was Jules Verne's *Around the World in Eighty Days.* An excellent student, she was easily accepted to Athens University, where at first she thought she wanted to be a historian. She was very interested in the turbulent history of modern Greece. Eleni had been only two years old when the seven-year dictatorship of the Greek generals came to an end and democracy was restored, but her parents discussed it often at the dinner table as she grew older. After entering the university, however, Eleni found that the history courses were a disappointment. The academic track that she was on allowed her to study both history and archaeology and then to make up her mind about which she would do. She decided on archaeology, specifically environmental archaeology.

Eleni had not known that there was such a thing until she attended some lectures by archaeologists who had done that kind of work abroad. It sounded fascinating to her. Taking an introductory course in the subject, she quickly learned that archaeology was not just about pottery and stone tools. It could also be about trees, animals, climate—in short, the great outdoors in which she had grown up. Athens University did not have a formal program in the subject, so Eleni began reading a great deal on her own. In one book about scientific method in archaeology, she read a short article by Cecilia Western, a pioneer in charcoal analysis and one of the first women to become prominent in the field. Eleni was bowled over by the idea that one could reconstruct the environment around an archaeological site by studying its charcoal. This was what she wanted to do.

Eleni knew that the Institute of Archaeology in London was one of the best places in Europe to study environmental archaeology. The other was the University of Sheffield. Cecilia Western had donated her entire charcoal collection to the institute, and of course Gordon Hillman and other archaeobotanists had given the gray building on Gordon Square an international reputation. The year that Eleni received her state scholarship from the Greek government to pursue a master's degree, the London institute was not offering the archaeobotany course, so she went to Sheffield, where Paul Halstead—the former Cambridge graduate student into whose apartment a very wet Michael Parker Pearson had burst so many years before—was in charge of the course. At Sheffield she learned how to identify thousands of plant species from their seeds, leaves, and stems; how to core for pollen samples; and important, how to use a microscope, which she had never done before.

With her master's degree from Sheffield, Eleni applied to the Institute of Archaeology to do her Ph.D. She was accepted by John Hather, the institute's wood expert. But Eleni was in a quandary. Her scholarship funding required that she begin working on her Ph.D. thesis right away. That meant that she needed charcoal to work on from an archaeological site. She found that she had two choices of material, and she had to decide within a week or two which she was going to tackle. One choice was to study the charcoal from a long-completed dig in Greece. Meanwhile Hather had spoken to Ian Hodder and found out that the Çatalhöyük dig had no wood specialist. At first Eleni was not sure what to do. Basing her Ph.D. on the Greek material would make her life much easier, and it would also make it easier for her to get a job in Greece later. She had never been to Turkey. Personally, she had no time for the stereotypes that some Greeks and Turks had about each other, or for the stereotypes that some other people held about the complex relationship between the two nations. Still, Eleni knew that it would be a big challenge to base her Ph.D. on a project in Turkey. She decided to go for it.

Eleni started her Ph.D. work at the institute in September 1997. Ian had invited her to come to Çatalhöyük that summer, but she had to finish her master's thesis at Sheffield and was not able to make the trip. She made plans to come out in 1998, but that year Kostas's team was refused entry. Eleni also fell victim to whatever decisions were being made behind the scenes by Turkish authorities. Her visa was denied. She was devastated, but she decided to continue working on charcoal specimens that the team exported back to London and to apply again the following year. When the time came, she put in her visa application and tried not to think about it too much. She began looking for other sites to work on. Then, in late June, just before the regular season was about to begin, she got e-mails from both Ian and Roger Matthews saying that she was on the permit. Once again, there was no explanation. Eleni, happy and excited, got ready to go to Turkey.

Eleni's arrival at Çatalhöyük in 1999 filled a critical gap in the otherwise impressive collection of archaeological specialties represented at the site. The archaeobotany team, led by Christine Hastorf, had grown considerably. It now included Julie Near, Andy Fairbairn, Amanda Kennedy, and several Turkish graduate students, including Meltem Agcabay. The previous year Arlene Rosen, an expert in the analysis of phytoliths—tiny fossil plants that are ubiquitous in an ancient site like Çatalhöyük—had also joined the team. Before long this formidable army of plant experts would join forces with Neil Roberts, who was leading the paleoecology team, and Doug Baird, whose crew was making great progress on the regional survey of the Konya Plain, to create a detailed portrait of Çatalhöyük's place in the larger landscape—thus giving the entire team the insights it needed to figure out why these early farmers had come to this area in the first place.

Eleni had been at Çatalhöyük only days when she realized that she had much more in common with the Turkish students than with anyone else on the dig, especially the Turkish women. She spent most of her free time laughing and talking with Nurcan, Meltem, and Banu Aydinoglugil, a member of the faunal team with whom she became good friends. Their body language, their way of laughing, their entire view of the world, seemed nearly identical to hers—and much different from that of the comparatively reserved British archaeologists she knew in England and on the dig. One day Eleni was talking to Louise Martin, who knew her from the institute in London, about the villagers who lived in the area around Çatalhöyük: "If I changed their religion and their clothes and changed the signs over the shops and in the roads, it would be just like I was in Greece."

As the weeks went by, Eleni's friendships with the Turks grew ever closer. And when Banu learned that Ian had arranged a scholarship for her to spend a year studying in London, she and Eleni made plans to be flatmates.

THE LONG SEASON team was back from holiday. Craig Cessford and Pete Boyer, a member of Neil Roberts's paleoecology team who was working in the deep sounding that year, drilled three cores into the bottom of the trench to see how much farther they had to go before they reached natural. They found fragments of clay, bone, obsidian, and charcoal down to about 999 meters above sea level; then they hit a thin layer of alluvium laid down by the river that had once flowed right next to the mound, followed by the marl of an extinct lake that had once covered much of the Konya Plain. This seemed like good news: natural might be a full meter closer than they had thought. In mid-July Craig spent a day and a half excavating two newborn babies that had been buried in baskets. Despite the encouraging results from the coring,

Craig, who had a tendency toward pessimism, was feeling the pressure. In his diary entries he began taking some shots at the specialists and other academic archaeologists. "The entire project . . . often feels like it is run to give academics something nice to do over the summer and they can turn up whenever they like for however long they like and do whatever they want and people who turn up for six months just have to put up with [it] because someone has an academic title and large ego," he wrote on August 1.

The next day things were going better. "Quite a good day, the first in a while," Craig wrote. "Re-read yesterday's diary, boy was I in a bad mood. Today I feel much better and although I still believe all the things that I said yesterday I would probably word them a bit more circumspectly, never mind this is multivocality in action as we get my views on different days and I shouldn't censor the person I was yesterday." One interesting development over the previous two weeks was that Wendy's hypothesis of a penning deposit in the deep sounding was looking stronger with the discovery of what looked to be a newborn sheep or goat. Could it be that pregnant animals were kept inside the settlement at certain times of the year?

Another day passed. It now appeared that the coring measurements were correct, but Craig and Pete might not have cored in the deepest deposits of the deep sounding. Back to pessimism again. "The amount left to dig looks really intimidating," Craig reported on August 3.

About a week later the team began to hit deposits of a light-colored material made up of fired lime. They were now at or below Mellaart's Level XII. Wendy was called in again. Her excitement was immediate. Up until now all the plaster they had found at Çatalhöyük had been made from the local clay. But at earlier Neolithic sites in the Near East, such as Jericho in Palestine and 'Ain Ghazal in Jordan, the plaster used to cover walls and floors had been made from limestone, which was heated to a high temperature and then mixed with water. Now they were finding evidence of what seemed to be lime burning at Çatalhöyük. If true, it would mean that during Çatalhöyük's earliest days its inhabitants had used fired lime-based plasters, implying a possible cultural link with settlements much farther east. They may have given up the practice later because of the great deal of fuel it used. Indeed, some archaeologists have speculated that the fairly rapid decline of 'Ain Ghazal and other settlements in the Levant about 8,000 years ago might have been due to the ravages their populations inflicted on the local environment in search of wood to burn.

On August 17, 1999, at three A.M., an earthquake measuring 7.4 on the Richter scale hit about fifty-five miles east of Istanbul, leaving more than 15,000 people dead and hundreds of thousands homeless. The epicenter was between Izmit and Bursa. Ayfer had family in both cities, as did many of the Turkish archaeologists. Ayfer eventually was able to get hold of her family; they were all okay, although the family summer home in Izmit had been destroyed. Başak and Julie began organizing blood donations and launched a fund-raising drive. The Thursday night theme party was dedicated to earthquake relief, and a thousand dollars was raised among the team members. Some of the Turkish team members went to the earthquake area to help with rescue efforts.

By late August it was beginning to look as though the deep sounding was going down into an area outside the earliest settlement of Çatalhöyük. The first occupants had probably built their homes closer to the center of the mound; the excavators were at the southern end. It was not clear if they were in a rubbish dump or an area where activities outside the houses took place. While somewhat disappointing, this was not all bad. Rubbish had a lot to say about the daily lives of Neolithic people, sometimes even more than the houses, especially if their inhabitants kept them particularly clean. The deep sounding was reaping a rich harvest of human and animal bones, obsidian, charcoal, and other plant remains. And a large number of fired clay balls were also found below Level XII. Their function was still a mystery.

On September 9, 1999, at 2:17 P.M, Craig Cessford and Jez Taylor, a professional digger who had most recently worked in London, were digging through a layer of animal bone, charcoal, clay objects, and painted plaster when they hit natural—three weeks ahead of schedule. Craig scooped up a good handful of the lake marl, put it in a plastic bag, and climbed up the ladder that led out of the deep sounding. He walked down the mound to the dig house. Just an hour before, James and Arlette Mellaart had left Çatalhöyük, after their latest visit to the site. Ian was away in Istanbul. Craig walked up to Shahina and handed her the bag without a word. Shahina put her hand in the bag and took out a little bit of the marl. It was wet, shiny, grayish white, and it had the consistency of smooth clay. She rolled it in her fingers and smiled. Someone walked by and said, “What’s that?” She anointed his forehead with the marl. Then she went around and anointed everyone she saw.

15 / Till Death Us Do Part

THE BACH TEAM was keeping Başak Boz and Lori Hager pretty busy. Nearly every day the two anthropologists were called up to the Goddess Pavilion to excavate another human burial. The first round of excavations in the south area and in Building 1 of the north area was now completed, giving the pair more time to concentrate on the BACH building. The first five seasons of full excavation, from 1995 to 1999, had yielded thirty-two skeletons from thirteen buildings in the south area, and sixty-two from Building 1 alone—an extraordinary number to be found in just one house. All of the burials except one had been within the buildings. The great majority were under the floors or platforms. The one exception, which Shahina had found during the 1999 season, was the skeleton of a man that had been buried in a rubbish or midden area between two buildings. Theya Molleson and

Peter Andrews, the leaders of the human remains team, had found that the man suffered from a crippling bone disease, which might have explained why his deformed body was treated differently.

Başak, a petite young woman, had grown up in several of Turkey's major cities, including Bursa, Izmir, and Konya. As an undergraduate paleoanthropology student at Ankara University during the early 1990s, Başak had met Peter Andrews, an anthropologist at the Natural History Museum in London; they were both working at a 15-million-year-old Miocene site called Paşalar in northwest Turkey, where excavations had turned up more than six hundred specimens of fossil apes. After receiving her bachelor's degree in 1992, Başak came to live in London for a couple of years and work as a volunteer with Peter in the museum. Başak soon got interested in studying human teeth, especially their microwear—microscopic marks made by chewing various foods, which can provide important clues about the diet of prehistoric humans. One day Theya, who also worked at the museum, walked into Peter's office and saw some scanning electron micrographs that Başak had taken of ape teeth from Paşalar. Peter and his colleagues had treated the teeth experimentally with various acids and sediments to see how the microwear pattern might be altered over time. Impressed with the micrographs, Theya, who was in charge of recruiting people for the human remains team, asked Başak if she was interested in working at Çatalhöyük. Soon afterward Başak began work at Haceteppe University in Ankara on her master's degree, which would be based on a study of the teeth wear at Çatalhöyük.

Lori Hager had earned her Ph.D. in anthropology at the University of California, Berkeley, in 1989. She now taught physical anthropology classes at the campus. Lori, whose long, wavy auburn hair and broad smile were frequently seen at Çatalhöyük's Thursday night parties, was an expert on sex differences among human skeletons. Yet her interest in this topic extended far beyond the technical details of how to tell the sexes apart. Lori was one of a number of mostly female anthropologists and archaeologists who believed that researchers had largely ignored the role of women in prehistory. She was particularly well known for editing a 1997 volume, *Women in Human Evolution*, featuring articles by herself and ten other leading women scholars examining the various ways in which leaving women out of the picture had led to a skewed view of human development. Some of Theya Molleson's earlier research had been critical to helping to redress this imbalance: her studies of the skeletons at Abu Hureyra in Syria had been among the first to examine the various tasks that men and women carried out in the economy of the early Neolithic period.

Başak and Lori had been called in to excavate a skeleton that the BACH team had uncovered in one of the three small rooms on the south side of Building 3. These rooms, which had been designated as Spaces 87, 88, and 89, were separated from the main building by a double mud-brick wall. The skeleton was found in Space 87. Why it had been put there, rather than under the floor of the much larger main portion of Building 3, was not clear. The skeleton had been placed in an oval-shaped pit, about three by four feet. The body was lying on its right side and very tightly flexed—so tightly, in fact, that it probably could not have been compressed into a smaller space. The skeleton's axis was oriented east-west and the top of the skull faced east.

A few days earlier Başak and Lori had excavated a different skeleton in this same pit, that of an adolescent between thirteen and fifteen years old. It was found lying in exactly the same orientation as the other. They had not been able to figure out whether the first skeleton was a male or a female, which was often the case with relatively immature children. The widening of the pelvis in women to accommodate the birth canal, which is the best indication of sex, does not take place until adolescence is well under way. Despite the teenager's youth, its teeth were in very bad shape; they had numerous cavities and their outer enamel was very thin. The pit also contained a particularly beautiful artifact: an intricately carved, highly polished belt buckle made from the bone of either a cow or a horse. The buckle was made up of two pieces, one with two carefully drilled holes, and the other with a sharply bent hook that was used to fasten the belt—which had probably been made from cloth or animal skin—around its wearer's waist. It was not clear whether the buckle had been buried together with one particular skeleton or was just put loosely into the burial pit.

Başak and Lori set to work, squeezing themselves into the little bit of room that remained in Space 87 once the pit had been opened by the excavators. Başak straddled the pit with her feet. Lori perched on the other side. After at least 8,000 years in the ground, the bones were likely to be very fragile. Başak and Lori had to take every possible precaution to avoid breaking them. Bone by bone, the skeletons had to be removed and taken down to the human remains lab. Başak blew the dust from the yellowish orange bones with an oven baster, and then began scraping away the larger clumps of dirt with a small scalpel. With the help of one of the BACH team excavators, who was stationed nearby behind a Leica surveying instrument mounted on a tripod, Basak took several levels. She held the point of a long metal staff on several parts of the skeleton in turn—the highest point of the skull, the leg and arm bones, and the ground on which the burial lay—while the surveyor called out a series of numbers. Lori entered these on a recording sheet held by a clipboard. These measurements would later be entered into the computer and help them draw a three-dimensional reconstruction of the skeleton.

"This looks like an older individual," Lori said, pointing to a telltale thickening of its vertebrae, a sign of osteoarthritis. "I would say it was at least forty years old." Başak nodded as she carefully lifted the lower jaw, which had become detached from the skull, and put it into a shallow cardboard box lined with paper towels. As Lori continued to take notes, Başak picked up a dental pick and began pulling out the smaller bones. The diagnosis of osteoarthritis seemed confirmed by the hand and foot bones, which were also thickened and enlarged.

While Başak worked on the smaller bones, Lori took out her own scalpel and started cleaning one of the clavicles. "This is one of my favorite bones," Lori said. "It has a nice curved shape, which makes it easy to figure out which side it comes from, left or right." Just when Lori thought she had a clear shot at lifting the clavicle, the end of it broke off. "Oh, there goes my nice clavicle," Lori said. Many of the bones were intact, but some were broken and out of place, making it difficult to tell what they were. "Is that a radius or an ulna?" Başak asked, pointing to a long, partly buried bone. The rib bones were all jumbled, and the femur was lying next to the long row of spinal vertebrae. The task was made even more difficult because some of the bones from the adolescent were still in the pit. The adult had apparently been buried later than the child. Although it was impossible to know how much time had passed between the two burials, the second burial had clearly disturbed the bones of the pit's younger resident. Başak, determined to take at least one bone out without breaking it, held her breath as she successfully lifted the juvenile's tibia—one of the lower leg bones—and placed it in a second box.

The dinner bell rang down at the dig house. The working day was over. They covered the burial with a plastic sheet. On arriving at the shelter the next morning, Başak and Lori decided to have some good photographs taken of the skeleton. In archaeology's old days they would have painstakingly drawn each tiny bone and bump on sketch paper, a lengthy process that increased the danger of the bones' drying out before they could be removed and transferred to the lab. But for the BACH team, which considered itself on the cutting edge of archaeological technology, little was worth doing unless it could be done on a computer. Başak and Lori called in the team's so-called Wonder Twins, Michael Ashley and Jason Quinlan. Michael and Jason were graduate and undergraduate students, respectively, who had worked closely with Ruth Tringham and other Berkeley anthropology faculty to develop computerized, multimedia teaching methods. At Çatalhöyük, they were key facilitators of Ruth's grand plan to meticulously record, through photography and video, every aspect of the BACH excavations, with the aim of creating an Internet-accessible digital archive. And, as students of Ruth, Michael and Jason had learned how to combine archaeological rigor with a touch of the dramatic.

The sturdy metal side supports and crossbars that kept the Goddess Pavilion shelter standing—and which even the fiercest Anatolian windstorm had yet to disturb—provided the perfect support for the Wonder Twins' considerable rappelling skills. With Michael spotting, Jason put on a harness and anchored himself to the tent post closest to the burial. Then, with the help of handgrips called ascenders, he made his way along a series of guide ropes until he was hovering right over the skeleton. Using a level attached to his digital camera, Jason made sure that the axis of his lens was exactly perpendicular to the axis of the burial—this to eliminate distortion of the image—and began clicking away. The photographs, once uploaded into the computer, would not entirely take the place of drawings, however. Başak and Lori would use the photos as a guide to creating three-dimensional representations of the skeletons.

Başak and Lori needed yet another day before they could remove all of the bones. At the end all that remained was the skull and two bones lying underneath it, the left humerus (long bone of the upper arm) and one of the scapulae (shoulder blades). The most critical step had come: removing the skull. Başak and Lori prepared a separate cardboard box with paper towels and placed it at the edge of the burial pit. They held their breaths and placed all four of their hands under the skull, lifting it together. The cranium was still filled with soil, some of which began to spill out into the pit. As they placed it into the box, the temporal, occipital, and parietal bones separated, leaving the skull in several pieces. Even in pieces, the skull and other bones of this ancient human would have much to tell.

Back in the lab Başak and Lori gave the skeleton a thorough anatomical examination. Since it was an adult, figuring out whether it was male or female posed little problem. While the best indicator is the width of the pelvis, the size and shape of the skull can also provide good clues. The pelvis of this skeleton was relatively narrow. But since there is a lot of variation among human skeletons, they also looked carefully at several other pelvic features just to be sure. The pubic bones of males and females, for example, are usually noticeably different, attaching in the middle of the pelvis at differing angles—again, wider angles in females and narrower angles in males. Yet the pubic bones, which are in the front of the pelvis, are quite fragile and often get damaged during archaeological excavations. Thus a better indicator is something called the sciatic notch, which is in the stronger, posterior section of these large bones.

Lori was an expert on the sciatic notch. A few years earlier she had published an important study showing that male-female differences in this notch were much greater in humans than in other apes. In humans the notch is clearly wider and shallower in females, and deeper and narrower in males. The distinction is less clear in gorillas, even less in bonobos, and weaker still in the common chimpanzee. Lori concluded that the sciatic notch, which is also more prominent in modern humans and extinct hominids than in apes, took its present form during the transition to bipedalism, and that the greater sex differences in this feature must have evolved later on in human evolution.

Başak and Lori were now able to conclude that the skeleton they had excavated in Space 87 was a male between forty-four and fifty years old, a ripe old age in Neolithic times. He had suffered from arthritis in his pelvis, spinal column, and hands. Later, when they finished excavating all of the burials in Space 87, a total of at least nine people had been pulled from this collective grave. The other skeletons included a woman about the same age as the older man—she suffered badly from osteoporosis, a debilitating decrease in bone density—another teenager who suffered from anemia, a child about eight or nine years old, and several infants, including one who was buried in a large basket. Had this group of people once made up a single family that lived together in Building 3? If so, why were they all buried together in this tiny space, and who put them there? Başak and Lori were not yet prepared to answer these questions, at least not until the entire BACH area excavation had been completed and some overall conclusions could be drawn about this complex building and who had lived in it. Meanwhile they could not help feeling a twinge of guilt about disturbing the rest of these prehistoric humans, who perhaps thought that they would be spending eternity together under a plaster floor.

NOTHING IN LIFE reflects our ideas, beliefs, and fears more accurately than our attitudes toward death. Our keen awareness of our mortality is part of what makes us human. "The idea of death, the fear of it, haunts the human animal like nothing else," anthropologist Ernest Becker wrote in his 1973 Pulitzer Prize–winning book *The Denial of Death*. This fear, Becker declared, "is a mainspring of human activity—activity designed largely to avoid the fatality of death, to overcome it by denying in some way that it is the final destiny for man." The close cultural link between life and death probably explains why burials and burial practices have long been a focus of interest for prehistorians, along with such expressions of material culture as pottery, figurines, and stone tools. Most anthropologists would agree that while we are still alive, we use our bodies as material culture, adorning them with clothes, hats, ornaments, hairstyles, makeup, and so forth; seen this way, there is little difference between the neck rings worn by Maasai women in Kenya and the lip rings worn by some body-piercing young people today. When we die, our bodies are transformed into another form of material culture, now available to our friends and family, who invest in our remains their own feelings about us and what we represent to them. The skull cults at early Neolithic sites like Jericho and Çayönü, in which heads were removed from bodies and manipulated in various apparently symbolic ways, were an early manifestation of this seemingly universal human habit. Likewise, when King Tutankhamen goes on tour with all of his gold grave goods, he is more than just an individual. He symbolizes—in our modern eyes, of course—the great Egyptian civilizations of the past.

Although the issue is hotly debated, many archaeologists believe that true burial practices—those that are accompanied by some sort of ceremony or ritual—only began with the advent of *Homo sapiens.* Some would go even further and insist that such behavior cannot be demonstrated before the Upper Paleolithic period, some 30,000 to 40,000 years ago. The opposing camp in the argument maintains that the Middle Paleolithic Neandertals, whom most anthropologists now assign to a separate species from modern humans, also engaged in deliberate burial; and the excavators of the incredible 300,000-year-old Sima de los Huesos ("Pit of the Bones") in northern Spain, where at least thirty-two hominid bodies were apparently thrown down a natural shaft leading to an underground cave, believe that this represented some sort of burial rite.

Using the most conservative definition, however, the earliest completely unambiguous burials are probably those at the 29,000-year-old open-air site of Sungir' in Russia, about 125 miles northeast of Moscow, which was excavated by Otto Bader between 1956 and 1970. Bader found the intact burials of one adult male and two children, a girl and a boy. The adult's grave contained 2,936 ivory beads. His forearms and biceps were decorated with about 25 polished ivory bracelets. The children were buried head to head in a second grave. The boy was covered with 4,903 ivory beads that were about two-thirds the size of those adorning the adult, but with the same oblong form. Around his waist the boy wore the apparent remains of a belt strung with more than 250 canine teeth from polar foxes. The girl was covered with 5,274 beads, the same size and form as those covering the boy; she had no belt, but at her side the archaeologists found a number of small, lancelike ivory objects and two batonlike objects made from antlers. Randall White, an archaeologist at New York University who studied the beads, determined that each one of them would have taken about an hour to make.

Most of us would probably be happy to have such a seemingly splendid send-off. Traditionally, most archaeologists would have concluded that the huge effort that went into the Sungir' burials meant that the man and the children were special people of some sort, particularly revered by the family, group, or community they belonged to. Many archaeologists have also considered the range of variation in the way people were buried as an indicator of the degree of social complexity within a settlement or community, that is, how ranked or statified that society was. One of the early ambitions of the New Archaeologists, including Lewis Binford, was to put this kind of analysis on a firmer scientific footing. But over the past two decades a number of post-processual archaeologists, including Ian Hodder and some of his former graduate students, have criticized the idea that there is a direct relationship between the fashion in which people are buried and the status that they had in life. A lot of their arguments are based on ethnographic studies on modern-day peoples. For example, the British anthropologist Jack Goody, in a 1960s study of the LoDagaa people of West Africa, reported that corpses were dressed in the garb of a chief or rich merchant regardless of what the deceased's social position had actually been in life.

One ethnoarchaeological demonstration of the danger of simply reading off social status from burial practices was carried out in the early 1980s by Michael Parker Pearson, who was studying with Ian Hodder at Cambridge University. Parker Pearson compared the current mortuary habits of people living in Cambridge and its surroundings with those of the Victorian-era residents of the city. As part of his research, he combed through the records of four funeral homes, tallying information on age, sex, occupation, religion, property values, type of coffin, number of automobiles hired for the funeral, manner in which the corpse was treated and dressed (including whether or not it was cremated), the number and size of death notices in the news media, and whether or not a monument was constructed over the burial place. He also toured the city's cemeteries, recording the details of Victorian tombs; here he was greatly aided by the frequent Victorian habit of noting the occupation of the deceased right on the tombstone, a practice that is rare today.

Parker Pearson's conclusions were simple: whereas in Victorian times tombstones quite closely reflected social status, with ostentatious monuments seemingly trying to outdo each other for pride of the cemetery, funerals today tend to be understated affairs for all social classes, whether rich, poor, or middle-class. This shift is also reflected in a dramatic increase in the number of people whose remains are cremated, which, in the United Kingdom, went from essentially zero in 1930 to about 60 percent of the population by 1975. Let archaeologists digging up Cambridge in the next millennium be warned: any assumptions that its twentieth-century residents lived in a classless, egalitarian society could be highly erroneous.

Despite these cautionary tales, however, there is still a great deal to be learned from prehistoric mortuary practices, especially about humanity's first steps toward settled existence. The rise of the Natufians in the Levant about 12,500 years ago was accompanied by an apparently abrupt and dramatic shift in burial habits. The Natufians, whom many archaeologists consider the earliest truly sedentary peoples, were the first to bury their dead on site, either in their houses or in adjacent cemeteries. Since Dorothy Garrod's pioneering excavations at Shukbah Cave in the 1920s, some 500 Natufian burials have been excavated at Natufian sites, the majority at Shukbah, 'Ain Mallaha, Hayonim Cave, Nahel Oren, and El-Wad, all in Israel. At the earlist Natufian villages, the settlers buried their dead in groups—possibly corresponding to family clusters—and often adorned the bodies with beads, bone pendants, and perforated teeth.

After this early stage Natufian burial practices underwent a significant change. During the so-called Late Natufian period, which roughly corresponds with the coming of the Younger Dryas cold front, the group burials gave way to individual interments, and few burials had ornaments of any kind. At the same time a new practice of removing the heads, and other so-called secondary burial habits that involved disturbing the primary burials and messing about with the bones, became common. Some archaeologists have speculated that the practice of transforming heads and other bones into portable objects corresponded to the more mobile lifestyle that the late Natufians adopted in the face of the severe downturn in the weather. When they moved, they could take their ancestors with them. Other explanations, including changes in attitudes toward death, could also have been responsible. One thing is sure: the skull cult became a widespread cultural phenomenon in the Near East, continuing well into the Neolithic period and spreading as far as Anatolia.

In some cases the skulls underwent special treatment. Kathleen Kenyon, who led the excavations at Jericho, described her first discovery of this remarkable Neolithic practice in her book *Digging Up Jericho:*

> Excavators are trained not to go burrowing into the walls of the trench or square to get out objects, however inviting they look. So the skull remained where it was until after digging had stopped. But a skull of an individual perhaps some seven thousand years old is something of a special case, so, after I had one morning finished drawing the section of the stratification, I rather unwillingly gave permission for the site supervisor to get it out . . . None of us were prepared for the object he produced in the evening . . . What we had seen in the side of the trench had been the top of a human skull. But the whole of the rest of the skull had a covering of plaster, molded in the form of features, with eyes inset with shells.

Equally dramatic evidence for skull cults was unearthed at Çayönü in southeastern Turkey, an early Neolithic site first dug during the 1960s by the American Robert Braidwood and Turkish archaeologist Halet Çambel. Later excavators, led by Mehmet Özdoğan, uncovered a special structure—which they named the Skull Building—where the skulls of 288 adults and 106 children had been deposited.

As the number of skulls found at Natufian and Neolithic sites piled up, archaeologists began to ponder what this ritual practice had represented to ancient peoples. They had plenty of ethnographic analogies from more recent cultures to inspire their imaginations. The Pitt-Rivers Museum in Oxford, for example, is stuffed with decorated skulls from islands in the Pacific Ocean where such cults were common. In the Solomon Islands, as late as the early twentieth century, the skulls of important people such as chiefs or priests would be put on display in wooden shrines, special huts, or on top of stone altars.

Nor are skull cults restricted to exotic peoples in faraway lands. There is evidence that at least two U.S. presidents may have engaged in the ritual. Author Alexandra Robbins, in her book about Yale University's secret Skull and Bones Society, *Secrets of the Tomb,* traced the fate of the skull of the Apache Indian chief Geronimo, who died in 1909 at Fort Sill, Oklahoma. Nine years later the skull was stolen from the fort, allegedly by Prescott Bush and other members of the society who were stationed there. According to the story, Bush and the others deposited the skull in a secret tomb at the society's Yale headquarters. If true, this would mean that Prescott Bush's son, George H. W. Bush, his grandson, George W. Bush, and presidential candidate John Kerry—all members of the Skull and Bones Society—may have engaged in the secret skull cult at one time or another.

In regards to Natufian and Neolithic skull cults, archaeologists have usually gravitated toward one or the other of two primary interpretations. The first would see the skulls as trophies from prehistoric warfare, the prizes of victory over enemies. But few experts today go for this explanation, mainly because there is little evidence that such battles actually took place. James Mellaart, during his 1960s excavations at Çatalhöyük, thought that some of the axes and daggers he found there were used in warfare, but physical anthropologists who have studied the bones at this and many other early sites seldom see the kind of traumatic injuries that would be expected if warfare had been a regular occurrence. The second and more popular theory has been that the skulls were part of some sort of ancestor worship. Kenyon favored this explanation for her findings at Jericho: "I have personally little doubt that we should regard the Jericho heads as those of venerated ancestors," she wrote in a 1956 article in *Antiquity*. Many archaeologists would go further and relate the skull cult to the dramatic transformation from mobile to sedentary societies then taking place in the Near East. In this view, as people became more dependent on the natural resources of a particular region, the ancestors would serve to establish claims to particular plots of land through family or clan lineages.

That kind of interpretation would extend more generally to the question of why Natufian and Neolithic peoples buried their dead under the floors of their houses, a practice that reached a high point at sites like Çatalhöyük and which has characterized many other societies down through the ages. Boston University archaeologist Patricia McAnany, in her 1995 book *Living with the Ancestors*—a study of the ancient Maya of Mexico and Guatemala, who buried their dead under the floors or in various shrines—came to a very similar conclusion: "Ancestor veneration as a creative social practice, is about naming and claiming—naming progenitors, naming descendants, and by virtue of these proper nouns establishing proprietary claims to resources." And Christine Hastorf, who has excavated burial centers at the 3,500-year-old site of Chiripa on the Bolivian shore of Lake Titicaca, concluded in one report on her research that "such memorials to group lineage and ancestor helped form the Chiripian individual . . . This spiral of action perpetuated the cultural memories through each generation creating and recreating the group as it coalesced into an emotionally connected society."

Lately some archaeologists have begun to feel that the ancestors are getting a little too much press. "There are too many ancestors in contemporary archaeological interpretation, and they are being asked to do too much," wrote James Whitley of Cardiff University in Wales, in a 2002 paper in *Antiquity* entitled, appropriately enough, "Too Many Ancestors." Whitley criticized his colleagues for too easily embracing this ubiquitous explanation for prehistoric burial practices. "The universal ancestor has gone from being a suggestion to becoming an orthodoxy without ever having had to suffer the indignation of being treated as a mere hypothesis. Ancestors are everywhere, and everything is ancestral." He was especially critical of some post-processual archaeologists who have invoked the ancestors in their own writings, including Michael Parker Pearson, who in one recent series of papers interpreted the use of the landscape surrounding Stonehenge in ancestral terms. "One of the great claims made by 'interpretative' or 'post-processual' archaeologists was that their interpretations, being contextual, respected the particularity of the time, people and period they were trying to examine . . . It is surely one of the ironies of modern archaeology that it is these same . . . 'post-processual' archaeologists, who are now so keen on ancestors, ancestors who are omnipresent and omnicompetent."

One alternative view which downplays the ancestors in favor of broader community themes comes from Ian Kuijt, an anthropologist at the University of Notre Dame in Indiana. Kuijt has analyzed the mortuary practices at a number of Natufian and Neolithic sites and concluded that skull cults and other secondary manipulations of skeletons formed part of community-wide ceremonies and rituals. The purpose of these shared rituals, Kuijt maintains, was to promote social cohesion and egalitarianism—or, at least, the perception of egalitarianism—in early villages. As support for this idea, Kuijt cites numerous ethnographic examples, such as the Ma'anyan people of southern Borneo, who unearth their dead after several years of burial and rebury them in a collective funeral festival that goes on for a full week. Kuijt's hypothesis has been challenged, however, because it assumes that social differentiation and inequalities had already begun to develop as early as Natufian times, a conclusion that some archaeologists find debatable.

The team at Çatalhöyük, which had now excavated nearly a hundred skeletons in well-defined stratigraphic contexts, was in a good position to tackle some of these nagging issues. But Ian Hodder was not quite ready to pronounce on the most fundamental question behind the burials, what the dead had meant to the living. He wanted to wait until all of the excavation results had been analyzed and cross-referenced, so that he and the team could make full use of their contextual approach. That would require at least one, and possibly more, "study seasons," during which the excavations would be held in abeyance while the team pored over data from the past several years, tracing the intricate patterns that modern archaeological interpretation relies upon. But while the meaning of death at Çatalhöyük remained shrouded in mystery, the human bones were beginning to reveal a lot about how the people here had lived, including whether or not men and women had lived as equals.

THE BONES OF A DEAD PERSON can say a great deal about who that person was in life. Indeed, forensic scientists working on modern-day criminal investigations use many techniques similar to those employed by physical anthropologists on prehistoric digs. Anthropologist Douglas Ubelaker of the Smithsonian Institution in Washington, D.C., coauthor of *Bones: A Forensic Detective's Casebook*, relates a case that began in

May 1980, when a pretty twenty-one-year-old woman from Puerto Rico disappeared after setting off to work from her apartment in Arlington, Virginia. Two days later her 1974 Pinto automobile was found, engulfed in flames, on a deserted road in Maryland. But she was not in it. The police had no other leads, so the case went into the missing persons file. Then, more than two years later, a group of berry pickers found some bones corresponding to the upper half of a human body, including a skull, scattered across a blackberry patch in rural Goochland County, Virginia. At first Virginia authorities made no connection with the earlier disappearance in Arlington. The state's deputy chief medical examiner sent the bones to Smithsonian anthropologist J. Lawrence Angel for an opinion.

Angel was not a forensic scientist by profession but a physical anthropologist who had worked on many archaeological sites over his long career. One of them was Çatalhöyük. In the 1971 volume of *Anatolian Studies,* Angel published a detailed report on the human bones from James Mellaart's excavations, which stood as one of the definitive accounts until the site was reopened by Ian Hodder's team. As Angel now examined the human remains from Goochland County, he noticed that one little finger bone had a strange diagonal cut in it, which could have happened either during the victim's lifetime or after death. He did not know what to make of it but noted it carefully in his report. Angel, together with an artist from Richmond, Virginia, then used the skull to make a reconstruction of the victim's head. A photograph of the reconstruction was published in the Richmond *News Leader,* which eventually led to the connection being made with the young woman from Arlington. The young woman's remains were sent to Puerto Rico, where she was buried by her family.

In 1991 Ubelaker was contacted by Goochland County authorities. Angel had died in 1986, and Ubelaker had taken over some of his forensic activities. A suspect had been arrested in the case. The prosecutor had read Angel's report and felt that the cut on the little finger might be important for the trial. Ubelaker traveled to Puerto Rico, where the skeletal remains, which had been put in a box and then buried in a coffin, were exhumed by local authorities so that he could examine them. In a small plastic bag, labeled "Goochland" in Angel's handwriting with an indelible pen, Ubelaker found the cut finger bone. Later, back in

Washington, he performed a series of experiments with a 1974 Pinto and the thigh bone of a chicken. If the Pinto's car door was slammed on the chicken bone, he found, it created a cut mark very similar to that on the young woman's little finger. Fortunately or unfortunately, the evidence never made it to court: the suspect pleaded guilty, and the case was over.

Angel's work on the skeletons from the Mellaart excavations, which he carried out in the late 1960s, led him to a number of interesting findings. Allowing for damage to the bones and the fact that some of them had gone missing in the years since the dig was shut down by Turkish authorities, he had a total of 216 adults and 72 infants and children to study. He found that adult women outnumbered men by 132 to 84, a significant difference. One striking finding was that 41 percent of the adults had a pathological condition called porotic hyperostosis, an abnormal porosity or sponginess of the bones—especially those of the skull—which is typical of anemic malaria sufferers. Angel speculated that Çatalhöyük's location on the Konya Plain, which was thought to have been often marshy during prehistoric times, meant that its population would have been exposed to the *Anopheles* mosquitoes that carry the malaria parasite. As for the high female death rate, Angel was able to determine that most of the "excess" deaths were concentrated in the fifteen-to-thirty-year age range—a strong indication that most of the women had died during childbirth or shortly afterward.

The new human remains team at Çatalhöyük has had a lot of advantages that Angel did not. Its members had the opportunity to participate in the excavations of nearly all the burials in Building 1 and the south area, and to carefully record every detail. And they had access to scientific methods that did not exist in the late 1960s. As a result, the team's lead anthropologists—Theya Molleson, Peter Andrews, and Başak Boz—were able to come to more detailed, and in some cases different, conclusions from those that Angel and Mellaart had arrived at.

One important difference was that the team found little evidence of secondary burial at Çatalhöyük. Mellaart believed that the corpses were put outside after death and defleshed in a process of "excarnation," possibly carried out by the vultures that were depicted in some of the artworks. But the intact skeletons found by the new team were inconsistent with such a practice, which would have caused much more disruption to the remains. In addition, only two skeletons out of ninety-four had actually been decapitated. Both were males. One, found in Building 1, had its skull and first cervical vertebra (atlas) removed without disturbing any of the rest of the spinal column. This body was laid out in a very contorted fashion: the lower part of the body was lying on its side, but the upper torso had been twisted around so that it was lying on its back. The second headless body had been found in Building 6 in the south area, during the Long Season. It was lying flat on its back. In this case the skull had been detached from the atlas vertebra, which, the team remarked in its final report, was "an extremely difficult undertaking even in the optimal conditions of a modern dissecting room, and it could only have been achieved after advanced decay of tissues." The team speculated that both bodies might have been laid out on their backs to make it easier to remove their heads later on.

The anthropologists did not find the same marked overrepresentation of females that had so impressed Angel, although they found it difficult to interpret this discrepancy—other than by assuming that Angel's sample, which included many skeletons too damaged to be analyzed, had not been representative. They did, however, confirm the high number of child, infant, and newborn burials, which together amounted to about two-thirds of the entire sample. The team rejected the possibility that this preponderance may have been due to a practice of infanticide, largely because there were not enough newborn deaths to make it likely. Rather, they concluded, the crowded conditions in the settlement, and the challenges of surviving in the early days of agriculture, may have led to a large number of childhood infections. But they did not think Angel was right that malaria was responsible for the widespread evidence of anemia. For one thing, the environmental reconstructions of the Konya region by Neil Roberts and his colleagues implied that conditions would have been too cold in the winter for the mosquitoes to survive; more likely, they thought, the anemia was due to low birth weight and malnourishment during infancy.

One of the most important things archaeologists want to know about the societies they study is what the people ate. This is especially true for the Neolithic period, when the agricultural revolution was dramatically altering the daily diet. Here the team got a big help from two archaeological scientists, Michael Richards, then at the University of Bradford in the UK, and Jessica Pearson, then at Oxford University. Richards and Pearson analyzed the ratios of carbon and nitrogen atoms in the human bones at Çatalhöyük. The tissues of the body are largely made up of these two elements, which come in different isotopic forms. Radioactive carbon 14 atoms allow archaeological sites to be accurately dated, but the great majority of carbon and nitrogen atoms are not radioactive but stable. Using what they call stable isotope analysis, bioarchaeologists can directly determine the dietary sources of carbon and nitrogen by measuring the ratios of carbon 12 and carbon 13 atoms, on the one hand, and of nitrogen 14 and nitrogen 15 atoms on the other. These ratios differ in a reproducible way, depending on what a person has been eating over the last years of his life. The material analyzed is normally the protein collagen, which is usually the best preserved organic component from bones (and which is also used in radiocarbon dating).

The results from Çatalhöyük were striking. Some fifty individuals were analyzed, from Building 1 and the south area. The south area people seemed to have similar diets, even when they came from different occupation levels. Their isotope profiles were consistent with consumption of a mixture of plants and animals such as sheep or goats, but it was clear that they had eaten little or no beef. The diet of the Building 1 people, however, was much more varied. They seemed to have eaten a higher overall proportion of animal meat, probably also sheep and goat, along with plant foods. But three individuals from Building 1 had isotope values that indicated they may indeed have eaten more beef.

Such wide variations in diet at one archaeological site are rare. Richards and Pearson, as well as the other members of the Çatalhöyük team, were hard put to make sense of them. It was possible that the result was due to the larger sample size in Building 1, which had so many skeletons buried under the floors. Or the finding could reflect a real difference. Some members of the community might have been away from the site for part of the year, thus partaking of a different diet, or some members of the community may have eaten better than others. But there was at least one clear result from the isotope work: there was no difference in diet between men and women. If some people had better access to high-value foods, this early social inequality was not along gender lines.

To some extent this conclusion did not come as a surprise. When Başak Boz completed her study of the human teeth, she too had found that there was little difference in their tooth wear or any other characteristics, except that women tended to have a few more cavities. And Naomi Hamilton, who had tried hard to find evidence for differences in the way men and women were buried—how their bodies were positioned, and what grave goods went in with them—could not come up with any differences. The team had been cautious about interpreting these findings, however, since how one is buried does not necessarily reflect one's status in life. But then Theya Molleson and Peter Andrews came up with yet another piece of evidence for male-female equality.

Theya and Peter had noticed early in the excavations that the inside of the ribs of the Neolithic skeletons were often covered with a black substance. When analyzed, it turned out to be carbon—soot from the fires in the mud-brick houses. With only a hole in the roof for ventilation, interiors must have been smoky indeed, especially during the winter months. The soot, Theya and Peter surmised, must have been in the lungs of the people before they died, and then was deposited on the inner surface of the ribs. In fact, Wendy Matthews, who had studied the wall plasters under her microscope, was able to distinguish between alternating bands of more sooty and less sooty plaster layers, which may have corresponded to these seasonal changes. When Theya and Peter plotted out the sex of the sooty skeletons, they found that both men and women were equally affected.

"This finding implies that we cannot argue, for example, that men had more of an outdoor and women more of an indoor life," Ian Hodder pointed out in a later article for *Scientific American*. "In fact, they appear to have lived quite similar lives in terms of the amount of time spent in the house." Another implication of these results, Ian wrote, was that it was unlikely Çatalhöyük was the kind of matriarchal society that James Mellaart and Marija Gimbutas had imagined. "We are not witnessing a patriarchy or a matriarchy," he concluded. "What we are seeing is perhaps more interesting—a society in which, in many areas, the question of whether you were a man or a woman did not determine the life you could lead."

As the anthropological data on human diet took on shape and meaning, the members of another team at Çatalhöyük were paying careful attention. For Louise and Rissa, the finding that few of the settlement's people ate beef seemed to confirm a trend they were seeing in the animal bones: sheep and goat, but not cattle, made up the major part of the "faunal assemblage." The earlier claims by James Mellaart and his own faunal analyst, Dexter Perkins, that Çatalhöyük had been a major center of cattle domestication and consumption were looking even shakier.

16 / Taming the Wild

I MADE MY FIRST TRIP to Çatalhöyük in 1998, on assignment from *Science* magazine to write an article about the site. I have been back every year since. Beginning with that first visit, I made it a point to always get together with Louise, Rissa, and the rest of the animal bone team for what I called a faunal session. We would stand around the long tables covered with bone fragments that were sorted into various piles corresponding to body parts and species. Some of the bones were nearly intact, but they represented only a small minority of the total. Louise and Rissa would explain what they had found that season and fill me in on their latest thinking about which species were domesticated and which were wild. Of all the labs at Çatalhöyük, the faunal lab seemed to have the most relaxed, easygoing atmosphere, despite the fact that the faunal team almost never stopped working, day or night. The tension that such intense labor might otherwise have generated was seemingly dissipated by the gentle rapport between Louise and Rissa.

During my visit in 1999, at the height of the Long Season, I stood with Louise, Rissa, and Sheelagh Frame around some trays of freshly washed bone that had just come out of the excavations in the deep sounding and in the off-site trench that Neil Roberts's team was digging on the north edge of the mound. The three were excited about the huge pieces of cattle bone that the diggers were finding. At the same time, smaller versions of the same bones often cropped up in the faunal assemblage. There were two possible explanations for this size difference, and the team was not sure which one was correct. Since domesticated animals tend to be markedly smaller than their wild counterparts, it could mean that both domestic and wild cattle were being consumed at Çatalhöyük, at least in the early days of the settlement. But the work of the past few seasons suggested that this size discrepancy might have continued throughout the thousand-year-long occupation of the settlement. Since the overall trend in the Near East was toward domestication of cattle as well as of sheep, goats, and pigs, it seemed odd that the Neolithic community would not rely more on domesticated animals over time.

The other possible explanation was sexual dimorphism, that is, size differences between males and females. Most mammal species, including humans, display sexual dimorphism to one degree or another. The aurochs *Bos primigenius*, the wild ancestor of modern cattle, is now extinct, but the American bison (also called the plains buffalo), which belongs to the same Bovidae family, displays enormous sexual dimorphism. A mature bull stands about six and a half feet at the shoulder and weighs nearly 2,000 pounds, while the female stands only five feet tall and weighs a diminutive 700 pounds.

In her diary that evening, Louise rehearsed the various arguments for and against these two explanations for the size differences. But she realized that it was way too early to come to any definite conclusion. That would require even more data, and perhaps most important, a much more sophisticated analysis of the animal bones than they had attempted at that point. Louise was prepared to be patient. She had been in the bone business since she was eighteen years old.

• • •

LOUISE MARTIN was born on January 14, 1963, in the English village of Henfield, about ten miles north of Brighton. When Louise was still young, the family moved to a larger house on a large plot of land. The family kept a donkey, some sheep, several dogs and cats, and a flock of chickens. Louise had her own pony. She also got a taste for travel at an early age. Her father's work took him throughout Europe and beyond, and he would often take the family with him.

Louise's father loved to tinker with old bits of machinery he found in junkyards and surplus stores, trying to figure out how they worked. One summer the family went to Greece for a holiday. Louise's mother just wanted to lie in the sun, but her father decided he was going to figure out how the ancient Greeks had created their beautiful sculptures. He got hold of a large piece of marble and a hammer and chisel, and sat on the beach working away at the smooth stone. Back in England he would take Louise and her brother to a large clay pit near their home, which had earlier been quarried by a cement company. Some paleontologists from the Natural History Museum in London had found a large extinct reptile there. The children would dig away at the clay with small geological picks, hoping to find some dinosaurs. They never did, but they did unearth the fossil shells of lots of ammonites, spiral-shaped mollusks that had lived in abundance on the English coast during the Mesozoic period, the age of the dinosaurs.

As a young girl, Louise was very shy and introverted. She was an average student at school, preferring the outdoors to the classroom. She loved to take long countryside walks and to dig up worms in the family garden. When Louise was about sixteen years old, she began to get the itch to travel independently. She learned that the Council for British Archaeology was looking for volunteers to work on digs abroad, so she signed up to work on an excavation on the outskirts of the French town of Chartres, home to one of the world's most spectacular cathedrals. It was a Gallo-Roman site, directed by a French archaeologist who was the son of the mayor of Chartres. For the first two weeks, Louise was incredibly bored. The team had found little of interest, and the stratigraphy made no sense to her. Then, gradually, the stratigraphy began to fall into place. One morning she hit something hard with her trowel. It was a cache of two buff-colored Roman amphorae, fully intact including the double handles, and each standing more than a half meter in height. Louise was bowled over.

Back at school she told her career counselor that she wanted to be an archaeologist. The counselor did not seem to know what archaeology was but assured Louise that she could study it when she went to university. Louise was crestfallen. Neither of her parents had attended a university. Her mother had left school at fourteen years, her father at sixteen. But she got up her nerve to apply to the Institute of Archaeology in London. What Louise did not know then was that the institute placed as much emphasis on the interest and enthusiasm the applicant showed in an interview as it did on grades. Louise's interview was conducted by Richard Reece, one of the institute's experts on the Roman Empire. Louise was bubbling over with excitement at the idea that she really might become an archaeologist. She was accepted into the undergraduate program.

That summer, while waiting for classes at the institute to begin, Louise spent some time in Israel traveling and working on various digs. But with a month of the summer left, she ran out of money. Louise decided to go back to Chartres for the remaining weeks, this time to help excavate the foundations of some medieval houses right near the cathedral. That decision would turn out to be one of the most important she ever made. It was there that she met W. A. B. Brown.

Barry Brown, as he was known to his friends, was a noted professor of dental anatomy at Kings College London. He was close to retirement and looking for something new to do with his time. Brown had volunteered to work on the Chartres dig for a month. He was nearly sixty years old, and Louise only eighteen, but somehow their senses of humor clicked and they immediately hit it off. Brown knew everything there was to know about teeth and quite a bit about bones too. He told Louise that he was working on a dental anatomy manual. He asked her if she wanted to take the photographs for it. Over the next three years Louise spent most of her Wednesday afternoons, when there were no classes at the institute, working in Brown's lab. That was when she began to take bones and teeth very seriously.

Louise took two classes from James Mellaart while she was at the institute, including his course on the Anatolian Neolithic and Chalcolithic. The class met each week in a small room on the institute's second floor. Out of eleven lectures, seven were totally devoted to Çatalhöyük. Louise took copious notes. On October 13, 1983, Mellaart told the class that the word *settlement* was a good, noncommital term to use to describe early Anatolian communities, rather than words such as *city, village,* or *town.* Louise put a star next to that note. A few weeks later Mellaart was telling the class about the Anatolian sites that preceded Çatalhöyük in the Neolithic sequence, including Aşikli Höyük in Cappadocia. He pointed out that while the sheep and goats at Aşikli appeared at first glance to be wild rather than domesticated animals, the archaeologist had to be very cautious about drawing conclusions from the bones alone without looking at the overall use of animals in a settlement. "Therefore a pile of bones is not a real indication of domestication or not," Louise recorded in her notes.

When it came time to do her undergraduate thesis, Louise conducted a study to look for new methods to determine the age of sheep teeth from their developmental stages. Upon graduating from the institute in 1985, she did not at first think about continuing on for a Ph.D. After all, she already was an archaeologist. She spent one summer digging in the Klithi Gorge in Greece, at a Paleolithic site directed by Newcastle University archaeologist Geoff Bailey. The remote site was very near where the teenage Ian Hodder had excavated briefly with Eric Higgs. The archaeologists lived in tents, cooked over an open camp fire, and washed their clothes in the river. Later she got a small grant from the British Museum that helped her go to Jordan and work on the animal bones at Tell es-Sa'idiyeh, a huge Bronze Age and Iron Age site that Jonathan Tubb of the museum had recently begun excavating. Tell es-Sa'idiyeh, in the heart of the central Jordan Valley, was thought to be the biblical city of Zarethan. Louise spent three years working there, and—just as Roger and Wendy had fallen in love with Iraq—fell in love with Jordan, its friendly people, and the valley's lush landscape.

While in Jordan, Louise had another fateful encounter. She met Andrew Garrard, then the director of the British Institute at Amman for Archaeology and History, the Jordanian equivalent of the BIAA in Ankara. There was an enormous amount of archaeology going on in Jordan at that time. Garrard and the British Institute were right in the middle of it all. The important Neolithic sites of 'Ain Ghazal and Beidha were under excavation, and everybody who was anybody in Near Eastern archaeology passed through at one time or another. Gordon Hillman was working there at the time, as was Douglas Baird, future leader of the Konya survey.

Andrew hired Louise to work as a faunal analyst on his own ambitious project in the Azraq Basin of eastern Jordan. Garrard had decided to test the so-called margins hypothesis first put forward in the late 1960s by Lewis Binford and his disciple Kent Flannery. Binford and Flannery had proposed that the Neolithic Revolution got under way when population pressures pushed some hunter-gatherers out of the optimal zones for plants and animals, whereupon they invented agriculture so that they could eat as well as those in the center. The center, most archaeologists assumed, was the Levantine Corridor, the Mediterranean strip of land that included Jericho and other early Neolithic sites. Eastern Jordan, on the other hand, was in what was considered the "Marginal Zone."

No one had ever gone into the margins and tried to thoroughly test the hypothesis, which Binford himself had argued was the only proper way to do archaeology. Garrard surveyed and excavated at some twenty sites in the Azraq Basin over many years. Louise's work, which focused largely on the gazelle, sheep, and goat bones, made a critical contribution. Another important contributor was archaeobotanist Susan Colledge, who also worked at Abu Hureyra, and who later went to work at the Institute of Archaeology. In the end Garrard concluded there was no evidence that plant and animal domestication had begun in the Marginal Zone; rather it had appeared in the Levantine Corridor first, and only after a time gap did it appear farther east. The margins hypothesis had been tested, and it had failed.

Garrard had become Louise's primary mentor. He encouraged her to do a Ph.D. thesis on the Azraq animal bones and suggested that she do it at Sheffield University, where Paul Halstead, by then a leading light in zooarchaeology, was on the faculty. Garrard himself was about to do a sabbatical year at Sheffield, and Sue Colledge was just starting her own Ph.D. work there. In short, Garrard had managed to transfer some of the key people on his Azraq team to the university. At Sheffield Louise had her first exposure to Ian Hodder's post-processual ideas. Ian's former graduate student Matthew Johnson was lecturing there, an inspiring teacher who seemed capable of converting entire classes of Sheffield undergraduates to the Hodderian point of view in the course of a single lecture, to the dismay of some of the processually oriented faculty. In the spring of 1994, just before she completed her Ph.D., Louise got a telephone call from someone claiming to be Ian Hodder. Louise spent much of the conversation trying to figure out which one of her friends was playing a joke on her.

"Oh hello, this is Ian Hodder here," said the man on the phone, in a voice so shy and halting that it could not possibly belong to the leader of one of the twentieth century's most influential archaeological movements. "Andy Garrard gave me your name. I, uh, was wondering whether you're at all interested in doing the animal bones at Çatalhöyük." After a while Louise began to wonder if perhaps it really was Ian Hodder, in which case she had been acting so uninterested in what he had to say that she had surely blown a huge opportunity. What Louise did not realize was that Ian had no interest in having big-name archaeologists at Çatalhöyük. He wanted people who were open to new ideas. Ian had to come up to Bradford, a city not far north of Sheffield, to give a talk the following week. He asked Louise if she could meet him there. They met in the seedy bar of the Bradford railway station. Ian did not want anything to drink, so Louise ordered an orange juice. A drunk came up to them and asked for some money. Ian ignored him and kept on talking about Çatalhöyük. Louise had to give the drunk a pound so he would go away.

JOB ONE FOR A zooarchaeologist is to try to identify the species of as many of the bones dug up by a site's excavators as possible. This task might not be difficult if each bone came out of the earth intact—that is, if every humerus, tibia, vertebra, scapula, metatarsal, and phalanx looked exactly like the ones illustrated in such helpfully titled volumes as *Bones for the Archaeologist* or the *Atlas of Animal Bones for Prehistorians*. Unfortunately, prehistoric humans tended to strip each animal of every bit of flesh and then smash open the bones to get at the nutritious bone marrow and to find good bits for making bone tools. This heavy processing, combined with the ravages of time, often leaves the faunal expert with a sorry pile of bone splinters and fragments, many of which are recovered only after the excavated soil has been put through a fine sieve. This can sometimes make species identifications difficult or even impossible, especially in the case of sheep and goats, which look very much alike. At Çatalhöyük, where both sheep and goat were plentiful, Louise and Rissa often had no choice but to lump together some of their bones into a general category known as "sheep/goat."

Under such conditions the zooarchaeologist's best friend is a reference collection. This is an assortment of disarticulated skeletons from modern animals that can be used to make species identifications and the kind of size and morphological comparisons critical to establishing whether a particular specimen is wild or domesticated. With training and experience, the expert can often identify an animal from the size and details of the bony ridges, depressions, or fossae where ligaments, muscles, and nerves once twitched with life. The teeth, which are often found intact, are particularly prized for the clues they can provide about species and the age at which the animal died. Archaeologists working in Europe or North America can often find such reference collections in their local natural history or university museums. In the Near East and many other parts of the world, faunal experts usually have to create their own collections the hard way—from scratch. It is sometimes a smelly, disgusting business.

Louise's first efforts, during the 1994 season, could have ended in disaster. One of the team members, aware of her eagerness to have the skeleton of an animal, any animal, rolled into the site one day with a dead fox tied to the roof of the dig's Land Rover. Following textbook procedure, Louise skinned the fox, trimmed away as much muscle tissue as possible, and then cut it up into several smaller portions. These she placed in several basins filled with washing powder she had bought at a supermarket in Çumra. Louise checked on progress every day for several days, but the rotting process was frustratingly slow. So, with the help of Sedrettin Dural, who, together with Mustafa Tokyağsun, served as one of the site's two guards, Louise put the animal parts in a larger metal container filled with water, piled kindling around it, and lit a fire to get it boiling. She then went off to do something else. A while later Sedrettin came running up to her shouting that the mound was on fire. This turned out to be an exaggeration: the dry grass had caught and a stream of flame was making its way toward the hill, but the tell was not really in danger. Sedrettin got out a water hose and quickly put the fire out, but Louise decided she was not going to have her fox bones any time soon. She buried the fox near the mound, hoping that nature would take its course and the microorganisms in the soil would do the job for her by the next season. But when she returned the following year, Louise discovered that part of the new dig house had been constructed over the spot. Inadvertently, the fox had become a foundation deposit.

By the 1997 season Louise and Rissa had yet to obtain a fully intact goat or sheep skeleton for the collection. One day Naomi Hamilton, who had been on a day trip to Konya, came into the faunal lab to announce that she had seen a dead goat by the side of the road. Louise and Rissa were thrilled. Then Naomi began to backtrack.

"Well," she said, "it looked like a goat. But maybe it wasn't a goat. I'm not totally sure." Louise's and Rissa's faces fell in unison. "In fact," Naomi continued, "I'm not sure it was really dead. Maybe it was just very tired."

With the help of Orrin Shane of the Science Museum of Minnesota—he was putting together the display panels for the Çatalhöyük visitor's center and had rented a hatchback automobile—the faunal team decided to organize an expedition to check out the situation. Louise and Rissa piled into the hatchback, with Shane at the wheel. Sure enough, on the side of the road just past the village of Küçükköy lay the carcass of a young donkey. While a donkey was not as urgently needed as a goat, it would make a nice addition to the collection. With some effort the three wrestled the donkey into the hatchback. Louise and Rissa flipped a coin to see who would ride in the back with the dead animal. Louise won, or lost, as the case may be. While Rissa loved working with dry bones, she was quite squeamish about the soft parts of an animal; indeed, as a high school student she had avoided taking biology classes precisely because she could not stand to do the required dissections of frogs and other beasts. Moreover, the donkey's stomach was somewhat swollen, a sure sign that it had been dead for at least a day or two. There was a distinct danger of a stomach gas explosion, an occupational hazard much discussed among zooarchaeologists.

On their return to Çatalhöyük they arranged with Shahina to have some of the Turkish workers dig a pit behind the dig house. The donkey would be buried in the pit and the slow decomposition process, which could take a year or two, would begin. The men seemed to know whom the donkey had belonged to—apparently someone who lived in the village. When Louise and Rissa expressed concern that the owner might be upset that they had taken it, the workers looked at each other and burst into laughter. Once the pit was dug, the donkey was pushed into it, along with a note expressing the animal's last words, which the men had written in Turkish: "Do not move me from my burial place, and do not disturb me."

The following season Louise and Rissa were working in the lab when Orrin Shane and one of his colleagues from the museum burst in excitedly to say that this time, for certain, they had seen a dead sheep on the side of the Konya road. "Uh-huh," said Rissa skeptically. Louise nodded in agreement. "Are you sure it's not another donkey?" They were sure. Once again they all piled into Orrin's vehicle, and once again, out on the side of the road, they came upon a dead donkey. At this point Louise and Rissa were giving up all hope of finding a sheep or a goat for the collection. Then Shane mentioned that he had received a private donation from a benefactor of the museum, to be used at his discretion. He offered to use part of it to buy a sheep and a goat from the local villagers. Louise and Rissa gratefully accepted. After lengthy negotiations with some of the people in Küçükköy, one specimen of each was purchased. The owners slaughtered the animals, and Ismail Salmancý, the dig's cook, carefully butchered them so as not to damage the bones. Ismail thought the goat meat looked old and tough, so he gave it away to some poor people in Çumra. The sheep meat was turned into kebabs and consumed at the dig's Thursday barbecue.

Louise and Rissa buried the goat skeleton before night fell, but by the time Ismail had finished butchering the sheep, it was too dark to see what they were doing. So they laid it out on a large piece of plastic on the floor of the faunal lab. The next morning, when Rissa walked into the lab to begin work, she was startled to see the sheep's rib cage heaving as if it were breathing. The dig's pet kitten had crawled into the chest cavity.

• • •

IF ALL IT TOOK was a pile of bones to figure out whether animals were domesticated or wild, the faunal team at Çatalhöyük could have closed the book on the issue in fairly short order. During the 1996 season the team recorded 11,634 pieces of animal bone; in 1997 the figure was 22,412; 1998 brought in another 30,826 pieces; and during the 1999 Long Season Louise, Rissa, and Sheelagh logged in 123,840 pieces of bone. The overwhelming majority of these bone pieces and fragments came from between the Neolithic buildings, from the midden areas that were used as rubbish dumps. As a general rule, the inhabitants of the mud-brick buildings do not seem to have thrown their animal bones on the floor and left them there. Indeed, several years of excavations, along with Wendy Matthews's micromorphological work, had demonstrated that the floors were kept very clean except in cooking areas, and even those were carefully raked out. When there were animal bones inside the houses, they often seemed to have been deposited in fairly deliberate ways—a habit of particular interest to Rissa, who had a long-standing interest in ritual feasting.

Despite this embarrassment of bone riches, however, only a small percentage of them were diagnostic, that is, identifiable as to species. Out of the 123,840 pieces of bone recorded in 1999, for example, the team was able to identify only 10 percent of them. And while 819 sheep bones and 402 goat bones were identified with a good degree of confidence, another 6,661 bones had to be lumped in the sheep/goat category.

In terms of animal domestication, the most important issues at Çatalhöyük were to determine the status of the sheep, goats, cattle, and pigs, the primary livestock in the Near East. The faunal expert who worked with Mellaart, Dexter Perkins, had concluded—based on a much smaller sample of bones—that the sheep and goats at the site were wild. Louise and Rissa now doubted that conclusion; they believed that many or most of the sheep and goats were domesticated, although wild sheep may still have been hunted. That would be consistent with the evidence that these animals were domesticated very early in the Near East. Perkins himself claimed that the sheep at the nearly 11,000-year-old site of Zawi Chemi Shanidar in the Kurdish region of Iraq were domesticated or at least under human control, although most zooarchaeologists have rejected his conclusions since. More recently, Melinda Zeder of the Smithsonian Institution in Washington, D.C., and Brian Hesse at the University of Alabama in Birmingham have come up with convincing evidence that goats, at least, were already domesticated in the Zagros Mountains of western Iran by 10,000 years ago. Since the most recent radiocarbon dating of Çatalhöyük, from samples taken from the 1999 deep sounding, indicates that it was first settled about 9,500 years ago, an assumption that the sheep and goats were domesticated was at least a reasonable working hypothesis.

Perkins really stirred up Near Eastern zooarchaeology, however, with his claims about the cattle at Çatalhöyük. Perkins concluded, in a 1969 paper in *Science*, that in the earliest stratigraphic layers the cattle were wild but that in later levels they were domesticated. Moreover, he counted many more cattle bones than those of either sheep or goats at the site. If he was correct, Çatalhöyük was a major center of cattle domestication in the Near East, as has been its reputation for decades in both the scientific and popular literature. Yet from the very beginning of their tenure at Çatalhöyük, Louise and Rissa had been questioning Perkins's conclusions.

The domestication status of the animals, although a key question for zooarchaeologists, was far from the only thing that Louise and Rissa were interested in. The relationship between humans and animals was important not only for understanding Çatalhöyük's economy, but also for gaining insights into the religious and ideological beliefs of its people. While Ian Hodder and many other team members had their doubts about goddess worship, there was little question that the bull—and cattle in general—had an important symbolic significance to the Neolithic settlers. In addition to the paintings and sculptures, many buildings had large cattle horns either attached to their walls or mounted on their plastered platforms. One of Ian's main aims in coming to Çatalhöyük had been to try to understand the art. Louise and Rissa had a big role to play in this endeavor. But as the bones piled up, so also did evidence accumulate for Rissa's hypothesis that some animals, especially cattle, were at times prepared in special ways and eaten as part of ritual feasts. These feasts seemed to involve more than just one household, and possibly marked some sort of major event such as the completion of a house or the birth of a child.

This trend had become quite clear by the 1998 season. After the 1999 Long Season the faunal team crunched out a number of interesting correlations in the faunal data. It compared the animal bones from some selected midden areas, which were assumed to represent normal daily consumption, with those found between the walls of some of the houses, which were more likely to correspond to "feasting deposits." The bones in one of the midden areas, for example, were 83 percent sheep/goat, 5 percent horse, and only 4 percent cattle. But in the presumed feasting deposits, the cattle made up 36.1 percent of the total. The team was also able to demonstrate that the cattle were processed differently in the two cases. The average length of the cattle bones in the midden areas was 4.36 centimeters, but in the feasting areas the average length was 12.28 centimeters, nearly three times as long. This result indicated that the bones had undergone much less processing, which would be more consistent with feasting than daily processing.

Rissa had spent countless hours during her career grinding out faunal statistics. But it was her ideas concerning what animals had to say about people that had really made her reputation.

WHEN RISSA WAS about four years old, she called her mother to the window of their home in rural Massachusetts. "Look, Mommy!" Rissa said. She pointed to a red bird in the bird feeder. Then she pointed to a picture of a red crossbill in the bird book she held open. The red crossbill, a member of the finch family, is a rare bird in New England. But Rissa's mother, who sometimes taught nature studies and knew her birds and wildflowers, could see that she had it right.

Rissa was born on September 27, 1957, in Boston. When she was thirteen years old, the family, which included her younger brother, moved to rural New Hampshire. In school she was interested in social studies, and especially in Native American cultures. She read at least ten of Sonia Bleeker's classic books about American Indians, including *The Cherokee: Indians of the Mountains* and *The Pueblo Indians: Farmers of the Rio Grande*. Rissa was such an obsessive reader that she would sometimes open up the telephone book in desperation. Shy and sensitive, she had a hard time socially. Her mother thought that she was not being challenged enough academically, so when it came time for Rissa to go to high school, her parents sent her to Miss Porter's School, a private school in Farmington, Connecticut.

Rissa took her first archaeology class at Miss Porter's. More important, the school's headmaster left after Rissa's sophomore year to take a job as head of a small American Indian museum in nearby Washington, Connecticut. Rissa had taken a course with him about American Indians, and she had written a term paper about the foods that the Indians ate. The headmaster asked her to revise it for the museum's newsletter. Rissa had her first publication.

That same year Yale University was running an archaeology field school at a prehistoric site in the area. The headmaster arranged for some students to participate, including Rissa. She did not find much other than a quartzite projectile point, but she had so much fun that she decided right away she wanted to be an archaeologist. The next year Stuart Struever, codirector of the excavations at prehistoric Koster and other sites in Illinois, came through town and gave a talk at the high school. Struever was one of the leading lights of the New Archaeology and also an early pioneer along with David French of botanical flotation techniques. He was recruiting people to come to the field school. Rissa wanted to do it, but she did not have the money to pay the school's fee. She went up to Struever after his lecture and asked if he would take her on as a volunteer. He said he didn't take volunteers but that if she still felt that strongly about it in two months, she should write to him. She had to pester Struever a number of times, but finally he agreed to take her on as a volunteer and give her room and board if she would work in the central processing laboratory in the evenings. When she arrived, he decided to pay her. The salary was small, but at sixteen years old, Rissa had become a professional archaeologist. The following year he offered her a job as a field supervisor.

One year, while excavating at Koster, Rissa came upon a deposit of charcoal mixed with a big concentration of fish bones. It was her first big faunal find, and she thought it was very cool. Rissa started hanging around the faunal lab. She loved the shapes of the bones and the process of sorting them, trying to recognize the patterns. Meanwhile Rissa's mother had a pretty good farm going at the family property in New Hampshire. When Rissa was home, she helped her mother with the chores. There were 6 milking cows, 2 pigs, 125 chickens, 6 geese, and a dog and a cat. On graduating from high school, Rissa decided to go to Harvard, where her father had also gone.

The most inspiring faculty member in Harvard's anthropology department at that time, Rissa's archaeology friends told her, was Ruth Tringham. Rissa took some courses and seminars with Ruth, who then invited her to come out to her site at Selevac, in the former Yugoslavia, where she and Mira were working. Somebody else was already doing the animal bones, so Rissa took on the bone tools, a specialty she continued to pursue at Çatalhöyük and other sites. Meanwhile she asked Harvard's Richard Meadow, a world authority on the fauna of Western Asia, to train her as a zooarchaeologist. Meadow agreed and became her bone mentor. When Rissa graduated from Harvard, she applied to the University of California at Berkeley, where Ruth was now teaching. Over the next several years she worked at Selevac with Ruth, at Neolithic Mehrgarh in Pakistan with a French team, and finally at Ruth's Opovo dig. Rissa's Ph.D., awarded in 1993, was based on her analysis of the animal bones at Opovo.

The title of Rissa's Ph.D. thesis was "Hunting, Herding and Feasting: Human Use of Animals in Neolithic Southeast Europe." Long before she arrived at Çatalhöyük, it became clear to Rissa that the domestication of animals was about much more than just getting hold of a steady supply of meat. With a few notable exceptions, such as her bone mentor Richard Meadow, most faunal experts tended to look at domesticated animals as "walking larders," as the British zooarchaeologist Juliet Clutton-Brock titled one of her books. That is, the primary emphasis was on their dietary value. But Rissa's work at Opovo had convinced her that the keeping of livestock, especially cattle, signaled profound changes in the nature of human society. She was also greatly influenced in her thinking by Richard Meadow's writings. "The key conceptual switch involved in animal domestication is a shift in focus from the dead to the living animal," she wrote later in a paper subtitled "Where's the Beef?" "For the most part, wild animals are considered a communal resource that can be appropriated only by killing them. Domestic animals, on the other hand, have owners who invest labor and other goods in their maintenance."

Once animals have owners, Rissa argued, they become a form of wealth rather than just something to eat. This shift seemed clear from ethnographic studies of pastoral communities around the world. In traditional East African societies, for example, cattle were often considered the equivalent of money. The animals are still used today in many parts of the world as bridewealth, a payment by the groom's family to the bride's family designed to guarantee the exclusivity of a marriage. Rissa's work on the animal bones at Neolithic Opovo suggested to her that the cattle at this site also functioned as wealth rather than mere food. The settlement was located at the edge of a plain, in an area not at all ideal for cattle raising, yet cattle made up 50 to 60 percent of the domestic animals at the village, even though its inhabitants also raised sheep, goats, and pigs. "This pattern strongly implies that cattle had value beyond their dietary contribution," Rissa wrote. In a provocative conclusion to her "Where's the Beef?" paper, Rissa suggested that the practice of using cattle as bridewealth may help explain how the Neolithic Revolution spread so quickly across Europe. The fate of the hunter-gatherer populations that lived in Europe before the arrival of farming has always been a mystery. Could it be, Rissa asked, that the incoming farmers used their cattle to marry the hunter-gatherer women and assimilate them into their agricultural societies?

THE 2000 AND 2001 SEASONS marked a new phase for most of the Çatalhöyük team. With Building 5 now on display to the public and the Long Season's deep sounding completed, most of the archaeologists now began working on the publication of what they had found during the 1995 to 1999 seasons. The one big exception was the BACH team, which, having begun later than everyone else, was still excavating Building 3.

The faunal team was still puzzling over the meaning of the cattle data from Çatalhöyük when it received a visit, in late July 2001, from Hijlke Buitenhuis, a Dutch zooarchaeologist who was handling the animal bones from the recent excavations at Aşikli Höyük and Musular, in Cappadocia. Buitenhuis had concluded that the cattle from Aşikli, which was occupied about one thousand years before Çatalhöyük, were clearly wild. He gave all of his bone measurements to Louise and Rissa. This was a terrific opportunity to make direct comparisons between data that had been gathered using similar methodologies and from sites that had been under excavation at about the same time. One of Louise's students at the Institute of Archaeology, Lisa Yeomans, had been working with her to analyze the measurements of the Çatalhöyük cattle, so Louise asked her to incorporate the Aşikli data into her database. It immediately became clear that the Çatalhöyük cattle were the same size as, and even a bit larger than, those at Aşikli.

When I arrived at the site a few days later, Louise and Rissa had begun saying that the cattle were "morphologically wild," meaning that the cattle may have been under some sort of human control and had not yet begun to reduce in size. Exactly why domesticated animals get smaller is not clearly understood, although many zooarchaeologists now believe that it is an adaptation to the conditions of being herded. Louise and Rissa were hesitant to say anything more until they had a chance to look more closely at the data.

Over the next year Rissa and Louise began crunching the data to see if they could make more sense out of what they were seeing; they continued during the 2002 season. They looked at the distribution of different body parts to see if perhaps the animals were being slaughtered off-site and only some of the parts were brought into the village; the answer seemed to be no. They pruned the data and ran various cross-checks to see how well they could distinguish whether the size differences were due to sexual dimorphism or domestication. They looked at cull patterns, whether cattle of certain sexes or ages were butchered more frequently, to see what that could tell them about sexual dimorphism and herding practices. They ran the data through the computer again and again, and every time they came up with the same answer. Then they ran it through some more.

Finally Louise and Rissa felt that they were ready to make it official. In October 2002 Rissa sent a message out to the Çatalhöyük team's e-mail list:

"The cattle were all wild."

17 / The Goddess and the Bull

ONE HOT DAY during the 2002 season, Burcu Tung, a Turkish graduate student at Cambridge University, was excavating in the south area when she found a small female figurine. The main excavations in the south area had been halted while the team wrote up the results of the previous seasons. But Ian, in consultation with the Turkish authorities, had decided to construct a huge, steel-framed shelter over the entire south area. In part its purpose was to provide shade for the excavators when they began digging there again in 2003, but it was also intended to make it easier for visitors to the site to view the excavated areas. To erect the shelter, it was necessary to dig foundation trenches on top of the Neolithic mound. Burcu and several other archaeologists were excavating these trenches to record any archaeological finds and structures before they were filled with concrete.

A crowd of archaeologists was already gathering around Burcu when she called out to Ian, who was standing on another part of the mound. The clay figurine Burcu held in her hand was less than an inch long and fairly crude. The head had been broken off, although that was common with the figurines found at Çatalhöyük and often seemed to have been done deliberately. The figurine was obviously meant to be a woman: it had breasts and a swollen abdomen, on which its stubby little arms rested. The legs, however, were truncated, and there were no feet. The team had found a lot of figurines over the years, but most were fairly schematic in shape. It was often difficult to tell whether they were humans or animals, let alone their gender. Most of the more detailed figurines that Mellaart had found during his 1960s excavations, such as the supposed goddess on her throne with two leopards, were unearthed in the later layers of the settlement, the occupation Levels I through IV. The figurine that Burcu had found was probably from Level III or IV.

The figurine was taken down to the finds room, where the staff working there logged it in and cleaned the dirt off it. A small opening was revealed in its back, and Ian was called in again. A seed of some sort was peeking out of this tiny cavity. Ian asked Meltem Agcabay, a member of the archaeobotany team, to have a look at it. Ian assumed that it would turn out to be the grain of a cultivated cereal of some sort. "After all, here we were, well into the Ceramic Neolithic, in the second half of the 7th millennium B.C., long after the origins of agriculture," he wrote in a later article entitled "The Lady and the Seed." Ian admitted that he was still influenced by "the mass of literature arguing for the centrality of female symbolism in the Neolithic of Anatolia and the Near East," which linked representations of women "to agricultural as well as human fertility. The seed should be a cereal. It should represent the crops on which the whole of settled life depended after the Neolithic Revolution."

Meltem put the figurine under a microscope and moved the seed about with a small brush. She got up from her chair and let Ian have a look. "It's a wild seed," Meltem said. In that case, Ian thought, it must have gotten there by accident when the figurine was fashioned out of soft clay and then fired in an oven. No one he talked to on the dig seemed to believe that explanation. The cavity was centered right in the middle of the back, and it did seem to have been created deliberately. The episode reminded Ian of something he had been trying to figure out for a long time. Why did the art at Çatalhöyük seem to focus on wild things rather than domestic? Why were there no paintings of wheat and barley stalks swaying in the wind, or pastoral scenes of shepherds tending their flocks? Why was it all bulls, leopards, and wild boar? Why did the sculptures of supposed breasts have vulture's beaks embedded in them? What was with the people of Çatalhöyük, anyway?

THE ÇATALHÖYÜK PROJECT had done a better job than most digs of making its results known promptly to the archaeological community, as well as to the general public. Archaeologists are notorious for taking years or even decades to issue their final site reports. But from the very early days of the excavations, an enormous amount of detailed information had been made available on the project's Web site (www.catalhoyuk.com), including summaries of each season's findings, the excavator diaries, and the project's annual newsletter. In addition the project had already published two volumes, *On the Surface* and *Towards Reflexive Method in Archaeology*, which covered the surface work as well as the post-processual approaches that the team was taking to the dig. Ian now arranged with Cambridge University's McDonald Institute for Archaeological Research, which was directed by Colin Renfrew, to publish four more volumes that would cover the excavation work between 1995 and 1999. The publication schedule called for all of them to appear by the end of 2004.

Now it was time for the team members to report their data, as well as make the first serious attempts to interpret what they meant. Craig Cessford was put on the payroll in Cambridge, and he and Shahina, who now worked for the project full-time, sat at their desks in the basement of the McDonald Institute cajoling people to get their submissions in on time and editing them when they did come in, as well as writing their own reports on the north and south areas. Ian, true to his principle of multivocality, did not insist that anyone had to follow a particular interpretative point of view in their papers. But he did want them to interpret, even if their trowels had been put away for the time being. As the manuscripts trickled in, it became possible for the first time to assemble a coherent picture of the life of Çatalhöyük, one of the largest Neolithic settlements ever discovered.

• • •

THE 1999 LONG SEASON had provided an opportunity to take samples for radiocarbon dating at many different stratigraphic levels, all the way down to the bottom of the mound. Craig Cessford himself took charge of this project. He selected ten samples of organic remains, from different levels in the stratigraphic sequence, that had been retrieved from the flotation machine, and sent them off to Oxford University's Radiocarbon Accelerator Unit. There Paul Pettit, the head of the unit's dating program, directed his staff to prepare the samples, a multistep process that removes most or all modern organic contamination, leaving just the original organic material. Pettit's crew then ran the samples through the unit's acclerator mass spectrometer, an enormous apparatus that takes up a very large room and is capable of counting the radioactive carbon 14 atoms. The end result was a series of raw radiocarbon dates on a computer screen, accompanied by their statistical margins of error.

The job of calibrating the raw results also fell to Craig, who, with the aid of computer programs especially designed to help the statistically challenged archaeologist, came up with the first reliable calibrated date for when the first residents of Çatalhöyük settled on the Konya Plain: about 7,500 years B.C., or 9,500 years ago. As Craig pointed out in a 2001 paper in *Antiquity* reporting these results, that date seemed to make the earliest evidence for occupation at Çatalhöyük at least one hundred years later than the last radiocarbon dates from Aşikli Höyük, ninety miles to the east. If the margin of error of radiocarbon dates was taken into account, that gap would not rule out the idea that the Çatalhöyük people might have come from the large settlement at Aşikli, but it did suggest that alternative possibilities should be considered. Excavations in Central Anatolia during the 1960s and 1970s had uncovered at least two sites closer to Çatalhöyük that might have overlapped in time with the larger settlement: Can Hasan III to the southeast, which had been excavated by David French, and the site of Suberde to the west, which had been excavated by the French archaeologist Jacques Bordaz.

While excavating individual sites that are spaced out geographically can give some hints about possible population movements in a region, such excavations usually focus on the kind of large tell sites that can make an archaeologist's career. That's one reason why, in recent years, the archaeological survey has become an increasingly important device for figuring out the prehistoric sequence of a region. Since 1995 Douglas Baird of the University of Liverpool and his hardy band of students and colleagues had been carrying out their Konya Plain survey, walking along irrigation channels, crisscrossing farmer's fields, and talking to local people all over the region. They also used remote sensing satellite imagery to help identify occupation sites. The survey area covered about a thousand square kilometers in the area around Çumra and south of Konya. This enormous work had paid off handsomely. On the alluvial fan of the Çarsamba River alone, Baird's team had found evidence of more than about forty sites, most from the Chalcolithic but a small number from the Neolithic as well.

The survey showed that there were six distinct phases of prehistoric settlement in the study area, stretching from pre-Neolithic sites dating around 17,000 B.C. to the so-called Middle Chalcolithic period from about 5,500 to 4,500 B.C. (The West Mound at Çatalhöyük, which was a possible candidate for where the East Mounders went after they abandoned the original settlement and which was now under excavation by Jonathan Last, Catriona Gibson, and Naomi Hamilton, had been dated to an earlier part of the Chalcolithic.) Where things really started to get interesting was in the so-called Aceramic Neolithic period, about 8,000 to 7,000 B.C., which was represented by at least four and possibly as many as six settlements. These villages were somewhat bigger than the ones that had preceded them in time, although they were still tiny compared to Çatalhöyük. Because these sites have not been excavated, it was difficult to assign exact dates to them, or to know to what extent they overlapped with Çatalhöyük. But one thing was clear: once the occupation of Çatalhöyük became well established, about 7,000 B.C., there was no definite evidence of any other contemporaneous settlement in the survey area. Not one. That did not mean that they did not exist, Baird commented in his volume report, only that they had not been found. If they did exist, they were likely to represent either mobile communities or "task groups" from Çatalhöyük or other communities lying outside the survey area. The closest known village from this time period was likely to have been at Can Hasan I, about thirty-five miles to the south.

The upshot of these results, Baird concluded, was that Çatalhöyük did not serve as some sort of "political, economic, administrative or religious center" for a network of surrounding communities. Rather it stood alone. Çatalhöyük was a place where, for whatever reasons, people had come together in unprecedented numbers.

Craig now set about trying to estimate what these numbers were. Since Mellaart's day, the population estimates for Çatalhöyük had ranged from 5,000 to 10,000 people, and over the years some journalists reporting on the site may have been guilty of using the higher number to impress people. Mellaart had claimed the higher figure during the 1960s, but in later publications he backed off somewhat and settled for somewhere between 5,000 and 7,000.

Roger Matthews, in his report on the surface scraping work in *On the Surface*, took another stab at it and came up with a similar range, 5,000 to 6,700. Part of the uncertainty was caused by the difficulty in knowing how many buildings were occupied at any given time in the life of the settlement and also how many occupants each building had. The task was also more complicated because the heights of the floors of the mud-brick buildings are often uneven from one building to the next, making it unclear whether two buildings belonged to the same occupation level or to different ones. In an attempt to get around this problem, Craig borrowed a formula used earlier by archaeologist Albert Ammerman and geneticist Luigi Luca Cavalli-Sforza, who had studied population movements of Neolithic farmers in Europe. The formula, which considers the three-dimensional volume of the mound rather than just a two-dimensional slice of it, is

$$N = VT/HP$$

where N is the number of buildings, V the overall volume of the mound, T the average life span of a building, H the volume of an individual building, and P the length of time the site was occupied. Once Craig had made that calculation, he then had to estimate how many people lived in a building. Here he relied on some previous estimates from ethnoarchaeological studies, which ranged from four to nine inhabitants. Clearly he was not going to be able to come up with exact numbers. But his calculations did give an average of about nine hundred buildings and a population range somewhere between 3,500 and 8,000 people. That meant that the only archaeological site in the Near

East that fell into the same order of magnitude for population was Abu Hureyra in Syria, whose excavators came up with a best estimate of 5,000 to 6,000 for this roughly contemporaneous settlement.

Whatever the real numbers, one would think that if up to 8,000 people came together on the Konya Plain during the Neolithic period, they would choose the most advantageous spot to live, where the soil was best for farming, the fruits of the forest were nearby for the picking, and the grazing lands were the most appetitizing for their sheep and goats. One would be wrong.

IN 1999 IAN MOVED from Cambridge to Stanford University in California. At long last Ian, Christine, Nicky, and Kyle were united as a family. While Christine remained in charge of the archaeobotany team at Çatalhöyük, after 1999 the responsibility for analyzing the copious plant remains at the site fell increasingly on the shoulders of Julie Near and Andy Fairbairn. Now Julie and Andy teamed up with Danièle Martinoli, an archaeobotanist from the University of Basel in Switzerland who had joined the group, to produce a final report on Çatalhöyük's agriculture.

Louise and Rissa had demonstrated that the people of Çatalhöyük ate both domesticated and wild animals, although domesticated sheep and goats made up most of the meat diet. The archaeobotany results showed that the villagers had cultivated wheat and barley, as well as lentils, peas, bitter vetch, and other legumes, from the first days of the settlement. This regime was complemented with an assortment of wild fruits and nuts—including hackberries, wild almonds, pistachios, plums, and acorns—as well as tubers from the club-rush plant. There was no evidence, however, to suggest that any of the cereals consumed had undergone domestication from wild to cultivated forms during the lifetime of the site, and very little evidence that legumes had done so. "The full suite of fully domesticated crops were present from the earliest phases of the site so far excavated and through the entire period of occupation," Andy, Julie, and Danièle concluded.

The use of wood, however, underwent some interesting changes over the life of the settlement. Eleni Asouti's analysis of the charcoal remains showed that in Çatalhöyük's earliest days, animal dung was probably a major source of fuel for fires, and timber somewhat less so. Since dung burns more slowly and lasts longer than wood, this result correlated well with the evidence for lime burning in the deepest parts of the 1999 deep sounding, since lime burning requires sustained high temperatures. The wood burned in the early levels consisted largely of willow, poplar, and elm. Later juniper and oak, which were also used for the timbers that supported the mud-brick houses, became much more prominent, and the use of dung for fuel seems to have declined although it did not disappear entirely. Eleni suggested that dung and wood may have been used for different purposes: dung would be more suitable for cooking, while wood would be better for providing heat and light.

The archaeobotanical results presented the team with a dilemma. Clearly, Çatalhöyük was an advanced agricultural community, whose livelihood was based heavily on cultivated crops. However, for a number of years Neil Roberts had been telling his colleagues that he thought the area around Çatalhöyük was flooded during most of the spring months back in Neolithic times. Now he made it official. All of the coring, pollen identification, chemical analysis, and other paleoecological work that Neil and his team had been doing since 1993 pointed to this conclusion. I was at Çatalhöyük during the 2001 study season, when Neil told a hot, stuffy room full of archaeologists that this was his final word on the subject. With the fan going full blast and the windows open to catch the light breeze off the surrounding wheatfields, Neil projected his slides onto the wall. Çatalhöyük had been smack in the middle of a marshy wetlands, a stark contrast to the comparatively arid conditions that exist on the Konya Plain today. Louise had heard it before, but she was still worried. "Where did they keep their animals?" she asked.

Back in 1982 Neil had published a paper in the *Journal of Archaeological Science* entitled "A Note on the Geomorphological Environment of Çatal Hüyük, Turkey," in which he was already taking issue with earlier interpretations of the site's ancient environment. Despite the presence today of profitable wheat and melon fields right around Çatalhöyük, Neil argued that most of the alluvial soils in which they grew had been laid down by the Çarsamba River after the first Neolithic settlers arrived. This meant, Neil wrote back then, that "the modern distribution of soil and water resources cannot be used directly to assess past agricultural potential in the vicinity of the site." Twenty years later Neil was sure about it.

Much of the Konya Plain is actually a basin, where a huge lake once stretched south and east of the city of Konya. About 12,000 years ago this lake dried out, leaving behind the marshlands. Then, about 2,000 years before Çatalhöyük was founded, oak and juniper trees sprouted on the foothills about seven miles from the site, although the immediate surroundings remained largely treeless. Just before the settlers arrived, some 9,500 years ago, the Çarsamba River, a distributary of which once ran right next to the mound, began depositing layers of broad alluvial sediments. The long buildup of alluvial soils that made the area good for farming today had only just begun when Çatalhöyük was founded. And when Neil and his team analyzed the sediments, they provided strong evidence that Çatalhöyük's mound had stood right in the middle of flood waters two or three months out of each year.

While this conclusion did pose some problems for Rissa's and Louise's sheep and goats, which prefer dry land, Rissa's own analysis of the bird bones from Çatalhöyük seemed to support it. Rissa teamed up with Kevin McGowan, an ornithologist at Cornell, to identify these birds. It turned out that 75 to 80 percent of them were waterbirds such as ducks, geese, and coots. In fact, the waterfowl they found suggested that there was some sort of standing water very near the settlement all year round, including marshlands and maybe even a lake.

These apparent wetlands conditions raised another issue: where were the fields of domesticated wheat, barley, and other crops that the project's archaeobotanists had found in abundance on the site? It was not impossible to farm these crops in marshy areas, especially if the farmers used hillocks, sand ridges, or other higher ground that might have peeked out from the marshes. They would just have had to be careful about when they sowed the crops and when they reaped them, to avoid the times when their fields would be flooded. Yet that scenario was contradicted by the work of Arlene Rosen of the Institute of Archaeology in London, an expert in the analysis of phytoliths—tiny fossil plant remains that are formed when silica, which enters plants from the soil, is deposited within the cells of a plant's outer epidermal tissues. The amount of silica that ends up in the phytolith depends on the nature of the soil it is grown in and how much water it is exposed to. When wheat is grown in irrigated fields with clay-rich alluvial soils, the longer exposure to silica from standing water leads to extensive phytolith formation and large cell clusters. But when wheat is grown under dry farming conditions, the phytoliths usually consist of single cells or small clusters.

Arlene's analysis of the wheat and barley phytoliths showed that they came from plants that had been dry-farmed, but the nearest land available for dry farming during most of the Neolithic occupation at Çatalhöyük was about seven miles away from the site. It was hard to believe, but the evidence was growing that the village had been located far from some of its major food sources, with all the transport problems that represented. Yet it was not impossible. Indeed, Eleni's analysis of the charcoal had already demonstrated that most of the wood used for construction on the site was oak and juniper, which came from the forests in the foothills—again, no closer than seven miles.

As far as Ian was concerned there was only one reasonable explanation for why the people of Çatalhöyük had chosen this spot on which to settle. It was rich in the alluvial clays and lake marls they needed to make the plaster on which they painted their artworks and out of which they fashioned their sculptures and figurines. "They were plaster freaks," Ian said. If Ian was right, then once again economic determinism would have been trumped by the exigencies of culture, religion, and ritual. Not everyone on the team was prepared to accept such a radical conclusion, nor were they sure that Ian could ever prove that it was right, but no one was able to come up with a better explanation.

> THE HOUSE AND THE BODY are intimately linked. The house is an extension of the person; like an extra skin, carapace or second layer of clothes, it serves as much to reveal and display as it does to hide and protect. House, body and mind are in continuous interaction, the physical structure, furnishing, social conventions and mental images of the house at once enabling, molding, informing and constraining the activities and ideas which unfold within its bounds.

This conception of the house, from anthropologists Janet Carsten's and Stephen Hugh-Jones' introduction to a collection of essays entitled *About the House: Lévi-Strauss and Beyond*, sums up the thinking of a large number of cultural anthropologists today. Ian Hodder's concept of the domus, which he first introduced in *The Domestication of Europe*, reflects a similar view of the house as something more than just a shelter with walls. After nearly a decade of work at Çatalhöyük, Ian believed that he saw plenty of evidence that the house was the center of socialization during the Neolithic, the key place where people learned social rules and became domesticated. In a paper he published with Craig Cessford in *American Antiquity* entitled "Daily Practice and Social Memory at Çatalhöyük," Ian spelled out these ideas in greater detail.

One of the big problems that archaeologists working in the Neolithic period had to deal with was how the incipient societies of the Near East regulated themselves socially, that is, how conflicts were resolved and how it was decided who was in charge—who the authority figures were. At some early Neolithic settlements in the Levant and even in southeastern Anatolia, there did appear to be central gathering places where community-wide rituals might have been performed, such as the impressive stone tower at Jericho, the skull house at Çayönü, and a possible temple complex at Aşikli Höyük. Yet even in those cases, the areas involved were not big enough to hold more than a small minority of the community. Moving farther west to Central Anatolia, there is much less evidence for such specialized areas. In fact, Mehmet Özdoğan, Turkey's leading Neolithic specialist, pointed out that Çatalhöyük and other Central Anatolian sites are notable for their apparent lack of social ranking.

At Çatalhöyük, Ian now suggested, the house itself was the basic unit of society. "The house is an important social, productive, and symbolic unit . . . It was also the main mechanism for creating social rules." In those days thousands of years before writing was invented, Ian argued, these rules were expressed in the way the house was constructed and the way that people moved about the house. "As a child grew up in a house at Çatalhöyük, it would have learned that different types of people were buried beneath certain platforms, that different plasters were used for different platforms, and that refuse was swept up more carefully from some areas . . . Because of the burial associations between different types of people and different parts of the house, it seems reasonable to assume that different people may have sat, eaten, and slept in different parts of the house. Social rules would have been learned through daily practice involving the movement of the body in the house."

Moreover, Ian wrote, these social rules did not have to be relearned every time a new house was constructed. By building one house right on top of another and burying their dead under the floors, the members of a family or extended family group created an intergenerational "social memory." As an example, Ian took the sequence of Building 5, which was built first, and Building 1, which came afterward. "Can we estimate how much overlap in population there could have been?" he asked. Craig and the other excavators of these buildings had obtained some forty radiocarbon dates, which allowed the sequence of many of the sixty burials under Building 1 to be determined. Some of the first burials in Building 1 were older individuals who were probably alive during much or most of the lifespan of Building 5, which was occupied for about seventy years. Likewise, two males who were buried toward the end of the lifetime of Building 1 were nearly as old as the building itself. While Ian's excavation team had only examined the two-building sequence of Buildings 5 and 1, James Mellaart, who had dug many more buildings, had demonstrated that the houses with the most burials were the ones that had been rebuilt one atop the other the most times.

"Domestic houses used for large numbers of burials," Ian concluded, ". . . may have been more closely tied to continuity and the preservation of a collective memory." But with all this domesticity about, why was the art focused on the wild rather than the tame? Why, for example, did the figurine that Burcu had found contain a wild seed rather than a cultivated one?

IN ADDITION TO her role as a cultural broker at Çatalhöyük, Ayfer Bartu continued her studies of the various interest groups that visited the site. The most frequent visitors were contingents of goddess worshippers, many of whom considered Çatalhöyük to be their equivalent of Mecca. Ayfer would often accompany the women to the top of the tell and observe their rituals and ceremonies. Sometimes these would consist of little more than holding hands in a circle and humming or chanting hymns to the Mother Goddess. At other times, however, the rites were more dramatic. One time a goddess group carried out its ceremonies on the mound in the presence of a number of local officials. One member of the group, who was engaged in a work of performance art dedicated to the Mother Goddess, reached down, scooped up a handful of soil, and slowly ate it, right in front of the mayor of Çumra. On another occasion a group of pilgrims in a tour bus, many of whom started crying as soon as they got out, climbed up the mound and set up an altar where they put their rings and other jewelry. After a round of singing and chanting, some of the women began taking off their tops and baring their breasts, tears streaming down their faces.

Cynthia Eller, in her 1993 study of the feminist spirituality movement in the United States, *Living in the Lap of the Goddess*, evoked the goddess movement's nostalgia for a mythical ancient paradise: "There was no war, people lived in harmony with nature, women and men lived in harmony with one another, children were loved and nurtured, there was food and shelter for all, and everyone was playful, spontaneous, creative, and sexually free under the loving gaze of the goddess." Seven years later, Eller published a sequel to her 1993 book, entitled *The Myth of Matriarchal Prehistory: Why an Invented Past Won't Give Women a Future*. As the title implies, Eller found little evidence for this fantasy. Among other things, she questioned what she saw as the tendency of goddess worshippers to see their revered deity in every artifact. "Were our ancestors so steeped in the sacred that every image they produced could not help but reveal their deepest values, the objects of their greatest reverence? Gimbutas, who seems to view every cup as a ritual vessel for pouring libations to the goddess, would probably say yes."

Since the 1970s, when Marija Gimbutas began popularizing the notion of prehistoric goddess worship, many other archaeologists—especially feminist archaeologists—have tried to point out what they see as serious flaws in her interpretation of the evidence. Ruth Tringham and Meg Conkey, in a 1998 article entitled "Rethinking Figurines," argued that the great majority of figurines from the Paleolithic and Neolithic of the Near East and Europe were schematic and did not clearly depict men or women. This was certainly the case at Opovo, where most of the nearly one hundred humanoid figurines found had been unceremoniously deposited in pits. And Ian's former graduate student Lynn Meskell, now at Columbia University in New York, commented in a paper in the same collection of essays—which Meskell entitled "Twin Peaks"—that "we have decided what is male and female, or sacred and profane, in the imagery of Çatalhöyük, rather than really knowing what the original inhabitants intended and in that sense it will always be *our* fiction."

Some of the goddess pilgrims who visited Çatalhöyük have been openly angry with Ian Hodder and the other archaeologists for their doubts about Neolithic matriarchies and goddess worship, as indicated by hostile comments they have left in the visitor's book. "Shockingly biased presentation. For shame," wrote one leading goddess leader after a visit in 2000. "Is it not more than possible that Mellaart presented a more accurate interpretation?" another visitor asked.

Nevertheless, Ian always tried to engage in dialogue with the goddess groups. One of his most successful attempts was an exchange of letters in 1998 with Anita Louise, a feminist spirituality leader who visited Çatalhöyük that same year. In the correspondence, which Ian decided to leave on the dig's Web site permanently after Anita Louise died of cancer in 2001, he responded in a conciliatory tone to a number of questions she had posed, particularly about the role of women in the Neolithic settlement:

> It is difficult to argue against the importance of women in the symbolism. Especially in the later levels at the site, the image of the enthroned or seated woman is powerful. There do not seem to be equivalent images of men, although as Naomi [Hamilton] would be quick to point out, most of our representations of humans are "sexless"—there is nothing on most figurines and clay models of humans to tell us whether they are men or women. The number of clear men and women figurines is not large. What is more, when we find these clay figures, they do not occur in special places. They seem to occur most frequently in "midden" (refuse) contexts. They do not occur in burials or in locations which would suggest special importance. The famous seated "Mother Goddess" was found in a grain bin—perhaps this has something to do with fertility, but we have no suggestion that grain bins were symbolically important. Most of the figurines are very small.

Naomi, in her final report on the figurines at Çatalhöyük, rejected any suggestions that even the "fat female" figurines found in more recent levels at the site—that is, in Level IV and later—represented goddesses. Rather, she wrote, this change in artistic imagery more likely signaled social and economic developments at the settlement, developments evidenced as well by changes in the styles and technology of the pottery and stone tools that took place around Level VI.

In his article "The Lady and the Seed," Ian suggested that these changes, which occurred during the last few hundred years of the settlement's millennium-long lifetime, may have indicated greater specialization in the production of craft items. It was not impossible that men and women also took on more specialized roles as time went on. But the art continued to reflect nondomestic themes, and social life continued to be focused at least in part on ritual feasting on wild animals, such as the wild cattle that must have been roaming around in the vicinity of Çatalhöyük. Was it possible, Ian asked, that domesticated plants and animals, whatever their importance to the settlement's economy, were simply not all that important to their psyches?

Recently I had a chance to talk to Ian a little more about this question. We discussed a couple of the papers in the upcoming volumes, one that had been written by Rissa along with a graduate student at Cambridge named Stephanie Meece, and another by Linda Donley-Reid, a former graduate student of Ian's who now worked in San Francisco as a psychoanalyst. Rissa and Stephanie had taken a close look at the animal symbolism at Çatalhöyük, particularly the artworks that the Mellaart excavations had uncovered. They found a number of interesting facts, including that although leopards are depicted in a number of sculptures and figurines, and the men running around after the bulls in the wall paintings seemed to be wearing leopard skins, this animal was never found in the faunal assemblage. Another thing they noticed was that despite the celebrity of the bull paintings at Çatalhöyük, there were very few of them. However, a large number of the houses that had been excavated during the Mellaart and Hodder digs had some sort of cattle remains in them, often horns stuck in the walls, scapulae, and so forth.

Linda Donley-Reid, who had worked for the famed paleontologist Richard Leakey in Kenya and later went on to do her Ph.D. with Ian, had attempted a psychoanalytic analysis of the Çatalhöyük art. In many of the images she saw an attempt to deal with the fear of death and a desire to use the power of the wild as protection and psychological support against the stresses and strains of Neolithic life. She also suggested that the capturing of wild cattle might have served as an initiation rite for young men. "If the Çatalhöyük wall murals were made and used by older men in the initiation of younger men," Linda wrote, "they would have established a powerful relationship between the power of the bull and men in the society."

Ian was less interested in who had caught the wild cattle than in what they meant to the community. He said that he now saw a parallel between the burial of the ancestors under the floors of the houses and the use of wild cattle symbolism within them. If the ancestors were necessary to establish the lineage of a particular family within a vertical sequence of houses as well as a social memory for the inhabitants of that house, it might also be the case that the capture and feasting on wild cattle—which seemed to take place among several households at once—represented an offering by the inhabitants of one house to secure the place of that house in the larger community. The placement of the horns in the walls or on the floors might symbolize the social memory that this offering had once been made. He also thought that the wild cattle might in some way be symbolic stand-ins for the ancestors.

Ian realized that he still had a long way to go before he solved the meaning of the art. Yet the project had done a great deal to put the art into some sort of archaeological context, which was one of its main goals. And while the attempts to link the paintings on the plaster walls with the life cycle of the houses had proved frustratingly difficult, Ian and Shahina had worked out some new excavation methods that might make this possible in the future. With time, and a lot more digging, the team might be able to penetrate even deeper into the minds of these prehistoric people.

BY THE END OF the 2003 season Ruth and Mira had largely wrapped up their excavations of Building 3 in the BACH area. They had amassed an enormous amount of data. They wanted to have a proper amount of time to digest it all, so they opted out of publishing their results in the four volumes that Ian was pushing to get finished. Neither of them wanted to make hasty interpretations after all their years of work. The one thing they did know for sure was that Building 3 had not been burned down when it was abandoned. Instead it had been closed up in a far different way. But that did not mean that they were wrong about the importance of fire in the Neolithic, which was, after all, one of the questions that had brought them to Çatalhöyük. Craig Cessford and Julie Near, having undertaken to analyze the burning episodes in Building 1 as well as Mellaart's reports of fires in Level VI and Level VII during his own excavations, concluded that many or most of the fires were indeed deliberate. So Ruth and Mira had been on the right track about that.

Mira did feel ready, however, to sketch at least an outline of the remarkable life story of Building 3, which in many ways differed from the other structures the team had excavated. When James Mellaart visited Çatalhöyük in 1999, he took one look at Building 3 and said to Ian, "At last you have a real Çatalhöyük shrine!"

One thing that set Building 3 apart was the series of three side rooms, Spaces 87, 88, and 89. For a long period during its early life, no one was buried under the floors of the main building; instead, it appeared, the first burials took place in Space 87, where Lori and Başak had found nine skeletons. Only after a major reconstruction of the interior, which involved moving a large oven and a number of other changes, did the burials in the main room begin with two children and one baby in a basket. Later the oven was moved back to its original location, and the house was subdivided by a screen wall made of plaster—a feature never seen before at Çatalhöyük. This screen wall apparently had some sort of plaster relief sculpture on it.

Mira estimated that Building 3 was occupied for somewhere between seventy-nine and ninety-five years. Like all Çatalhöyük houses, it was abandoned in a ritual fashion. But fire had nothing to do with it. Onto the collapsed roof, which had fallen into the center of the house, were placed the remains of an oven, the skull of a bull, and the two skulls of a boy and a young woman. In 1999, the year the skulls were found, Mira had not wanted to speculate about them, other than to say that they were placed there deliberately. Now she was struggling between two opposing hypotheses. The first was that the skulls represented some sort of human sacrifice after an opposing clan or family had attacked the inhabitants of this house and killed some of its occupants. In this scenario, the victors would have placed the skulls in the house to warn this clan not to expand its presence on the mound.

But Mira preferred another explanation. "The second scenario is closer to my heart," she said. "The unusual presence of the skulls could simply indicate the ending of what was initially a very promising household line. Their placement together, with foreheads touching, expresses to me a sense of emotion and gentleness. They might have been siblings, perhaps the last offspring in the household who were unfortunately killed in an accident." The accident might have involved the collapsed roof, she said. "Or it may have taken place outside the settlement." Either way, Ruth and Mira had probably come as close as anyone possibly could to putting faces on the people of Çatalhöyük.

DURING MY VISIT to Çatalhöyük in 2001, Ayfer Bartu announced her engagement to Can Candan, a filmmaker she had known since her days as a student at Robert College in Istanbul. Can (pronounced "John") was spending some time at the site working on a documentary about the excavations. On the following Thursday morning Ayfer and Can were told that under no circumstances should they leave Çatalhöyük that evening. They were not told anything more.

What they did not know was that Julie Near and John Swogger were organizing one of the most memorable Thursday night parties Çatalhöyük would ever see: Ayfer and Can's Mock Wedding. That same year a new wing of the dig house, which was to be used for a seminar room and laboratories, had been inaugurated. During the planning of the wing, Shahina had convinced Ian to have the builders construct a rooftop terrace over it. Ian didn't like the idea. He told Shahina a rooftop terrace smacked of the old style of the British Empire, and besides the red tape to get permission to do it would be formidable. Shahina continued to pester him, and finally he agreed as long as she did all the paperwork.

It was now, up to the rooftop terrace, that a reluctant Ayfer and Can were dragged, knowing that something was up, but also knowing that there was nothing that they could do about it. Julie slipped a white robe around Ayfer's shoulders and put a wedding veil on her head, while John put a top hat made from purple paper on Can's head. Everyone else was in costume. Ian was dressed as a vicar, John as the lecherous uncle of the bride, and Julie as the floozy whom Can had spurned to marry Ayfer. I came as a radio reporter. I had attached a Sony Walkman to my belt and tied a screwdriver to it with a string. I went around holding the screwdriver upside down, poking the handle into people's faces and asking them for their reaction. Several people asked me in all seriousness if I really was recording them.

Ian took his place before the couple and began reading the vows:

IAN: We have come together in the presence of the goddess to witness the marriage of Ayfer and Can and to ask her blessing on them. The next bit, I want you to know, came from a real goddess Web site—this is a direct quote:

> Marriage is a commitment to a spiritual journey and a life of becoming, a partnership with the earth, a nurturing of who we really are. It combines two separate hearts into one."

So, may the goddess protect you and keep you fertile, and may you have many little leopards, and this is just for you, Ayfer, may your breasts be full of sweet milk and not vulture beaks.

CAN: I feel left out.

IAN: And may there never be any strange orange staining with medium-sized aggregates in your living room. I am now required to ask if anyone here present knows of any just cause or reason why these two should not be joined together in holy matrimony, apart from the fact that Can is a man, which isn't allowed in a goddess wedding. So are there any?

AYFER: Yes . . .

IAN: So, do you, Can, promise to love, cherish, and respect the multivocality of Ayfer, till death do you part, and do you also promise not to use your drinking glass as a shaving cup, not to throw solids down the sink, and to switch the bloody modem off after use?

CAN: Yes, I do.

IAN: And do you, Ayfer, promise to love, cherish, and respect the multivocality of Can, till death do you part, and do you also promise not to use your glass as a toothbrush holder, to always put another beer in the refrigerator when you take a cold one out, unless of course you like warm beer, and to always throw used toilet paper into the bin provided and not into the toilet?

AYFER: No, I don't, I'm not sure . . .

IAN: We are now coming to the most solemn part. I need the ring.

JULIE: I've forgotten the ring!

IAN: So, do you Ayfer and Can take each other to be lawfully wedded earth soul-partners, to have and to hold for richer or poorer, in sickness and in health, till death do you part and your heads be removed neatly from your bodies leaving small obsidian cut marks on the surface of the foramen magnum?

AYFER AND CAN (TOGETHER): I do!

IAN: So, in the name of the goddess, the bull, and the holy vulture, I pronounce you man and wife.

The CD player was turned on, and the dancing began. The British Embassy bar, which had been brought up to the terrace for the occasion, was stocked with libations. Sonya Atalay, a former Ph.D. student of Ruth Tringham's who had supported herself during her undergraduate years at the University of Michigan tending bar at a nightclub called The Nectarine, poured the drinks. Mavili Tokyağsun, a cigarette in one hand and a borrowed video camera in the other, recorded the events.

I danced a few turns with Rissa and Julie, and then decided to take a rest. I walked over to the banister at the edge of the terrace. The Neolithic settlement seemed to glow faintly in the light of the full moon. The breeze rippled through the canvases of the tents covering Building 5 and the BACH area. As I gazed out at the mound, I tried to do what I am sure many people before me had done: imagine this ancient village teeming with people, the laughter of its children, the people on their own roofs tending fires, chipping obsidian, sewing animal skins into clothes. For a few moments I could almost see them. Then they faded away in the moonlight. Yet the bond between us and them was almost palpable. Without us, they would be forgotten, buried in their monument, just as they had been for the nine millennia that passed before James Mellaart and his friends came along and found them. And without them, we would have no reason to be out here on this isolated spot on the Konya Plain. Our community would never have come together. Past and present, locked in an embrace that spanned 9,000 years.

I listened to the party behind me, but I kept staring ahead. I could hear the laughter of my friends, their voices, the accents of at least ten different nationalities. They had come here because of a shared passion to understand this prehistoric community, a curiosity that transcended national boundaries and linked us all in our common humanity. As I gazed over the ancient mound, it occurred to me that if we could understand a little better why we all wanted to live together, maybe we would get better at doing it.

Epilogue

By the beginning of the 2002 season, Ian and Shahina had become convinced that the project needed to radically shift gears in its excavation strategy. Since the launch of full-scale digging seven years before, the team had concentrated on excavating one building at a time. This was also the basic approach adopted by a new team from Poznan, Poland, which had arrived in 2001 to open up a fresh excavation area at the highest point on the mound, very near the summit area where the Greek team had worked previously. Now, with the BACH excavations winding up, Building 1 completed, and work in the south area temporarily suspended, it was time to make some decisions about the project's future course.

Shahina had felt for some time that putting every building under the high-definition archaeological microscope was beginning to result in diminishing returns. Ruth and Mira had shared similar concerns with both Ian and Shahina. The team had learned a great deal about the life cycle of individual houses but very little about how the Neolithic community as a whole was organized. One day, toward the end of the 2002 season, Shahina said to Ian, "Let's open up a big area and expose a lot of houses at one occupation level." Ian's first reaction was a nervous laugh. He knew how much such an ambitious plan was likely to cost. But he had also felt for some time that the survival of the project required a fresh approach.

The idea was not to duplicate what Mellaart had already done, and certainly not to "move earth" at Mellaart's amazing pace during the 1960s of one building each day. On the other hand, as Ian put it later, "it was time to return to the bigger picture." Ian pointed out that there were a number of questions remaining to be answered: "Were these buildings organized into groups? What was the social geography of the town? Were there bureaucratic or ceremonial centers that regulated the 3000 to 8000 people that lived there? How had the whole thing worked?"

Ian and Shahina also had pragmatic reasons for wanting to ramp up the scale of the excavations. From the very beginning of the dig, Ian had struggled with the conflict between doing contextual, high-definition archaeology—which diminished the chances of quickly finding the paintings, sculptures, and other artwork the site was famous for—and the increasing desire of some of the sponsors, as well as the Turkish authorities, to see the kind of spectacular results that could be put on public display. The new strategy was an attempt to accomodate these two often competing goals. To ensure that valuable information was not lost when the pace picked up, Ian and Shahina developed a two-tier excavation system: Fast Track and Full-On Sampling. At first, Fast Track meant that no sampling took place, but after many of the specialists took exception to this the scheme was modified so that limited sampling was done in some Fast Track buildings. After a period of adjustment, the excavators and specialists got better at negotiating together over which buildings would fall into which tracks.

As the 2003 season approached, Ian and Shahina made plans to open up a huge, forty-meter by forty-meter trench just south of Building 5 and the BACH area. Shahina assembled a crew of 26 excavators to work in what was now called the 4040 area. The crew was supervised by

Jez Taylor—the digger who, together with Craig Cessford, had reached natural during the 1999 Long Season—and another British contract archaeologist named Joann Lyon.

Meanwhile, there were some important changes in personnel among the team members. Ian had asked the specialists to commit for another five years if they were going to stay with the project. Some of them felt it was time to move on. The leaders of the archaeobotany lab, Christine Hastorf, Andy Fairbairn, and Julie Near, all left for other projects and other pursuits. They were replaced by the husband-and-wife team of Amy Bogaard from the University of Nottingham and Mike Charles from the University of Sheffield. Naomi Hamilton also departed, as well as Theya Molleson and Peter Andrews of the human remains team, who were replaced by Clark Larsen of Ohio State University and Simon Hillson of the Institute of Archaeology in London.

Another new arrival was a baby named Aysun, the daughter of Mavili Tokyağsun. Mavili had found a nice new husband, a construction materials salesman from Konya, where she now lived when not working at Çatalhöyük.

As for Ruth and Mira, now that the BACH excavations were over, Ruth had happily signed on to dig in the 4040 area, while Mira had decided to take a break from excavating and carry out a study of the clay and other building materials used at Çatalhöyük.

To prepare the 4040 area for excavation, the team went back to the surface scraping technique that had worked so well during the project's early years. The scraping revealed about sixty-five internal spaces or rooms, although it was not yet possible to determine how many buildings these represented. The structures appeared to be grouped into definite sectors, and there were two gaps between the buildings that looked something like streets, although they could also have been rubbish dumping areas.

Once the scraping was done, there was still enough time left in the season to carry out limited excavations. A number of human burials immediately appeared at the surface, evidently from buildings whose foundations had been been destroyed by the erosion at the top of the mound. Some of these skeletons were adorned with elaborate jewelry, including armbands made from copper and alabaster and long strings of beads.

Meanwhile a separate group of excavators had resumed digging in the south area, under the enormous steel-frame shelter that had been erected there in 2002. Just before the end of the season, this team found two segments of red, geometric-style wall paintings in a stucture designated Building 17. And the Polish team, made up of twelve archaeologists from the Polish Academy of Sciences and the University of Poznan and led by Arkadiusz Marciniak and Lech Czerniak, made what may have been one of the most spectacular discoveries Çatalhöyük had seen in recent years: the apparent remains of a nearly intact roof that had collapsed during Neolithic times. The roof, now lying at an angle, was nearly eight inches thick, measured about eight meters by at least three meters, and was made up of plaster layers interspersed with ashy deposits. Although bits of fallen roof had been found before, including a nice specimen in the BACH building, this new find represented the best chance yet for the team to study what kinds of activities the people of Çatalhöyük had carried out under the Anatolian sky.

The new excavation strategy was already showing a lot of promise, in part because the team was now excavating some of the later occupation levels, where the most exciting discoveries were likely to be made. The team looked forward to the 2004 season with the keen anticipation that the project was about to turn a major page in its history.

THE PEOPLE OF Çatalhöyük occupied this spot on the Konya Plain for more than one thousand years. Then the settlement was abandoned. Where did they go? Did they die out, due to disease or famine? Or, as Mellaart had suggested, did they move across a distributary of the Çarsamba River to the West Mound, a smaller Chalcolithic settlement with lots of painted pottery? There was a problem with this tempting hypothesis, however. While neither the abandonment of the East Mound nor the first settlement of the West Mound had been precisely dated, the first rough estimates made by the Hodder team had indicated that there might be a gap of at least a few hundred years between the two sites.

In 1998, to get at this and other questions about the West Mound, Jonathan Last and several other excavators began digging there. Each morning they would trudge across the dry, dusty channel between the mounds where the river once had flowed. This first short season had revealed the corner of a mud-brick building on the highest part of the settlement. After a one-year hiatus to work on the deep sounding in 1999, Jonathan, joined first by Naomi Hamilton and then by Catriona Gibson of the Wessex Archaeology contract unit, began a more intensive round of excavations, which led to further exposure of the structure now called Building 25.

The calibrated radiocarbon dates from the bottom of the East Mound had shown that the people of Çatalhöyük first settled on the Konya Plain about 7500 B.C. More recently, samples from Level II of the East Mound had yielded calibrated dates of 6480 to 6220 B.C. It was not possible to date Level I, because most of this occupation layer had been highly disturbed by erosion. However, Craig Cessford had calculated that the mound had grown higher by between 1.7 and 2.4 meters per century, meaning that the very last occupation of the settlement ended sometime between 6200 and 5900 B.C.

Meanwhile Craig had the Oxford radiocarbon unit date samples from Building 25. The results indicated that Building 25 had been occupied between 6030 and 5700 B.C. The team knew that the depth of archaeological deposits underneath Building 25 was 4.9 meters. Assuming the same growth rate as that for the East Mound, the West Mound would have been founded some two or three hundred years before Building 25 was constructed—and probably overlapped with the last occupation of the East Mound. Mellaart's original hypothesis now seemed to be on much firmer ground. Jonathan and Craig concluded that the two mounds should be seen as part of the same overall occupational sequence, and that the people of the East Mound may have simply moved across the river.

This new view of Çatalhöyük's history raised all sorts of questions, especially because there were marked cultural differences between the East and West mounds. For one thing, the arrangement of buildings and use of space was much different. And Jonathan, as the dig's pottery specialist, could not help but notice that the painted ceramics found on the Chalcolithic West Mound, which had red-on-white geometeric designs, differed greatly from the plain pottery on the East Mound. While the East Mound pottery had undergone some interesting technological changes after Level VII, including a shift from tempering with straw or chaff to mineral tempering using sand or mineral-rich clays, it was never painted. On the other hand, the wall paintings that had made the East Mound famous were found less frequently in its later levels, and there was no indication so far that the walls of West Mound buildings had been painted.

Jonathan, who was familiar with the painted pottery from David French's excavations of Can Hasan, had noted that this nearby site also had no Çatalhöyük-type wall paintings. In a paper in the *Journal of Material Culture*, Jonathan proposed that this shift from painting the walls to painting the pots might have represented a change in the social structure of these Central Anatolian sites from a more inward-looking to a more outwardly expansive worldview as the Neolithic period gave way to the Chalcolithic. The wall paintings on the interior walls of houses, he pointed out, would probably only be seen by its residents; the pots, on the other hand, would be seen by everyone, and could have been traded among other settlements in the area.

There was another dramatic finding during the 2003 season at the West Mound. Sheelagh Frame, who was in charge of analyzing the animal bones from the site, had finally collected enough samples to conclude that the sheep and goats were domestic—and so, most likely, were the cattle. The cattle bones fell well within the domestic size range and were distinctly smaller than the wild cattle from the East Mound.

Sheelagh's conclusions raised yet more questions. For one thing, it was not clear whether the cattle had been domesticated by the settlers themselves or brought in from other villages in Anatolia, perhaps farther east. Nor was it yet possible to determine when the shift from wild to domesticated cattle took place. Although all of the cattle analyzed from the East Mound so far were wild, the project was only now beginning to excavate occupation levels higher than Level VI. The new excavation strategy, with its emphasis on later levels, promised to eventually fill this gap in the faunal team's understanding of how the use of animals had evolved.

One important implication of all of these findings was that the distinction between the Neolithic and the Chalcolithic, at least on the Konya Plain, might not be nearly as sharp as previously thought. Only further excavations, both of the later stratigraphic layers of the East Mound and the early levels of the West Mound, could determine whether the cultural changes that led to the Chalcolithic originated in the later occupation levels of the East Mound.

IN 2004 THE TEAM was back up to full strength. Nearly 100 archaeologists flocked to Çatalhöyük for what promised to be one of the most exciting seasons since the excavations began. They were not disappointed. In mid-July, Lori Hager had been called in to investigate some disarticulated human bones in Building 42 in the south area, when she uncovered a typical Mellaart-style fat lady figurine carved from stone, the first of its kind found by the Hodder team. A few days later, excavators working in another part of the south area spotted the two front feet of an animal that had been buried next to a human skeleton. Further excavation revealed that the animal was a young lamb that had been interred with its front feet sticking straight up. This was the first time that the Çatalhöyük team had found an animal treated the same way as a human.

Later in the month, another first for the Hodder team: the excavators working in the 4040 area found a small obsidian mirror.

The team was on a roll. On July 28, Başak Boz, while excavating another human grave in Building 42, found some fragments of plaster near a skull. Just what she had found became clear the following morning, after she had exposed more of the burial: the front of the skull had been covered with white plaster, forming a new nose and face. A red ochre–based paint had been applied to the forehead, nose, and eyes. The skull was reminiscent of those found at Jericho and other sites in the Near East, although it bore some stylistic differences. Most important for the team, it was the first plastered skull ever found at Çatalhöyük, and only the second time that such a skull had shown up in Anatolia.

Başak's timing could not have been better. The next day was the annual press tour. Some thirty journalists, mostly from the Turkish press, were expected to visit. One of the conservators, James Hales of the Institute of Archaeology in London, was called up to the mound. James, along with Ian, Shahina, Başak and Lori, crouched around the skull, discussing how best to keep its fragile shell from falling apart before it could be lifted out and taken to the conservation lab. Other team members crowded in to get a look. Jason Quinlan and Michael Ashley, the Wonder Twins, hovered over the group, photographing the skull and recording the conversation on videotape. The skull, of course, would be left in place until the press had come and gone.

Notes

Introduction

PAGE

1 *"archaeologist is digging"*: Wheeler 1956, 13. Italics in the original.
2 *pattern of bone sutures:* Interview with Başak Boz.
2 *"All I know"*: Interview with Mirjana Stevanovic.
2 *"The Mystery of Communities"*: Balter 1998.
2 *Sir John Lubbock:* Bahn 2001, 43.
3 *Jared Diamond:* Diamond 1997.
3 *one of the largest:* Bahn 2001, 80.
3 *enormous village:* Cessford in press/d.
5 *Publishing my article:* Balter 1999.

Chapter 1: "It's Neolithic!"

7 *Late in the afternoon:* Interviews with James Mellaart and David French; Mellaart 1967, p. 27; Mellaart 1978, p. 12; Pearson and Connor 1967a, 32.
8 *"filthy Roman muck"*: Interview with David French.
8 *Hacilar: Anatolian Studies* 8:127 (1958); Lloyd 1963, 105.
9 *"no sign whatever"*: Lloyd 1956, 53.
9 *excavations on Cyprus:* Le Brun 1997, 12.
9 *more than a dozen new settlements: Anatolian Studies* 9:31 (1959).
10 *considerable mounds:* Lloyd 1963, 14.
10 *5,000 mounds:* Ibid., 98.
10 *left Iraq for Turkey:* Collon 1996.
10 *good example was Jericho:* Kenyon 1957.
10 *mound was huge:* Mellaart 1967, 30.
11 *should have opened archaeologists' eyes:* Mellaart 1975, 124.
11 *Garstang had found:* Ibid.
11 *toasted their discovery:* Interview with James Mellaart.
11 *"make sure it was still there"*: Pearson and Connor 1967a, 32.
12 *"Even more important": Anatolian Studies* 9:33 (1959).
12 *call him Jimmy:* Interviews with Mellaart contemporaries and younger archaeologists.

12 *Mellaart's account:* Interviews with James Mellaart; Mellaart's scholarship application to the BIAA, February 24, 1951.
12 *Vermeer forgery:* www.museumbredius.nl.
12 *mother's death marked him:* Interviews with anonymous contemporaries.
12 *Atlantic Wall:* home.zonnet.nl/atlanticwall/start.htm.
13 *Adriaan de Buck:* millennium.arts.kuleuven.ac.be/egyptology/coffintexts; www.touregypt.net/featurestories/coffintext.htm.
13 *so-called Sea Peoples:* Bray and Trump 1982, 184; Scarre and Fagan 1997, 184.
13 *became an enthusiast:* Interview with James Mellaart; Mellaart 1978, 7.
14 *Wheeler-Kenyon school:* Lucas 2001, 36.
14 *Stratigraphic Revolution:* Ibid., 47; Renfrew and Bahn 1996, 33; "Kidder, Alfred V.," *Encyclopædia Britannica* 2003 Encyclopædia Britannica Premium Service, accessed 19 February 2003, www.britannica.com/eb/article?eu=46446.
14 *borrowed the concept:* Wheeler 1954, 57; Renfrew and Bahn 1996, 24.
14 *a scientific discipline:* Renfrew and Bahn 1996, 24.
14 *Thomas Jefferson:* Ibid., 21; Wheeler 1954, 20 and 58–59.
15 *the lift it needed:* Wheeler 1954, 24–26.
15 *Boucher de Crèvecoeur de Perthes:* Ibid.; *Encyclopædia Britannica* 2003 Encyclopædia Britannica Premium Service, accessed 18 February 2003, www.britannica.com/eb/article?eu=16106.
15 *"no right way of digging":* Wheeler 1954, 15.
15 *Heinrich Schliemann: Encyclopædia Britannica* 2003 Encyclopædia Britannica Premium Service, accessed 18 February 2003, www.britannica.com/eb/article?eu=67867.
15 *"We may be grateful to Schliemann":* Wheeler 1954, 59.
15 *Pitt-Rivers:* Ibid., 13; Renfrew and Bahn 1996, 31.
15 *archaeological campaigns:* Wheeler 1954; Wheeler 1956.
15 *Frederick Kenyon:* www.gospelcom.net/chi/DAILYF/2002/08/daily-08-23-2002.shtml; Kenyon 1940, 288, 289.
15 *Verulamium is still heralded:* Bray and Trump 1982, 261.
16 *his leading disciple:* Lucas 2001, 38; Kathleen Kenyon biography: www.pef.org.uk/s/Kenyon.htm; "Kenyon, Dame Kathleen," *Encyclopædia Britannica* 2003 Encyclopædia Britannica Premium Service, accessed 19 February 2003 www.britannica.com/eb/article?eu=46184.
16 *Kenyon at Sutton Walls:* Callaway 1979, 122–25.
16 *technique Wheeler and Kenyon:* Kenyon 1953, 69.
16 *skeletons of men and boys:* www.hereford.uk.com/history/ironage.asp; www.smr.herefordshire.gov.uk/hist_periods/iron_age.htm.
16 *invited him:* Interview with James Mellaart.
16 *The British, with schools:* www.britac.ac.uk/institutes/.
16 *In January 1948 the BIAA:* Matthews 1998, 1.
17 *Lloyd, having spent:* Collon 1996.
17 *he proposed:* Scholarship application to the BIAA, February 24, 1951.
17 *application was accepted:* Letter from BIAA secretary to James Mellaart, May 5, 1951.
17 *£150:* Interview with James Mellaart; letter from BIAA secretary to Mellaart, May 22, 1951.
17 *on foot:* Interview with James Mellaart; Mellaart 1978, 8.

17 *he had spotted:* Ibid.; Mellaart 1967, 27.
17 *his Anatolian surveys: Anatolian Studies* 9: 175 (1954).
17 *Mellaart served:* Kenyon 1957, 21; Interviews with James Mellaart and Charles Burney.
17 *remains farther down:* Interviews with James Mellaart and Charles Burney; Kenyon 1957, 67–8.
18 *a godsend:* Letter from Seton Lloyd to the BIAA Council of Management, November 12, 1954; interviews with Dominique Collon and Charles Burney.
18 *mound of Beycesultan:* Matthews 1998, 61; Lloyd 1963, 87.
18 *This was Copper Age Hacilar: Anatolian Studies* 8:6 (1958); Matthews 1998, 53.
18 *Mellaart as assistant director:* Letter from Hugh Beaver to James Mellaart, January 23, 1958.
18 *His discovery:* Interviews with Charles Burney, David French, David Hawkins, and other contemporaries.
18 *"Mellaart's West Anatolian survey":* Lloyd 1963, 102.
19 *a sprawling* yali: Arlette Mellaart 2002, 62; Interviews with Arlette Mellaart and Ian Todd.
19 *Museum of the Ancient Orient:* Arlette Mellaart 2002.
19 *Arlette began sitting in:* Interview with Arlette Mellaart.
19 *Bittel was an expert:* Kurt Bittel was director of the institute 1938–44 and again 1954–60: E-mail from A. Juren Meister of the German Archaeological Institute; Lloyd 1956, 38 et seq.
19 *the Hittites:* Bray and Trump 1982, 111.
19 *Bittel brought over:* Interview with Arlette Mellaart.
19 *red burnished pot:* Interview with James Mellaart.
19 *James and Arlette were married:* Interview with Arlette Mellaart.
20 *levels at Fikirtepe:* Özdoğan and Başgelen 1999, 206 et seq., 212 et seq.
20 *see it today:* Interview with Arlette Mellaart.

Chapter 2: A Prehistoric Art Gallery

21 *began hatching plans:* Interviews with James and Arlette Mellaart.
21 *abundant pottery: Anatolian Studies* 9:51 (1959).
21 *Turkish workman:* Interviews with James and Arlette Mellaart and Ian Todd.
21 *Bronze Age palace:* Lloyd 1963, 87; Lloyd and Mellaart 1962.
22 *female figurines: Anatolian Studies* 11:39 (1961).
22 *"Mellaart has discovered": Time,* February 24, 1961, 34.
22 *The British press: Daily Telegraph,* January 16, 1961.
22 *three-page color spread:* Mellaart 1961b.
22 *"The Anatolian 'Fertility Goddess'": Anatolian Studies* 11:59 (1961).
22 *"it can only be hoped":* Ibid., 61.
22 *Mellaart arrived at Çatalhöyük:* Mellaart 1962b, 41.
22 *grant from Wenner-Gren Foundation:* Letter from the Hanover Bank to BIAA secretary, January 27, 1961.
23 *Can Hasan:* French 1962.
23 *seemed like a blotch:* Interviews with James and Arlette Mellaart; Mellaart 1967, 171; Mellaart 1962b.
23 *Five or six red men:* Mellaart 1967, 98, 158, and 171.

24 *Teilelat Ghassul:* Todd 1976, 33; Bahn 2001, 166 and 439.
24 *wide time gap:* "Painting, Western," *Encyclopædia Britannica* 2003 Encyclopædia Britannica Premium Service, accessed 6 March 2003, www.britannica.com/eb/article?eu=115369.
24 *earliest known paintings:* Ibid.; Mellaart 1962b, 57.
24 *dozens of wall paintings:* Mellaart 1967, 77 and 131; Mellaart 1966; Mellaart 1964.
24 *"town plan":* Mellaart 1967, 133 and 176–77.
24 *Mellaart became obsessed:* Interviews with James Mellaart and Ian Todd; Mellaart 1998.
24 *At Jericho:* Kenyon 1954.
24 *At Jarmo:* Braidwood 1960.
25 *Hawkins answered the call:* Mellaart 1962b, 41; Interviews with James and Arlette Mellaart.
25 *Hawkins's advice:* Interview with Ian Todd; letter from Elizabeth French to Paolo Mora, January 24, 1962; see also Matero 2, 71.
25 *plaster adhered:* Letter from Elizabeth French to Paolo Mora, January 24, 1962.
25 *horizontal excavation:* Wheeler 1954, 149.
26 *"railway time-table without a train":* Ibid.
26 *forty mud-brick buildings:* Mellaart 1962b, 44; Mellaart 1962a, 2.
26 *nearly two hundred buildings:* Interview with James Mellaart; Düring 2001, 3.
26 *an acre of the tell:* Interview with James Mellaart; Todd 1976, 15.
26 *took to calling it a city:* Mellaart 1964.
26 *a major boost:* Jacobs 1970, 31.
27 *he numbered the layers:* Mellaart 1967, 49–53.
27 *settlement's maximum population:* Düring 2001, 3.
27 *each house was built:* Mellaart 1967, 54 et seq.; Todd 1976, 24 et seq.
27 *By counting the number:* Todd 1976, 31.
28 *series of raised platforms:* Todd 1976, 29.
29 *Most of the bodies:* Ibid., 64 et seq.; Mellaart 1967, 204.
29 *"secondary" rather than primary burials:* Mellaart 1967, 204; Bahn 2001, 71.
29 *"Upon death the corpse":* Mellaart 1967, 204.
29 *suggested by wall paintings:* Todd 1976, 67–9.
30 *questioned whether the bodies:* Ibid., 67.
30 *differences in the way man and woman:* Todd 1976, 71–72.
30 *grave goods:* Ibid., 69–70.
30 *eight obsidian mirrors:* Vedder in press/b; Mellaart 1963, Plate XXVb.
30 *the earliest known:* Vedder in press/b; Thorpe 1994, 248–55, quoted in Vedder.
31 *allowed scholars to accurately date:* Renfew and Bahn 1996, 123.
31 *Willard Libby:* "Libby, Willard Frank," *Encyclopædia Britannica* 2003 Encyclopædia Britannica Premium Service, accessed 12 March 2003, www.britannica.com/eb/article?eu=49247.
31 *whose ages were already known:* Arnold and Libby 1949, 678.
32 *Mellaart had given the method:* Mellaart 1967, 52.
32 *stratigraphic levels at Hacilar:* Mellaart 1967, 25.
32 *Mellaart had assumed:* Todd 1976, 98.
32 *Mellaart collected samples:* Ibid., 100–101; Cessford 2001.
32 *University of Pennsylvania and at a French facility:* Mellaart 1967, 12.

32 *The earliest date:* Ibid., 52; Todd 1976, 98 et seq.
32 *thrived at the same time:* Mellaart 1975, 283 et seq.
33 *"After its primary precursor":* Mellaart 1967, 9.
33 *an enthusiastic account: Daily Telegraph.* June 22, 1961.
33 *Mellaart himself published:* Mellaart 1962a, 2.
33 *international media:* For example, *Der Spiegel,* April 24, 1963, 97; *Times* (London), July 10 and 24, 1963, June 30, 1965, February 16, 1966.
33 *two-part photo-essay:* Mellaart 1963b; Mellaart 1963c.
34 *Back in Mellaart's day:* Interview with James Mellaart.
34 *failed to land:* Letter from Seton Lloyd to Winifred Lamb, March 10, 1960.
34 *not always generously:* Interview with James Mellaart; numerous letters of complaint in BIAA files.
34 *Lloyd took over:* Collon 1996.
34 *prestigious Institute of Archaeology:* Harris 1997/1998.
34 *found Mellaart troublesome:* Numerous memos in BIAA archives.
34 *Lloyd tended to indulge:* Interview with Dominique Collon.
34 *his job would also end:* Minutes of the Council of Management meeting, January 22, 1960.
34 *Michael Gough: Anatolian Studies* 11:2 (1961).
34 *Gough, a former major:* Interview with Hugh Elton.
35 *little love lost:* Interviews with James and Arlette Mellaart, other anonymous sources.
35 *each season might be his last:* Interviews with James and Arlette Mellaart and Ian Todd.

Chapter 3: The Dorak Affair

36 *about a dozen people:* Seasonal preliminary reports in *Anatolian Studies.*
36 *Whirling Dervishes:* "Mawlawiyah," *Encyclopædia Britannica* 2003 Encyclopædia Britannica Premium Service, accessed 27 March 2003, http://www.britannica.com/eb/article?eu=52809.
36 *an archaeology student:* Interview with Ian Todd.
37 *exposing the artworks:* Interview with Ian Todd; Todd 1976, 35.
37 *Viola Pemberton-Pigott:* Interview with Viola Pemberton-Pigott.
37 *leopards changed their spots:* Interview with Ian Todd; Todd 1976, 57.
38 *danger lurked:* Mellaart 1967, 126; Todd 1976, 61.
38 *juxtaposition of life and death:* Mellaart 1967, 183.
38 *outstretched arms and legs:* Mellaart 1967, 46 and 81.
38 *Obliterating their faces:* Ibid., 82.
38 *"goddesses" galore:* Ibid., 203.
38 *most spectacular:* Ibid., 157.
38 *"A belief in a goddess":* Mellaart 1962b, 57.
39 *enormous bull heads:* Mellaart 1967, 42, 48, 118–30.
39 *Mellaart concluded:* Ibid., 178–202.
39 *parallels he saw:* Ibid., 201.
40 *absence of phalluses and vulvae:* Ibid., 201–202.
40 *"emphasis on sex in art":* Ibid., 202.
40 *spiritual, cultural, and trade center:* Mellaart 1975, 100 and 106.

40 *"As the only source of life"*: Mellaart 1967, 202.
40 *Marija Gimbutas:* Gimbutas 1989, xx.
40 *estimated 5,000:* Todd 1976, 122–23; Cessford in press/d.
41 *Helbaek had earlier worked:* Braidwood 1960.
41 *"The deposits of carbonized grain"*: Helbaek 1964, 121.
41 *Perkins's findings:* Perkins 1969.
42 *Renfrew's research:* Dixon et al. 1968; Renfew and Bahn 1996, 356.
42 *Ian Todd drove Renfrew around:* Interview with Colin Renfrew.
43 *another ten years' work:* Mellaart 1967, 227.
43 *"We were devastated"*: Interview with Arlette Mellaart.
43 *"Who is your enemy"*: Interview with James Mellaart; Pearson and Connor 1967b, 10.
43 *making his own inquiries:* Pearson and Connor 1967a.
44 *fabulous Bronze Age treasure:* Ibid.
44 *Aşikli Höyük:* Todd 1966.
44 *small wooden box:* Interview with Viola Pemberton-Pigott.
45 *it never existed:* Anonymous interviews with numerous Mellaart contemporaries and other archaeologists.
45 *question the authenticity:* Broodbank 2000, 97; Basch 1987, 91–3; Bahn 2001, 122.
45 *Seton Lloyd believed:* Interview with Dominique Collon.
45 *committee of inquiry:* Report of the *Ad Hoc* Committee on the Dorak Affair (undated; concerning meeting of 10 May 1968); Minute 891 of the meeting of the BIAA Council of Management, 14 June 1968.
45 *third possibility:* Anonymous interviews with Mellaart contemporaries.
45 *Mellaart's own accounts:* Interview with James Mellaart; "English translation of the Turkish version of Mr. Mellaart's original letter to the Director of Department of Antiquities in Ankara [18 July 1960], as approved by him"; Pearson and Connor 1967a, 34–37.
45 *"official" version:* "English translation of the Turkish version of Mr. Mellaart's original letter to the Director of Department of Antiquities in Ankara [18 July 1960], as approved by him."
46 *He told Seton Lloyd:* Pearson and Connor 1967b, 7.
46 *"Almost miraculously"*: Lloyd 1967, 32.
46 *stunning confirmation:* Lloyd 1963, 83–85.
47 *Anna responded:* Letter from Anna Papastrati to James Mellaart, October 1958 (photograph published in Pearson and Connor 1967a, facing 161).
47 *supposedly from Hacilar:* "English translation of the Turkish version of Mr. Mellaart's original letter to the Director of Department of Antiquities in Ankara [18 July 1960], as approved by him"; Pearson and Connor 1967a.
47 *Mellaart claimed that he reported:* Pearson and Connor 1967b, 7; Report of the *Ad Hoc* Committee on the Dorak Affair (undated; concerning meeting of 10 May 1968).
47 *changed his story:* Pearson and Connor 1967b, 7; interviews with James and Arlette Mellaart.
48 *Lloyd apparently accepted:* Pearson and Connor 1967b, 7.
48 *authorities went to Izmir:* Pearson and Connor 1967a.

48 *Sotheby's:* Catalogue of Greek, Roman, Egyptian and Near Eastern Antiquities, Sotheby and Co., 1962.
48 Milliyet *launched:* Pearson and Connor 1967b, 7 and 10.
48 *two streets with that name:* Pearson and Connor 1967a, 96–102.
49 *"Quite apart from straightforward":* Letter to Richard Barnett from Seton Lloyd, July 19, 1964.
49 *"someone capable of greater tact":* Ibid.; see also letter from Michael Gough to Seton Lloyd, April 3, 1965.
49 *department's attitude:* Letter from Michael Gough to Seton Lloyd, April 3, 1965.
49 *Case against him was dismissed:* Ibid.
49 *no more eager:* Letter from Michael Gough to Seton Lloyd, April 29, 1965.
49 *appointed Oliver Gurney:* Letter to James Mellaart from James Bowker, May 25, 1965; letter from Michael Gough to Seton Lloyd, June 2, 1965.
49 *authorities seemed to know:* Letter to James Mellaart from James Bowker, May 25, 1965; *Anatolian Studies* 16:165 (1966); Report to Department of Antiquities and Museums by Nemika Altan, August 21, 1965; letter from Seton Lloyd to Michael Gough, September 3, 1965.
49 *Ian Todd designated:* Letter from Oliver Gurney to Michael Gough, June 5, 1965; interview with Ian Todd.
50 *one of the most successful:* Mellaart 1966.
50 *she wandered into:* Report by Nemika Altan to Department of Antiquities and Museums, September 22, 1965; interview with Nemika Altan.
50 *four of the Beycesultan men:* Interviews with Nemika Altan and Ian Todd; Mellaart 1966, 165.
51 *decision to allow Mellaart:* Letter from Michael Gough to Oliver Gurney, August 29, 1965; letter from Michael Gough to Seton Lloyd, August 30, 1965.
51 *much more concerned:* Letter to Directorate of the British Institute of Archaeology at Ankara from Mehmet Önder, director general of antiquities and museums, March 7, 1966.
51 *own worst enemy:* Anonymous interviews with Mellaart contemporaries.
51 *He later insisted:* Interview with James Mellaart; Minutes of the meeting of the BIAA Council of Management, October 28, 1966.
51 *Mellaart's four-page report:* Royal Ontario Museum *Archaeological Newsletter,* New Series, No. 9, February 1966.
52 *Turkish scholar at New York University:* Minutes of the BIAA Policy Committee, April 14, 1966.
52 *press campaign went on:* Numerous clippings in BIAA archives.
52 *campaign was endangering:* Minutes of the meeting of the BIAA Council of Management, October 28, 1966.
52 *elected to the council:* Unsigned letter to James Mellaart, March 7, 1966.
52 *stand out in the hall:* Interview with James Mellaart; Minutes of the meeting of the BIAA Council of Management, October 28, 1966.
52 *Mellaart's "indiscretions":* Ibid.
52 *voted unanimously:* Ibid.
52 *discovered Aşikli Höyük:* Esin and Harmankaya 1999.
53 *small wall painting:* Todd 1998, 19.
53 *In 1969 he replaced: Anatolian Studies* 19:3 (1969).

53 *Pamela Pratt:* Interview with Pamela (Pratt) French.
53 *chief painting conservator:* Interview with Viola Pemberton-Pigott.
53 yali *burned down:* Interview with Arlette Mellaart.
53 *"A plume of smoke":* Arlette Mellaart 2002.
53 *typewritten manuscript:* This manuscript is mentioned in Pearson and Connor 1967a, 160–61, and was viewed by the author at the Mellaart home.

Chapter 4: Ian Hodder

55 *"Çatalhöyük and I":* Hodder 1990, 20.
55 *Mellaart's class:* Interview with Ian Hodder.
56 *Ian Hodder was born:* Interviews with Ian Hodder.
57 *For B. W. Hodder:* Interview with B. W. Hodder.
57 *event that most marked his life:* Interview with Ian Hodder.
57 *from Singapore to Nigeria:* Interview with B. W. Hodder.
57 *markets of the Yoruba:* Ibid.; interview with Ian Hodder.
58 *Fishbourne:* Bahn 2001, 154.
58 *Higgs had founded:* Ibid., 191 and 343.
59 *grueling conditions:* Interviews with Ian Hodder and Andrew Sherratt.
59 *offer an undergraduate degree:* Harris 1997/98, 3–5.
60 *"What in fact is Archaeology?":* Wheeler 1954, 16.
60 *was looted:* Lawler 2003.
60 *"The archaeologist is digging":* Wheeler 1954, 13. Italics in the original.
60 *"culture history":* Trigger 1989, 148 et seq.; Flannery 1967.
61 *defined as a shared body:* Flannery 1967.
61 *"We find certain types of remains":* Childe 1929, v–vi, quoted in Johnson 1999, 16.
61 *archaeologists assumed either:* Trigger 2003, 4.
61 *the main purpose:* Lucas 2001, 43–51.
61 *promoting the Pecos Classification:* Bahn 2001, 235 and 351.
61 *archaeologists working in Palestine:* Balter 2000.
61 *firmly entrenched:* Interview with Bruce Trigger.
62 *"Here then are the beginnings":* Mellaart 1965, 135.
62 *"It is this kind of material":* Ibid., 10.
62 *became dissatisfied:* Renfrew and Bahn 1996, 34–35; Childe 1936.
62 *charismatic but very different men:* Renfrew and Bahn 1996, 36–39; Trigger 1989, 294–319.
62 *a child of 1930s:* Sabloff 1998, 49–64.
62 *deep, booming voice:* Ibid., 72–75; interviews with Andrew Sherratt, Ian Hodder, and anonymous Binford acquaintances.
62 *the exact opposite:* Interview with Andrew Sherratt.
63 *had his fill of typology:* Trigger 2003, 8.
63 *Midwestern Taxonomic Method:* Trigger 1989, 190.
63 *"little Linnaean beings":* Binford 1972, 8–9.
63 *had written a manifesto:* Ibid., 10.
63 *Binford declared:* Binford 1962.
63 *one of his heroes:* Sabloff 1998, 8–10.
63 *culture was the extrasomatic:* Cited in Binford 1962, 218.

63 *"We cannot afford"*: Ibid., 224.
64 *"Practical men"*: Clarke 1973; many thanks to Andrew Sherratt for pointing this quote out to me.
64 *Carl Gustav Hempel:* "Hempel, Carl Gustav," Encyclopædia Britannica 2003 Encyclopædia Britannica Premium Service, accessed 2 June 2003, www.britannica.com/eb/article?eu=40816.
64 *Following Hempel:* Binford and Binford 1968, 17; Johnson 1999, 40.
64 *"paleo-psychology"*: Binford 1965, 204.
64 *enthusiastic advocate:* Clarke 1968, 568–634.
64 *much more interested:* Shennan 1989, 843.
64 *"Certainly, scientific aids"*: Clarke 1968, 635.
65 *"Archaeology, is archaelogy"*: Clarke 1973.
65 *1968, the year that student protests:* I am indebted to Stephen Shennan for making this association for me; Shennan 1989, 831.
65 *revolution had not yet come:* Interview with Ian Hodder; Harris 1994, vii.
66 *rest of his career:* Interviews with B. W. Hodder and Ian Hodder.
66 *published a shorter version:* Hodder and Hassall 1971.
66 Models in Archaeology: Clarke 1972.
66 *Binford challenged:* Binford 1973, 227–54.
66 *Clarke's chief rival:* Interviews with Andrew Sherratt, Stephen Shennan, and Bruce Trigger.
66 *overturned the traditional view:* Renfrew 1973a, 93–182; Johnson 1999, 30–32.
67 *For his doctoral work:* Interview with Ian Hodder; Hodder and Orton 1976.
67 *trace the adoption:* Hodder and Orton 1976, 241.
68 *"equifinality"*: Ibid., 239–41; interview with Ian Hodder.
68 *His early death:* Interviews with Ian Hodder and Andrew Sherratt; "A Bone to Pick: Interview with Paul Halstead," *assemblage* (1998), http://www.shef.ac.uk/assem/4/4halst1.html.
68 *more closely allied:* Interviews with Stephen Shennan.
68 *Françoise Hivernel:* Interviews with Ian Hodder and anonymous sources.
69 *Ian would go to Kenya:* Interview with Ian Hodder; Hodder 1982b.
69 *Baringo area:* Hodder 1982, 14–15.
69 *"ethnoarchaeology"*: David and Kramer 2001.
69 *"living archaeology"*: Ibid., 6.
69 *"keep my archaeology dead"*: Ibid., 31.
69 *among the Nunamiut:* Sabloff 1998, 95–96, Appendix by Jeremy A. Sabloff; Binford 1983a, 109–43.
69 *archaeologists did not know enough:* Sabloff 1998, 95, Appendix by Jeremy A. Sabloff.
70 *Binford was able to convince:* Binford 1983a, 33–59.
70 *decided to launch his own:* Interview with Ian Hodder; Hodder 1982b.
70 *different cultures reflected:* Binford 1965.
72 *One hot morning:* Interview with Ian Hodder; Hodder 1982b, 125–84.
73 *His entire world:* Interview with Ian Hodder.

Chapter 5: Return to Çatalhöyük

74 *"So, Ian said"*: "Recantation, reflection, revision . . . ," interview with Michael Parker Pearson, *assemblage* no. 2 (1997), www.shef.ac.uk/assem/2/2rrr.html.
74 *became known as "processualism"*: Johnson 1999, 30.
75 *less charismatic figure:* Anonymous interviews.
75 *not delivering:* Trigger 2003, 122.
75 *failed to discover any universal laws:* Sabloff 1998, 84; Trigger 2003, 122.
75 *too many limitations:* Sabloff 1998, 85–86.
75 *ignore religion and ideology:* Ibid., 91.
76 *defined it as a shared body:* Flannery 1967, 119.
76 *"extrasomal" means:* Binford 1962, 218.
76 *"meaningfully constituted"*: Hodder 1982b, 186.
76 *"play an active part"*: Ibid., 12.
76 *three women who made pottery:* Ibid., 122–24.
77 *"Binford provides no evidence:"* Ibid., 191.
77 *graduate students eager:* This section is based on interviews with Henrietta Moore, Michael Parker Pearson, Christopher Tilley, Daniel Miller, Paul Halstead, Ian Hodder, Colin Renfrew, and anonymous sources; see also Hodder 1982a, vii.
78 *works by Claude Lévi-Strauss:* Milner and Browitt 2002, 102–104.
78 *Pierre Bourdieu:* Ibid., 86–91; Bourdieu 1970.
78 *Michel Foucault:* Milner and Browitt 2002, 118–19.
78 *Louis Althusser:* Ibid., 111–12.
78 *postmodern view:* Appignanesi and Garratt 2003.
78 *infused Ian's students:* Interviews with Henrietta Moore and Christopher Tilley.
79 *burst out of the shower:* "A Bone to Pick: Interview with Paul Halstead," *assemblage* no. 4 (October 1998), www.shef.ac.uk/assem/4/4halst1.html; interviews with Paul Halstead and Michael Parker Pearson.
79 *he was embarrassed:* Interview with Ian Hodder.
79 *Binford came to Cambridge:* Interviews with Paul Halstead, Michael Parker Pearson, Ian Hodder, Daniel Miller, and Colin Renfrew; "A Bone to Pick: Interview with Paul Halstead," *assemblage* no. 4 (October 1998), www.shef.ac.uk/assem/4/4halst1.html; Binford 1983a, 17.
79 *"This is horseshit!"*: "A Bone to Pick: Interview with Paul Halstead," *assemblage* no. 4 (October 1998), www.shef.ac.uk/assem/4/4halst1.html.
79 *attacking Binford for positions:* Ibid.; interview with Paul Halstead.
79 *"This 'discussion' began"*: Binford 1983a, 17. Italics in the original.
80 *"You'll find out"*: Interviews with Paul Halstead and Daniel Miller; "A Bone to Pick: Interview with Paul Halstead," *assemblage* no. 4 (October 1998), www.shef.ac.uk/assem/4/4halst1.html.
80 *the first manifesto:* Hodder 1982a.
81 *undisputed ringleaders:* Trigger 2003, 2.
81 *now in its third edition:* Hodder and Hutson 2003.
81 *"does not espouse one approach"*: Hodder 1991, 181.
81 *"The alternative is"*: Ibid., 187.
82 *"This is a little book"*: Binford 1988, 875.
82 *dig at Haddenham:* Hodder 1992.

83 *Christine Hastorf was born:* Interviews with Christine Hastorf.
83 *The Etruscans:* Bray and Trump 1982, 86.
85 *Ian and Christine had first met:* Interview with Christine Hastorf.
85 *In January 1985:* Ibid.
85 *Mimbres Valley ceramics:* Conkey and Hastorf 1990, vii.
86 *asked him to write a paper:* Hodder 1987.
86 *At UCLA Ian tried out:* Interviews with Ian Hodder and Christine Hastorf.
86 *A forthcoming book:* Hodder 1990.
87 *"There's lots of symbolism in Peru":* Interview with Christine Hastorf.
87 *The unspoken rule:* Interviews with anonymous archaeologists.
87 *One of his main jobs:* Interviews with David French, Charles Burney, and anonymous sources.
87 *kept the institute's copy:* Interview with anonymous source.
87 *he did his best:* Interview with David French.
87 *the three of them sat:* Interviews with David French, Ian Hodder, and Christine Hastorf; dates from David French's diary, personal communication.
88 *French could easily guess:* Interview with David French.
88 *"you're probably thinking":* Interview with Christine Hastorf.
88 *the grand tour:* Interviews with Ian Hodder and David French; dates from David French's diary, personal communication.
88 *first stop was Aşikli Höyük:* Esin and Harmankaya 1999.
88 *Ian scurried excitedly:* Interview with Ian Hodder.
89 *resigned himself:* Interview with David French.
89 *meet in Istanbul:* Interview with Ian Hodder.
89 *mildly encouraging:* Ibid.
89 *Timothy Daunt:* Interviews with Ian Hodder and Timothy Daunt.
90 *tentative permission:* BIAA News Release, "Excavation to Be Resumed at Turkey's Most Important Neolithic Site," 18 March 1974.
90 *wrote up the news:* Pearson 1974.
90 *The council had even approached:* Interview with Colin Renfrew.
90 *a joint letter:* "Bid to Reinstate Mellaart," *Sunday Times* (London), 31 March 1974.
90 *plan had to be scuttled: Anatolian Studies* 25:3 (1975).
90 *another BIAA working group:* Interview with Pamela (Pratt) French.
90 *Ian sat in an armchair:* Interviews with Ian Hodder and James and Arlette Mellaart.

Chapter 6: On the Surface

91 *his journey to Çatalhöyük:* Interview with James Conolly.
91 *Andrew Garrard:* Interviews with James Conolly and Andrew Garrard.
92 *the first to jump aboard:* Interviews with Ian Hodder, Roger and Wendy Matthews; Hodder 1996, xv.
92 *Ian had asked Roger:* Interviews with Ian Hodder and Roger Matthews.
92 *James excitedly fired:* Interview with James Conolly.
93 *new building in Çumra:* Interviews with Adnan Baysal and Naomi Hamilton.
93 *decrepit wooden bar:* Interviews with James Conolly and Roger Matthews.
93 *Roger was the last:* Ibid.

93 *caught the bar:* Ibid.
94 *Naomi Hamilton:* Interviews with Naomi Hamilton.
94 *He was insistent:* Interview with Roger Matthews.
94 *wear headscarves:* Interviews with Naomi Hamilton and Wendy Matthews.
94 *tourist guidebooks:* Brosnahan and Yale 1996.
94 *Roger recalled:* Interview with Roger Matthews.
94 *"Çatalhöyük and I":* Hodder 1990, 20.
95 *Ian had no intention:* Matthews and Hodder 1993.
95 *Only about 3 percent:* Hodder 1996, 2.
95 *Binford and his colleagues:* Binford 1972, 163–81.
95 *Abu Salabikh:* Matthews and Postgate 1987.
95 *His primary aim:* Hodder 1996, 6.
96 *As Ian had recruited:* Interview with Ian Hodder.
96 *more conventional goals:* Ibid., pp. 2–6.
97 *end of the Ice Age:* Roberts 1998, 22–23.
97 *V. Gordon Childe coined the term:* Childe 1928.
97 *demonstrated that sedentism:* Balter 1998.
98 *Whirling Dervishes:* "Mawlawiyah," *Encyclopædia Britannica* 2003 Encyclopædia Britannica Premium Service, 10 July 2003, www.britannica.com/eb/article?eu=52809.
98 *Ian proposed to transform:* Interview with Ian Hodder; Hodder 1996, 1.
98 *journeyed to Konya:* Interview with Wendy Matthews.
98 *only thirty days:* Matthews and Hodder 1993.
99 *birds would sit in the road:* Interviews with James Conolly and Wendy Matthews.
99 *his or her mission:* Interview with Adnan Baysal; Hodder 1996.
100 *the two had a talk:* Interview with Christine Hastorf.
100 *Ian relied heavily:* Interview with Ian Hodder; Hodder 1996, xv.
100 *what remained of Mellaart's:* Wendy Matthews 1993.
101 *"Wendy tools":* Anonymous interviews with several archaeologists.
101 *Micromorphology is a relatively:* "High Definition Archaeology," *World Archaeology* 29(2):151–312 (1997).
101 *she cut out a number:* Wendy Matthews 1993.
101 *labor-intensive surface collection:* Matthews and Hodder 1993.
102 *For the surface scraping:* Ibid.
102 *Roger loved this kind:* Interview with Roger Matthews.
102 *Roger and Wendy Matthews loved Iraq:* Interviews with Roger and Wendy Matthews.
102 *the world's first cities:* Scarre and Fagan 1997.
103 *he met James Mellaart:* Interview with Charles Burney.
103 *present at the fateful council meeting:* Minutes of the 74th Meeting of the Council of Management, 28 October 1966.
104 *reestablished their friendship:* Interview with Charles Burney.
104 *eccentric British millionaire:* Interview with Roger Matthews.
104 *Binford, visiting Cambridge:* Ibid.
104 *his doctoral work:* Ibid.
105 *Wendy was born:* Interview with Wendy Matthews.
106 *The school's London-based council closed:* Interview with Roger Matthews.
106 *Tell Brak:* Bahn 2001, 65.

107 *small meeting in Cambridge:* Interviews with Roger and Wendy Matthews.
107 *feminist archaeologist Ruth Tringham:* http://ls.berkeley.edu/dept/anth/tringham.html; Tringham 1991.
107 *a group of women holding hands:* Interviews with Tom Strasser and Wendy Matthews.
108 *too patiently:* Interview with Tom Strasser.
108 *Naomi Hamilton was happy:* E-mail from Naomi Hamilton.
108 *among the first to embrace:* Interview with Margaret Conkey; see also Hodder 1991, 168–72.
108 *Ian had worked behind the scenes:* Interview with Margaret Conkey.
108 *now-classic collection:* Gero and Conkey 1991.
109 *in the article he wrote:* Hodder 1987.
109 *entitled* On the Surface: Hodder 1996.
109 *buildings he called "shrines":* Mellaart 1967, 77 et seq.
109 *select body of priests:* Ibid., 175.
109 *"priestly quarter":* Ibid., 77–79; Hodder 1996, 5–6.
110 *Ritchey found a continuity:* Hodder 1996, 7–17.
110 *Matthews's surface-scraping work:* Ibid., 79–99.
110 *The scraping had revealed:* Ibid., 85 and 86.
110 *Wendy's micromorphology work:* Ibid., 312–21.
111 *This appeared to be the case:* Ibid., 317–20.
111 *"The coincidence of this change":* Ibid., 319–20.
112 *"the site as a whole":* Ibid., 361.
112 *the world's first city:* Jacobs 1969, 31–36.
112 *"an elaborate village":* Hodder 1996, 361.
112 *some resemblance to figurines:* Gimbutas 1989, xv–xxi.
113 *Naomi found that nearly half:* Hamilton 1996, 215–29.
113 *"Women's rites or women's rights?":* Ibid., 226.
113 *"women tamely embraced":* Ibid.
114 *"My challenges to orthodoxy":* Ibid., 227.

Chapter 7: At the Trowel's Edge

115 *Roger Matthews had been:* Interview with Shahina Farid.
116 *The site was just below:* Museum of London Archaeology Service (1998); www.archaeology.freewire.co.uk/thames.html; www.kalwall.com/4.html; news.bbc.co.uk/2hi/uk_news/politics/480426.stm.
116 *She had met Roger and Wendy:* Interviews with Shahina Farid, Roger Matthews, and Wendy Matthews.
116 *Bronze Age temple at Saar:* Bahn 2001, 387.
116 *Wendy had chosen Saar:* Interview with Shahina Farid.
117 *"I've been under a lot of pressure":* Ibid.
117 *theory was a waste of time:* Ibid.
117 *meet Ian for lunch:* Ibid.; Interview with Roger Matthews.
118 *Tille Höyük:* Blaylock 1998.
118 *Roger and Wendy had been raving:* Interview with Roger Matthews.
118 *best in the business:* Ibid., also interview with David French.
118 *Shahina Farid was born:* Interviews with Shahina Farid.

119 *glittering exhibition:* www.egyptianartcenter.com/tototiti/kingtut.html.
119 *exhibit about the destruction:* www.royalacademy.org.uk/?lid=843.
120 *at Boxgrove:* Pitts and Roberts 1998.
121 *so impressed with Shahina's skill:* Interview with Mark Roberts.
121 *She earned a reputation:* Interviews with David French and anonymous colleagues.
122 *Queen Boudica's torching:* www.molas.org.uk/s/siteDetails.asp?siteID=ngt00_2.
123 *a constant flow of information:* Interviews with Shahina Farid, Nerissa Russell, Roddy Reagan, and other Çatalhöyük team members.
123 *an unusual cluster:* Interview with Shahina Farid; catal.arch.cam.ac.uk/catal/archive_rep99/andrews99.html.
123 *"reflexivity":* Hodder 1999a, 80–104; Hodder 1997.
124 *begins "at the trowel's edge":* Hodder 1999a, 92.
124 *filmmakers and film students:* catal.arch.cam.ac.uk/catal/TAG_papers/karlsruhel.htm.
124 *pear-shaped mound:* catal.arch.cam.ac.uk/catal/Archive_rep95/east1.gif.
124 *assigned Roger to begin digging:* catal.arch.cam.ac.uk/catal/Archive_rep95/rjm95b1.html.
125 *idea was to excavate down:* catal.arch.cam.ac.uk/catal/Archive_rep95/farid95.html.
125 *the sheer terror:* Interview with Ian Hodder.
125 *In one video clip:* Çatalhöyük Video Data, CH95.1, file 3.mov.
126 *A few days later:* Çatalhöyük Video Data, CH95.1, file Ch95i13.mov.
127 *considerable progress:* catal.arch.cam.ac.uk/catal/Archive_rep95/farid95.html.
127 *his strategy for Building 1:* catal.arch.cam.ac.uk/catal/Archive_rep95/rjm95b1.html.
128 *Wendy's brand:* catal.arch.cam.ac.uk/catal/Archive_rep95/wmatthews95.html.
129 *The grid system:* Barker 1993, 37–47.
129 *"At all stages of the excavation":* catal.arch.cam.ac.uk/catal/Archive_rep95/rjm95b1.html.
130 *Space 70 had gone through:* catal.arch.cam.ac.uk/catal/Archive_rep95/rjm95b1.html.
131 *Louise and Rissa had come:* Interviews with Louise Martin and Nerissa Russell.
131 *They wanted to know:* catal.arch.cam.ac.uk/catal/Archive_rep95/martin95.html.
131 *found expert who analyzed:* Perkins 1969.
131 *zooarchaeologists have found:* Interviews with Nerissa Russell and Louise Martin.
131 *part of a humerus:* catal.arch.cam.ac.uk/catal/Archive_rep95/martin95.html.
132 *Mellaart's seventieth birthday:* Interviews with Shahina Farid, Louise Martin, and Ian Hodder.

Chapter 8: Dear Diary

134 *grant from the European Union:* Hodder 1996, xv. The grant was for 150,000 ECU, converted to dollars at the 1 January 1996 rate, www.oanda.com/convert/fxhistory.
135 *the pressure-cooker atmosphere:* Interviews with numerous Çatalhöyük team members.
136 *peeking voyeuristically:* Interview with Louise Martin.

136 *entirely excavate Building 1:* catal.arch.cam.ac.uk/catal/Archive_rep96/rog-matthews96.html.
136 *In the South area:* catal.arch.cam.ac.uk/catal/Archive_rep96/farid96.html.
136 *team made up of Greek archaeologists:* catal.arch.cam.ac.uk/catal/Archive_rep96/kotsakis96.html; interview with Kostas Kotsakis.
137 *her diary entry for August 4:* catal.arch.cam.ac.uk/catal/database/Diary.html
137 *his diary entry for August 9:* Ibid.
138 *Turkish authorities had laid down:* Interview with Ian Hodder.
138 *paying for the actual fieldwork:* Hodder 1996, xv.; Interview with Ian Hodder.
138 *financed by Leon Levy:* www.fas.harvard.edu/_semitic/ashkelon/ashkelon_dig2.html.
138 *Ian concluded:* Interview with Ian Hodder; Hodder 1999a, 165–69; Hodder 2000, 4.
139 *Çatalhöyük Research Trust: Çatal News 1: The Newsletter of the Çatalhöyük Research Trust,* January 1995; interview with Ian Hodder.
139 *recruited Colin Renfrew:* www.mcdonald.cam.ac.uk/McD/Staff/Renfrew.htm.
139 *David Attenborough:* "Attenborough, Sir David," *Encyclopædia Britannica* 2003 Encyclopædia Britannica Premium Service, accessed 7 October 2003. www.britannica.com/eb/article?eu=11296.
139 *director for Turkish operations of Visa:* Interview with Ian Hodder.
140 *Koç Group:* www.kocbank.com.tr/_eng/kocgroup.asp.
140 *first bank accounts:* Hodder 2000, 4.
140 *its own motivation:* Interview with Ian Hodder; interview with Glaxo Wellcome representative in Turkey after she had had a few Efes beers.
140 *had not occupied Anatolia:* "Turkic Peoples," *Encyclopædia Britannica* 2003 Encyclopædia Britannica Premium Service, accessed 9 October 2003, www.britannica.com/eb/article?eu=75778.
140 *One day James Conolly:* Interview with James Conolly; Hodder 1999, 166.
140 *types of obsidian tools:* catal.arch.cam.ac.uk/catal/Archive_rep96/conolly96.html.
141 *analysis of the pottery:* catal.arch.cam.ac.uk/catal/Archive_rep96/last96.html; interviews with Jonathan Last.
141 *Ian himself later admitted:* Hodder 1999, 166.
141 *On September 3 he confided:* catal.arch.cam.ac.uk/catal/database/Diary.html.
142 *Roger's point of view:* Roger Matthews' Excavation Diary, 15 August 1996.
142 *reached the plaster floors:* Ibid., 21 August 1996.
142 *"at least two skulls":* Ibid., 24 August 1996.
143 *As she troweled away:* Interviews with Shahina Farid.
144 *Wendy's preliminary:* Balter 1998.
145 *principle behind flotation:* Interviews with Christine Hastorf; Renfrew and Bahn 1996, 229–30.
145 *Hans Helbaek, the pioneering:* Helbaek 1964.
146 *David French, who built:* Interview with Christine Hastorf; French 1971; Weaver 1971.
146 *Hillman's version of the machine:* Interviews with Christine Hastorf; Renfrew and Bahn 1996, 229.
146 *large sample of soil:* catal.arch.cam.ac.uk/catal/Archive_rep96/hastorf96.html.
147 *that year's team:* Ibid.

147 *turned into a disaster:* Interviews with Nerissa Russell, Mirjana Stevanovic, and Ruth Tringham.
148 *team at Abu Hureyra:* Moore et al. 2000, 327–422.
148 *charred many of the plant remains:* Wright 2003.
148 *Study of einkorn wheat:* Heun et al. 1997.
148 *Christine was eager:* Interview with Christine Hastorf.
148 *Christine had never considered:* Ibid.
149 *Some important new findings:* catal.arch.cam.ac.uk/catal/Archive_rep95/butler95.html; catal.arch.cam.ac.uk/catal/Archive_rep96/hastorf96.html.
150 *sixty-two figurines:* catal.arch.cam.ac.uk/catal/Archive_rep96/hamilton96.html.
151 *various grave goods:* Ibid.
151 *shards of pottery:* catal.arch.cam.ac.uk/catal/Archive_rep96/last96.html.
151 *Louise Martin and Rissa Russell had never met:* Interviews with Louise Martin and Nerissa Russell.
151 *something was wrong:* catal.arch.cam.ac.uk/catal/Archive_rep96/russmartin96.html.
151 *"It is likely":* Ibid.
152 *Tringham, who was visiting:* Diary entries of Shahina Farid and Roger Matthews, 25 August 1996. catal.arch.cam.ac.uk/catal/database/Diary.html.
152 *"Interesting discussion last night":* Ibid., 25 August 1996.
152 *BACH team:* www.mactia.berkeley.edu/catal/.
153 *Ephesus:* Bahn 2001, 141.
153 *"Catch the Wind":* Interviews with Nerissa Russell.
153 *Around the time:* Roger Matthews diary entries for 19 and 21 September 1996, catal.arch.cam.ac.uk/catal/database/Diary.html.
154 *Peter Andrews:* www.nhm.ac.uk/palaeontology/v&a/pja/pja.html.
154 *Theya had recently completed:* Molleson 1994.
154 *X-rayed the bones and teeth:* Molleson and Andrews 1996.
155 *"The results give tentative support":* Ibid., 269.

Chapter 9: The Neolithic Revolution

157 *Cappadocia, in east Central:* "Cappadocia," *Encyclopædia Britannica* 2003 Encyclopædia Britannica Premium Service, accessed 22 October 2003, http://www.britannica.com/eb/article?eu=20473; Brosnahan and Yale 1996, 549.
157 *Aşikli Höyük:* Esin and Harmankaya 1999.
157 *Calibrated radiocarbon dates:* Gérard and Thissen 2002.
158 *right around the time:* According to recent calibrated radiocarbon dates; see Cessford 2001.
158 *Did the settlers:* Gérard and Thissen 2002.
158 *site of Pinarbaşi:* Watkins 1996.
158 *called Musular:* Özbaşaran 1999.
158 *Mihriban was reluctant:* Interview with Mirhiban Özbaşaran.
159 *yielded a radiocarbon date:* Gérard and Thissen 2002.
159 *surface survey of Aşikli:* Todd 1966.
159 *more than 6,000 pieces:* Ibid., 139.

159 *Renfrew and his colleagues:* Dixon et al. 1968.
159 *Aşikli was made up:* Esin and Harmankaya 1999, 124.
160 *Vere Gordon Childe:* Trigger 1980; Harris 1994; Tringham 1983; Green 1981; Sherratt 1998; Barton 2000.
160 *Mortimer Wheeler concluded:* Cited in Trigger 1980, 16.
160 *others have pointed out:* Ibid., 14–15.
161 *Max Mallowan, once commented:* Ibid., 17.
161 *"He had an acute visual memory":* Ibid., 11.
161 *"an economic revolution":* Childe 1957, 23.
161 *the word* Neolithic: Bahn 2001, 43.
162 *"The Neolithic of the Near East":* Özdoğan 1999, 9.
162 *the later Urban Revolution:* Childe 2003, 140–78.
162 *Childe left Edinburgh:* Bahn 2001, 89.
162 *he was very popular:* Trigger 1980, 17–18.
162 *either fell or jumped:* www.bbc.co.uk/history/historic_figures/childe_gordon.shtml; Barton 2000; Green 1981, 152–54.
162 *he left the royalties:* Barton 2000.
162 *installed a bust:* Harris 1994, vii.
163 *Another in a long series:* Roberts 1998.
163 *variations in the earth's orbit:* Roberts 1998, 60.
163 *endure another ice age:* Ibid.
163 *"variability selection":* Potts 1996; Balter 2002.
163 *while the Neandertals:* Balter 2001.
163 *covered by ice sheets:* Roberts 1998, 7 and 62–63.
163 *terms Pleistocene and Holocene:* Bahn 2001, 194–95 and 361.
164 *earliest Holocene:* Roberts 1998, 22–23.
164 *known as the Oasis Theory:* Watson 1995, 23–24; Childe 2003, 66–85.
164 *Raphael Pumpelly:* Pumpelly, Raphael W., *Encyclopædia Britannica* 2003 Encyclopædia Britannica Premium Service, accessed 29 October 2003, www.britannica.com/eb/article?eu=63466.
164 *Childe was much vaguer:* Watson 1995, 23–4.
164 *generally wetter:* Roberts 1998, 143.
164 *number of other explanations:* For this overall historical perspective on explanations for agriculture I am indebted to two main sources: Watson 1995 and Wright 1971.
165 *Jarmo in Iraq:* Watson 1995, 24–26; Braidwood and Braidwood 1950; Braidwood 1952.
165 *excavations at Jarmo:* Braidwood 1960.
165 *Tepe Sarab in western Iran:* Ibid.
165 *The hilly flanks theory:* Ibid.; Watson 1995, 25.
165 *"The multiple occurrence":* Braidwood 1960.
165 *"settled in":* Ibid.
165 *marginality or edge hypothesis:* Watson 1995, 27.
165 *"the original affluent society":* Sahlins 1968; Sahlins 1972, 1–40.
167 *"Adopting the Zen strategy":* Sahlins 1972, 2.
167 *Kent Flannery:* Watson 1995, 26–27; Flannery 1965.

167 *"like a chicken"*: Binford 1983a, 197.
168 *a proper explanation:* Renfrew and Bahn 1996, 441–74.
168 *"The adoption of cultivation"*: Childe 2003, 71.
169 *research in the New World:* Pringle 1998; Roush 1997.
169 *called the Natufians:* Bar-Yosef et al. 1991; Bar-Yosef 1998.
169 *"Through gaps in the leafy trees"*: Mithen 2003, 29–30.
169 *Jean Perrot:* Ibid., 29; www.diplomatie.gouv.fr/culture/culture_scientifique/archeologie/israel/ (in French).
170 *Dorothy Garrod:* Bahn 2001, 162; Smith 1997.
170 *Wadi en-Natuf:* Bahn 2001, 312.
170 *she assumed:* Mithen 2003, 32–33.
170 *Some archaeologists questioned:* Edwards 1989; Kaufman 1992; Rafferty 1985.
170 *questions of terminology:* Rafferty 1985, 113–16.
170 *Dolní Věstonice:* Klíma 1954.
171 *Terra Amata:* www.musee-terra-amata.org/.
171 *called Ohalo II:* Nadel and Werker 1999; ohalo.haifa.ac.il.
171 *site of Hayonim Cave:* Bahn 2001, 188.
172 *Lieberman looked at:* Lieberman 1991; Lieberman 1993a.
172 *other Natufian sites:* Lieberman 1993b.

Chapter 10: The Domesticated Human

174 *processual explanations dominated:* Harris 1996, 1–2.
174 *"strong techno-environmental bias"*: Bender 1978, 207.
174 *"unacceptable"*: Ibid., 208.
174 *Sahlins's intention:* Sahlins 1972.
175 *"Leadership plays"*: Bender 1978, 213.
175 *"we should not be constrained"*: Cited in Bender 1978, 214.
176 *tell of Mureybet:* Mellaart 1975, 42–48; see also numerous mentions in Cauvin 2.
176 *complete with horns:* Cauvin 2000, 28.
178 *an influential paper:* Flannery, 1972; see also Flannery 2002.
178 *Cauvin along with some other:* Cauvin 2000, 128–32; Saidel 1993, and Flannery's response, Flannery 1993.
178 *"Geometric forms"*: Cauvin 2000, 130.
179 *still actively debating:* "Review Feature," *Cambridge Archaeological Journal* 11:105–21 (2001).
179 *came across Cauvin's work:* Hodder 1990.
179 *He spent six months:* Ian Hodder's curriculum vitae; interviews with Ian Hodder and Christine Hastorf.
179 *analysis of the symbolism:* Hodder 1987.
180 *epiphany in the Nuba hut:* Hodder 1990, 6–8.
180 *all about the domestication:* Ibid., 48.
181 *brain thoroughly picked:* Interview with Ruth Tringham; Hodder 1990, ix.
181 *site of Lepenski Vir:* Hodder 1990, 21–31.
181 *Dragoslav Srejović:* Bahn 2001, 420.
181 *"As at Çatalhöyük"*: Hodder 1990, 27.
181 *so-called linear tombs:* Ibid., 142–56.
182 *chose to call the* domus: Hodder 1990, 38, 44–5.

183 *Walter Bagehot:* "Bagehot, Walter," *Encyclopædia Britannica* 2004 Encyclopædia Britannica Premium Service, accessed 10 April 2004, www.britannica.com/eb/article?eu=11883.
183 *"Man, being the strongest":* Bagehot 2003, 26.
183 *"The domus became":* Hodder 1990, 39.
183 *his 1980 book:* Wilson 1983 (second edition).
183 *Ian did not see:* Interviews with Ian Hodder and Peter Wilson.
183 *"a dominant cultural symbol":* Wilson 1988, 4.
184 *called the Younger Dryas:* Moore and Hillman 1992.
185 *mostly treeless steppe:* Hillman 1996.
185 *"a vast expanse":* Ibid., 189.
185 *hunting was good:* Clutton-Brock 1999, 18–19; Davis 1987, 140–43.
186 *pollen analysis had shown:* Roberts 1998, 29–33.
186 *temperatures suddenly dropped:* Moore and Hillman 1992, 482–83.
186 *identified from macrofossils:* Ibid., 36–40.
186 *cores taken through the ice:* Mayewski 1993; Taylor et al. 1997.
186 *new pollen analysis:* Moore and Hillman 1992, 484–85; Baruch and Bottema 1991.
187 *Meanwhile, at Abu Hureyra:* Moore and Hillman 1992, 487–88.
187 *Late Natufian stage:* Ibid., 491.
188 *"significant catalyst":* Ibid.
188 *Ian had pointed out:* Hodder 2001.
188 *"long drawn-out domestication":* Ibid., 109.
189 *"Göbekli Tepe":* Özdoğan and Başgelen 1999, 78–80.
190 *rise of the primates:* Klein 1999, 62–143; "Primate," *Encyclopædia Britannica* 2003 Encyclopædia Britannica Premium Service, accessed 10 November 2003, www.britannica.com/eb/article?eu=108392.
191 *5,000 or more extinct species:* Fleagle 2002.
191 *All living primates share:* "Primate," *Encyclopædia Britannica* 2003 Encyclopædia Britannica Premium Service, accessed 10 November 2003, www.britannica.com/eb/article?eu=108392; Klein 1999, 66–68.
191 *have Meissner's corpuscles:* Ibid.; www.microscopyu.com/galleries/confocal/meissnerscorpusclesprimate.html.
191 *Their manual dexterity:* Klein 1999, 92–93.
191 *24 million years ago:* Ibid., 88–90.
191 *two species:* de Waal 2002.
191 *"make love, not war":* Ibid., 41.
192 *the better model:* Zihlman 1978.
192 *Our brains get bigger:* Aiello and Dunbar 1993; see also Dunbar 1996.
193 *Humans get modern:* Stringer and McKie 1996.
193 *convincingly symbolic expressions:* McBrearty and Brooks 2000.
193 *"ratchet effect":* Tomasello 1999.
193 *great intensification:* Gamble 1999.
193 *"release from proximity":* Rodseth et al. 1991.
194 *"You may see your sister":* Gamble 1999, 43.
194 *Gordon Hillman's vision:* Hillman 1996.
194 *original affluent society:* Sahlins 1972.
194 *"Agriculture not only raised":* Ibid., 37.

Chapter 11: Fault Lines and Homecomings

196 *Nurcan Yalman:* Interview with Nurcan Yalman.

197 *the Silk Road:* "Silk Road." *Encyclopædia Britannica.* 2004. Encyclopædia Britannica Premium Service, accessed. 18 Mar. 2004, www.britannica.com/eb/article?eu=69534.

197 *Kitaro:* www.domo.com/artist/kitaro-bio.html

197 *excavations at Çayönü:* Asli Özdoğan 1999.

197 *Tille Höyük:* Blaylock 1999.

197 *created a sensation:* Anonymous interviews.

197 *Ataturk Dam:* "Ataturk Dam," *Encyclopædia Britannica* 2004 Encyclopædia Britannica Premium Service, accessed 18 March 2004, www.britannica.com/eb/article?eu=10160.

197 *"I cried for two years":* Interview with Nurcan Yalman.

198 *Mavili Tokyağsun:* Interview with Mavili Tokyağsun, translated by Burcu Tung; interviews with Ayfer Bartu and Shahina Farid.

200 *It soon became clear:* Interviews with Ian Hodder, Shahina Farid, Nerissa Russell, Wendy Matthews, Roger Matthews, Roddy Regan, Naomi Hamilton, James Conolly, and others; see also Carolyn Hamilton 2000 and Shahina Farid 2000.

200 *a sharp fault line:* Shahina Farid's excavator diary, 30 August 1996.

200 *"Please no more samples!":* Shahina Farid's excavator diary, 10 August 1996.

200 *Wendy had been "adamant":* Ibid., 15 August 1996.

200 *"Laboratory staff demands":* Carolyn Hamilton 2000, 124.

201 *often tease Wendy:* Interviews with Roderick Regan and James Conolly.

201 *ready to debate:* Interview with Roderick Regan.

201 *he was going to quit:* Interviews with Roderick Regan and Ian Hodder.

201 *members of the team suspected:* Anonymous interviews.

201 *"For me the major worry":* Ian Hodder's excavator diary, 25 August 1996.

201 *a meeting of all the diggers:* Ibid.

202 *"Why are the excavators":* Nerissa Russell's private diary, 23 September 1996.

202 *excavators videotaped:* Ibid.; interviews with Nerissa Russell and Shahina Farid.

203 *Thirty-one years:* Interviews with James and Arlette Mellaart and Ian Hodder.

204 *Before Ian could invite:* Interview with Ian Hodder.

204 *Engin Özgen:* www.getty.edu/conservation/resources/newsletter/13_1/profile1.html; interviews with Ian Hodder and Roger Matthews.

204 *a formidable presence:* Interviews with David French, David Hawkins, and Charles Burney.

204 *Mellaart published:* Mellaart 1978; Mellaart 1975.

205 *Mellaart began showing:* Interviews with Dominique Collon, David Hawkins, Harriet Crawford, and anonymous sources; letter from John Evans to the author, 10 October 2002.

205 *painstaking reconstruction:* Ibid.; interviews with James Mellaart; Mellaart 1991.

205 *Two of them approached:* Interviews with Dominique Collon, David Hawkins, and Harriet Crawford; letter from John Evans to the author, 10 October 2002. There are differing accounts of the circumstances surrounding the seminar that took place in June 1987, as evidenced in these interviews as well as other documents. See for example the letter from David Harris in *Oriental Rug Review*

11(4):46 (April/May 1991), taking issue with Collon's account in her *Hali* article cited below, and response in private letter from Dominique Collon to David Harris, 10 April 1991.

205 *particularly keen memory:* Interview with David Hawkins.

206 *a flyer announcing:* Copy provided by Dominique Collon.

206 *belonged to Edith Porada:* Interviews with Dominique Collon and David Hawkins.

206 *Then Collon, who had carefully:* Interview with Dominique Collon.

206 *a stiff drink:* Ibid.

206 *four-volume work:* Mellaart et al. 1989. Many of the reconstructed paintings are also reproduced in Bennett 1990.

207 *"it seems now likely":* Mellaart 1967, 152; see also 108, 111, 118, 152–55, and 170.

207 *Mellaart had electrified: Oriental Rug Review* 10/6:18 (1990); Bennett 1990; Eiland 1993.

207 *"Kilims that had been":* Eiland 1993, 860.

207 *given prominent coverage:* "The Discovered Kilim," *Hali* 50:97–99 (April 1990).

207 *recalled Mellaart's explanations:* Collon 1990, 121; interview with James Mellaart.

207 *"This would explain":* Collon 1990, 121.

207 *"numerous discrepancies":* Ibid., 123.

207 *two lengthy articles:* Mallett 1990; Mallett 1993.

208 *none of the participants:* Ibid.; interviews with Ian Todd, Viola Pemberton-Pigott, and anonymous sources.

208 "Bluntly put": Lamberg-Karlovsky 1992, 38.

208 *"he introduced me":* Ibid., 39.

208 *"competent scholar":* Ibid.

208 *Yet Mellaart stuck:* Mellaart 1991. Mellaart also repeated many of the points in this article in interviews with the author.

208 *"minority of the whole":* Ibid., 86.

208 *"extreme care":* Ibid.

208 *"drawings, tracings, notes":* Ibid.

208 *"not those found afterwards":* Ibid.

206 *"These disputed paintings":* Ibid., 87.

206 *"have to put disclaimers":* Ibid.

206 *quoted a lengthy section:* Ibid.

206 *Ian Hodder, at the time:* Interview with Ian Hodder.

206 *to distance the new team:* Interviews with anonymous members of the Çatalhöyük team.

206 *Mellaart's visit to Çatalhöyük:* Interviews with Ian Hodder, Shahina Farid, Christine Hastorf, and Louise Martin; Ian Hodder's excavator diary, 16 September 1996.

210 *"What a grotty building!":* Interview with Ian Hodder.

210 *where was the deep sounding?:* Interview with Shahina Farid.

210 *Mellaart lit up:* Interview with Roderick Regan.

211 *a good time to invite:* catal.arch.cam.ac.uk/catal/Archive_rep96/hodder96intro.html; Ian Hodder's excavator diary, 28 September 1996; Nerissa Russell's private diary, 25 September 1996.

211 *Ian joked that he thought:* Interview with Nerissa Russell.
212 *Stone bead disappeared:* Nerissa Russell's private diary, 25 September 1996; Ian Hodder's excavator diary, 28 September 1996.
212 *Ian's emotions:* Ian's excavator diary, 28 September 1996.
212 *To Julie Near:* Interview with Julie Near.
212 *"Excellent therapy":* Nerissa Russell's private diary, 25 September 1996.
212 *Turkish news media:* Ian Hodder's excavator diary, 28 September 1996.
213 *represented a helicopter:* Interview with Nerissa Russell.
213 *He was worried:* Ian Hodder's excavator diary, 28 September 1996.
213 *inauguration of the dig house:* Nerissa Russell's private diary, 27 September 1996.
213 *Işik took Ian aside:* Ian Hodder's excavator diary, 28 September 1996.
213 *David Shankland:* Interview with David Shankland; www.bris.ac.uk/anthropology/staff/shankland.
214 *members of the Council hesitate:* Interviews with anonymous sources.
214 *he had been chosen:* Interview with Roger Matthews.
214 *Ian had voiced similar doubts:* Ian Hodder's excavator diary, 3 September 1996.
214 *"We truly have lost":* Roger Matthews' excavator diary, 3 September 1996.
215 *"I came away from it":* Roger Matthews' excavator diary, 9 September 1996.
215 *"We have been defeated":* Ibid., 28 September 1996.
215 *"We have plotted":* Ibid.
215 *a total lunar eclipse:* antwrp.gsfc.nasa.gov/apod/ap960926.html.
216 *Julie began to wonder:* E-mail to the author from Julie Near. I am very grateful to Julie for sharing her thoughts and feelings, which form the basis of this account.
216 *Doug Baird's survey:* catal.arch.cam.ac.uk/catal/Archive_rep96/baird96.html.
216 *celebrate Rissa's birthday:* Nerissa Russell's private diary, 27 September 1996; interview with Nerissa Russell.
217 *Ian had heard:* Interview with Ian Hodder.
217 *He picked Shahina:* Interviews with Ian Hodder and Shahina Farid.

Chapter 12: Burning Down the House

218 *Analysis of Building 1:* Roger Matthews 1996.
219 *Building 1 greatly resembled:* Ibid.
220 *Wendy had taken:* Wendy Matthews 1996.
221 *"female and male zones":* Roger Matthews 1996.
222 *Ruth Tringham was born:* Interviews with Ruth Tringham; see also "An Interview with Ruth Tringham," www.scanet.org/tringham.html.
223 *Stuart Piggott:* Bahn 2001, 358.
223 *Wayland's Smithy:* Ibid., 472–3.
223 *called Bylany:* Ibid., 73.
224 *Nea Nikomedeia:* Whittle 1996, 58–59; Bahn 2001, 313.
224 *agricultural way of life:* Whittle 1996.
224 *Childe, who had a keen interest:* Trigger 1980, 92–95 and 124–28
224 *In 1966 Bruce Chatwin:* Shakespeare 1999, 188–200.
225 *Considerably annoyed:* Ibid., 208; interview with Ruth Tringham.
225 *Citroën van:* Interview with Ruth Tringham.
225 *tour of Russia:* Ibid.

225 *"Tringham was sick"*: Shakespeare 1999, 210.
225 *Chatwin, in his own account*: Chatwin 1989, 59–62.
225 *Specializing in the microwear*: Renfrew and Bahn 1996, 307–10.
225 *Stuart Piggott*: www.britarch.ac.uk/ba/ba19/ba19obit.html: www.cpa.ed.ac.uk/bulletinarchive/1996–1997/01/obit1.html.
225 *Wessex Culture*: Bahn 2001, 473.
226 *Sitagroi*: Ibid., 412.
226 *timber-framed house*: Renfrew 1970.
226 *site called Selevac*: Bahn 2001, 402.
226 *Vinča culture*: Ibid., 468.
227 *One was Rissa Russell*: Interviews with Nerissa Russell and Ruth Tringham.
227 *Ruth would later tell*: Interviews with Ruth Tringham and Mirjana Stevanovic.
227 *Mira was born*: Interviews with Mirjana Stevanovic.
228 *dig at Gomolava*: Bahn 2001, 170.
228 *under Ruth's influence*: Interview with Mirjana Stevanovic.
228 *did not always agree*: Ibid.
229 *pageantry of invasions*: Gimbutas 2001, xx–xxi.
229 *"Once there was a great place"*: Tringham 2000, 134.
229 *"Our model"*: cited in Tringham 1994, 178.
229 *settlement called Opovo*: Tringham et al. 1992; Stevanovic 1997.
230 *J. Desmond Clark*: www.berkeley.edu/news/media/releases/2002/02/15 clark.html.
230 *never forgave her*: Interview with Ruth Tringham.
230 *novel excavation strategy*: Interviews with Mirjana Stevanovic; Stevanovic 1997.
231 *In a major paper*: Stevanovic 1997.
231 *habit of house burning*: Ibid., 339.
232 *She was still doing*: Interview with Ruth Tringham.
232 *The Wedge conference*: Gero and Conkey 1991.
232 *"How do you envisage"*: Tringham 1991, 93–94.
234 *"My wish to retain respectability"*: Ibid., 95.
235 *Ruth flung herself*: Interview with Ruth Tringham.

Chapter 13: "Always Momentary, Fluid and Flexible"

236 *Gavin Lucas had been one*: Interview with Gavin Lucas.
237 *"Two new, articulated inhumations"*: Gavin Lucas's excavator diary, 16 August 1997
237 *five bone rings*: Ibid., 18 August 1997.
238 *Mellaart's strategy when a painting*: Interviews with Ian Todd and Pamela French.
238 *art history of this particular wall*: Lucas 1997.
239 *"Because the wall plaster"*: Ibid., emphasis in the original.
239 *The team had been forced*: Many thanks to Shahina Farid for her clear explanation.
240 *"Fruits of the earth"*: Nerissa Russell's private diary, 11 August 1997.
240 *for the BACH team*: Tringham 1997.
241 *took on a new confidence*: Interviews with anonymous archaeologists at Çatalhöyük.

242 *The beer consumed:* Nerissa Russell's private diary, 13 September 1997.
242 *had got well past the stage:* Farid 1997.
243 *"It's been too long":* Shahina Farid's excavator diary, 15 September 1997.
243 *Shahina had an experience:* Many thanks to Shahina for her detailed e-mail account, on which this description is closely based.
244 *as Ian himself admitted:* Hodder 1996, 7.
244 *"How we excavate":* Ibid., 692.
244 *"A 'floor' context":* Ibid.
245 *Kennewick Man:* Holden 2004.
245 *finds in the Holy Land:* Balter 2000.
245 *"Within the global communities":* Hodder 1997, 700.
245 *Fekri Hassan:* www.ucl.ac.uk/archaeology/staff/profiles/hassan.htm.
246 *a blistering attack:* Hassan 1997.
246 *"an ethos that celebrates":* Ibid., 1021.
246 *"Whether a group":* Ibid., 1024.
246 *Ian's strategy of raising money:* Anonymous interviews with numerous archaeologists in Europe and the United States.
246 *"His advocacy for":* Hassan 1997, 1025.
246 *"nostalgic pleasure":* Hodder 1998b.
246 *"We cannot assume":* Ibid., 217.
247 *Laura Nader, the sister:* anthropology.berkeley.edu/nader.html.
247 *Ian rang Ayfer up:* Interview with Ayfer Bartu.
247 *Ayfer Bartu was born:* Ibid.
247 *earthquake measuring 7.4:* quake.wr.usgs.gov/research/geology/turkey/.
248 *defines heritage tourism:* Cited in Hargrove 2002, 10.
248 *Nelson Graburn:* anthropology.berkeley.edu/graburn.html.
249 *At Çatalhöyük Ayfer began:* Bartu 2000.
249 *the site's "cultural broker":* Interview with Ayfer Bartu.
250 *to see the mayor of Çumra:* Interview with Ayfer Bartu; Hodder 1999, 168–69.
250 *ultranationalist MHP:* Hodder 1999, 168: news.bbc.co.uk/2/hi/europe/325138.stm.
250 *Around the same time:* Interview with Ayfer Bartu.

Chapter 14: The Long Season

252 *Seven detectable phases:* Lucas 1997b.
252 *Building 5, as the house underneath:* Hodder 1998; Cessford 1998.
253 *"I have risen":* Craig Cessford's excavator diary, 20 July 1998.
253 *Craig was born on December 24:* Interviews with Craig Cessford.
254 *Raunds Area Project:* museums.ncl.ac.uk/raunds/.
254 *Caerwent:* www.bbc.co.uk/wales/about/rr-3-3.shtml.
254 *Craig met Anja Wolle:* Interview with Anja Wolle.
255 *Frank Matero and his conservation team:* Matero 2000.
255 *"Hopefully we can work around him":* Craig Cessford's excavator diary, 9 August 1998.
255 *"In terms of progress":* Ibid., 7 September 1998.
257 *In 1998 the team was made up:* Hodder 1998a.

257 *One Thursday evening:* Many thanks to Julie Near and John Swogger for their highly detailed memos.
259 *the Kara Dag, a huge volcanic formation:* www.arcl.ed.ac.uk/arch/pinarbasi/location.htm.
259 *village of Binbirkilise:* Louise Martin's private diary, 30 August 1997.
259 *monitoring of the water table:* Hodder 1999b.
260 *In 1970 a team:* Cohen 1970.
260 *excavations by Neil's team:* Merrick et al. 1997.
260 *The Long Season as it was called:* Interviews with Shahina Farid, Craig Cessford, Jez Taylor, Sheelagh Frame, Richard Turnbull, Başak Boz, Andy Fairbairn, Julie Near, John Swogger, and other members of the team; excavator diaries.
261 *Ian and Shahina had discussed:* Interview with Shahina Farid.
261 *Ian raised over $500,000:* Hodder 1999.
261 *mapped out the strategy:* Shahina Farid's excavator diary, 17 April 1999.
262 *put them in a biscuit tin:* Interview with Craig Cessford; Richard Turnbull's excavator diary, 8 May 1999.
262 *According to Mellaart's measurements:* Craig Cessford's excavator diary, 15 May 1999.
263 *"The excavated skeleton":* Charlie Newman's excavator diary, 16 May 1999.
263 *an unusual grave:* Başak Boz's excavator diary, 3 June and 6 June 1999.
263 *they were penning deposits:* Shahina Farid's excavator diary, 9 June 1999.
263 *"I feel really drained":* Craig Cessford's excavator diary, 17 June 1999.
263 *Craig was also worried:* Ibid., 22 June 1999.
264 *environmental archaeologist:* Renfrew and Bahn 1996, 211–52.
264 *Kostas had not brought:* Interview with Kostas Kotsakis.
264 *Neolithic site of Sesklo:* www.mnsu.edu/emuseum/archaeology/sites/europe/sesklo.html.
264 *Imia-Kardak affair:* Hickok 1998.
265 *Eleni Asouti was born:* Interviews with Eleni Asouti.
268 *drilled three cores:* Craig Cessford's excavator diary, 4 July 1999.
269 *"The entire project":* Ibid., 1 August 1999.
269 *"Quite a good day":* Ibid., 2 August 1999.
269 *"The amount left to dig":* Ibid., 3 August 1999.
269 *made up of fired lime:* Balter 1999, 891.
270 *an area outside the earliest:* Craig Cessford's excavator diary, 26 and 28 August 1999.
270 *they hit natural:* Ibid., 8 September 1999.
271 *anointed everyone:* Interview with Shahina Farid.

Chapter 15: Till Death Us Do Part

272 *The first five seasons:* Molleson et al. in press/d.
273 *Başak, a petite young woman:* Interview with Başak Boz.
273 *site called Paşalar:* www.sunysb.edu/anthro/lmartin.html.
273 *especially their microwear:* King et al. 1999.
273 *Lori Hager had earned:* ls.berkeley.edu/dept/anth/hager.html.
273 *well known for editing:* Hager 1997.

274 *Theya Molleson's earlier research:* Molleson 1994, 70–75.
274 *the BACH team had uncovered:* Hager and Boz 2002; observation of the excavation of the second skeleton by the author.
274 *The widening of the pelvis:* Interviews with Başak Boz and Lori Hager; Mays 1998, 33–42.
274 *polished belt buckle:* Stevanovic and Tringham 2002.
276 *computerized, multimedia teaching:* www.mactia.berkeley.edu.
276 *digital archive:* Lopez 2002.
277 *Since it was an adult:* Mays 1998, 33–42.
277 *called the sciatic notch:* Ibid., 33 and 36.
277 *Lori was an expert:* Hager 1996.
278 *was a male between forty-four:* Hager and Boz 2002.
278 *all of the burials in Space 87:* Ibid.
278 *"The idea of death":* Becker 1973, ix.
279 *true burial practices:* Gargett 1989; Kooijmans, Louwe, et al. 1989; Pettit 2002a; Pettit 2002b; Parker Pearson 1999, 148–54.
279 *Sima de los Huesos:* Arsuaga et al. 1997; Klein and Edgar 2002, 147–53.
279 *Site of Sungir':* Klein and Edgar 2002, 265–66; www.insticeagestudies.com/library/Ivory/ivory4.html.
279 *Otto Bader:* Bahn 2001, 46.
279 *the intact burials:* www.insticeagestudies.com/library/Ivory/ivory4.html.
280 *about an hour to make:* Klein and Edgar 2002, 266.
280 *One of the early ambitions:* Parker Pearson 1982, 99–101; Parker Pearson 1999, 27–32.
280 *the LoDaaga people:* Goody 1962.
280 *Pearson compared:* Parker Pearson 1982.
281 *a dramatic increase:* Ibid., 108.
281 *The Natufians, whom:* Byrd and Monahan 1995.
281 *500 Natufian burials:* Ibid; Weinstein-Evron 2003.
281 *Natufian burial practices underwent:* Byrd and Monahan 1995, 283.
281 *archaeologists have speculated:* Ibid.
282 *In some cases the skulls:* Bienert 1991.
282 *more mobile lifestyle:* Kuijt 1996; Grosman 2003.
282 *"Excavators are trained":* Kenyon 1957, 60–61.
282 *unearthed at Çayönü:* Çambel and Braidwood 1970.
282 *named the Skull Building:* Özbek 1995.
282 *Pitt-Rivers Museum:* Bienert 1991, 20.
282 *In the Solomon Islands:* www.deathonline.net/disposal/exposure/solomon.cfm.
283 *Secret Skull and Bones Society:* Robbins 2003, 7, 14, 144–46.
283 *skulls as trophies:* www.deathonline.net/disposal/exposure/solomon.cfm.
283 *there is little evidence:* Peterson 2002, 64–65 and 83–84.
283 *some sort of ancestor worship:* Bienert 1991, 20.
284 *"Ancestor veneration":* McAnany 1995, xi.
284 *"such memorials to group lineage":* Hastorf 2003.
284 *"There are too many ancestors":* Whitley 2002.
284 *"The universal ancestor":* Ibid.
284 *"One of the great claims":* Ibid.
284 *One alternative view:* Kuijt 1996; Kuijt 2.

285 *Ma'anyan people:* Kuijt 2000, 144.
285 *social differentiation and inequalities:* Ibid., 156–57; Peterson 2002, 21–23.
285 *case that began in May 1980:* Ubelaker and Scammell 1992, 1–15 and 200–205.
287 *adult women outnumbered men:* Angel 1971, 78. As there are discrepancies between the table and the text of this paper, I have used the figures in the table.
287 *women had died during childbirth:* Ibid., 80.
287 *little evidence of secondary burial:* Andrews et al., in Hodder in press/d.
288 *only two skeletons:* Ibid.
288 *The anthropologists did not find:* Ibid.
288 *Child, infant, and newborn burials:* Molleson et al. in Hodder in press/d.
288 *that malaria was responsible:* Ibid.
289 *the ratios of carbon and nitrogen:* Richards et al. 2003.
289 *much more varied:* Ibid., 75.
290 *When Başak Boz completed:* Boz in Hodder in press/d.
290 *And Naomi Hamilton, who:* Hamilton in Hodder in press/d.
290 *a black substance:* Molleson in Hodder in press/d.
290 *Wendy Matthews, who had studied:* Interview with Wendy Matthews.
290 *"This finding implies":* Hodder 2004, 79.
290 *"We are not witnessing":* Ibid., 83.
291 *The earlier claims:* Richards et al. 2003; interviews with Nerissa Russell and Louise Martin.

Chapter 16: Taming the Wild

293 *explanations for this size difference:* Frame with Russell and Martin 1999; interviews with Louise Martin, Nerissa Russell, and Sheelagh Frame.
293 Bos primigenius: Clutton-Brock 1999, 84–85; "Bison," *Encyclopædia Britannica* 2004 Encyclopædia Britannica Premium Service, accessed 28 April 2004, http://www.britannica.com/eb/article?eu=82455.
293 *Louise rehearsed the various arguments:* Louise Martin's private diary, 30 August 1999.
294 *Louise Martin was born:* Interview with Louise Martin.
294 *Louise's father:* Obituary, *Independent* 22 January 2002, 22; www.alanmacfarlane.com/FILES/gerry.html.
295 *buff-colored Roman amphorae:* Interview with Louise Martin; www.potsherd.uklinux.net/atlas/Ware/GAUL
295 *his course on the Anatolian:* Louise Martin's lecture notes, 1983. Thanks, Louise!
296 *digging in the Klithi gorge:* E-mail from Geoff Bailey.
296 *bones at Tell Es-Sa'idiyeh:* www.thebritishmuseum.ac.uk/ane/anereextell.html.
297 *so-called margins hypothesis:* Binford 1968; Binford 1983.
297 *it had failed:* Garrard et al. 1996.
299 *such helpfully titled volumes:* Cited in Davis 1987, 32.
299 *bone splinters and fragments:* Ibid., 26; interviews with Louise Martin and Nerissa Russell.
299 *"sheep/goat":* Davis 1987, 32–33.
299 *in Europe and North America:* Ibid., 32.
299 *with a dead fox:* Interview with Louise Martin.
300 *Science Museum of Minnesota:* www.smm.org/catal/.

300 *Carcass of a young donkey:* Interview with Louise Martin and Nerissa Russell.
300 *she was quite squeamish:* Interview with Nerissa Russell.
301 *The donkey would be buried:* Interviews with Louise Martin and Nerissa Russell.
301 *The following season:* Ibid.
301 *a private donation:* E-mail from Orrin Shane.
301 *to buy a sheep and a goat:* Interviews with Louise Martin and Nerissa Russell.
302 *During the 1996 season:* Archive reports for 1996–99.
302 *able to identify only:* Frame 1999, Table 19.
302 *faunal expert who worked:* Perkins 1969.
302 *Zawi Chemi Shanidar:* Davis 1987, 151; Clutton-Brock 1999, 74.
303 *in the Zagros Mountains:* Zeder and Hesse 2000.
303 *Perkins really stirred up:* Perkins 1969.
303 *Rissa's hypothesis:* Russell and Martin 1998.
304 *faunal team crunched out:* Frame with Martin and Russell 1999.
304 *The red crossbill:* research.amnh.org/ornithology/crossbills/.
304 *Rissa was born:* Interviews with Nerissa Russell.
305 *Miss Porter's School:* www.missporters.org/.
305 *prehistoric Koster:* Bahn 2001, 244.
306 *Harvard's Richard Meadow:* www.cirs.net/researchers/AnthropologyArchaeology/Meadow.htm.
306 *Rissa's Ph.D. thesis:* Russell 1993.
306 *titled one of her books:* Clutton-Brock 1988.
306 *"The key conceptual switch":* Russell 1998a.
307 *the cattle from Aşikli:* Buitenhuis 2002, 183–89.
308 *began crunching the data:* Interviews with Nerissa Russell and Louise Martin.

Chapter 17: The Goddess and the Bull

309 *decided to construct:* Farid 2002.
309 *A crowd of archaeologists:* Hodder 2003.
310 *a lot of figurines:* Hamilton 1996.
312 *The 1999 Long Season had provided:* Cessford 2001; Cessford in Hodder in press/b.
312 *Radiocarbon Accelerator Unit:* www.rlaha.ox.ac.uk.
312 *Can Hasan III:* Cessford 2001.
312 *Suberde:* Cessford 2001.
313 *their Konya Plain survey:* Baird 1996.
313 *On the alluvial fan:* Baird 2001.
313 *The survey showed:* Baird in Hodder in press/a.
314 *what these numbers were:* Cessford in Hodder in press/d.
315 *The archaeobotany results showed:* Fairbairn et al. in Hodder in press/d.
315 *"The full suite":* Ibid.
315 *analysis of the charcoal remains:* Asouti in Hodder in press/d; see also Asouti and Hather 2001.
316 *he made it official:* Balter 2001; Roberts et al. in Hodder in press/c.
316 *Neil had published a paper:* Roberts 1982.
316 *Rissa's own analysis:* Russell and McGowan in Hodder in press/d.
317 *analysis of phytoliths:* Rosen in Hodder in press/d.

318 *As far as Ian was concerned:* Balter 2001.
318 *"plaster freaks":* Ibid.
318 *"The house and the body":* Carsten and Hugh-Jones 1995, 2.
319 *In a paper he published:* Hodder and Cessford 2004.
319 *central gathering places:* Ibid., 18.
319 *Mehmet Özdoğan:* Özdoğan 2002.
320 *contingents of goddess worshippers:* Interview with Ayfer Bartu.
321 *Cynthia Eller:* Eller 1995, 161.
321 *"were our ancestors":* Eller 2000, 133.
321 *when Marija Gimbutas:* Gimbutas 2001.
321 *in a 1998 article:* Tringham and Conkey 1998.
321 *"we have decided":* Meskell 1998.
322 *hostile comments:* Çatalhöyük Visitor's Center visitor book, 24 May 2000.
322 *an exchange of letters:* catal.arch.cam.ac.uk/catal/goddess.html.
322 *Naomi, in her final report:* Naomi Hamilton in Hodder in press/b.
323 *"The Lady and the Seed":* Hodder 2003b.
323 *a close look at the animal symbolism:* Russell and Meece in Hodder in press/a.
323 *bull paintings:* Mellaart 1967, 136.
323 *attempted a psychoanalytic analysis:* Donley-Reid in Hodder in press/a.
323 *Neither of them wanted:* Interview with Ruth Tringham.
323 *Building 3 had not been burned:* Interview with Mirjana Stevanovic.
325 *many or most of the fires:* Cessford and Near in Hodder in press/a.
325 *life story of Building 3:* Interview with Mirjana Stevanovic.
325 *"At last you have":* Ibid.
326 *Ayfer and Can's Mock Wedding:* Author's notes.
326 *Shahina had convinced Ian:* Interview with Shahina Farid.
327 *reading the vows:* Transcribed by Freya Swogger from her video of the event.

Epilogue

331 *had become convinced:* Interviews with Ian Hodder and Shahina Farid.
332 *"Let's open up":* Interview with Shahina Farid.
332 *"It was time":* Hodder 2003c.
332 *specialists took exception:* Anonymous interviews.
333 *Ian had asked:* Interviews with numerous specialists.
333 *sixty five internal spaces:* Jeremy Taylor and Joann Lyon 2003. "Excavation of the 4040 Area." Çatalhöyük 2003 Archive Report.
334 *nearly intact roof:* Hodder 2003c.
334 *West Mound, a smaller:* Gibson and Last 2003.
335 *calibrated radiocarbon dates:* Interview with Craig Cessford.
335 *Cessford had calculated:* Ibid.
335 *painted ceramics:* Interviews with Jonathan Last.
336 *Jonathan proposed:* Last 1998.
336 *cattle bones:* Gibson and Last 2003.
336 *In 2004:* This section based on author's 2004 visit.

Bibliography

Aiello, Leslie C., and R. I. M. Dunbar. 1993. "Neocortex Size, Group Size, and the Evolution of Language." *Current Anthropology* 34(2):184–93.

Andrews, Peter, Theya Molleson, and Başak Boz. Forthcoming. "The Human Burials at Çatalhöyük." In Hodder in press/d.

Angel, J. Lawrence. 1971. "Early Neolithic Skeletons from Çatal Hüyük: Demography and Pathology." *Anatolian Studies* 21:77–98.

Appignanesi, Richard, and Chris Garratt. 2003. *Introducing Postmodernism.* Icon.

Arnold, J. R., and W. F. Libby. 1949. "Age Determinations by Radiocarbon Content: Checks with Samples of Known Age." *Science* 110:678.

Arsuaga, J. L., J. M. Carretero, C. Lorenzo, A. Gracia, I. Martínez, J. M. Bermúdez de Castro, and E. Carbonell. 1997. "Size Variation in Middle Pleistocene Humans." *Science* 277:1086–88.

Asouti, Eleni. Forthcoming. "Woodland Vegetation and the Exploitation of Fuel and Lumber at Neolithic Çatalhöyük: Report on the Wood Charcoal Macro-remains." In Hodder in press/d.

Asouti, Eleni, and Jon Hather. 2001. "Charcoal Analysis and the Reconstruction of Ancient Woodland Vegetation in the Konya Basin, South-Central Anatolia, Turkey: Results from the Neolithic Site of Çatalhöyük East." *Vegetation History and Archaeobotany* 10:23–32.

Atalay, Sonya. Forthcoming. "Domesticating Clay: The Role of Clay Balls, Mini Balls and Geometric Objects in Daily Life at Çatalhöyük." In Hodder in press/b.

Atalay, Sonya, and Christine A. Hastof. Forthcoming. "Foodways at Çatalhöyük." In Hodder in press/a.

Bagehot, Walter. 2003. *Physics and Politics.* IndyPublish.com.

Bahn, Paul, ed. 2001. *The Penguin Archaeology Guide.* Penguin.

Baird, Douglas. 1996. "The Konya Plain Survey: Aims and Methods." In Hodder 1996, 41–46.

———. 2001. "Konya Plain Survey." *Anatolian Archaeology* 7:16.

———. Forthcoming. "The History of Settlement and Social Landscapes in the Early Holocene in the Çatalhöyük Area." In Hodder in press/a.

Balter, Michael. 1998. "The Mystery of Communities." *Science* 282:1442–45.

———. 1999. "A Long Season Puts Çatalhöyük in Context." *Science* 286:890–91.

———. 2000. "Baedeker's Guide, or Just Plain 'Trouble'?" *Science* 287: 29–30.

———. 2001a. "Did Plaster Hold Neolithic Society Together?" *Science* 294:2278–81.

———. 2001b. "What—or Who—Did In the Neandertals?" *Science* 293: 1980–81.

———. 2002. "Why Get Smart?" *Science* 295:1225.

Balter, Michael. 2003. "Early Date for the Birth of Indo-European Languages." *Science* 302: 1490–1491.
Balter, Michael. 2004. "Search for the Indo-Europeans." *Science* 303:1323–26.
Bar-Yosef, Ofer. 1998. "The Natufian Culture in the Levant, Threshold to the Origins of Agriculture." *Evolutionary Anthropology* 6(5):159–77.
Bar-Yosef, Ofer, and François R. Valla, eds. 1991. *The Natufian Culture in the Levant.* International Monographs in Prehistory.
Barker, Philip. 1993. *Techniques of Archaeological Excavation.* Routledge.
Barnett, William K., and John W. Hoopes. 1995. *The Emergence of Pottery: Technology and Innovation in Ancient Societies.* Smithsonian Institution Press.
Barton, Huw. 2000. "*In memoriam* V. Gordon Childe." *Antiquity* 74:769–70.
Barstow, Anne. 1978. "The Uses of Archeology for Women's History: James Mellaart's Work on the Neolithic Goddess at Çatal Hüyük." *Feminist Studies* 4:7–18.
Bartu, Ayfer. 2000. "Where Is Çatalhöyük? Multiple Sites in the Construction of an Archaeological Site." In Hodder 2000, 101–10.
Baruch, Uri, and Sytze Bottema. 1991. "Palynological Evidence for Climatic Changes in the Levant ca. 17,000–9,000 B.P." In Bar-Yosef and Valla 1991, 11–20.
Basch, Lucien. 1987. *Le musée imaginaire de la marine antique.* Institut Hellénique pour la Préservation de la Tradition Nautique.
Becker, Ernest. 1973. *The Denial of Death.* Free Press.
Bender, Barbara. 1978. "Gatherer-Hunter to Farmer: A Social Perspective." *World Archaeology* 10(2):204–22.
Bennett, Ian. 1990. "The Mistress of All Life." *Hali* 50 (April): 116–29.
Betancourt, Philip P., et al., eds. 1999. *Meletemata: Studies in Aegean Archaeology Presented to Malcolm H. Wiener.* Université de Liège.
Bienert, Hans-Dieter. 1991. "Skull Cult in the Prehistoric Near East." *Journal of Prehistoric Religion* 5:9–23.
Binford, Lewis R. 1962. "Archaeology as Anthropology." *American Antiquity* 28:217–25.
———. 1965. "Archaeological Systematics and the Study of Culture Process." *American Antiquity* 31:204.
———. 1968. "Post-Pleistocene Adaptations." In Binford and Binford 1968, 313–41.
———. 1972. *An Archaeological Perspective.* Seminar Press.
———. 1973. "Interassemblage Variability—the Mousterian and the 'Functional' Argument." In Renfrew 1973b. 227–254.
———. 1983a. *In Pursuit of the Past.* University of California Press.
———. 1983b. *Working at Archaeology.* Academic Press.
———. 1988. "Review of Hodder, *Reading the Past: Current Approaches to Interpretation in Archaeology*." *American Antiquity* 53:875–76.
———. 1989. *Debating Archaeology.* Academic Press.
Binford, Sally R., and Lewis R. Binford, eds. 1968. *New Perspectives in Archaeology.* Aldine.
Blaylock, Stuart. 1998. "Rescue Excavations by the BIAA at Tille Höyük, on the Euphrates, 1979–1990." In Roger Matthews 1998, 111–26.
Bourdieu, Pierre. 1970. "The Berber House or the World Reversed." *Social Science Information* 9:150–70.
Boyer, Peter. 1999. "Excavations in the KOPAL Area." Çatalhöyük 1999 Archive Report. catal.arch.cam.ac.uk/catal/Archive_rep99/boyer99.html.

Boz, Başak. Forthcoming. "Oral Health of Çatalhöyük Neolithic People." In Hodder in press/d.

Braidwood, Robert J. 1952. "From Cave to Village." *Scientific American*, October, 62–66.

———. 1960. "The Agricultural Revolution." *Scientific American*, September 131–148.

Braidwood, Robert J., and Linda Braidwood. 1950. "Jarmo: A Village of Early Farmers in Iraq." *Antiquity* 24:189–95.

Bray, Warnick, and David Trump, eds. 1982. *The Penguin Dictionary of Archaeology*. Penguin.

Broodbank, Cyprian. 2000. *An Island Archaeology of the Early Cyclades*. Cambridge University Press.

Brosnahan, Tom, and Pat Yale. 1996. *Turkey: A Lonely Planet Survival Kit*. Lonely Planet.

Buitenhuis, Hijlke. 2002. "The Transition from Foraging to Farming: The Archaeozoological Perspective in Anatolia." In R. T. J. Cappers and S. Bottema, eds. *Studies in Early Near Eastern Production, Subsistence, and Environment*. No. 6. 2002. Berlin: Ex Oriente, 183–89.

Byrd, Brian F., and Christopher M. Monahan. 1995. "Death, Mortuary Ritual, and Natufian Social Structure." *Journal of Anthropological Archaeology* 14:251–87.

Callaway, J. A. 1979. "Dame Kathleen Kenyon, 1906–1978." *Biblical Archaeologist* 42:122–25.

Çambel, Halet, and Robert Braidwood. 1970. "An Early Farming Village in Turkey." *Scientific American*, March, 50–56.

Carsten, Janet, and Stephen Hugh-Jones. 1995. "Introduction." In Janet Carson and Stephen Hugh-Jones, eds. *About the House: Lévi-Strauss and Beyond*. Cambridge University Press.

Cauvin, Jacques. 2000. *The Birth of the Gods and the Origins of Agriculture*. Cambridge University Press. Translation by Trevor Watkins.

Cessford, Craig. 1998. "The Excavation of the North Area 1998." Çatalhöyük 1998 Archive Report. catal.arch.cam.ac.uk/catal/Archive_rep98/cessford98.html.

———. 2001. "A New Dating Sequence for Çatalhöyük." *Antiquity* 75:717–25.

———. Forthcoming. "Absolute Dating at Çatalhöyük." In Hodder in press/b.

———. Forthcoming. "Estimating the Neolithic population of Çatalhöyük." In Hodder in press/d.

Cessford, Craig, and Julie Near. Forthcoming. "Fire, Burning and Pyrotechnology at Çatalhöyük." In Hodder in press/a.

Chatwin, Bruce. 1989. *What Am I Doing Here*. Picador.

Childe, V. Gordon. 1927. *The Dawn of European Civilization*. Kegan Paul, Trench, Trubner & Co.

———. 1928. *The Most Ancient East: The Oriental Prelude to European History*.

———. 1929. *The Danube in Prehistory*.

———. 1936. *Man Makes Himself*. Library of Science and Culture.

———. 1957. *New Light on the Most Ancient East*. Grove Press.

———. 2003. *Man Makes Himself*. Spokesman.

Clarke, David L. 1968. *Analytical Archaeology*. Methuen.

———, ed. 1972. *Models in Archaeology*. Methuen.

———. 1973. "Archaeology: The Loss of Innocence." *Antiquity* 47:6–18.

Clutton-Brock, Juliet. 1988. *The Walking Larder*. Taylor & Francis.

———. 1999. *A Natural History of Domesticated Animals*. Cambridge University Press.

Cohen, Harold R. 1970. "The Palaeoecology of South Central Anatolia at the End of the Pleistocene and the Beginning of the Holocene." *Anatolian Studies* 20:119–37.

Cohen, Mark Nathan. 1977. *The Food Crisis in Prehistory: Overpopulation and the Origins of Agriculture*. Yale University Press.

Collon, Dominique. 1990. "Subjective Reconstruction?" *Hali* 53(Sept):119–23.

———. 1996. "A Long Interval in Iraq." *Guardian*, January 10.

Conkey, Margaret W., and Christine A. Hastorf, eds. 1990. *The Uses of Style in Archaeology*. Cambridge University Press.

Conkey, Margaret W., and Ruth Tringham. 1995. "Archaeology and the Goddess: Exploring the Contours of Feminist Archaeology." In Stanton and Stewart 1995, 199–247.

Courbin, Paul. 1982. *Qu'est-ce que l'archéologie? Essai sur la nature de la recherche archéologique*. Payot.

———. 1988. *What Is Archaeology?* Trans. Paul Bahn. University of Chicago Press.

David, Nicholas. 1982. "Inferences from Artifacts": review of *Symbols in Action*. *Science* 216:1402.

David, Nicholas, and Carol Kramer. 2001. *Ethnoarchaeology in Action*. Cambridge University Press.

David, Nicholas, Judy Sterner, and Kodzo Gavua. 1988. "Why Pots Are Decorated." *Current Anthropology* 29:365–98.

Davis, Simon J. M. 1987. *The Archaeology of Animals*. Yale University Press.

de Waal, Frans B. M., ed. 2002. *Tree of Origin: What Primate Behavior Can Tell Us about Human Social Evolution*. Harvard University Press.

Diamond, Jared. 1997. *Guns, Germs, and Steel: A Short History of Everybody for the Last 13, Years*. Vintage.

Dixon, J. E., J. R. Cann, and Colin Renfrew. 1968. "Obsidian and the Origins of Trade." *Scientific American*. March, 38–46.

Donley-Reid, Linda. Forthcoming. "Figurines, Wall Murals and Daggers: Objects and Art as Emotional Support for Cognitive Development and the Fear of Death." In Hodder in press/a.

Douglas, Mary. 2002. *Purity and Danger*. Routledge.

Dunbar, Robin. 1996. *Grooming, Gossip, and the Evolution of Language*. Harvard University Press.

Düring, Bleda S. 2001. "Social Dimensions in the Architecture of Neolithic Çatalhöyük." *Anatolian Studies* 51:1–18.

Edwards, Phillip C. 1989. "Problems of Recognizing Earliest Sedentism: The Natufian Example." *Journal of Mediterranean Archaeology* 2(1):5–48.

Eiland, Murray L., III. 1993. "The Past Re-made: The Case of Oriental Carpets." *Antiquity* 67:860.

Eller, Cynthia. 1995. *Living in the Lap of the Goddess: The Feminist Spirituality Movement in America*. Beacon Press.

———. 2000. *The Myth of Matriarchal Prehistory: Why an Invented Past Won't Give Women a Future*. Beacon Press.

Esin, Ufuk, and Savas Harmankaya. 1999. "Aşikli." In Özdoğan and Başgelen 1999, 115–32.

Fairbairn, Andrew, Julie Near, and Danièle Martinoli. Forthcoming. "Macrobotanical Investigation of the North, South and KOPAL Area Excavations at Çatalhöyük East." In Hodder in press/d.

Farid, Shahina. 1997. "Mellaart Area." Çatalhöyük 1997 Archive Report. catal.arch.cam.ac.uk/catal/Archive_rep97/farid97.html.

———. 2002. "South Area Shelter." Çatalhöyük 2002 Archive Report. catal.arch.cam.ac.uk/catal/Archive_rep02/a08.html.

Flannery, Kent V. 1965. "The Ecology of Early Food Production in Mesopotamia." *Science* 147:1247–56.

———. 1967. "Culture History v. Cultural Process: A Debate in American Archaeology." *Scientific American*, August, 119.

———. 1972. "The Origins of the Village as a Settlement Type in Mesoamerica and the Near East: A Comparative Study." In Ucko 1972, 23–53.

———. 1993. "Will the Real Model Please Stand Up: Comments on Saidel's 'Round House or Square?'" *Journal of Mediterranean Archaeology* 6(1):109–17.

———. 2002. "The Origins of the Village Revisited: From Nuclear to Extended Households." *American Antiquity* 67(3):417–33.

Fleagle, John G. 2002. "The Primate Fossil Record." *Evolutionary Anthropology* 11 (Supplement 1): 20–23.

Foley, Robert. 1997. *Humans before Humanity*. Blackwell.

Frame, Sheelagh, with Nerissa Russell and Louise Martin. 1999. "Animal Bone Report." Çatalhöyük 1999 Archive Report. catal.arch.cam.ac.uk/catal/Archive_rep99/framemartin99.html.

French, D. H. 1962. "Excavations at Can Hasan." *Anatolian Studies* 12:27–40.

———. 1971. "An Experiment in Water Sieving." *Anatolian Studies* 21: 59–64.

Galbraith, John Kenneth. 1958. *The Affluent Society*. The New American Library.

Gamble, Clive. 1999. *The Palaeolithic Societies of Europe*. Cambridge University Press.

Gargett, Robert H. 1989. "Grave Shortcomings: The Evidence for Neandertal Burial." *Current Anthropology* 30(2):157–90.

Garrard, Andrew, Susan Colledge, and Louise Martin. 1996. "The Emergence of Crop Cultivation and Caprine Herding in the 'Marginal Zone' of the Southern Levant." in Harris 1996-b.

Gérard, Frédéric, and Laurens Thissen. 2002. *The Neolithic of Central Anatolia*. Yayinlari.

Gero, Joan M., and Margaret W. Conkey, eds. 1991. *Engendering Archaeology: Women and Prehistory*. Basil Blackwell.

Gibson, Catriona and Last, Jonathan. 2003. "West Mound Excavations." Çatalhöyük 2003 Archive Report. catal.arch.cam.ac.uk/catal/Archive_rep03/all.html.

Gimbutas, Marija. 2001. *The Language of the Goddess*. Thames and Hudson.

Goodison, Lucy, and Christine Morris. 1998. *Ancient Goddesses*. British Museum Press.

Goody, Jack. 1962. *Death, Property and the Ancestors: A Study of the Mortuary Customs of the LoDagaa of West Africa*. Tavistock. Cited in Parker Pearson 1982.

Gray, R. D. and Atkinson, Q. D. 2003. "Language-tree divergence times support the Anatolian theory of Indo-European origin." *Nature* 426: 435–439.

Green, Sally. 1981. *Prehistorian: A Biography of V. Gordon Childe*. Moonraker.

Grosman, Leore. 2003. "Preserving Cultural Traditions in a Period of Instability: The Late Natufian of the Hilly Mediterranean Zone." *Cultural Anthropology* 44(4):571–80.

Hager, Lori. 1996. "Sex Differences in the Sciatic Notch of Great Apes and Modern Humans." *American Journal of Physical Anthropology* 99(2):287–300.
———. 1997. *Women in Human Evolution*. Routledge.
Hager, Lori D., and Başak Boz. 2002. "Human Remains 2002." Çatalhöyük 2002 Archive Report. catal.arch.cam.ac.uk/catal/Archive_rep02/a04.html.
Hamilton, Carolyn. 2000. "Faultlines: the Construction of Archaelogical Knowledge at Çatalhöyük." In Hodder 2000, 119–127.
Hamilton, Naomi. 1996. "Figurines, Clay Balls, Small Finds and Burials." In Hodder 1996a, 215–29.
———. Forthcoming. "The Figurines." In Hodder in press/b.
———. Forthcoming. "Social Aspects of Burial." In Hodder in press/d.
Hargrove, Cheryl M. 2002. "Heritage Tourism." *CRM* No. 1, 10. crm.cr.nps.gov/archive/25-01/25-01-4.pdf.
Harris, David. 1991. Letter. *Oriental Rug Review* 11(4):46.
———. ed. 1994. *The Archaeology of V. Gordon Childe*. University College London Press.
———. 1996a. "Introduction: Themes and Concepts in the Study of Early Agriculture." In Harris 1996b, 1–2.
———, ed., 1996b. *The Origins and Spread of Agriculture and Pastoralism in Eurasia*. Smithsonian Institution Press.
———. 1997/1998. "Sixty Years On: The Institute of Archaeology, 1937–97." *Archaeology International* 1:3.
Hassan, Fekri A. 1997. "Beyond the Surface: Comments on Hodder's 'Reflexive Excavation Methodology,'" *Antiquity* 71:1020–25.
Hastorf, Christine A. 1991. "Gender, Space, and Food in Prehistory." In Gero and Conkey 1991, 132–59.
———. 2003. "Community with the Ancestors: Ceremonies and Social Memory in the Middle Formative at Chiripa, Bolivia." *Journal of Anthropological Archaeology* 22:328.
Helbaek, Hans. 1964. "First Impressions of the Çatal Hüyük Plant Husbandry." *Anatolian Studies* 14:121.
Heltzer, M., and E. Lipinski. 1988. *Society and Economy in the Eastern Mediterranean (c. 1500–1 B.C.)*. Peeters Publishers.
Heun, Manfred, et al. 1997. "Site of Einkorn Wheat Domestication Identified by DNA Fingerprinting." *Science* 278: 1312–14.
Hickok, Michael Robert. 1998. "The Imia/Kardak Affair, 1995–6: A Case of Inadvertent Conflict." *European Security* 74(1):118–36.
Hillman, Gordon. 1996. "Late Pleistocene Changes in Wild Plant-Foods Available to Hunter-Gatherers of the Northern Fertile Crescent: Possible Preludes to Cereal Cultivation." In Harris (1996b).
Hodder, Ian, ed. 1982a. *Symbolic and Structural Archaeology*. Cambridge University Press.
———. 1982b. *Symbols in Action*. Cambridge University Press.
———. 1986. *Reading the Past: Current Approaches to Interpretation in Archaeology*. Cambridge University Press.
———. 1987. "Contextual Archaeology: An Intrepretation of Çatal Hüyük and a Discussion of the Origins of Agriculture." *Bulletin of the Institute of Archaeology*, 43–56.

———. 1990. *The Domestication of Europe*. Blackwell.
———. 1991. *Reading the Past: Current Approaches to Interpretation in Archaeology*. Cambridge University Press.
———. 1992. "The Haddenham Causewayed Enclosure—a Hermeneutic Circle." In Ian Hodder. 1992. *Theory and Practice in Archaeology*. Routledge.
———, ed. 1996a. *On the Surface: Çatalhöyük 1993–5*. McDonald Institute for Archaeological Research.
———. 1996b. "Re-Opening Çatalhöyük." In Hodder 1996a, 1–18.
———. 1997. "Always Momentary, Fluid and Flexible: Towards a Self-reflexive Excavation Methodology." *Antiquity* 71: 691–700.
———. 1998a. "Introduction and Summary." Çatalhöyük 1998 Archive Report. catal.arch.cam.ac.uk/catal/Archive_rep98/hodder98.html.
———. 1998b. "Whose Rationality? A Response to Fekri Hassan." *Antiquity* 72:213.
———. 1999a. *The Archaeological Process: An Introduction*. Blackwell.
———. 1999b. "Introduction: Çatalhöyük 1999." Çatalhöyük 1999 Archive Report. catal.arch.cam.ac.uk/catal/Archive_rep99/hodder99en.html.
———, ed. 2000. *Towards Reflexive Method in Archaeology: The example of Çatalhöyük*. McDonald Institute for Archaeological Research.
———. 2001. "Symbolism and the Origins of Agriculture in the Near East." In "Review Feature." *Cambridge Archaeological Journal* 11:107–12.
———. 2003a. *Archaeology beyond Dialogue*. University of Utah Press.
———. 2003b. "The Lady and the Seed." In Hodder 2003a, 155–63.
Hodder, Ian. 2003c. "Introduction." Çatalhöyük 2003 Archive Report. catal.arch.cam.ac.uk/catal/Archive_rep03/a01.html.
———. 2004. "Women and Men at Çatalhöyük." *Scientific American* January, 66–73.
———, ed. Forthcoming. *Çatalhöyük Perspectives: Themes from the 1995–99 Seasons*. McDonald Institute Monographs/British Institute of Archaeology at Ankara, in press/a.
———, ed. Forthcoming. *Changing Materialities at Çatalhöyük: Reports from the 1995–99 Seasons*. McDonald Institute Monographs/British Institute of Archaeology at Ankara, in press/b.
———, ed. Forthcoming. *Excavating Çatalhöyük: South, North and KOPAL Area Reports from the 1995–99 Seasons*. McDonald Institute Monographs/British Institute of Archaeology at Ankara, in press/c.
———, ed. Forthcoming. *Inhabiting Çatalhöyük: Reports from the 1995–99 Seasons*. McDonald Institute Monographs/British Institute of Archaeology at Ankara, in press/d.
Hodder, Ian, and Craig Cessford. 2004. "Daily Practice and Social Memory at Çatalhöyük." *American Antiquity* 69(1):17–40.
Hodder, Ian, and Mark Hassall. 1971. "The Non-Random Spacing of Romano-British Walled Towns." *Man (New Series)* 6:391–407.
Hodder, Ian, and Scott Hutson. 2003. *Reading the Past: Current Approaches to Interpretation in Archaeology*. Cambridge University Press.
Hodder, Ian, and Clive Orton. 1976. *Spatial Analysis in Archaeology*. Cambridge University Press.
Holden, Constance. 2004. "Scientists Hope Ruling Will Lead Them to Bones." *Science* 303:943.
Jacobs, Jane. 1970. *The Economy of Cities*. Vintage.

Johnson, Matthew. 1999. *Archaeological Theory: An Introduction.* Blackwell.
Joyce, Rosemary A., and Susan D. Gillespie, eds. 2000. *Beyond Kinship: Social and Material Reproduction in House Societies.* University of Pennsylvania Press.
Kaufman, Daniel. 1992. "Hunter-Gatherers of the Levantine Epipalaeolithic: The Socioecological Origins of Sedentism." *Journal of Mediterranean Archaeology* 5(2):165–201.
Kenyon, Frederick. 1940. *The Bible and Archaeology.* Harper & Row.
Kenyon, Kathleen. 1953. *Beginning in Archaeology.* Frederick A. Praeger.
———. 1954. "Ancient Jericho." *Scientific American* April, 76–82.
———. 1956. "Jericho and Its Setting in Near Eastern History." *Antiquity* 30:184–95.
———. 1957. *Digging Up Jericho.* Frederick A. Praeger.
King, Tania, Peter Andrews, and Başak Boz. 1999. "Effect of Taphonomic Processes on Dental Microwear." *American Journal of Physical Anthropology* 108:359–73.
Klein, Richard G. 1999. *The Human Career: Human Biological and Cultural Origins.* University of Chicago Press.
Klein, Richard G., and Blake Edgar. 2002. *The Dawn of Human Culture.* John Wiley & Sons.
Klíma, Bohuslav. 1954. "Palaeolithic Huts at Dolní Věstonice, Czechoslovakia." *Antiquity* 28:4–14.
Kooijmans, L. P. Louwe, et al. 1989. Comments on "On the Evidence for Neandertal Burial." *Current Anthropology* 30(3):322–30.
Kuijt, Ian. 1996. "Negotiating Equality through Ritual: A Consideration of Late Natufian and Prepottery Neolithic A Mortuary Practices." *Journal of Anthropological Archaeology* 15:313–36.
———. 2000a. "Keeping the Peace: Ritual, Skull Caching, and Community Integration in the Levantine Neolithic." In Kuijt 2b, 137–164.
———, ed. 2000b. *Life in Neolithic Farming Communities: Social Organization, Identity, and Differentiation.* Kluwer Academic/Plenum Publishers.
Lamberg-Karlovsky, C. C. 1992. " 'Constructing' the Past." *Review of Archaeology* 13:38.
Last, Jonathan. 1998. "A Design for Life: Interpreting the Art of Çatalhöyük." *Journal of Material Culture* 3(3): 355–378.
Last, Jonathan. Forthcoming. "Pottery from the East Mound." In Hodder in press/b.
Lawler, Andrew. 2003. "Ten Millennia of Culture Pilfered amid Baghdad Chaos." *Science* 300: 402–403.
Leach, Edmund. 1973. "Concluding Address." in Renfrew 1973b, 761–71.
Le Brun, Alain. 1997. *Khirokitia: A Neolithic Site.* Bank of Cyprus Cultural Foundation.
Lee, Richard B., and Irven DeVore, eds. 1968. *Man the Hunter.* Aldine.
Levy, Philip. 2000. "Always a Handmaiden—Never a Bride." *Archaeology.* Online features, www.he.net/_archaeol/online/features/history/.
Lieberman, D. E. 1991. "Seasonality and Gazelle Hunting at Hayonim Cave: New Evidence for 'Sedentism' during the Natufian." *Paléorient* 17(1):47–57.
———. 1993a. "Life History Variables Preserved in Dental Cementum Microstructure." *Science* 261:1162–64.
———. 1993b. "The Rise and Fall of Seasonal Mobility among Hunter-Gatherers: The Case of the Southern Levant." *Current Anthropology* 34(5):599–631.
Lloyd, Seton. 1956. *Early Anatolia.* Penguin.
———. 1963. *Mounds of the Near East.* Edinburgh University Press.

———. 1967. *Early Highland Peoples of Anatolia*. Thames and Hudson.

Lloyd, Seton, and James Mellaart. 1962. *Beycesultan Volume I: The Chalcolithic and Early Bronze Age Levels*. BIAA.

Lopez, Michael Ashley. 2002. "Real Webs and Virtual Excavations: A Role for Digital Media Recording in Archaeological Site Management." *UNESCO Virtual Congress*, October–November.

Lovejoy, C. Owen. 1981. "The Origin of Man." *Science* 211:341–50.

Lucas, Gavin. 1997a. "The Excavation of Building 1, North Area." Çatalhöyük 1997 Archive Report. catal.arch.cam.ac.uk/catal/Archive_rep97/lucas97.html.

———. 1997b. "Summary of the New Phasing for Building 1, North Area." Çatalhöyük 1997 Archive Report (supplement of 3 December 1997). catal.arch.cam.ac.uk/catal/Archive_rep97/phasing97.html.

———. 2001. *Critical Approaches to Fieldwork*. Routledge.

Mallett, Marla. 1990. "A Weaver's View of the Çatal Hüyük Controversy." *Oriental Rug Review* 10/6:32–43. Available at www.marlamallett.com/chupdate.htm.

———. 1993. "An Updated View of the Çatal Hüyük Controversy." *Oriental Rug Review* 13/2:24–31. Available at www.rugreview.com/orr/132marl.htm.

Mallory, J. P. 1989. *In Search of the Indo-Europeans: Language, Archaeology and Myth*. Thames and Hudson.

Matero, Frank. 2000. "The Conservation of an Excavated Past." In Hodder 2, 71–88.

Matthews, Roger. 1996. "The Excavation of Building 1, North Area." Çatalhöyük 1996 Archive Report. catal.arch.cam.ac.uk/catal/Archive_rep96/rogmatthews96.html.

———, ed. 1998. *Ancient Anatolia: Fifty Years' Work by the British Institute of Archaeology at Ankara*. BIAA.

———. 2003. *The Archaeology of Mesopotamia: Theories and Approaches*. Routledge.

Matthews, Roger, and Ian Hodder. 1993. "Çatalhöyük 1993." Çatalhöyük 1993 Archive Report. catal.arch.cam.ac.uk/catal/Archive_rep93/rmatthews93.html.

———. 1994. "Çatalhöyük 1994." Çatalhöyük 1994 Archive Report. catal.arch.cam.ac.uk/catal/Archive_rep94/hodder94.html.

Matthews, Roger J., and Nicholas J. Postgate. 1987. "Excavations at Abu Salabikh, 1985–86." *Iraq* 49:91–119.

Matthews, Wendy. 1993. "Analysis of Field Section from 1960's Excavations." Çatalhöyük 1993 Archive Report. catal.arch.cam.ac.uk/catal/Archive_rep93/wmatthews93.html.

———. 1996. "Microstratigraphy, Micromorphology and Sampling Report." Çatalhöyük 1996 Archive Report. catal.arch.cam.ac.uk/catal/Archive_rep96/wmatthews96.html.

Mayewski, P. A., et al. 1993. "The Atmosphere during the Younger Dryas." *Science* 261:195–97.

Mays, Simon. 1998. *The Archaeology of Human Bones*. Routledge.

McAnany, Patricia A. 1995. *Living with the Ancestors: Kinship and Kingship in Ancient Maya Society*. University of Texas Press.

McBrearty, Sally, and Alison S. Brooks. 2000. "The Revolution That Wasn't: A New Interpretation of the Origin of Modern Human Behavior." *Journal of Human Evolution* 39:453–563.

Mellaart, Arlette. 2002. "Reflections on a Lost Summerhouse." *Cornucopia* 5(25):62–71.

Mellaart, James. 1961. "By Neolithic Artists of 7500 Years Ago—Statuettes from Hacilar, Unique for Quantity, Variety, Beauty and Preservation." *Illustrated London News*, February 11, 229–31.
———. 1962a. "The Beginnings of Mural Painting." *Archaeology* 15(1):2.
———. 1962b. "Excavations at Çatal Hüyük." *Anatolian Studies* 12:41–66.
———. 1963a. "Excavations at Çatal Hüyük, 1962, Second Preliminary Report." *Anatolian Studies* 13:43–104.
———. 1963b. "Çatal Hüyük in Anatolia: Excavations which Revolutionise the History of the Earliest Civilisations." Part I. *Illustrated London News* January 26.
———. 1963c, pp. 118–121. "Çatal Hüyük in Anatolia: Excavations which Revolutionise the History of the Earliest Civilisations." Part II. *Illustrated London News*. February 2, 160–64.
———. 1964. "A Neolithic City in Turkey." *Scientific American* April, 94–104.
———. 1965. "Çatal Hüyük West." *Anatolian Studies* 15:135–56.
———. 1966. "Excavations at Çatal Hüyük, 1965, Fourth Preliminary Report." *Anatolian Studies* 16:165–91.
———. 1967. *Çatal Hüyük: A Neolithic Town in Anatolia*. McGraw-Hill.
———. 1975. *The Neolithic of the Near East*. Scribner's.
———. 1978. *The Archaeology of Ancient Turkey*. The Bodley Head.
———. 1991. "James Mellaart Answers His Critics." *Hali* 55 (February):86–87.
———. 1998. "Çatal Hüyük: The 1960s Seasons." In Roger Matthews 1998, 38.
Mellaart, James, Udo Hirsch, and Belkis Balpinar. 1989. *The Goddess from Anatolia*. Adenau.
Merrick, Jamie, Peter Boyer, and Neil Roberts. 1997. "Archive Report on Work by the KOPAL Team 1997." Çatalhöyük 1997 Archive Report. catal.arch.cam.ac.uk/catal/Archive_rep97/roberts97.html.
Meskell, Lynn. 1998. "Twin Peaks." In Goodison and Morris 1998, 46–62.
Milner, Andrew, and Jeff Browitt. 2002. *Contemporary Cultural Theory: An Introduction*. Routledge
Mithen, Steven. 2003. *After the Ice: A Global Human History 20,–5 B.C.* Weidenfeld & Nicolson.
Molleson, Theya. 1994. "The Eloquent Bones of Abu Hureyra." *Scientific American*, August, 70–75.
Molleson, Theya, and Peter Andrews. 1996. "Trace Element Analyses of Bones and Teeth from Çatalhöyük." In Hodder 1996, 265–70.
Molleson, Theya, Peter Andrews, and Başak Boz. Forthcoming. "Reconstruction of the Neolithic People of Çatalhöyük." In Hodder in press/d.
Moore, A. M. T., and G. C. Hillman. 1992. "The Pleistocene to Holocene Transition and Human Economy in Southwest Asia: The Impact of the Younger Dryas." *American Antiquity* 57(3):482–94.
Moore, A. M. T., G. C. Hillman, and A. J. Legge. 2. *Village on the Euphrates*. Oxford University Press.
Museum of London. 1995. "Jubilee Line Extension Project." May.
Museum of London Archaeology Service. 1998. *The Big Dig: Archaeology and the Jubilee Line Extension*. June. www.archaeology.freewire.co.uk/thames.html; www.kalwall.com/4.htm; news.bbc.co.uk/2/hi/uk_news/politics/480426.stm.
Nadel, Dani, and Ella Werker. 1999. "The Oldest Ever Brush Hut Plant Remains from Ohalo II, Jordan Valley, Israel (19, BP)." *Antiquity* 73:755–64.

Newton, Maryanne W., and Peter I. Kuniholm. 1999. "Wiggles Worth Watching—Making Radiocarbon Work. The Case of Çatal Höyük." in Betancourt 1999, 527–37.

Özbaşaran, Mihriban. 1999. "Musular: A General Assessment on a New Neolithic Site in Central Anatolia." In Özdoğan and Başgelen 1999, 147–56.

Özbek, Metin. 1995. "Dental Pathology of the Prepottery Neolithic Residents of Çayönü, Turkey." *Rivista di Antropologia (Roma)* 73:101.

Özdoğan, Asli. 1999. "Çayönü." In Özdoğan and Başgelen 1999, 35–63.

Özdoğan, Mehmet. 1999. "Preface." in Özdoğan and Başgelen 1999, 9.

———. 2002. "Defining the Neolithic of Central Anatolia." In Gérard and Thissen 2002, 253–61.

Özdoğan, Mehmet, and Nezih Başgelen, eds. 1999. *Neolithic in Turkey: The Cradle of Civilization*. Arkeoloji Ve Sanat Yayinlari.

Parker Pearson, Michael. 1982. "Mortuary Practices, Society and Ideology: An Ethnoarchaeological Study." In Hodder 1982a, 99–101.

———. 1999. *The Archaeology of Death and Burial*. Texas A&M University Press.

Pearson, Kenneth. 1974. "New Hope for the Dig That Died," *Sunday Times* (London), 24 March.

Pearson, Kenneth, and Patricia Connor. 1967a. *The Dorak Affair*. Michael Joseph.

———. 1967b. "The Strange Case of James Mellaart." *Horizon* Summer, 4–15.

Perkins, Dexter. 1969. "Fauna of Çatal Hüyük: Evidence for Early Cattle Domestication in Anatolia." *Science* 164:177–79.

Peterson, Jane. 2002. *Sexual Revolutions: Gender and Labor at the Dawn of Agriculture*. Altamira Press.

Pettit, Paul. 2002a. "When Burial Begins." *British Archaeology* August, 8–13.

———. 2002b. "The Neanderthal Dead: Exploring Mortuary Variability in Middle Palaeolithic Eurasia." *Before Farming* 1(4):1–19.

Pitts, Michael, and Mark Roberts. 1998. *Fairweather Eden*. Arrow.

Potts, Rick. 1996. *Humanity's Descent: The Consequences of Ecological Instability*. William Morrow.

Price, Douglas T., and Anne Birgitte Gebauer. 1995. *Last Hunters, First Farmers: New Perspectives on the Prehistoric Transition to Agriculture*. School of American Research Press.

Pringle, Heather. 1998. "The Slow Birth of Agriculture." *Science* 282:1446–50.

Rafferty, Janet E. 1985. "The Archaeological Record on Sedentariness: Recognition, Development, and Implications." *Advances in Archaeological Method and Theory* 8:113–56.

Renfrew, Colin. 1970. "The Burnt House at Sitagroi." *Antiquity* 44:131–34.

———. 1973a. *Before Civilization*. Penguin.

———, ed. 1973b. *The Explanation of Culture Change: Models in Prehistory*. University of Pittsburgh Press.

———. 1998. *Archaeology and Language: The Puzzle of Indo-European Origins*. Pimlico.

Renfrew, Colin, and Paul Bahn. 1996. *Archaeology: Theories, Methods, and Practice*. Thames and Hudson.

Richards, M. P., J. A. Pearson, et al. 2003. "Stable Isotope Evidence of Diet at Neolithic Çatalhöyük, Turkey." *Journal of Archaeological Science* 30:67–76 (2003).

Robbins, Alexandra. 2003. *Secrets of the Tomb*. Little, Brown.

Roberts, Neil. 1982. "A Note on the Geomorphological Environment of Çatal Hüyük, Turkey." *Journal of Archaeological Science* 9:341–48.
———. 1998. *The Holocene: An Environmental History*. Blackwell.
Roberts, Neil, et al. Forthcoming. "The KOPAL Research Program at Çatalhöyük (1996–2001)." In Hodder in press/c.
Rodseth, Lars, et al. 1991. "The Human Community as a Primate Society." *Current Anthropology* 32(1):240.
Rosen, Arlene. Forthcoming. "Phytolith Indicators of Plant and Land Use at Çatalhöyük." In Hodder in press/d.
Roush, Wade. 1997. "Squash Seeds Yield New View of Early American Farming." *Science* 276:894–95.
Russell, Nerissa. 1993. "Hunting, Herding and Feasting: Human Use of Animals in Neolithic Southeast Europe." Ph.D. thesis, University of California, Berkeley.
Russell, Nerissa. 1998. "Cattle as wealth in Neolithic Europe: where's the beef?" in D. W. Bailey, ed. *The Archaeology of Value: Essays on Prestige and the Processes of Valuation*, 42–54. British Archaeological Reports, International Series no. 730.
Russell, Nerissa, and Louise Martin. 1998. "Çatalhöyük Animal Bone Report." Çatalhöyük 1998 Archive Report: catal.arch.cam.ac.uk/catal/Archive_rep98/martin98.html.
Russell, Nerissa, and Kevin J. McGowan. Forthcoming. "Çatalhöyük Bird Bones." In Hodder in press/d.
Russell, Nerissa, and Stephanie Meece. Forthcoming. "Animal Symbolism at Çatalhöyük." In Hodder in press/a.
Sabloff, Paula L. W. 1998. *Conversations with Lew Binford*. University of Oklahoma Press.
Sahlins, Marshall. 1968. "Notes on the Original Affluent Society." In Lee and DeVore 1968, 85–89.
———. 1972. *Stone Age Economics*. Aldine de Gruyter.
Saidel, Benjamin Adam. 1993. "Round House or Square? Architectural Form and Socio-Economic Organization in the PPNB." *Journal of Mediterranean Archaeology* 6(1):65–108.
Scarre, Christopher, and Brian Fagan. 1997. *Ancient Civilizations*. Longman.
Shakespeare, Nicholas. 1999. *Bruce Chatwin*. Vintage.
Shane, Orrin C., and Mine Küçük. 1998. "The World's First City." *Archaeology* 51(2):43–7.
Shennan, Stephen. 1989. "Archaeology as Archaeology or as Anthropology? Clarke's *Analytical Archaeology* and the Binfords' *New Perspectives in Archaeology* 21 Years On." *Antiquity* 63:834.
Sherratt, Andrew. 1997–1998. "Gordon Childe: Right or Wrong?" *Archaeologia Polona* 35–36: 363–78.
Singer, I. 1988. "The Origins of the Sea Peoples and Their Settlement on the Coast of Canaan." In Heltzer and Lipinski 1988, 239–50.
Smith, Pamela Jane, et al. 1997. "Dorothy Garrod in Words and Pictures." *Antiquity* 71:265–70.
Stanton, Domna C., and Abigail J. Stewart, eds. 1995. *Feminisms in the Academy*. University of Michigan Press.
Stevanovic, Mirjana. 1997. "The Age of Clay: The Social Dynamics of House Destruction." *Journal of Anthropological Archaeology* 16:334–95.

Stevanovic, Mirjana, and Ruth Tringham. 2002. "The Excavation of the BACH 1 Area 2002." Çatalhöyük 2002 Archive Report. catal.arch.cam.ac.uk/catal/Archive_rep02/a03.html.

Stringer, Chris, and Robin McKie. 1996. *African Exodus: The Origins of Modern Humanity*. Pimlico.

Struever, Stuart. 1968. "Flotation Techniques for the Recovery of Small-Scale Archaeological Remains." *American Antiquity* 33:353–62.

Taylor, K. C., et al. 1997. "The Holocene–Younger Dryas Transition Recorded at Summit, Greenland." *Science* 278:825–27.

Thorpe, James. 1994. *Ancient Inventions*. Ballantine.

Todd, Ian. 1966. "Aşikli Hüyük—A Protoneolithic Site in Central Anatolia. *Anatolian Studies* 16:139–63.

———. 1976. *Çatal Hüyük in Perspective*. Cummings.

———. 1998. *Kalavasos-Tenta*. Bank of Cyprus Cultural Foundation.

Tomasello, Michael. 1999. *The Cultural Origins of Human Cognition*. Harvard University Press.

Trigger, Bruce G. 1980. *Gordon Childe: Revolutions in Archaeology*. Columbia University Press.

———. 1989. *A History of Archaeological Thought*. Cambridge University Press.

———. 2003. *Artifacts and Ideas*. Transaction.

Tringham, Ruth. 1983. "V. Gordon Childe 25 Years After: His Relevance for the Archaeology of the Eighties." *Journal of Field Archaeology* 10:85–100.

———. 1991. "Households with Faces: The Challenge of Gender in Prehistoric Architectural Remains." In Gero and Conkey 1991, 93–131.

———. 1994. "Engendered Places in Prehistory." *Gender, Place and Culture* 1(2):178.

———. 1997. "BACH Area." Çatalhöyük 1997 Archive Report. catal.arch.cam.ac.uk/catal/Archive_rep97/tringham97.html.

———. 2000. "The Continuous House: A View from the Deep Past." In Joyce and Gillespie 2000, 115–34.

Tringham, Ruth, et al. 1992. "Excavations at Opovo, 1985–1987: Socioeconomic Change in the Balkan Neolithic." *Journal of Field Archaeology* 19(3): 351–86.

Tringham, Ruth, and Margaret Conkey. 1998. "Rethinking Figurines." In Goodison and Morris 1998, 22–45.

Ubelaker, Douglas, and Henry Scammell. 1992. *Bones: A Forensic Detective's Casebook*. HarperCollins.

Ucko, P. J., et al., eds. 1972. *Man, Settlement and Urbanism*. Duckworth.

Vedder, James. Forthcoming. "The Obsidian Mirrors of Çatalhöyük." In Hodder in press/b.

Watkins, Trevor. 1996. "Excavations at Pinarbaşi: The Early Stages." In Hodder 1996, 47–58.

Watson, Patty Jo. 1995. "Explaining the Transition to Agriculture." in Price and Gebauer 1995, 23–24.

Weaver, M. E. 1971. "A New Water Separation Process for Soil from Archaeological Excavations." *Anatolian Studies* 21:65–68.

Weinstein-Evron, M. 2003. "In B or Not in B: A Reappraisal of the Natufian Burials at Shukbah Cave, Judaea, Palestine." *Antiquity* 77:96–101.

Wheeler, Mortimer. 1954. *Archaeology from the Earth*. Penguin.

———. 1956. *Still Digging: Interleaves from an Antiquary's Notebook*. Michael Joseph.

Whitley, James. 2002. "Too Many Ancestors." *Antiquity* 76:119.
Whittle, Alasdair. 1996. *Europe in the Neolithic: The Creation of New Worlds.* Cambridge University Press.
Wilson, Peter. 1983. *Man, the Promising Primate.* Second edition. Yale University Press.
———. 1988. *The Domestication of the Human Species.* Yale University Press.
Wright, Gary A. 1971. "Origins of Food Production in Southwestern Asia: A Survey of Ideas." *Current Anthropology* 12(4/5):447–77.
Wright, Patti. 2003. "Preservation or Destruction of Plant Remains by Carbonization?" *Journal of Archaeological Science* 30(5):577–83.
Yengoyan, Aram A. 1985. *Proceedings of the Prehistoric Society* 51:333.
Zeder, Melinda, and Brian Hesse. 2000. "The Initial Domestication of Goats *(Capra hircus)* in the Zagros Mountains 10, Years Ago." *Science* 287:2254–57.
Zihlman, Adrienne, et al. 1978. "Pygymy Chimpanzee as a Possible Prototype for the Common Ancestor of Humans, Chimpanzees and Gorillas." *Nature* 275:744–46.

Acknowledgments

ACKNOWLEDGING ALL OF THE PEOPLE who helped me in the preparation of this book has been a humbling experience. Once everyone is thanked, there is very little this writer can take credit for, other than having read most of the references in the bibliography and, of course, putting all the pieces together with, one hopes, a modicum of literary artistry.

Like most nonfiction works, this book is based on what I have read, what people told me, and what I saw and heard. I would have seen and heard very little at Çatalhöyük were it not for Ian Hodder, the project's director, and Shahina Farid, the dig's field director. Their willingness to give me completely unrestricted access to the excavation site as well as to the project's staff and documents made this book possible. Over a period of six years, they also subjected themselves to endless interviews and questions. The same must be said for James and Arlette Mellaart, who welcomed me into their home on many occasions, and for whose help in reconstructing the 1960s excavations at Çatalhöyük I am very grateful.

I want to single out some other members of the current excavation team who were particularly generous with their time: Nerissa Russell, Louise Martin, Roger Matthews, Wendy Matthews, and Craig Cessford, along with Eleni Asouti, Ayfer Bartu, James Conolly, Andrew Fairbairn, Naomi Hamilton, Christine Hastorf, Jonathan Last, Julie Near, Roderick Regan, Arlene Rosen, Mirjana Stevanovic, John Swogger, Ruth Tringham, and Anja Wolle, as well as Tom Higham from the Oxford radiocarbon unit.

A special thank you is also owed to Ian Todd, David French, Pamela French, Nemika Altan, and Viola Pemberton-Pigott for digging deep into their memories of Çatalhöyük's early days. Likewise, to the staff and managing council of the British Institute of Archaeology at Ankara for opening their archives to me, especially Timothy Daunt, Hugh Elton, Gina Coulthard, and Gülgün Girdivan, plus Nilgün Girdivan for providing translations.

Thanks are due to a large number of other members of the current excavation team and people closely associated with the project, who subjected themselves to interviews or helped in other ways, sometimes without realizing it: Meltem Agcabay, Mary Alexander, Peter Andrews, Michael Ashley, Sonya Atalay, Banu Aydinoglu, Douglas Baird, Adnan Baysal, Åsa Berggren, Peter Boyer, Başak Boz, Ann Butler, Can Candan, Tristan Carter, Christina Clements, Becky Coombs, Anwen Cooper, Amanda Cox, Sarah Cross, Lech Czerniak, Linda Donley-Reid, Louise Doughty, Warren Eastwood, Martin Emele, Oğuz Erdur, Freya Evans-Swogger, Richard Evershed, Lindsay Falck, Sheelagh Frame, Duncan Garrow, Catriona Gibson, Lori Hager, Carolyn Hamilton, Katerina Johnson, Amanda Kennedy, Kostas Kotsakis, Peter Kuniholm, Duncan Lees, Gavin Lucas, Arkadiusz Marciniak, Frank Matero, Kevin McGowan, Stephanie Meece, David Meiggs, William Middleton, Slobodan Mitrovic, Sharon Moses, Theya Molleson, Maryanne Newton, Jackie Ouchikh, Emin Murat Özdemir, Serap Özdol, Jessica Pearson, Melih Pekperdahci, Tolga Pekperdahci, Jason Quinlan, Tiffany Raszick, Tim Ready, David Reese, Michael Richards, Neil Roberts, Orrin Shane, David Shankland, David Small, Thomas Strasser, Josephine Stubbs, Jez Taylor, Mavili Tokyağsun, Mustafa Tokyağsun, Burcu Tung, Ali Türkcan, Richard Turnbull, James Vedder, Trevor Watkins, Sharon Webb, Willeke Wendrich, Nurcan Yalman, Lisa Yeomans.

I spoke with many archaeologists, anthropologists, and other experts whose insights and perspectives were essential to this book. Special thanks to Richard Bradley, Meg Conkey, Clive Gamble, Andrew Garrard, Steven Mithen, Henrietta Moore, Michael Parker Pearson, Colin Renfrew, Andrew Sherratt, Chris Tilley, Bruce Trigger, and Peter Wilson; and a grateful nod to Ofer Bar-Yosef, Stuart Blaylock, Charles Burney, John Chapman, Susan Colledge, Dominique Collon, Nicholas David, Ufuk Esin, John Evans, Nigel Goring-Morris, Chris Gosden, Paul Halstead, David Hawkins, Gordon Hillman, B. W. Hodder, Helen

Leach, Steven LeBlanc, Mark Leone, David Lewis-Williams, Daniel Lieberman, Lynn Meskell, Daniel Miller, Mehmet Özdoğan, Rick Potts, Robert Preucel, Mark Roberts, Steven Rosen, Curtis Runnels, Marshall Sahlins, Stephen Shennan, Olga Soffer, Chris Stinger, Ian Tattersall, Peter Ucko, Richard Wrangham, Karen Wright, and John Yellen. I am saving for last one person who may be surprised to find himself singled out here: Mark Patton, the archaeologist who, many years ago, took me in hand at Neolithic La Hougue Bie, on the island of Jersey, and really opened the door on the world of archaeology to me for the first time. Thank you, Mark.

This book began as an assignment for *Science*. A number of the magazine's editors were involved in the many articles I was allowed to write about Çatalhöyük over the years, including Daniel Clery, Tim Appenzeller, and Richard Stone, who each time easily convinced news editor Colin Norman that, yes, there was something new to say about the excavations. I want to save a very special thank you for Elizabeth Culotta, the editor who first insisted that I go to Çatalhöyük and who, I am sure without intending to, changed my life. Other colleagues who have provided invaluable support and friendship include Ann Gibbons, Heather Pringle, Carl Zimmer, Rick Harmon, Heidi Yorkshire, Joseph Anthony, Marc Cooper, Torene Svitil, and Frank Clancy.

Without the constant support and enthusiasm of my agent, Heather Schroder, and my editors at Free Press, Elizabeth Stein and Stephen Morrow, the hard job of writing this book would have been impossible. And thanks to Maris Kreizman for handling the heavy lifting on the production end of this process.

Finally, to my wife, Catherine, and my daughter, Emma—to whom this book is dedicated: Thank you for so many sacrifices, and for not kicking me out of our nuclear family.

Index

About the Author

MICHAEL BALTER worked for many years as a political, environmental, and travel writer with hundreds of features in the *Los Angeles Times, Travel & Leisure, Islands, Bon Appétit,* and the *International Herald Tribune.* Currently he is a Paris correspondent for *Science* magazine and also serves as one of the magazine's chief archaeology and human evolution writers. He lives in Paris, France, and can be reached at www.MichaelBalter.com.